Essay Index

The Poetry of Meditation

The Poetry of Meditation

A STUDY IN ENGLISH RELIGIOUS LITERATURE

OF THE SEVENTEENTH CENTURY BY LOUIS L. MARTZ

New Haven and London: Yale University Press

Essay Index

Distributed in Great Britain, Europe, Asia, and
Africa by Yale University Press Ltd., London; in
Canada by McGill University Press, Montreal; and
in Latin America by Centro Interamericano de Libros
Académicos, Mexico City.

Originally published as Volume 125
in the Yale Studies in English

FOR EDWINE

Contents

vii

Illustrations

Preface to the First Edition

THE present study began in an effort to discover precedents for the unusual construction of John Donne's *Anniversaries*, with their surprisingly precise division and subdivision into formal sections. Poetical traditions, it seemed, could not explain the significance of this construction: it seemed rather that the answer must lie somewhere in the realm of devotional practices—somewhere, perhaps, in that vast variety of meditative methods summed up in Pourrat's *Christian Spirituality*. The results of this exploration were presented, in rather tentative form, in an article on the *Anniversaries* that appeared in *ELH: A Journal of English Literary History* for December, 1947; I am indebted to the editors of *ELH* for permission to include the major portion of that article in the sixth chapter of this book.

In the course of this exploration it appeared that the practices of methodical meditation held deep implications for the whole body of Donne's poetry, and especially for the "Holy Sonnets," which seemed to stem directly from the *Spiritual Exercises* of the Jesuit order. At the same time, these meditative practices appeared to have close relationships to the poetry of Herbert, Crashaw, Vaughan, and Marvell. Through the generous grant of a fellowship from the John Simon Guggenheim Memorial Foundation, I was able to spend the academic year 1948–49 pursuing the further implications of this study, chiefly at the Huntington Library. During this year I learned from Miss Helen Gardner that she was well advanced in the preparation of an edition of Donne's *Divine Poems*, making full use of the manuscripts, and studying the order, dating, and significance of the "Holy Sonnets" from a standpoint similar to my own. I therefore decided to limit my comments on the dating and biographical significance of the "Holy Sonnets" to a discussion of points treated in Grierson's edition—hoping that my questioning of the Gosse-Grierson assumptions would support whatever conclusions Miss Gardner might present. Her admirable edition of the *Divine Poems* has now appeared, and I have been able to include some references to it in my footnotes; but I have let my text stand as it was. I shall be most pleased if my comments on the "Holy Sonnets," written in a different context, will lend support to Miss Gardner's acute conclusions on these matters. I should also like to point out the recent appearance of Miss Rosemond Tuve's *Reading of George Herbert*, a very helpful study which I wish I could have had before me earlier; I have included some references to this in my footnotes, but in the text of my book I have used only Miss Tuve's article on "The Sacrifice," which appeared in 1950.

A word, I think, is needed about my use of translations of the meditative treatises. Some of these are easily available in good modern translations: the Newman Press, for example, offers good and inexpensive editions of the *Spiritual Exercises* of St. Ignatius Loyola, the *Spiritual Combat* attributed to Lorenzo Scupoli, the *Introduction to the Devout Life* by St. François de Sales, and the *Treatise on Prayer and Meditation* by San Pedro de Alcántara (which contains the essence of the much longer treatise by Fray Luis de Granada, frequently cited throughout this study). Nevertheless, wherever feasible, I have taken my quotations from the older English versions; though these often are more properly called adaptations than translations. It seemed to me that the analogies with poetry of the sixteenth and seventeenth centuries emerged more clearly in these older versions; furthermore, these are often works of considerable literary value in their own right, works that have great significance for what Chambers might call "the continuity of English prose" during these centuries. In presenting passages from these older versions, I have modernized the use of "s," "u," and "v," and have expanded abbreviations.

I am greatly indebted to the Clarendon Press for permission to make extensive quotations from their standard editions of Donne, Herbert, Crashaw, and Vaughan, as listed in my bibliography; to the Newman Press for permission to quote extensively from their editions of the *Spiritual Combat* and the *Spiritual Exercises*, as listed in my bibliography; to the Oxford University Press for permission to quote from the poetry of Gerard Manley Hopkins (see bibliography); to the Macmillan Company for permission to quote from

The Collected Poems of W. B. Yeats (New York, 1933; copyright by Macmillan, 1933); to Harcourt, Brace, and Company for permission to quote from T. S. Eliot's *Collected Poems, 1909–1935* (New York, 1936; copyright by Harcourt, Brace, 1936); to Alfred A. Knopf for permission to quote from Wallace Stevens' *Transport to Summer* (New York, 1947; copyright by Wallace Stevens, 1947); and to Random House for permission to quote from *The Collected Poetry of W. H. Auden* (New York, 1945; copyright by W. H. Auden, 1945). I am also very grateful to M. André Fabius for his kind permission to reproduce here the painting by Georges de la Tour in his collection; to the Pierpont Morgan Library for permission to reproduce portions of three books in their possession; and to the Yale University Library for permission to reproduce portions of four books in their possession. I owe a great debt to the staff of the Huntington Library for many favors and courtesies extended to me over the better part of a year, and also to the staffs of the Folger Shakespeare Library, the Pierpont Morgan Library, the Houghton Library of Harvard University, the William Andrews Clark Memorial Library of the University of California at Los Angeles, and the Yale University Library, especially to Miss Marjorie Wynne, librarian of the Rare Book Room at Yale. I should like also to thank Roger Thomas, Librarian of Dr. Williams's Library, London, for sending me a microfilm of the Williams manuscript of George Herbert's poems.

I have been greatly helped by my friend Maynard Mack, through his careful reading of the manuscript, and through many ambulatory conversations on these matters; and I am deeply indebted to other friends and colleagues who have helped in many ways: to Evelyn Hutchinson and Laurence Michel for their valuable criticism of my manuscript; to Benjamin Nangle for his scrupulous reading of the proofs and many helpful suggestions along the way; to Charles Seymour, Jr., for his careful and interested aid in selecting an appropriate frontispiece; to John Pope, Frederick Hilles, and Talbot Donaldson for their friendly advice and encouragement on various occasions; to Stuart Small and Edmund Silk for advice in translations from the Latin; to José Arrom for advice in matters of Spanish; and to Giovanni Previtali for advice in matters of Italian. I am particularly grateful to Don Cameron Allen for his thoughtful criticism of my preliminary work on the *Anniversaries* and for his encouragement of this project in its early stages. I owe many thanks to Mrs. Louise Lindemann, Mrs. Ellen Weld, and Miss Jeanette Fellheimer for helping to prepare the manuscript for press. Finally, I owe a great debt to one who encouraged this study by scholarly precept and example, but did not live to see it finished: Robert J. Menner. I have tried to make it meet, in some measure, his ideals of scholarship.

L.L.M.

Saybrook College
Yale University

Preface to the Second Edition

I am glad to have the opportunity in this new edition to perform some revisions and to note a number of recent publications that bear upon the subject of this book. Only a few minor revisions appear in the body of the book; the major changes occur in the Conclusion, which has been extensively rewritten and completely reset, within the limits required by the original pagination. The Conclusion originally spoke of establishing the nature of a "meditative style," but I am now convinced that this term is inaccurate. It seems better to speak of the "meditative poem," a genre that may be composed in different styles. Thus we find Southwell composing meditative poems in the old Elizabethan style of Gascoigne and the poetical miscellanies; we find Crashaw composing meditative poems in the style of the continental baroque; and we find Donne, Herbert, Vaughan, and Marvell composing meditative poems in what is usually called the metaphysical style. From this standpoint, we may go on to conceive the possibility that other poems in this genre exist among the works of Milton, among the poems of Wordsworth or Coleridge, among the poems of Yeats or Eliot—to say nothing of the Psalms or of other poetry in foreign tongues.

This revision of terminology has been influenced by a number of recent studies in continental poetry of the sixteenth and seventeenth centuries. I should note first the discriminating study of French poetry in this era by Odette de Mourgues, *Metaphysical, Baroque, & Précieux Poetry* (Oxford, Clarendon Press, 1953), which treats a number of poems that may be regarded as meditative. Next, I should like to mention the important article by Professor Edward M. Wilson, "Spanish and English Religious Poetry of the Seventeenth Century," [1] which describes the tradi-

1. *Journal of Ecclesiastical History*, 9 (1958), 38–53; also "A Key to Calderón's *Psalle et sile*," in *Hispanic Studies in Honour of I. González Llubera* (Oxford, Dolphin Book Co., 1959), pp. 1–12.

tion of sacred parody in Spanish poetry, suggests certain Spanish influences upon English poetry of the time, and indicates clearly that meditative poems were being composed in Spain by Lope de Vega, Luis de León, José de Valdivielso, and others; in another article Professor Wilson shows that Calderón's long poetical sequence, "Psalle et Sile," follows the principles of Ignatian meditation. Finally, my thoughts on these matters of genre and style have been greatly aided by the reading of two works that have just appeared from the Yale University Press: *Baroque Lyric Poetry*, by Lowry Nelson, Jr., and *European Metaphysical Poetry*, by Frank J. Warnke; the latter work, along with other kinds of poetry, prints and translates about forty examples of what might be called "meditative poetry in the metaphysical or baroque style," composed by French, Dutch, German, Spanish, and Italian poets.

It seems clear from these various studies that poetry of the meditative kind, closely akin to the poetry treated in the present book, appeared in many languages of Europe during the sixteenth and seventeenth centuries, under the stimulation of the widespread practice of meditative exercises. The Art of Meditation constituted one of the great developments in European culture; its influence penetrated to the center of the European consciousness in that period.

To demonstrate the impact of these exercises upon the English consciousness, I have quoted extensively from contemporary English versions of the continental meditative treatises. Certainly a Donne or a Herbert or a Crashaw had no need to read these treatises in such translations. But my point was not to suggest that any of these English poets had read any particular version of these treatises: it was to show that these methods had already entered into the English language, that the treatises had become a part of the popular culture of the era, that the meditative poetry of this time, like all great poetry, was arising from and expressing a central concern of the age.

The distribution of these meditative treatises in the English language was in fact greater than it may have appeared from the evidence available for the first edition of this study. In 1956 A. F. Allison and D. M. Rogers issued their admirable "Catalogue of Catholic Books in English Printed Abroad or Secretly in England,

1558–1640," [2] which lists nearly a thousand books, about one-third of which have not been previously recorded; this had been preceded in 1955 by Allison's detailed catalogue and study, "Franciscan Books in English, 1559–1640." [3] Through these listings, and through various articles in the new journal *Recusant History*, a large amount of new information has been published that serves to reinforce and correct materials previously available on this subject. Every title in this book that comes under the above categories should be verified by consulting the above lists, for new and more accurate information is often there provided. For example, the anonymous treatise *The Societie of the Rosary*, referred to several times in my second chapter, is now identified as the work of Southwell's fellow Jesuit, Henry Garnet; the first two editions of the treatise appear to have been printed secretly in England, in 1593–4 and in 1596–7; the many copies still in existence seem to indicate a distribution in considerable numbers. The English version of Bellarmine's *Ascent of the Mind to God* bears the words "Printed at Doway, 1616"; this is now identified as a book printed secretly in England, with a false attribution of place, such as frequently occurred. The first English version of Scupoli's *Spiritual Combat* bears the imprint, "Printed at Antwerp, 1598"; but it now appears to have been printed secretly in England, and to have been the work of another of Southwell's fellow Jesuits, John Gerard. The small anonymous treatise, "The Practical Methode of Meditation," which for convenience I referred to by the name "Gibbons" (see below, p. 14n), now appears to be the work of the English Jesuit, Edward Dawson, who spent a number of years in England during the earlier part of the seventeenth century. I should judge that the versions and editions of meditative treatises listed by Allison and Rogers represent at least twice the number of such books mentioned in my own study.

For the effect of these meditative exercises upon the creation of

2. Published as Vol. 3, nos. 3 and 4, of *Biographical Studies* (Bognor Regis, Arundel Press, 1956), a publication that in 1957 changed its title to *Recusant History*.

3. *Biographical Studies*, 3 (1955), 16–65. Additional evidence concerning the activities of the underground priests in England, including their publications, will be found in Christopher Devlin's *Life of Robert Southwell*, London, Longmans, 1956.

English poetry, additional evidence has now become available through the publication of *The Sonnets of William Alabaster*, edited by G. M. Story and Helen Gardner (Oxford University Press, 1959). Previously, William Alabaster (1568–1640) has probably been best known through Miss Guiney's publication of five of his sonnets, along with a short biography, in her *Recusant Poets* of 1938. The present edition at last brings before us all the known sonnets of Alabaster (77 of them, plus two doubtful attributions), with an informative general introduction by Mr. Story, a joint textual introduction, and a very helpful commentary on the poems by Miss Gardner. The implications of these sonnets deserve consideration here in some detail.

From this edition we learn that the crucial period for Alabaster's poetry came in 1597–8, when he gave up a promising career in the English church, announced his conversion to Roman Catholicism, and decided to enter the Society of Jesus, according to the underground Jesuit, John Gerard, who guided Alabaster in performing the *Spiritual Exercises* of Ignatius Loyola. Actually, Alabaster never entered into Roman orders, and he ultimately returned to service in the English Church; but his violent and painful conversion to Romanism led him to express his problems in religious poetry that clearly illustrates the impact of Counter-Reformation methods of devotion upon the spirituality of Elizabethan England. Mr. Story stresses the elements of continuity in English devotional traditions during the sixteenth century; and it is certainly true that remnants of the old religion provided the ground upon which the influence of continental Catholicism could work. At the same time he senses in Sonnet 15 a representation of the Ignatian mode of meditation by the "three powers of the soul"—memory, understanding, and will:

> My soul a world is by contraction,
> The heavens therein is my internal sense,
> Moved by my will as an intelligence,
> My heart the element, my love the sun.
> And as the sun about the earth doth run,
> And with his beams doth draw thin vapours thence,
> Which after in the air do condense,

And pour down rain upon the earth anon,
So moves my love about the heavenly sphere,
And draweth thence with an attractive fire
The purest argument wit can desire,
Whereby devotion after may arise.
And these conceits, digest by thoughts' retire,
Are turned into april showers of tears.

Miss Gardner's commentary clarifies the action of the meditative process here described: "As the sun draws up vapours from the earth, which it returns as rain, so love draws from the contemplation of heavenly things material for the intellect. These notions, digested in the privacy of thought, are turned into the tears of devotion which return to heaven" (p. 49). This process, Mr. Story notes, "is the immemorial method of Christian meditation; yet it is so with a difference. For one thing the sonnet form in which the meditation is cast belongs to the sixteenth century, and for another the temper of the verse is new. It is a metaphysical poem" (p. xxviii). Here the term "metaphysical" serves to associate Alabaster with Donne, reinforcing the resemblance that the above sonnet bears to Donne's Holy Sonnets, apparently composed at least ten years later. I would argue, however, that the temper of Alabaster's verse is new primarily because a new mode of religious apprehension lies within it and behind it: the meditative mode of the late sixteenth century, which developed a peculiar concentration out of the older methods of Christian devotion. The essential nature of this poetry is well represented in the title that the editors have chosen for Alabaster's sonnets, following a manuscript reported by Collier: *Divine Meditations*. The title, as readers of Miss Gardner's definitive edition of Donne will realize, is the same as the title given in some manuscripts to Donne's Holy Sonnets. The collocation is right, for both sets of sonnets appear to spring from the same spiritual discipline.

Thus we find that Alabaster's sonnets often begin in accordance with the several ways of opening a formal meditation, as advised by the devotional writers of the century: by a "composition of place," by a composition through "some similitude or comparison," or by a "simple proposing" of the subject (see below, pp. 27–30).

Some of the sonnets open with dramatic compositions in which the speaker makes himself present at a scene in the life of Christ:

> When without tears I look on Christ, I see
> Only a story of some passion,
> Which any common eye may wonder on;
> But if I look through tears Christ smiles on me.
> Yea, there I see myself, and from that tree
> He bendeth down to my devotion . . .

Or we may have the second kind of composition, performed by creating some "similitude": "His death begins within a farm, within/The farm of Jewry"; "My soul within the bed of heaven doth grow." In other sonnets we find both modes of "composition" combined, with a vivid effect of double concreteness:

> Behold a conduit that from heaven doth run,
> And at Christ's side a double stream doth vent . . .

> Behold a cluster to itself a vine,
> Behold a vine extended in one cluster,
> Whose grapes do swell with grace and heavenly lustre,
> Climbing upon a Cross with lovely twine . . .

Or, at other times, we have the firm "proposing" of a problem for meditation: "What meaneth this, that Christ an hymn did sing"; "When all forsake, whose courage dare abide?" And we have, of course, the frequent colloquies, sometimes with the self: "Sink down, my soul, into the lowest cell"; more often with Christ: "Jesu, thy love within me is so main"; "Lo here I am, lord, whither wilt thou send me?" Or we may have this curious address to St. Peter, keeper of the King's presence: "Ho, God be here, is Christ, my lord, at leisure?"

Beyond these dramatic openings, a more significant kinship with Donne may be found in the steady presence, throughout Alabaster's sonnets, of that "intellectual, argumentative evolution" long ago pointed out by Grierson as a prime quality of Donne's poetry. This development in Alabaster's sonnets is inseparable from the process of formal meditation. Sometimes, as in a few of Donne's Holy Sonnets, we can see the whole process of a meditation recapitulated. Thus in Alabaster's third sonnet we have first the presentation of place, combined with a memory of the Old Testament "type":

> Over the brook of Cedron Christ is gone,
> To entertain the combat with his death,
> Where David fled beforetime void of breath,
> To scape the treacheries of Absolom.

Then follows the intellectual analysis, developing the brook into a conceit:

> Go let us follow him in passion,
> Over this brook, this world that walloweth,
> A stream of cares that drown our thoughts beneath,
> And wash away all resolution:
> Beyond the world he must be passed clear,
> That in the world for Christ will troubles bear.

Finally, we have the expression of "affections," the direction of the will, expressed in a colloquy of self-address and a plea to Christ:

> Leave we, O leave we then this miry flood,
> Friends, pleasures, and unfaithful good.
> Now we are up, now down, but cannot stand,
> We sink, we reel, Jesu stretch forth thy hand.

This is pedestrian enough, a sample of Alabaster in his weaker moments; but here in rudimentary form we can, I think, see the process of mind that dominates most of the sonnets: the deliberate evocation of the spirit of devotion through the use of analysed images.

The better sonnets rise to higher levels through a more complex dramatization, where the speaker not only addresses himself, but projects a certain aspect of himself upon the scene, and there subjects that part of himself to sustained analysis and judgment. One of the best examples of this higher level of achievement is found in Sonnet 33, "Ego Sum Vitis," where lust is turned to spiritual love through the interposition of the Vine upon the Cross:

> Now that the midday heat doth scorch my shame
> With lightning of fond lust, I will retire
> Under this vine whose arms with wandering spire

Do climb upon the Cross, and on the same
Devise a cool repose from lawless flame,
Whose leaves are intertwist with love entire,
That envy's eye cannot transfuse her fire,
But is rebated on the shady frame;
And youthful vigour from the leaved tier,
Doth stream upon my soul a new desire.
List, list, the ditties of sublimed fame,
Which in the closet of those leaves the choir
Of heavenly birds do warble to his name.
O where was I that was not where I am?

The powers of the soul are here so thoroughly wrought together
that the poem presents one sustained movement from the graphic
"composition" to the paradoxical realization of the will. It is a poem
that, despite a certain ruggedness of phrasing, would not disgrace
the works of Herbert or Vaughan. And it is not an isolated ex-
cellence: at least twenty of Alabaster's sonnets can equal or sur-
pass this poem. Alabaster, though often clumsy and excessively
intellectual, is a true poet; the body of his work here represents
much more than a footnote to the history of English literature.[4]

His Donne-like poetry arises without any evidence of Donne's
influence; his sonnets appear to anticipate Donne's by at least a
decade. As a result, Alabaster's sonnets cast further doubt upon
the adequacy of the phrase, "The School of Donne," as applied to
Herbert, Vaughan, Marvell, or Crashaw. When we consider the
full range of the many traditions, religious and poetical, that have
entered into the poetry of these writers, the influence of Donne
inevitably recedes in significance. "En conclusion," says M.
Denonain in his impressive study of these poets, "il apparaît donc
préférable d'écarter toute notion d' 'Ecole,' et il convient de
ne jamais employer qu'avec une extrême prudence le titre de
Disciple ou même d'émule de John Donne."[5]

As for Donne himself, I believe that meditative techniques are

4. I wish to thank the editors of *Modern Language Notes* for permission
to include here some remarks on Alabaster's work that originally formed
part of a review in that periodical.

5. Jean-Jacques Denonain, *Thèmes et Formes de la Poésie "Métaphysique"*
(Paris, Presses Universitaires de France, 1956), pp. 94–5.

essential to the dominant qualities of Donne's poetry; but that is far from saying that they are responsible for all of Donne's poetry. Donne wrote in many genres besides the meditative: satire, Ovidian elegy, funeral elegy, epistle, song, epigram, epitaph, epithalamion—and the sermon. In all these genres he displays the style that we call metaphysical. And in some of them we may discern the impingement and even the amalgamation of meditative elements, along with the other qualities of the poem. In Satire 3, in a few of the "Songs and Sonets" (such as "The Extasie" or the "Nocturnall"), and in the great *Anniversaries*, the meditative element has become so strong that the poems almost, if not quite, enter into the meditative genre. Most of his *Divine Poems* seem to belong essentially to this genre, although they also participate in other genres: the sonnet, the liturgy, the hymn. As Wellek and Warren say in their wise discussion of "Literary Genres": "Genre should be conceived, we think, as a grouping of literary works based, theoretically, upon both outer form (specific meter or structure) and also upon inner form (attitude, tone, purpose—more crudely, subject and audience). The ostensible basis may be one or the other (e.g., 'pastoral' and 'satire' for the inner form; dipodic verse and Pindaric ode for outer); but the critical problem will then be to find the *other* dimension, to complete the diagram." Modern theory of genres, they go on to say, "supposes that traditional kinds may be 'mixed' and produce a new kind (like tragicomedy)" [6]—or, as one might say here, like the genre of meditative poetry.

In attempting to grasp the nature of this genre, I have placed a heavy emphasis upon the practice of meditation according to the "three powers of the soul," because we find here the central, indispensable action of the Art of Meditation. From that center all other aspects of the meditative action flow. Sometimes we find that central action rehearsed in summary before our eyes and ears, in line with the usual advice for "What is to be done after Meditation" (see below, pp. 123–4). We may also find the whole process of a spiritual exercise recorded at greater length in sequences of poetry, or in poems of considerable length, as Wilson

6. René Wellek and Austin Warren, *Theory of Literature* (New York, Harcourt, Brace, 1949), pp. 241, 245.

has shown in regard to Calderón's "Psalle et Sile." Similarly, John Malcolm Wallace has shown how the thirty-seven poems by Traherne in the Dobell Manuscript may be interpreted as a five-part meditation in general accord with the full development of a spiritual exercise.[7] And Mrs. Nancy Pollard Brown, in an interesting paper delivered at the meetings of the Modern Language Association in 1959, has argued convincingly that Southwell's long poem, "Saint Peters Complaint," bears a structure related to the sacrament of penance and develops in close accord with the Ignatian meditation "upon sins," the second exercise in the First Week of the *Spiritual Exercises*. I have therefore moderated my original harsh comments on this poem's lack of unity (see below, p. 193).

In other meditative poems we may find only "some part" of the total action set down in poetical form; and yet the poem may contain an implied relation to the total process of meditation. Miss Gardner, for example, has interpreted some of Donne's Holy Sonnets as representing the preludes of the Ignatian meditation, while in the same sonnets I would see an operation of the "three powers" (see below, p. 51n). There is no contradiction here: the sonnets may be validly approached from either point of view, since the preludes are designed to evoke, in brief, a full awareness of the subject-matter and of the ultimate aim of the exercise; indeed the preludes assume that the whole matter of the meditation has been carefully planned and "pre-meditated."

It seems appropriate to conclude here by quoting at length the account of the operation of the "three powers" given by Gerard Manley Hopkins in his incomplete commentary on the Jesuit Exercises. The passage clearly shows how, to a man of great poetic imagination, the action of this trinity of powers is inseparably one; and it will also allow me to follow the good advice of my friend John E. Smith, who has pointed out that my comments on this action ought to have mentioned the prime source of the conception of the three powers of the soul, in Augustine's great treatise, the *De Trinitate*. The name of Augustine comes in easily here, since Hopkins' account shows the influence of Duns Scotus, who in this aspect of his thought remains a follower of the Augustinian tradition:

7. "Thomas Traherne and the Structure of Meditation," *ELH*, 25 (1958), 79–89.

On the contemplating Persons, Words and Actions—These three points belong to the three powers, memory, understanding, and will. Memory is the name for that faculty which towards present things is Simple Apprehension and, when it is question of the concrete only, γνῶσις, ἐπίγνωσις, the faculty of Identification; towards past things is Memory proper; and towards things future or things unknown or imaginary is Imagination. When continued or kept on the strain the act of this faculty is attention, advertence, heed, the being *ware*, and its habit, knowledge, the being *aware*. Towards God it gives rise to *reverence*, it is the sense of the *presence* of God. The understanding, as the name shows, applies to words; it is the faculty for grasping not the fact but the meaning of a thing. When the first faculty just does its office and falls back, barely naming what it apprehends, it scarcely gives birth to the second but when it keeps on the strain ('attendere, advertere, et contemplari') it cannot but continuously beget it. This faculty not identifies but verifies; takes the measure of things, brings word of them; is called λόγος and reason. By the will here is meant not so much the practical will as the faculty of fruition, by which we enjoy or dislike etc, to which all the intellectual affections belong. For all three faculties are the mind, the intellect, νοῦς. I ought to have added that the second faculty ends in admiration, which issues in *praise*, and the third in enjoyment, which issues in love, which issues in *service*.[8]

8. *The Sermons and Devotional Writings of Gerard Manley Hopkins*, ed. Christopher Devlin (London, Oxford University Press, 1959), p. 174; cf. Devlin's commentary, pp. 298–9, 344ff.

GEORGES DE LA TOUR OF LORRAINE, 1593–1652
Collection André Fabius, Paris

The Poetry of Meditation

Such thought—such thought have I that hold it tight
Till meditation master all its parts,
Nothing can stay my glance
Until that glance run in the world's despite
To where the damned have howled away their hearts,
And where the blessed dance;
Such thought, that in it bound
I need no other thing,
Wound in mind's wandering
As mummies in the mummy-cloth are wound.

WILLIAM BUTLER YEATS
Oxford, Autumn 1920

Introduction

THE SEVENTEENTH-CENTURY painting that forms the frontis-piece provides an emblem of all the central concerns of the present study. Georges de la Tour, like John Donne, is one of the rediscoveries of the twentieth century; and the admiration that both have evoked in our own time may be traced to the same fundamental causes. I do not mean simply the photographic realism of the composition, but rather the way in which every detail of the work is controlled by a human figure in profound meditation. This person's thoughts are not abstract: the left hand, with its sensitive, tapered fingers, probes the eyesocket of a skull; the arm, so delicately clothed, conveys a rude sensation to the brain. Meanwhile the eye is focused on a mirror, where we are accustomed to pursue the work of preparing "a face to meet the faces" that we meet: yet here the inquiring eye meets "the skull beneath the skin," a skull that seems to devour the book on which it rests. Sight and touch, then, meet to form these thoughts, meditative, piercing, looking through the mirror, probing whatever lies beyond. For me, at least, it suggests simultaneously Donne and Yeats: Donne in his shroud and Yeats in his tower, especially the figure that ends *A Vision*: "Day after day I have sat in my chair turning a symbol over in my mind, exploring all its details, defining and again defining its elements, testing my convictions and those of others by its unity, attempting to substitute particulars for an abstraction like that of algebra." [1]

Such meditation is the subject of this study: intense, imaginative meditation that brings together the senses, the emotions, and the intellectual faculties of man; brings them together in a moment of dramatic, creative experience. One period when such meditation flourished coincides exactly with the flourishing of English religious poetry in the seventeenth century. There is, I believe, much more

1. W. B. Yeats, *A Vision* (New York, Macmillan, 1938), p. 301.

than mere coincidence here, for the qualities developed by the "art of meditation" (as Joseph Hall described it) are essentially the qualities that the twentieth century has admired in Donne, or Herbert, or Marvell. Those qualities, some thirty years ago, received their classic definition in the introduction to Grierson's anthology, *Metaphysical Lyrics and Poems*, and in Eliot's essay inspired by that volume. Developed in a series of influential books issued during the 1930's, the definition views Donne as the master and father of a new kind of English poetry, with these distinguishing marks: an acute self-consciousness that shows itself in minute analysis of moods and motives; a conversational tone and accent, expressed in language that is "as a rule simple and pure"; highly unconventional imagery, including the whole range of human experience, from theology to the commonest details of bed and board; an "intellectual, argumentative evolution" within each poem, a "strain of passionate paradoxical reasoning which knits the first line to the last" and which often results in "the elaboration of a figure of speech to the farthest stage to which ingenuity can carry it"; above all, including all, that "unification of sensibility" which could achieve "a direct sensuous apprehension of thought, or a recreation of thought into feeling," and made it possible for Donne to feel his thought "as immediately as the odour of a rose." [2]

If it can be shown that the art of meditation played a fundamental part in the development of these qualities, important consequences may follow for the literary critic and historian. It may be easier for us to see Donne's originality, not as a meteoric burst, but as part of a normal, central tendency of religious life in his time. The "metaphysical poets" may be seen, not as Donne and his school, but as a group of writers, widely different in temper and outlook, drawn together by resemblances that result, basically, from the common practice of certain methods of religious meditation. The direct influence of one of these poets upon another, though considerable, would thus become secondary: individual mastery of the art of meditation would lie behind the poetry and be the essence of their kinship. Even the

2. T. S. Eliot, "The Metaphysical Poets," *Selected Essays, 1917–1932* (New York, Harcourt Brace, 1932), pp. 242, 245–8. *Metaphysical Lyrics and Poems of the Seventeenth Century*, ed. Herbert J. C. Grierson (Oxford, Clarendon Press, 1921), p. xxxiv.

deep and intimate influence of Herbert upon Vaughan would have been, perhaps, of little avail for poetry had not Vaughan himself become a fervent adept in meditative practices, especially in the widespread practice of meditation on the "creatures." Similarly, although both the personal and the poetical relationship between Donne and Herbert was very close, we may do Herbert a serious injustice if we see him only as a gifted disciple, transmuting through his own smaller personality a way of writing essentially made possible by Donne. We may have been attributing to Donne's example many qualities in Herbert's poetry which could better be attributed to the art of meditation, independently fertilizing the lines of both poets.

In short, the present study attempts to modify the view of literary history which sees a "Donne tradition" in English religious poetry. It suggests instead a "meditative tradition" which found its first notable example not in Donne but in Robert Southwell. Such a tradition could explain a number of embarrassing problems which cannot be adequately explained with Donne as our basing-point. Nearly everyone has recognized, for instance, that Crashaw's poetry is very unlike Donne's, while close students of Crashaw have pointed out his marked affinity with Southwell and his occasional echoes of Herbert. At the same time, as Herbert's editors have pointed out, there is evidence of strong poetical kinship between Southwell and Herbert, a kinship which appears very close indeed when examined in detail.[3] Moreover—though this lies outside the scope of the present study—in their habit of meditating on the "creatures," it is possible to find a fundamental link between Vaughan, Marvell, Traherne, and even Milton. This is not to deny the great influence of Donne upon the course of English poetry, but only to argue that a broader and greater tradition than that which stems from Donne's poetry lies behind the abundant variety and versatility of English religious poetry in the seventeenth century. The realm of meditation is broad

3. See Austin Warren, *Richard Crashaw, A Study in Baroque Sensibility* (Louisiana State University Press, 1939), pp. 114–18, 135–6; A. F. Allison, "Some Influences in Crashaw's Poem 'On a Prayer Booke Sent to Mrs. M. R.,'" *RES, 23* (1947), 36–7. *The English Works of George Herbert*, ed. George Herbert Palmer (3 vols., Boston and New York, Houghton Mifflin, 1905), *1*, 95. *The Works of George Herbert*, ed. F. E. Hutchinson (2d ed., Oxford, Clarendon Press, 1945), pp. 476, 477, 497, 504, 510, 512, 529, 539, 542, 543, 549.

enough to hold Jesuit and Puritan, Donne and Milton, the baroque
extravagance of Crashaw and the delicate restraint of Herbert. The
"poetry of meditation," I believe, would be a more accurate, a more
flexible, a more helpful term, both historically and critically, than
the much debated term "metaphysical poetry."

At the same time, as my references to Yeats may have suggested,
a study of this art of meditation bears a strong relation to the poetry
of our own day, so greatly influenced by two poets whose work
bears the unmistakable imprint of the same Jesuit methods of meditation: Donne and Hopkins. In thus recovering an ancient way of
meditation, Hopkins might be seen as the forerunner of a new era
of meditative poetry, represented in the later poetry of Yeats and
Eliot and found also in portions of the work of Allen Tate, Richard
Eberhart, Dylan Thomas, or Robert Lowell. As in the seventeenth
century, the growth of a poetry of meditation since the time of
Hopkins is paralleled by a rapid increase in the number of meditative
treatises written or translated for English readers. Most of the important treatises used in the present study are in fact easily available
in modern English translations, as they were in the day of Donne. I
do not mean to say that Yeats used them; but through his studies of
the occult he came upon related ways of meditation. These are matters, however, which cannot be discussed until the relationship between poetry and meditation in the seventeenth century has been
thoroughly explored. I shall return to modern poetry at the close of
this study; meanwhile, from time to time, brief allusions to modern
poets and critics may serve to reinforce one of the major issues of
this book: that the art of meditation represents yet another aspect
of the deep affinity between the seventeenth and the twentieth centuries.

2

Within the past thirty years students of religious thought have
given us an impressive view of the growth of meditative exercises
as they flourished on the Continent during the sixteenth and seventeenth centuries.[1] Above all, Pierre Pourrat, in the three volumes

1. See especially E. Allison Peers, *Studies of the Spanish Mystics*, 2 vols.,
London, The Sheldon Press, 1927–30; Pierre Debongnie, *Jean Mombaer de
Bruxelles*, Louvain, Librarie Universitaire, 1927: a study of the growth of

of his learned and subtle *Christian Spirituality*,[2] has traced the development of all kinds of spiritual exercises, from the early Fathers of the Church down to the end of the seventeenth century. It was from Pourrat's third volume that the present study took its origin, for there he has described in rich detail the leading and the lesser figures in the great movement toward methodical religious meditation which matured on the Continent in the middle of the sixteenth century, finding its first great landmark in the Pope's approval of the *Spiritual Exercises* of St. Ignatius Loyola in 1548. Behind St. Ignatius, as Watrigant has shown,[3] lay various methods of meditation that had long exerted, and continued to exert, a powerful influence: the practices of methodical meditation in the Low Countries, as collected in the mammoth *Rosetum exercitiorum spiritualium et sacrarum meditationum* of Mauburnus (1494); the medieval meditations on the life of Christ by the pseudo-Bonaventure and Ludolph the Carthusian; the exercises of García de Cisneros, Abbot of Montserrat (1500); and the scrutiny of the "inward man" counseled by the *Imitation of Christ* and other popular medieval treatises of its kind.

In the middle of the sixteenth century, under the stimulus of the Counter Reformation and its spearhead, the Jesuit order, new treatises on meditation began to appear by the dozens, and after the opening of the seventeenth century, by the scores and by the hundreds. Among these, the three most popular came, significantly, from three different countries. From Spain came the *Book of Prayer and Meditation* (1554) by Fray Luis de Granada, who was, as Miss White and Miss Hagedorn have shown,[4] the most popular of all

intricate methods of meditation in the Low Countries, based upon the pioneer work of Henri Watrigant; Henri Bremond, *A Literary History of Religious Thought in France*, trans. K. L. Montgomery, 3 vols., London, S.P.C.K., 1928–36.

2. Translated by W. H. Mitchell and S. P. Jacques, 3 vols., London, Burns, Oates, and Washbourne, 1922–7.

3. H. Watrigant, "La genèse des Exercices de Saint Ignace de Loyola," *Études*, 71 (1897), 506–29; 72, 195–216; 73, 199–228.

4. Helen C. White, *English Devotional Literature* [*Prose*], *1600–1640*, University of Wisconsin Studies in Language and Literature, No. 29 (Madison, 1931), pp. 104–9. Maria Hagedorn, *Reformation und Spanische Andachtsliteratur: Luis de Granada in England*, Leipzig, Bernhard Tauchnitz, 1934.

these meditative writers in England at the beginning of the seventeenth century. From Italy came the *Spiritual Combat* (1589), attributed to Lorenzo Scupoli, but perhaps the work of a group of Theatine writers: [5] this was a treatise which, throughout Europe, was equaled in popularity only by the *Imitation of Christ*; it was available in two different English translations during our period.[6] And from France came the *Introduction to the Devout Life* by St. François de Sales (1609), a manual destined to supersede Luis de Granada's in the permanence of its appeal; as Miss White has shown,[7] Yakesley's translation enjoyed a considerable vogue in seventeenth-century England.

It may seem surprising, at first glance, that such potent works of the Counter Reformation, all strongly tinged with Jesuit influence, could have penetrated to an England in the throes of religious revolution, fearful of Rome and its works, and especially hostile to the Jesuits. But a number of modern studies, set together, provide us with overwhelming evidence that the channels of communication between England and the Catholic Continent were ample to carry the meditative methods of the Counter Reformation into England. The most recent of these studies is A. C. Southern's *Elizabethan Recusant Prose, 1559–1582*,[8] which shows in elaborate detail how Catholic books in English were printed at Antwerp, Louvain, Rouen, Paris, Douay, Rheims—or in some cases at secret presses in England itself—and were distributed among the English people by missionary priests and other regular agents. Among these were four influential treatises on meditation. One was Richard Hopkins' attractive translation (Paris, 1582) of the first part of Luis de Granada's *Book of Prayer and Meditation:* a translation that by the year 1633 had gone through at least three more continental printings and, in a version adapted to Protestant views, six London editions. Two more were translations of meditative treatises by the popular Jesuit writer, Gaspar Loarte: *Instructions and Advertisements, How to meditate the Misteries of the Rosarie* (1579?); and *The*

5. See Pourrat, *3*, 239–40.

6. See below, Chap. 3, sec. 2.

7. *Devotional Literature*, pp. 111–13; Miss White is right in conjecturing that the confiscated London edition of 1637 was Yakesley's translation.

8. London, Sands and Co., 1950.

Exercise of a Christian Life (1579), a treatise very similar to that of Luis de Granada. The latter of these saw at least four more editions by 1634, but its major importance lies in the fact that it stimulated the composition of the famous *Christian Directory* (Rouen, 1582) by the English Jesuit, Robert Persons. Thurston, Southern, and Miss White have all given detailed accounts of the vogue of Persons' book in England,[9] both in its original form and in a Protestant adaptation by Edmund Bunny, which stirred up a bitter controversy between creator and adaptor: the Catholic version went through seven continental editions by 1633, and Bunny's adaptation through some twenty editions by 1640.

These works mark the beginning of a flood of such continental treatises, which Miss White has briefly recorded [10] and which it is our purpose to examine in detail in the course of this study. Toward the end of the sixteenth century and during the first half of the seventeenth century, these continental works of meditation poured into England, through English translations and adaptations made both by recusants abroad and by Anglicans at home. Such an eager reception of the works of continental Catholicism suggests the satisfaction of a deep inner need. It was a fact, lamented by writers of every persuasion, that English devotional life had been shattered by the rapid upheavals and bitter controversies of the sixteenth century's middle years. England was, for a time, almost completely cut off from the rapid development of meditation that was, at exactly this time, maturing on the Continent. Miss Helen White, in her new study, *The Tudor Books of Private Devotion*,[11] has shown

9. Herbert Thurston, "Catholic Writers and Elizabethan Readers. I.—Father Parsons' 'Christian Directory,'" *The Month, 82* (1894), 457–76. Southern, pp. 182–92, 467–9. White, *Devotional Literature*, pp. 144–9. The original edition of 1582 bore the title, *The Firste Booke of the Christian Exercise, appertayning to Resolution;* Bunny's adaptation of 1584 bore the title, *A Booke of Christian Exercise, appertaining to Resolution;* in his revised edition of 1585 Persons changed his title to *A Christian Directorie . . . commonly called the Resolution.*

10. *Devotional Literature*, pp. 116–49. See also Joseph B. Collins, *Christian Mysticism in the Elizabethan Age* (Baltimore, Johns Hopkins Press, 1940), pp. 121–9.

11. University of Wisconsin Press, 1951. See also Miss White's important article, "Some Continuing Traditions in English Devotional Literature," *PMLA, 57* (1942), 966–80. An authoritative account of the popularity of

how attempts were made to compensate for this disruption by re-vision of the primers, by collections of prayers for various occa-sions, and by various guides to good life. But these were not enough: set beside the continental works that I have mentioned, these Eng-lish books are dull and dry. The Catholic exiles on the Continent could feel this difference acutely; and it was their feeling that Eng-land was drifting away from the main stream of Christian devotion that led them to distribute these continental meditative treatises among their countrymen at home.

Thus Richard Hopkins, in the Dedicatory Epistle to his transla-tion of Fray Luis de Granada's treatise (1582), tells us that Stephen Harding had some fourteen years before "perswaded me earnestlie to translate some of those Spanishe bookes into our Englishe tounge, affirminge, that more spirituall profite wolde undoubtedlie ensewe thereby to the gayninge of Christian sowles in our countrie from Schisme, and Heresie, and from all sinne, and iniquitie, than by bookes that treate of controversies in Religion." Similarly, Robert Persons, in the preface to the first edition of his *Directory* (1582), declares that his "principall cause and reason" for conceiving this book was "to the ende our countrye men might have some one suf-ficient direction for matters of life and spirit, among so manye bookes of controversies as have ben writen, and are in writinge dailye." These controversies are doubtless necessary, he adds, "yet helpe they little oftentymes to good lyfe, but rather do fill the heades of men with a spirite of contradiction and contention, that for the most parte hindereth devotion. . . ." In the same vein, though with a sharper tone, John Heigham, in the preface to his translation of the *Meditations* of the Jesuit Luis de la Puente (St. Omer, 1619), reproaches the "deceaved Protestants" of England with having no knowledge of the contemplative life because their doctrine is all definition and speculation.

Such charges, though partisan, were in the main true: collections of scattered prayers, scraps of liturgy, and bundles of precepts were ineffectual when compared with the rich imaginative exercises

---

Protestant "Guides to Godliness" is given by Louis B. Wright, *Middle-class Culture in Elizabethan England* (Chapel Hill, University of North Carolina Press, 1935), chap. 8.

by which the Counter Reformation was cultivating the realm of "devotion." Consequently, in an England shaken by a threefold controversy, Catholic against Anglican against Puritan, it is not surprising to find, from the evidence of printed English books, that by the opening of the seventeenth century a large proportion of the English public had taken to its heart the fruits of the Counter Reformation in the realm of inward devotion. These continental practices of meditation combined with the older traditions of primer and private prayer, and with the inward surge of Puritanism, to produce in the seventeenth century an era of religious fervor unmatched in English history.

The evidence of this reunion with the central tendency of continental Catholic spirituality constitutes the matter of the following study. Quotations from English translations and adaptations of Catholic books will, I hope, show, by their simple eloquence, how firmly the meditative methods of the Continent became embedded in English life and literature of the seventeenth century.

But other aspects of the continental impact upon England would need to be considered before the case could be complete: the activities of the missionary priests among the educated classes in England; the establishment of English Catholic colleges and monastic houses abroad, and their close connections with English Catholics at home. Convincing surveys of these personal relationships with the Continent will be found in the studies of Mathew, Hughes, or Pollen; [12] and from these general studies one can launch into massive detail. There are, for example, the famous *Diaries* of the English college at Douay,[13] with their accounts of the comings and goings

12. David Mathew, *Catholicism in England, 1535–1935,* London, Longmans, Green, 1936; rev. ed. 1949. Philip Hughes, *Rome and the Counter-Reformation in England,* London, Burns, Oates, and Washbourne, 1942. John Hungerford Pollen, *The English Catholics in the Reign of Queen Elizabeth . . . . 1558–1580,* London, Longmans, Green, 1920.

13. *Records of the English Catholics under the Penal Laws,* ed. Fathers of the Congregation of the London Oratory, with introductions by Thomas Francis Knox, 2 vols., London, 1878–82; vol. *1: The First and Second Diaries of the English College, Douay;* Knox's long introduction to this volume is especially helpful. *The Douay College Diaries, Third, Fourth and Fifth, 1598–1654,* ed. Edwin H. Burton and Thomas L. Williams, 2 vols., London, 1911 (Publications of the Catholic Record Society, vols. *10, 11*).

of students and visitors to and from England, and the sending out of
"seminary priests." There is the learned study by Peter Guilday,
The English Catholic Refugees on the Continent, 1558–1795,[14]
which relates in great detail the activities of the English monastic
orders after their expulsion—an illuminating survey of the cultivation of the contemplative life among thousands of Englishmen on
the Continent. Or one may turn to the authoritative books dealing
with four of the most important missionary priests of the period,
three of them among the most eminent English devotional writers
of the time. Two volumes of contemporary documents record the
life and writings of the English Benedictine, Augustine Baker; while
we have a similar collection of materials relating to Robert Persons,
a masterly study of the life and works of Robert Southwell by
Pierre Janelle, and the recent new translation of the journal of the
Jesuit John Gerard, Southwell's colleague in the English mission.[15]
But of all these, the figure of Robert Southwell is the most significant
for our purposes here, for he combines within himself all the aspects
of the Counter Reformation which are important to our present
study.

First of all, as one of about three hundred missionary priests operating in England near the end of the sixteenth century,[16] Southwell managed to spend no less than nine consecutive years in England, between 1586 and his execution in 1595; during this time he
published books from his own secret press, ministered to several
noble families, and wrote devotional tracts and poems as a part of
his mission. The history of the publication of Southwell's works in

14. London, Longmans, Green, 1914.

15. *The Life of Father Augustine Baker, O.S.B. (1575–1641) by Fr. Peter
Salvin and Fr. Serenus Cressy*, ed. Justin McCann, London, Burns, Oates, and
Washbourne, 1933. *Memorials of Father Augustine Baker*, ed. Justin McCann
and Hugh Connolly, London, 1933 (Publications of the Catholic Record
Society, vol. *33*). *Letters and Memorials of Father Robert Persons*, vol. *1*
(to 1588), ed. L. Hicks, London, 1942 (Publications of the Catholic Record
Society, vol. *39*); the long introduction consists of an excellent life of Persons.
Pierre Janelle, *Robert Southwell the Writer*, London, Sheed and Ward,
1935. John Gerard, *The Autobiography of an Elizabethan*, trans. Philip
Caraman, London, Longmans, Green, 1951.

16. See Knox's introduction to the Douay *Diaries*, p. lxiv; cited above, n.
13.

Mœoniæ.
OR,

CERTAINE

excellent Poems and spirituall Hymnes:

*Omitted in the laſt Impreſſion of Peters
Complaint ; being needefull there-
unto to be annexed , as being both Di-
uine and Wittie.*

All compoſed by R. S.

LONDON
Printed by Valentine Sims, for
John Busbie
1 5 9 5.

Title-page of Robert Southwell's *Moeoniae*, 1595
(*Yale University Library*)

England illustrates with particular vividness the way in which the Elizabethan government would prosecute an individual Catholic while leaving his published works free to accomplish their purposes. In 1591, while Southwell was being hotly chased by the pursuivants, Gabriel Cawood issued, "under the hand of the Lord Archbishop of Canterbury," [17] Southwell's prose meditation, *Marie Magdalens Funeral Teares;* this proceeded to run through seven subsequent editions in London by 1636, to say nothing of two editions on the Continent, and produced a number of English imitations which have been recorded by Janelle and Thurston.[18] In the year of Southwell's execution six editions of his works appeared openly in London, all evidently prompted by the recent notoriety of his career.[19] Three of these were attributed on the title-page to "R.S.," and one, *The Triumphs over Death*, contained three prefatory poems flaunting the name of the celebrated author, the last of which defied the Puritans to object to the publication of so devout a work:

17. See *A Transcript of the Registers of the Company of Stationers of London; 1554-1640*, ed. Edward Arber (5 vols., London, 1875-94), *2*, 281b: entry of Nov. 8, 1591.

18. Janelle, pp. 309-10; Herbert Thurston, "Catholic Writers and Elizabethan Readers. III.—Father Southwell, the Popular Poet," *The Month, 83* (1895), 383-99.

19. Southwell was executed on Feb. 22 (o.s.), 1594/5; on April 5, Gabriel Cawood entered *Saint Peters complaynt, with other Poems* for publication (*Stationers' Register*, ed. Arber, *2*, 131); aside from Cawood's edition of this work, two others were published in this year by John Wolfe (see Appendix 3a). There were also two issues of *Moeoniae*, and one of the *Triumphs*, where the title-page, like that of *Moeoniae*, shows how far from surreptitious these publications were: *The Triumphs over Death: or, A Consolatorie Epistle, for afflicted mindes, in the affects of dying friends. First written for the consolation of one: but now published for the generall good of all, by R. S. the Author of S. Peters Complaint, and Moeoniae his other Hymnes. London. Printed by V. S.* [Valentine Sims] *for Iohn Busbie, and are to be sold at Nicholas Lings shop at the West end of Paules Church, 1595.* Both of the last two works were also duly entered for publication, *Moeoniae* on Oct. 17, the *Triumphs* on Nov. 20 (*Stationers' Register*, ed. Arber, *3*, 3b, 5). For full details of the publication of Southwell's works see Janelle's bibliography and James H. McDonald, *The Poems and Prose Writings of Robert Southwell, S. J. A Bibliographical Study*, Oxford, Roxburghe Club, 1937.

Yet if perhappes our late sprung Sectaries,
   Or, for a fashion, Bible-bearing hypocrites,
Whose hollowe hearts doe seeme most holy wise,
Do, for the Authors sake, the worke despise,
      I wish them weigh the worke, and not who writes:
      But they that leave what most the soule delights,
Because the Preachers, no precisian, sure,
To reade what *Southwell* writ will not endure.

In all, Southwell's various works went through at least twenty editions in London alone between the years 1591 and 1636, and through
at least two Edinburgh and five continental editions as well.

From all such evidence it seems clear that there were easy ways
by which the continental methods of meditation could, and did,
reach a large body of educated Englishmen, particularly those of
a High Church tendency, who were by no means averse to all
things Roman. There is, then, reason to consider the thesis that
English religious poetry of the seventeenth century represents the
impact of the continental art of meditation upon English poetical
traditions. That impact was exerted to some extent through the
example of continental religious poetry: Southwell and Crashaw
make this plain. But fundamentally, I shall argue, the Counter
Reformation penetrated to English literature through methods of
religious meditation that lay at the heart of the century's spiritual
life and provided a radiant center for religious literature of every
kind.

3

What, exactly, was the meaning of the term "meditation" during
the sixteenth and seventeenth centuries? It seems at first acquaintance with the devotional books of the time that the terminology
is a hopeless chaos: "meditation" is often used loosely and interchangeably with other terms that are used with a similar vague-
ness: "contemplation," "consideration," "prayer," "mental prayer,"
"good thoughts," "spiritual exercises," "examination of conscience."
Thus we find Fray Luis de Granada explaining: "Praier (to define
it properlie) is a petition we make unto Almightie God, for such

thinges as are apperteining to our salvation. Howbeit, praier is also
taken in another more large sense; to wit: for every lifting up of
our heart unto God." According to this view, he notes, "both meditation and contemplation, and every other good thought may be
also called a Prayer." [1]

But as the sixteenth century progressed the term "meditation"
gradually took on a more sharply delimited significance; by the beginning of the seventeenth century all the most important spiritual
writers are agreed upon the place and significance of "meditation"
as describing a particular stage and process in the spiritual life. The
meaning of the term among the English Jesuits at the opening of
the seventeenth century is plainly stated in a treatise on "The Practical Methode of Meditation" prefaced to a translation by the Jesuit
Richard Gibbons:

> Meditation which we treate of, is nothing els but a diligent
> and forcible application of the understanding, to seeke, and
> knowe, and as it were to tast some divine matter; from whence
> doth arise in our affectionate powers good motions, inclina-
> tions, and purposes which stirre us up to the love and exercise
> of vertue, and the hatred and avoiding of sinne. [2]

Meditation, then, is not simply diligent thinking but thinking deliberately directed toward the development of certain specific emotions: a distinction clearly announced by St. François de Sales in
his *Treatise on the Love of God* (1616):

> Every meditation is a thought, but every thought is not
> meditation; for we have thoughtes, to which our mynd is caried
> without aime or pretention at all, by way of a simple musing,
> as we see flies flie from one flowre to an other, without drawing
> any thing from them: And be this kind of thought as attentive
> as it may be, it can never beare the name of meditation; but

1. Luis de Granada, *Of Prayer, and Meditation* [trans. Richard Hopkins]
(Douay, 1612), p. 19.

2. The treatise is prefaced to Gibbons' translation: *An Abridgment of
Meditations of the Life, Passion, Death, and Resurrection of our Lord and
Saviour Iesus Christ. Written in Italian by the R. Father Vincentius Bruno
of the Society of Iesus* [St Omer], 1614. I use the name Gibbons to refer to
this prefatory treatise, but it may not be his work: see Appendix 3c.

must be called a simple thought. Sometimes we consider a thinge attentively to learne it's causes, effectes, qualities; and this thought is named studie, in which the mynd, is like locustes, which promiscuously flie upon flowres, and leeves, to eate them and nourishe themselfes therupon: but when we thinke of heavenly things, not to learne but to love them, that is called to meditate: and the exercise thereof Meditation: in which our mynd, not as a flie, by a simple musing, nor yet as a locust, to eate and be filled, but as a sacred Bee flies amongst the flowres of holy mysteries, to extract from them the honie of Divine Love.

He then sums up his distinctions to produce the central definition of the term upon which the present study is based:

In fine, thoughtes, and studies may be upon any subiect, but meditation in our present sense, hath reference onely to those obiectes, whose consideration tend's to make us good and devote. So that meditation is an attentive thought iterated, or voluntarily intertained in the mynd, to excitate the will to holy affections and resolutions.[3]

In short, the aim of meditation is the state of "devotion" which Persons has described as the end of his treatise, and which is thus exactly defined by St. François de Sales in his *Introduction to the Devout Life*:

Brieflie, devotion, is nothing els but a spirituall swiftnesse and nimblenesse of love, by which charitie worketh our actions in us, or we by her, with readiness of will, and alacritie of mind; And as it is the office of charitie, in what degree soever it be, to make us keepe the commandements of God generally and universally: so is it the proper function of devotion, to fullfill the commandements with promptnesse, fervour, and nimble vigour of our minds, as it were delighting, and reioycing in doing our dutie towards, God and man.[4]

3. St. François de Sales, *A Treatise of the Love of God*, [trans. Thomas Carre, i.e., Miles Pinkney], (Douay, 1630), pp. 324–5.
4. St. François de Sales, *An Introduction to a Devoute Life*, [trans. John Yakesley], (3rd ed., Rouen, 1614), p. 29.

Meditation, then, cultivates the basic, the lower levels of the spiritual life; it is not, properly speaking, a mystical activity, but a part of the duties of every man in daily life. It is not performed under the operations of special grace, but is available to every man through the workings of ordinary grace. Its activities are thus limited to the first two of St. Bernard's three "degrees of truth":

> We rise to the first by humble effort, to the second by loving sympathy, to the third by enraptured vision. In the first truth is revealed in severity, in the second in pity, in the third in purity. Reason, by which we analyze ourselves, guides us to the first, feeling which enables us to pity others conducts us to the second; purity by which we are raised to the level of the unseen, carries us up to the third.[5]

This third degree of truth represents the spiritual activity which modern writers are accustomed to call "infused contemplation," the work of special grace, the realm of mystical experience, properly so called. Nevertheless, for the achievement of this third stage, the activities of the first two stages of the traditional "threefold way" are usually regarded as almost indispensable. Puente makes the point very clearly when he describes contemplation as "a single viewe of the eternall veritye, without variety of discourses, penetrating it with the light of heaven, with great affections of admiration, and love; unto the which ordinarily no man arriveth, but by much exercize of meditation, and discourse." [6]

Meditation thus comes to be regarded, during our period, as an exercise essential for the ordinary conduct of "good life" and almost indispensable as preparation for the achievement of the highest mystical experience: "now when one names meditation," says St. François de Sales, "we understand a holy thinge, and that by which we begin mysticall Divinitie." [7] Hence the terms "meditation" and "contemplation" tend to flow together in the devotional treatises

5. St. Bernard, *The Twelve Degrees of Humility and Pride*, trans. Barton R. V. Mills (London, S.P.C.K., 1929), p. 40.

6. Luis de la Puente, *Meditations upon the Mysteries of our Holie Faith, with the Practise of Mental Prayer touching the same*, [trans. John Heigham], (2 vols., St. Omer, 1619), *1*, 29. The original work appeared in 1605.

7. *Love of God*, p. 324.

of our period. We find Fray Diego de Estella writing in his popular *Book of the Vanity of the World* (1562):

> In my meditation is the fire kindeled, sayth the Prophet David. For to kyndle the fire of gods love in thy will, and to have the more perfect knowledge of God, meditation, and Contemplation, be both most necessarie: Betwixt both which there is no other difference, but that meditation is an exercise more paynefull and difficult in the matters perteynynge to God: And contemplation is more easie and sweete to them that have had the exercise thereof. [8]

Much the same attitude is adopted in the more precise account of the Jesuit Richeome:

> Contemplation is more then meditation, and as it were the end thereof, and it groweth and springeth upon it many tymes, as the braunch doth upon the body of the tree, or the flowre upon the branch. For the understanding having attentively, and with many reasons to and fro meditated the mystery, and gathered divers lights togeather, doth frame unto her self a cleere knowledge, wherof without further discourse, one way or other, she enjoyeth (as I may say) a vision which approcheth to the knowledge of Angells, who understand without discourse. [9]

Clearly, these views of Fray Diego and Richeome lie behind the repeated definitions of St. François de Sales, who was deeply influenced by both these writers: "Meditation considereth by peecemeale the obiectes proper to move us; but contemplation beholdes the obiect it loves, in one simple and recollected looke, and the consideration so united, causeth a more lively and strong motion." "After we have moved a great many different pious affections by the multitude of considerations of which meditation is composed, we doe in the end gather together the vertue of all these affections,

8. Diego de Estella, *The Contempte of the World, and the Vanitie thereof,* trans. "G. C.," ([Douay?], 1584), f. 213v.

9. Louis Richeome, *The Pilgrime of Loreto,* trans. "E.W." (Paris, 1629), p. 50. The original work appeared in 1604.

from which by the . . . mixture of their forces, doth spring a certaine quintessence of affection . . . called a contemplative affection." [10]

Such views as these would appear to describe the state which
modern writers call "acquired," or "active," or "ordinary" contemplation, a state in which the intellectual powers are still strongly,
though more quietly, at work, and which lies below the "infused"
state of mystical experience proper. But this is a modern distinction which, according to Pourrat,[11] was only beginning to take
shape in the seventeenth century. The incentive for meditation
offered by some of the most popular writers of the time was the
possibility of achieving the highest reaches of mystical experience.
This is evident in such a work as the *Third Spiritual Alphabet* of
Fray Francisco de Osuna, the mystical treatise which had so profound an effect upon St. Teresa. Fray Francisco insists that "the
chief reason for which I wrote this book was to draw everyone's
attention to this exercise of recollection"—the term which the
Spanish mystics, notably St. Teresa, use to describe the withdrawal
from the world of sense-perceptions that marks the road to the
heights of mystical contemplation. Fray Francisco makes it plain
that a good many of his fellow-religious have objected to recommending these "exercises" to those living in the world, but he declares that this experience of contemplation is, and ought to be,
open to all, including the married.[12] Likewise, in his famous *Institutio Spiritualis* (1551) we find Louis de Blois (Blosius) urging
that everyone may hope for at least a taste or hint or glance of the
Mystical Oneness. His central theme is stated at the outset of his
twelfth chapter: "Mystical Union is often vouchsafed to the Soul
that is constant in Perseverance." And he proceeds to explain:

10. *Love of God*, pp. 336, 339.
11. See Pourrat, *3*, 221-3. Cf. Alban Goodier, *An Introduction to the
Study of Ascetical and Mystical Theology* (Milwaukee, Bruce Publishing
Co., 1938), Lecture 16; Auguste Poulain, *The Graces of Interior Prayer*, trans.
Leonora L. Yorke Smith (London, Kegan Paul, Trench, Trübner, 1910),
chap. 4.
12. Francisco de Osuna, *The Third Spiritual Alphabet*, trans. "by a Benedictine of Stanbrook" (Westminster, Md., Newman Bookshop, 1948), pp.
138-43. The original work appeared in 1527.

If the spiritual beginner is careful to exercise his soul daily in the manner laid down, and thus to unite himself to God; if, through internal conversations and loving desires, he strives without ceasing to join himself to God; if he takes care to persevere constantly in self-denial and mortification and never gives up his holy purpose, either on account of his frequent falls or because he becomes discouraged by the innumerable distractions of his mind, he will certainly arrive at perfection and mystical union, if not in this life at least in death.[13]

And the method that he is urging his readers to follow is the difficult "negative way" of "Dionysius the Areopagite"—the way later developed by St. John of the Cross.

Even more important is the fact that a full "treatise on contemplation" is included in one of the two most popular devotional treatises of the Middle Ages: the *Meditations on the Life of Christ* attributed to St. Bonaventure.[14] In the middle of this book, on the occasion of Christ's visit to the house of Martha, the writer takes the opportunity to discuss at length the nature of the contemplative life and its relation to the active life, in accordance with the long-established symbolism of Mary and Martha. This is explicitly compiled from the works of St. Bernard and given mainly through quotations from his works: the result is a full, though very simply presented, treatise on mystical theology, a guide to the highest reaches of contemplation; and thus both the lower levels of meditation and the higher levels of contemplation are urged upon the reader within the covers of a treatise devoutly followed by millions throughout Europe—and England.

I have discussed this relation between meditation and contemplation at such length because it is important to recognize that in the seventeenth century the two terms were not so widely separated from one another as they tend to be in the distinctions of modern students of mystical theology; writers of the seventeenth

13. Louis de Blois, *A Book of Spiritual Instruction: Institutio Spiritualis*, trans. Bertrand A. Wilberforce (2d ed., London, Art and Book Co., 1901), p. 95.

14. *Meditations on the Life of Christ, attributed to St. Bonaventure*, trans. Sister M. Emmanuel (St. Louis, B. Herder Book Co., 1934), chaps. 45–58.

century imply that the state of meditation blends so easily, so gradually, into that of contemplation that a firm distinction can be made
only between the extremes of each state. From this point of view
we can see why the term "mystical" may, with some justice, be
applied to the English meditative poets. Meditation may end with
a state of "devotion"; it may go beyond this into something very
close to a state of mystical contemplation; and it is certainly true
that in portions of the work of Crashaw, Vaughan, and Traherne,
and even in portions of the work of Donne and Herbert, we seem
to touch the state of mystical "recollection" which Miss Underhill has thus described: "the subject of meditation begins to take
on a new significance; to glow with life and light. The contemplative suddenly feels that he knows it, in the complete, vital, but
indescribable way in which one knows a friend. More, that through
it hints are coming to him of mightier, nameless things." The subject of meditation "becomes a symbol through which [he] receives
a distinct message from the transcendental world." [15]

Nevertheless, it is wise to be wary in dealing with the appearance
of mystical terminology in this poetry: it is not by any means valid
to argue that the poetry is therefore the product of mystical experience. The meditative writers of the time are constantly using
the threefold way of the mystics as a framework for purely ascetic
and devotional exercises: mystical terms provide powerful metaphors frequently used in cultivating the realm of devotion. The
term "mystical," then, may on occasion be valid when applied to
certain passages in the works of these writers, or when used to describe the general tendency of the spiritual efforts represented in
these writings. But most of the poetry with which we are here dealing appears clearly to lie within the realm of meditation leading to
devotion; and for this reason the term "meditative" seems to me
more accurate than "mystical" when applied to English religious
poetry of the seventeenth century.

4

The study of this poetry of meditation falls conveniently into
two closely related parts. The first four chapters will explore the

15. Evelyn Underhill, *Mysticism* (6th ed. London, Methuen, 1916), pp.
376–7.

great variety of devotional practices that constitute the art of
meditation. We are dealing here with the roots of religious life in
the seventeenth century, and the materials may be of some interest
to students of religious history in this period. But my major concern is not with a survey of devotional life; it is rather with those
aspects of meditation that may be called potential poetry: those
aspects that provided a discipline and cultivated an outlook akin
to that which we find expressed in English religious poetry of the
seventeenth century. The materials here, I hope, will provide an
illuminating context in which to read this poetry: I have tried to
place examples of the poetry in such a way that they may be seen
as symbols of one of the great movements of European culture. At
the same time, the prose quotations from meditative handbooks of
the time will perhaps convey their own implications for the development of English prose. The exploration ends with the year
1650—a date that is not merely convenient but is symptomatic of
profound changes in English religious life and in English poetry.
It is the date of the appearance of Richard Baxter's *The Saints
Everlasting Rest*, a book which represents a new direction in the
development of English Puritanism. And it is the date of Vaughan's
Silex Scintillans, a book so different from Herbert's *Temple* that
it too may be seen as symbolizing a profound change. We shall, in
places, look forward briefly to these changes and their significance
for English literature, but the subject as a whole lies beyond the
scope of the present study. I am mainly concerned with the earlier
and tightly connected group of Catholic and Anglican poets, in
whose works the continental art of meditation is most clearly manifested.

The second part of the study turns to consider in detail the work
of three of these poets: Southwell, Donne, and Herbert. The four
chapters here will develop further certain aspects of meditation
that have been touched upon in the first part and will introduce a
few other aspects that are more suitably discussed in relation to
these particular poets. But the chief aim of Part 2 is to examine the
many ways in which meditation seems to have coalesced with
strictly poetical traditions of the Renaissance. Poetry and meditation are by no means synonymous; and yet there is, I believe, a middle ground of the creative mind in which the two arts meet to

form a poetry of meditation. The purpose of Part 2 is to find that middle ground. In Southwell's poetry the steps toward that meeting of the arts are so deliberately taken that we can almost mark them on a chart; but they are early steps, frequently clumsy and faltering. Donne's *Anniversaries*, with their combination of religious meditation and Petrarchan eulogy, display a rich development of the tendencies suggested by Southwell and bring within the bounds of two long poems many of the ways of meditation that have been discussed in Part 1. Finally, in Herbert's *Temple* all the popular modes of the short poem in the Renaissance are grouped together in a unity that grows, I believe, from a profound meditative discipline.

In the course of the study I shall treat from the standpoint of meditation many passages of poetry which can be, and have been, fruitfully studied from the standpoint of absolute criticism, or from the standpoint of rhetoric, liturgy, sermon-writing, emblem-books, or the history of ideas. My concern with the art of meditation does not attempt in any way to discredit or disregard the importance of these approaches to the poetry under discussion. All our studies are partial; all need to be set together for a full view of literature. The present study is focused on one aspect of the period; my aim is to convince the reader that this is one among the several necessary methods of approaching a full understanding of English literature in the seventeenth century.

PART 1

The Art of Meditation

Wilt thou love God, as he thee! then digest,
My Soule, this wholsome meditation,
How God the Spirit, by Angels waited on
In heaven, doth make his Temple in thy brest.

John Donne, Holy Sonnet 15

CHAPTER 1

The Method of Meditation

> Our Meditation must *proceed* in due order, not troubledly, not preposterously: It begins in the understanding, endeth in the affection; It begins in the braine, descends to the heart; Begins on earth, ascends to Heaven; Not suddenly, but by certaine staires and degrees, till we come to the highest.
>
> Joseph Hall, *The Arte of Divine Meditation*, 1606

DURING the latter half of the sixteenth century and the first half of the seventeenth, all the important treatises on meditation show a remarkable similarity in fundamental procedure. A large part of this similarity is directly due to the widespread influence of the *Spiritual Exercises* of St. Ignatius Loyola, disseminated throughout Europe by religious counselors and by dozens of Jesuit treatises. The *Exercises* mark the beginning of a new epoch; as Brou says, from the time of their composition (1521–41) "the methods, the treatises of prayer, the collections of meditations, the retreats began to multiply, above all in the seventeenth century." [1] At the same time it is important to remember that the *Exercises* do not stand alone in their kind, but represent a summary and synthesis of efforts since the twelfth century to reach a precise and widely accepted method of meditation. The older methods and treatises which underlie the *Exercises* continued to exert strong influence in their own right. In explaining the methods of meditation followed during our period I shall therefore take the Jesuit manual as a base or skeleton, but shall constantly cite other writers of every affiliation,

---

1. Alexandre Brou, *Les Exercices Spirituels de Saint Ignace de Loyola. Histoire et Psychologie* (2d ed., Paris, P. Téqui, 1922), p. 217. See also James Brodrick, *The Origin of the Jesuits*, London, Longmans, Green, 1940; and *The Progress of the Jesuits* (*1556–79*), London, Longmans, Green, 1947.

in an effort to show both the central pattern and the delicate re-
finements it received at various hands. The entire course of these
spiritual exercises constitutes what the seventeenth century came,
consistently, to call "mental prayer"—the term which has come
down to the present day. In this process of mental prayer, meditation proper formed the major component: the rest of the process
consisted either of preparation for the meditation or of "affections"
flowing from it. Consequently the phrases "method of meditation"
and "method of mental prayer" are used synonymously during our
period. For convenience, I shall simply use the term "meditation."

The *Exercises* of St. Ignatius were designed to be performed during approximately a month set apart for extraordinary devotional
intensity. He divided his materials into four "weeks." The first is
purgative, being devoted to meditations on sin and hell; the second is
given over to meditations (St. Ignatius calls them "contemplations")
on the life of Christ from the Incarnation to Palm Sunday; the third
deals with the events of Passion Week; and the fourth deals with
events from the Resurrection to the Ascension. During this month
these exercises were normally performed five times daily, for periods
of about one hour apiece; a great part of the remainder of the day
was given over to preparing for, and examining the results of, these
devotions.

As the *Exercises* grew in popularity, their methods were adapted
for use during an hour or two of daily meditation. The adaptation
was based on the old medieval practice of setting apart a period for
meditation every morning and every evening, a practice popularized during the sixteenth century by such writers as Fray Luis de
Granada, San Pedro de Alcántara, Gaspar Loarte, and Juan de Avila.
The usual procedure was to set forth two sequences of seven meditations each: one, normally followed in the evening, was devoted
chiefly to self-knowledge and the fear of God. Thus in Fray Luis
de Granada we have the following typical sequence: (1) the knowledge of ourselves and of our sins; (2) the miseries of this life; (3) the
hour of death; (4) the Day of Judgement; (5) the pains of Hell;
(6) the glory and felicity of the Kingdom of Heaven; (7) the benefits of God. Such a sequence obviously accorded very well with the
nightly practice of examining the conscience. The seven morning

meditations then dealt with the life of Christ from the washing of the apostles' feet to the Resurrection.

Thus all the central aspects of the Christian faith were set forth for meditation in regular rotation and, more important, with a method for each period that developed a regular sequence of beginning, middle, and end: preparatory steps; meditation proper, divided into "points"; followed by "colloquies," in which the soul speaks intimately with God and expresses its affections, resolutions, thanksgivings, and petitions. St. Ignatius for his first exercise advises "a preparatory prayer and two preludes, three principal points and a colloquy," [2] and elsewhere expands the procedure to include three preludes, five points and three colloquies.

The preparatory prayer is a simple, short request for grace in the proper performance of the exercise. But the first prelude is the famous "composition of place, seeing the spot"—a practice of enormous importance for religious poetry. For here, says St. Ignatius, "in contemplation or meditation on visible matters, such as the contemplation of Christ our Lord, Who is visible, the composition will be to see with the eyes of the imagination the corporeal place where the thing I wish to contemplate is found." (p. 20) And this, as his followers make clear, is to be done with elaborate, exact detail. We must see, says the English Jesuit Gibbons,

> the places where the thinges we meditate on were wrought, by imagining our selves to be really present at those places; which we must endeavour to represent so lively, as though we saw them indeed, with our corporall eyes; which to performe well, it will help us much to behould before-hande some Image wherin that mistery is well represented, and to have read or heard what good Authors write of those places, and to have noted well the distance from one place to another, the height of the hills, and the situation of the townes and villages. And the diligence we employ heerin is not lost; for on the well making of this *Preludium* depends both the understanding of the mystery, and attention in our meditation. (§ 2, ¶ 10)

2. *The Text of the Spiritual Exercises of Saint Ignatius, Translated from the Original Spanish*, with preface by John Morris (4th ed., Westminster, Md., Newman Bookshop, 1943), p. 20.

Even more important for the poet, St. Ignatius directs that one must also use the image-forming faculty to provide a concrete and vivid setting for a meditation on invisible things; for example, in meditation upon sins, he says, "the composition will be to see with the eyes of the imagination and to consider that my soul is imprisoned in this corruptible body, and my whole self in this vale of misery, as it were in exile among brute beasts." (pp. 20–1) We must attempt, says the Jesuit Puente,

> to procure with the imagination to forme within our selves some figure, or image of the things wee intende to meditate with the greatest vivacity, and propriety that wee are able. If I am to thinke upon hell, I will imagine some place like an obscure, straight, and horrible dungeon full of fier, and the soules therin burning in the middest of those flames. And if I am to meditate [on] the birth of Christ, I will forme the figure of some open place without shelter, and a childe wrapped in swadling cloutes, layed in a manger: and so in the rest. (*1*, 23)

Or, Gibbons adds, if we are meditating on Heaven, we may visualize

> the spatious plesantnes of that celestiall Countrie, the glorious companie of Angels and Saintes. Yf on Gods iudgment which must passe upon us, our Saviour sitting on his Iudgment Seate, and we before him expecting the finall Sentence: if on death, our selves laied on our bed, forsaken of the Physitians, compassed about with our weeping friends, and expecting our last agony.

Whatever the subject, he insists, we must find "some similitude, answerable to the matter." (§ 2, ¶ 11)

The way in which a Jesuit would develop these "similitudes" in actual practice is shown in a passage from the Latin exercises of Robert Southwell, printed from a manuscript in which he appears to have recorded meditations pursued while he was undergoing preparation to enter the order, somewhere around the year 1580. The following passage appears to offer three alternative "compositions" for the meditation on sin advised for the first exercise of the First Week:

Consider first how thou wert the captive and slave of the devil, bound hand and foot by the chains of sin and at the very gates of hell. Thy King, hearing of this, laid aside His royal majesty, His power, His attendants, and His state, clothed Himself in coarse and torn garments and came into this vale of tears. For thirty-three years He sought thee, wandering about hidden and unknown and suffering many injuries and misfortunes. As He was praying for thee, with many tears and with sweat of blood, thy sins rushed in upon Him, tortured and scourged Him, and put Him to a shameful death, whilst thou didst go free.

Next regard thyself as a son who has left his Father and wandering far has at length fallen in with the army of His enemies. They have made thee a miserable captive, and cast thee into the filthy dungeon of thy sins. Thy Father, hearing of thy fate, has sent thy brethren to seek thee, but they have all been captured and put to death by thy enemies. Then thy Father Himself, moved with pity for thee, has left His household, put on the garb of a slave and willingly become an exile and a wanderer in search of thee. At length he too has fallen in with the army of thy enemies, and after most painful tortures has been put to death. But by His death thou hast been freed.

Or again think of Him as the Good Shepherd who has left His sheep upon the mountains and sought thee far and wide in the desert. He has been torn by thorns and has been without protection from the rains and storms, but at length He has found thee amongst the wolves. He has freed thee, but the wolves have attacked Him and He has been slain.[3]

The modern practice of capitalization has, in the translation, somewhat disturbed the effect of graceful familiarity given by the Latin original; but what is most important here is the easy colloquial style into which the composition falls: the practice of dramatizing theological points, after the manner of Gospel parables, has become almost second nature to the meditator. It is this habit of feeling

3. *Spiritual Exercises and Devotions of Blessed Robert Southwell, S.J. Edited for the first time from the Manuscripts*, with intro. by J.-M. de Buck and translation by P. E. Hallett (London, Sheed and Ward, 1931), pp. 47–8.

theological issues as a part of a concrete, dramatic scene that the meditative writers of our period stress as all important for the beginning of a meditation.

Fray Luis de Granada and St. François de Sales strongly advise this method in meditations on the life of Christ, death, hell, judgment, Paradise, and similar matters where the dramatic setting can be easily visualized, "that by meanes of such a representation of these thinges, the consideration and feelinge of them maie be the more lively in us." St. François de Sales notes that "we may use some similitude or comparison, to help our consideration" in dealing with "invisible mysteries," but he fears that this may weary the mind with "searching out curious inventions," and he prefers, with Fray Luis, that we begin with "a simple proposing" of any "wholly spirituall" matter.[4]

It is clear from the various practices mentioned by these writers that there were three different ways of performing this imaginary "composition." The first is to imagine oneself present in the very spot where the event occurred: "to see the arrangements in the holy sepulchre, and the place or house of our Lady, beholding all the parts of it in particular, and likewise her chamber and oratory." The second is to imagine the events as occurring before your eyes "in the very same place where thou art." And the third is performed when persons "imagin that everie one of these thinges whereupon they meditate passeth within their owne harte"—a method strongly recommended by Fray Luis, although St. François de Sales warns that this method is "to subtil and hard for young beginners." Whatever the method, the result is that "By the meanes of this imagination, we lock up our spirit as it were within the closet of the mysterie which we meane to meditate." The effect is an intense, deliberate focusing of the "mind and thought . . . within the bounds, and limits of the subiect . . . either by imaginarie representation, if the matter may be subiect to the sences; or by a simple proposing and conceit of it, if it be a matter above sence," or, for those following St. Ignatius, some concrete similitude dramatizing even spiritual matters.[5]

4. Luis de Granada, pp. 303–4; St. François de Sales, *Introduction*, pp. 126–7, 129; unless otherwise identified, all subsequent references to St. François allude to his *Introduction*.

5. St. Ignatius, p. 71; St. François de Sales, pp. 126–9; Luis de Granada,

The point toward which I am working is perhaps already evident: that such practices of "composition" or "proposing" lie behind the vividly dramatized, firmly established, graphically imaged openings that are characteristic of the poets we are considering. We recall those grand and passionate openings of Donne's "Holy Sonnets," where the moment of death, or the Passion of Christ, or the Day of Doom is there, now, before the eyes of the writer, brought home to the soul by vivid "similitudes":

> Oh my blacke Soule! now thou art summoned
> By sicknesse, deaths herald, and champion;
> Thou art like a pilgrim, which abroad hath done
> Treason, and durst not turne to whence hee is fled,
> Or like a thiefe . . . .

> This is my playes last scene, here heavens appoint
> My pilgrimages last mile; and my race
> Idly, yet quickly runne, hath this last pace,
> My spans last inch, my minutes latest point . . . .

> Spit in my face you Jewes, and pierce my side,
> Buffet, and scoffe, scourge, and crucifie mee . . . .

> What if this present were the worlds last night?

> At the round earths imagin'd corners, blow
> Your trumpets, Angells . . . .

Hutchinson has noted how, "after the example of Donne," Herbert also "often begins with an abrupt question or other provocative phrase, so that the problem gets stated at the outset: 'What is this strange and uncouth thing?,' 'Who says that fictions onely and false hair Become a verse?,' 'Kill me not ev'ry day,' 'The harbingers are come. See, see their mark.' " [6] We may wonder whether all this

---

p. 304. Cf. Gaspar Loarte, *The Exercise of a Christian Life,* [trans. Stephen Brinkley], ([Rheims?], 1584), p. 67, where he explains that the points of meditation "are in suche wise to be meditated, as though they happed even in that instant before thine eyes, in the selfe same place where thou art, or within thy soule: or otherwise imagining thou wert in the very places where suche thinges happed . . . ."

6. F. E. Hutchinson, "George Herbert," in *Seventeenth Century Studies Presented to Sir Herbert Grierson* (Oxford, Clarendon Press, 1938), p. 157.

is due to Donne's example. Is it not rather that Herbert is himself
an adept in meditative practices, adept in proposing the subject,
adept in the composition of introductory similitudes?

> What doth this noise of thoughts within my heart?

> The shepherds sing; and shall I silent be?

> Lord, how can man preach thy eternall word?
>   He is a brittle crazie glasse . . . .

>   I have consider'd it, and finde
> There is no dealing with thy mightie passion. . . .

> O blessed bodie! Whither art thou thrown?
> No lodging for thee, but a cold hard stone?

>   O day most calm, most bright,
> The fruit of this, the next worlds bud,
> Th' indorsement of supreme delight,
> Writ by a friend, and with his bloud . . . .

Or best of all, the opening of "The Collar," with its dramatic
sacrilege against the Communion table, "God's board":

> I struck the board, and cry'd, No more.
> I will abroad.

And we can go beyond Donne and Herbert to find, perhaps, these
habits of composition in the visualization, the colloquial ease, and the
similitude of:

> I saw Eternity the other night
> Like a great *Ring* of pure and endless light . . . .

But these are matters which here will be suggestive only: we must
return to them after considering the structure of the whole meditative process.

2

After these imaginative preliminaries there follows in the Jesuit
exercises yet another prelude, of the utmost importance for the construction and outcome of the total exercise. For here the meditator
asks of God "that which I wish and desire" to achieve in the whole

exercise. This petition, says St. Ignatius, "ought to be according to the subject-matter, *i.e.*, if the contemplation is on the Resurrection, the petition ought to be to ask for joy with Christ rejoicing; if it be on the Passion, to ask for grief, tears, and pain in union with Christ in torment"; or, in the meditation on sins, "it will be to ask for shame and confusion at myself, seeing how many have been lost for one sole mortal sin, and how many times I have merited to be lost eternally for my so many sins." (p. 21) "It is a thing of especiall moment," adds the Jesuit Tomás de Villacastín, "that before we begin our Prayer, we foresee and know the fruit which we ought to gather thereof." [1] And not only is the end foreseen, but the specific progress of the meditation toward this end is carefully charted and practiced beforehand.

Thus Puente, in urging the reader to "premeditate" the "matter of the meditation," declares that "ordinarilie meditation cannot be attentive, nor recollected, if the matter bee not first prepared, well digested, and divided into pointes." (*1*, 16, 25) And St. Ignatius himself gives these graphic directions:

> After having lain down, when I want to go to sleep, to think for the space of an *Ave Maria* of the hour when I have to rise, and for what purpose, briefly recapitulating the Exercise which I have to make.
>
> When I awake, not admitting other thoughts, immediately to turn my mind to that which I am going to contemplate in the first Exercise at midnight, bringing myself to confusion for my many sins, proposing examples to myself, as if a knight were to stand before his king and all his court, covered with shame and confusion, because he had grievously offended him, from whom he had first received many gifts and many favours. And thus too in the second Exercise, considering myself as a great sinner, and in chains, imagining, namely, that bound in fetters I am about to appear before the Supreme, Eternal Judge, taking an example from how prisoners bound in chains, and de-

1. Tomás de Villacastín, *A Manuall of Devout Meditations and Exercises, Instructing how to pray mentally. Drawne for the most part, out of the spirituall Exercises of B. F. Ignatius*, [trans. H. More], ([St. Omer], 1618), p. 40. The original appeared c. 1610.

serving of death, appear before their temporal judge; and I will dress myself, turning over these or other like thoughts, according to the subject-matter. (pp. 28–9)

Much the same general advice is given by the writers of other orders, such as Fray Luis de Granada, who says in his picturesque way:

> I thinke it also requisite here to advertise, that when a man mindeth to use the exercise of praier in the morninge, he doe goe to bedde with this care over night: and like as those that intende to bake the next daie, doe use to laie the leven over nighte, even so must a man with a godly carefulnes prevente and recommende over nighte unto our Lorde that thinge, which he intendeth to meditate the nexte daie followinge. And in the morninge so soone as he awaketh, he ought forthwith to occupie his harte with this holie thought, before anie other doe enter therein. (pp. 301–2)

The procedure thus "premeditated" involved a studied and foreseen movement according to the "three powers of the soul": [2] the memory, the understanding, and the will, in a natural and almost inevitable sequence thus precisely set forth by the Jesuit Puente:

> 1. . . . with the memory to be mindefull of God our Lorde, with whom wee are to speake, and to negociate; and to be mindefull also, of the mysterie that is to bee meditated, passing thorough the memorie, with clearnesse, and distinction, that which is to be the matter of the meditation. . . .
>
> 2. . . . with the understanding to make severall discourses, and considerations about that mysterie, inquyring, and searching out the Verities comprehended therein, with all the causes, proprieties, effectes, and circumstances that it hath, pondering them very particularly. In such sort that the Understanding may forme a true, proper, and entire conceipt of the thing that it meditateth, and may remaine convinced, and persuaded to receive, and to embrace, those truthes that it hath meditated, to propound them to the Will, and to move it therby to exercize its Actions.

2. St. Ignatius, p. 20.

> 3. . . . with the freedom of our will to draw forth sundry
> Affections, or vertuous Actes, conformable to that which the
> Understanding hath meditated . . . as are Hatred of our
> selves; Sorrowe for our Sinnes; Confusion of our owne misery;
> Love of God; trust in his mercye; prayses of God; thankesgiv-
> ing for benefits received; desire to obtaine true vertues . . .
> resignation of our selves to the Will of God . . . . (*1*, 3–4)

This threefold sequence was followed not only for every "mystery" but for every one of the three or more points into which the
Jesuits were accustomed to divide each subject: "in every Mysterie and point we take in hand, of all the meditations of the books
following, we are to exercise these three powers in Prayer . . . ." [3]

Writers outside the Jesuit order tend to be less specific about the
operation of these three powers, yet the basic procedure is the
same. Fray Luis de Granada, for example, agrees that "our will is
a blinde power, that cannot step one foote, unlesse the understanding doe goe before, and illuminate, and teach it, what thing it ought
to desire, and withall how much it ought to will and desire, the
same." (pp. 29–30)

The full theological implications of this stress upon the "three
powers" are not often made explicit in the popular treatises: they
are either taken for granted or regarded as too theoretical for the
layman. But a man with even slight theological training would
have realized that the three powers of the soul were regarded as
analogous to the Trinity, and that through the integration of this
trinity within man he might come to know and feel in himself the
operation of the higher Trinity: might (in St. Bernard's terminology) achieve through the reformed operation of these powers a
renewal, a refreshing, of the defaced Image of God within man.
This view was clearly set forth for every layman in one of the most
popular meditative books in English: the *Meditations* attributed to
St. Bernard and largely composed of passages taken from his works.
Nothing, the book declares, "is more like to that most excellent
and highest Wisdome, then a reasonable Soule, which through
Memory, Understanding, and Will, consisteth in that unutterable
Trinity." And this is the central point in exhorting the reader to

3. Tomás de Villacastín, p. 37.

meditation, for the soul "cannot consist and abide" in the Trinity "unlesse it remember, understand, and love the same."

> The minde is the Image of God, in which are these three things, *Memory*, *Understanding*, and *Will*, or *Love*. Wee attribute to the *Memory*, all which wee know, although we thinke not of it. Wee attribute to the *Understanding*, all which we finde to bee true in thinking, which wee also commit unto *Memory*.

> By *Memory*, wee are like to the Father, by *Understanding* to the Sonne, by *Will* to the holy Ghost.[4]

This whole view is set forth in its full implications in the works of St. Bonaventure, especially in the third section of his great treatise on meditation and contemplation, the *Itinerarium Mentis in Deum*.[5] But I think, for a rich summary of the whole position, I cannot do better than quote from the best of all modern commentators on St. Bonaventure, Étienne Gilson:

> Just as the Father engenders the eternal knowledge of the Word Who expresses Him, and as the Word is in turn united with the Father by the Holy Spirit, so memory or thought, big with the ideas which it encloses, engenders the knowledge of the intellect or word, and love is born from both as the bond which unites them. It is no accidental correspondence that is here described; the structure of the creative Trinity conditions and therefore explains the structure of the human soul.[6]

Now, with this trinity of powers integrated through meditation, the climax, the aim and end, of the whole exercise is achieved when the soul thus reformed is lifted up to speak with God in colloquy and to hear God speak to man in turn. These colloquies, according

4. *Saint Bernard His Meditations*, trans. "W.P." (4th ed., London, 1631–2), Pt. 2, pp. 6, 9.

5. See the translation of this treatise by "Father James" in *The Franciscan Vision*, London, Burns, Oates, and Washbourne, 1937.

6. Étienne Gilson, *The Philosophy of St. Bonaventure*, trans. Illtyd Trethowan and F. J. Sheed (New York, Sheed and Ward, 1938), p. 224.

to St. Ignatius, must conclude every exercise, and may be addressed to the Father, or to the Son, or to the Virgin—or to all in sequence —and they are to be performed "by speaking as one friend speaks to another, or as a servant to his master; at one time asking for some favour, at another blaming oneself for some evil committed, now informing him of one's affairs, and seeking counsel in them." (p. 23) St. Ignatius' followers expand these suggestions in rich, dramatic detail. Sometimes, says Puente, "wee are to speake unto him as a sonne speaketh unto his Father"; sometimes "as a poore wretch doth to a riche and mercifull man, begging of him an almes"; at other times, "as a sicke man speaketh to a Phisitian, declaring unto him his infirmities, and desiring remedie therof: or as a man that hath a processe, or as one that is guiltye speaketh to a Judge"; or as a "scholler speaketh unto his master, requyring of him light, and Instruction"; or "as one friend speaketh unto another, when he talketh with him of some waighty affaire." And on some occasions, Puente continues, "if confidence, and love shall so farre imbolden us," the soul may even speak to God (after the manner of St. Bernard and other medieval mystics) "as the bride speaketh to her spouse in severall Colloquyes, wherewith the book of Canticles is replenished." Moreover, "albeit praier is properly a speche, and colloquy with our Lord," we may nevertheless "speake therin to our selves, and have conference with our owne soule. Sometimes our selves (as S. Paul saieth) exhorting our selves, and reviving our selves in the affections, and petitions rehearsed. Other times reprehending our selves for our faultes, and for our want of zeale, and being ashamed of our selves that wee serve almightie God so negligentlie." [7] St. François de Sales, as usual, sums up beautifully the whole range of possibilities in colloquy, when he advises that "Amidst these affections and resolutions" which follow from meditation "it is good to use colloquies, or familiar talke, as it were somtime with God our Lord, somtime with our blessed Ladie, with the Angels, and persons represented in the mysterie which we meditate, with the Saints of heaven, with our selves, with our owne hart, with sinners, yea and with insensible creatures." (p. 139)

All these parts of a given exercise will, when properly performed, flow into one inseparable, inevitable sequence: the imaginative

7. Puente, 1, 8–9.

"composition" will in the meditation proper be recalled by the memory, whose responsibility is to "lay open to the view of our understanding the persons, wordes, and workes contained in the first point," thus "setting before our eyes the point or Mysterie on which we are to meditate." [8] Similarly, the acts of the colloquy are inseparable from the affections of the will. Without expecting any hard and fast divisions, then, we should expect to find a formal meditation falling into three distinguishable portions, corresponding to the acts of memory, understanding, and will—portions which we might call composition, analysis, and colloquy. And, if my present argument for the impact of these practices upon English poetry has any validity, we should expect to find, in at least a few poems, some total structure resembling the structure of a full spiritual exercise. For Robert Southwell was a Jesuit. John Donne was reared in a devout Catholic family, and his uncle, Jasper Heywood, was one of the leading Jesuit missionaries in England during Donne's childhood: it would be reasonable to suppose that Donne was subjected to a strong Jesuit influence during his formative years. George Herbert, as Nicholas Ferrar says in the preface to the *Temple*, "abounded in private devotions"; we may well suppose that these may have included some of the meditative exercises which we have described: methods, perhaps, such as were advised in a book venerated by the Ferrars at Little Gidding, St. François de Sales' *Introduction to the Devout Life*.[9]

The meditative process would, of course, be working in cooperation with many other elements to form the character of this poetry. In particular, the principles of Renaissance logic and rhetoric would be in evidence,[10] for these methods of meditation are in themselves adaptations of ancient principles of logic and rhetoric. This is made especially clear in one of the great prototypes of the central method of meditation practiced during our period: the *Scala Meditationis* of Wessel Gansfort, which will be dealt with

8. Gibbons, § 2, ¶ 12; Tomás de Villacastín, p. 37.

9. See Alan L. Maycock, *Nicholas Ferrar of Little Gidding* (London, S.P.C.K., 1938), pp. 283–4.

10. See the elaborate study of these matters by Rosemond Tuve, *Elizabethan and Metaphysical Imagery*, Chicago, University of Chicago Press, 1947.

later in this chapter.[11] Gansfort's long treatise, dating from the latter part of the fifteenth century, is filled with references to the logical and rhetorical methods of Aristotle, Cicero, Raymond Lull, Rudolf Agricola, and others; his *Scala* adapts and transforms the methods of these writers for the purpose of interior "oratory" and debate. And this is true of all the meditative treatises: all the ways of speaking and writing that a man has learned will inevitably help to form the thoughts of the "whole soul." At the same time, the enormous popularity of methodical meditation in this era may be attributed to the fact that it satisfied and developed a natural, fundamental tendency of the human mind—a tendency to work from a particular situation, through analysis of that situation, and finally to some sort of resolution of the problems which the situation has presented. Meditation focused and disciplined the powers that a man already possessed, both his innate powers and his acquired modes of logical analysis and rhetorical development. The process of meditation, then, is not an isolated factor in this poetry; it exists, I believe, as a fundamental organizing impulse deep within the poetry.

3

Let us look first at one of the better-known poems of Robert Southwell, "New Prince, new pompe":

> Behold a silly tender Babe,
>   In freesing Winter night;
> In homely manger trembling lies,
>   Alas a pittious sight:
> The Innes are full, no man will yeeld
>   This little Pilgrime bed;
> But forc't he is with sillie beasts,
>   In Crib to shrowd his head.
> Despise him not for lying there,
>   First what he is enquire:
> An orient pearle is often found,
>   In depth of dirtie mire.
> Waigh not his Crib, his wodden dish,

11. See Johan Wessel Gansfort, *Opera* (Groningen, 1614), pp. 194–326.

> Nor beasts that by him feede:
> Waigh not his Mothers poore attire,
> Nor Iosephs simple weede.
> This stable is a Princes Court,
> The Crib his chaire of state:
> The beasts are parcell of his Pompe,
> The wodden dish his plate.
> The persons in that poore attire,
> His royall liveries weare,
> The Prince himselfe is com'n from heaven,
> This pompe is prized there.
> With ioy approach ô Christian wight,
> Doe homage to thy King;
> And highly prayse his humble pompe,
> Which he from heaven doth bring.[1]

The first eight lines seem to form a "composition, seeing the spot"; the next two lines seem explicitly to begin the analytical acts of the understanding: "First what he is enquire"—as in Puente's directions, "inquyring, and searching out the Verities comprehended therein." And then, in the last four lines, the poem seems clearly to "draw forth sundry Affections, or vertuous Actes, conformable to that which the Understanding hath meditated." The affections of the will are not expressed in colloquy but rather in an exhortation addressed simultaneously to the self and to the reader.

Clear examples of colloquies concluding a threefold sequence may be found in two other poems by Southwell: "Sinnes heavie loade" and "Christs sleeping friends." These two poems are widely separated in Grosart's edition, and indeed they originally appeared in separate volumes of Southwell's works, but they form a pair of meditations on Christ's Agony in Gethsemane, each presented in seven stanzas of identical form.[2] The first two stanzas of "Sinnes heavie loade" suggest the acts of composition and memory, with a

---

1. For my procedure in quoting Southwell's poetry see Appendix 3, a.
2. In the manuscripts the poems are grouped with "Christs bloody sweate," which comes in between the two: see McDonald, pp. 21, 24, 26, 28, 45–6; "Sinnes heavie loade" first appeared in the "augmented" edition of *Saint Peters Complaint*, 1602; "Christs sleeping friends" in *Moeoniae*, 1595.

few touches of paradoxical analysis that prepare the way for the operations of the understanding:

> O Lord, my sinnes doe over-charge thy brest,
>   The poyse therof doth force thy knees to bow;
> Yea flat thou fallest with my faults opprest,
>   And bloodie sweat runs trickling from thy brow:
> But had they not to earth thus pressed thee,
> Much more they would in hell have pestred mee.
>
> This Globe of earth doth thy one finger prop,
>   The world thou doo'st within thy hand embrace;
> Yet all this waight, of sweat drew not a drop,
>   Ne made thee bow, much lesse fall on thy face:
> But now thou hast a loade so heavie found,
> That makes thee bow, yea fall flat to the ground.

Then, in the third stanza, begins the formal, theological analysis of the scene, continuing for four stanzas of elaborately argued paradox. I quote the fifth and sixth stanzas:

> Thou minded in thy heaven our earth to weare,
>   Doo'st prostrate now thy heaven, our earth to blisse;
> As God, to earth thou often wert severe:
>   As man, thou [seal'st] a peace with bleeding kisse.
> For as of soules thou common Father art,
> So is she Mother of mans other part.
>
> She shortly was to drink thy dearest blood,
>   And yeeld thy soule a way to sathans cave;
> She shortly was thy corse in tombe to shrowd,
>   And with them all thy deitie to have:
> Now then in [one] thou ioyntly yeeldest all,
> That severally to earth should shortly fall.

And finally, in the last stanza, we have this colloquy (petition):

> O prostrate Christ, erect my crooked minde,
>   Lord let thy fall my flight from earth obtaine;
> Or if I needes must still in earth be shrin'd,

> Then Lord on earth come fall yet once againe:
> And either yeeld in earth with me to lie,
> Or else with thee to take me to the skie.

The companion-poem follows this general pattern, but with significant variations. In its first two stanzas the memory reviews the events in elaborate detail:

> When Christ with care and pangs of death opprest
>   From frighted flesh a bloody sweate did raine,
> And full of feare without repose or rest
>   In agonie did watch and pray in vaine,
> Three sundrie times hee his disciples findes
> With heavy eies, but farre more heavy mindes,
>
> With milde rebuke he warned them to wake:
>   Yet sleepe did still their drowsie sences hold:
> As when the sunne the brightest shew doth make,
>   In darkest shroudes the night birdes them infolde,
> His foes did watch to worke their cruell spight,
> His drousie friendes slept in his hardest night.

The next three stanzas analyze the significance of these events by drawing an extended parallel between them and the sleeping of "Ionas" in the ship and under the shade of the "ivy" plant. Then comes, first, a colloquy with Christ, symbolized as the plant that withered while Jonah slept:

> O gratious plant, O tree of heavenly spring,
>   The paragon for leafe, for fruit and flower,
> How sweete a shadow did thy branches bring
>   To shrowd these soules that chose thee for their bower?
> But now while they with *Ionas* fall asleepe,
> To spoile their plant an envious worme doth creepe.

And finally, a stanza which is simultaneously a colloquy with the slumbering disciples and an exhortation to every sinner:

> Awake you slumbring wights lift up your eies,
>   Marke *Iudas* how to teare your roote he strives,
> Alas the glorie of your arbor dies,

> Arise and guarde the comforte of your lives.
> No *Ionas* ivy, no *Zacheus* tree,
> Were to the world so great a losse as he.

In these three, frequently awkward, poems, every reader will perhaps have been struck by a phrase here, a line or two there, which holds a tantalizing prefiguration of the much greater poetical achievements of Donne and Herbert; but what I should like to stress at this point is the way in which the total movement of these poems resembles, in its rudiments, the "intellectual, argumentative evolution" of Donne's or Herbert's poetry: the "strain of passionate, paradoxical reasoning which knits the first line to the last," and performs this knitting through close analysis and elaboration of concrete imagery. Southwell seems to be struggling toward the qualities that Hutchinson has thus accurately described as the dominant characteristic of Herbert: "Almost any poem of his has its object well defined; its leading idea is followed through with economy and brought to an effective conclusion, the imagery which runs through it commonly helping to knit it together." Southwell's poems give that impression of a "predetermined plan" which Palmer has noted as a characteristic of many of Herbert's poems,[3] and which is also, I think, a strong characteristic of Donne's. May it not be that all three poets are working, to some extent, under the influence of methods of meditation that led toward the deliberate evolution of a threefold structure of composition (memory), analysis (understanding), and colloquy (affections, will)?

4

The "Holy Sonnets" seem to bear out this conjecture. Holy Sonnet 12 bears a very close resemblance to the conclusion of St. Ignatius Loyola's second exercise for the First Week, a "meditation upon sins," where the fifth and last point is:

> an exclamation of wonder, with intense affection, running through all creatures in my mind, how they have suffered me to live, and have preserved me in life; how the angels, who are the sword of the Divine Justice, have borne with me, and have

3. *Works of Herbert*, ed. Hutchinson, p. xlix; *Works of Herbert*, ed. Palmer, *1*, 142.

guarded and prayed for me; how the saints have been interceding and praying for me; and the heavens, the sun, the moon, the stars, and the elements, the fruits of the earth, the birds, the fishes, and the animals; and the earth, how it is it has not opened to swallow me up . . . .

The whole to conclude with a colloquy of mercy, reasoning and giving thanks to God our Lord, for having given me life till now, and proposing through His grace to amend henceforward. (pp. 24–5)

In Sonnet 12 this problem, simply and firmly proposed in the opening line, is elaborated with a single, scientific instance in the first quatrain:

> Why are wee by all creatures waited on?
> Why doe the prodigall elements supply
> Life and food to mee, being more pure then I,
> Simple, and further from corruption?

The problem is then examined in greater detail through a shift to direct questioning of the animals, which runs through the next six lines:

> Why brook'st thou, ignorant horse, subjection?
> Why dost thou bull, and bore so seelily
> Dissemble weaknesse, and by'one mans stroke die,
> Whose whole kinde, you might swallow and feed upon?
> Weaker I am, woe is mee, and worse then you,
> You have not sinn'd, nor need be timorous.

The "colloquy of mercy" then appears to follow, as the speaker addresses himself, the representative of all mankind, "reasoning," developing the sense of "wonder," and implicitly "giving thanks":

> But wonder at a greater wonder, for to us
> Created nature doth these things subdue,
> But their Creator, whom sin, nor nature tyed,
> For us, his Creatures, and his foes, hath dyed.

Puente's development of this Ignatian topic will provide, perhaps, a more convincing proof of our argument for Jesuit influence here:

The fourth pointe, shall bee, to breake out with these considerations into an exclamation, with an affection vehement,
and full of amazement; As, that the creatures have suffered me,
I having so grievously offended their Creator, and benefac-
tor . . . . That the elements, the birdes of the aire, the fishes of
the sea, the beastes, and plantes of the earthe have helped to sus-
taine mee. I confesse that I deserve not the breade I eate, nor the
water I drinke, nor the aire I breathe in: neither am I worthy
to lift up myne eyes to heaven . . . . (*1*, 70–1)

At the same time, it seems that Holy Sonnet 15 bears some general relation to St. Ignatius' "Contemplation for obtaining love,"
a special meditation, annexed to the Fourth Week, which aims at
achieving "an interior knowledge of the many and great benefits
I have received, that, thoroughly grateful, I may in all things love
and serve His Divine Majesty." The meditation opens by calling
to mind

the benefits received, of my creation, redemption, and particular gifts, dwelling with great affection on how much God
our Lord has done for me, and how much He has given me of
that which He has; and consequently, how much He desires
to give me Himself in so far as He can according to His Divine ordinance; and then to reflect in myself what I, on my
side, with great reason and justice, ought to offer and give to
His Divine Majesty. (pp. 74–5)

This seems to be exactly what the speaker is so deliberately telling
himself to do in Sonnet 15:

Wilt thou love God, as he thee! then digest,
My Soule, this wholsome meditation,
How God the Spirit, by Angels waited on
In heaven, doth make his Temple in thy brest.
The Father having begot a Sonne most blest,
And still begetting, (for he ne'r begonne)
Hath deign d to chuse thee by adoption,
Coheire to'his glory, 'and Sabbaths endlesse rest.
And as a robb'd man, which by search doth finde

His stolne stuffe sold, must lose or buy'it againe:
The Sonne of glory came downe, and was slaine,
Us whom he'had made, and Satan stolne, to unbinde.
'Twas much, that man was made like God before,
But, that God should be made like man, much more.

In lines 3 and 4 there may be a reminiscence of a part of the "second point" of this exercise, where one is advised to "consider how God dwells in creatures . . . and so in me, giving me being, life, feeling, and causing me to understand: making likewise of me a temple . . . ." But the resemblances are only general, and of course the sonnet does not trace the progress of a complete exercise: it is analysis only, understanding; part of a complete exercise.

This, I believe, is what we should expect to find in most of the "Holy Sonnets" (and in most of the other religious poems of the time related to the art of meditation): a portion of an exercise which has been set down in explicit poetry; especially the colloquy, in which the "three powers" fuse, become incandescent, as Fray Luis de Granada says: "When we talke unto almightie God, then the understanding mounteth up on highe, and after it followeth also the will, and then hath a man commonly on his parte greater devotion, and attention, and greater feare, and reverence of the majestie of almightie God, with whom he speaketh . . . ." (p. 309) The complete exercise was long—an hour or more in duration—and its deliberate, predominantly intellectual method would not, for most of its course, provide material for poetry. Now and then a poet might recapitulate an exercise in miniature, or compose a poem that developed under the impulse of his frequent practice of the stages in a full sequence; but more often we should expect the poetry to reflect chiefly the final stages of the sequence. Furthermore, the formal procedure for a full exercise was not by any means necessarily followed on every occasion. All the meditative treatises explain that this full framework is provided as an aid for beginners or as a method to fall back upon in times of spiritual dryness. Even the Jesuit exercises, which might appear to prescribe the most rigorous of all plans, are actually very flexible, for St. Ignatius expects them to be performed under the direction of a priest who will adapt them to the needs and capacities of each individual. Adepts in meditation are encouraged, both by the Jesuits and by other writers, to

follow the lead of their affections. Thus we find Tomás de Villacastín warning that "the infinite goodnes and liberality of God is
not tyed to these rules" (p. 55); Fray Luis de Granada explaining
that he has set down "diverse and sundrie poyntes, to the intent,
that emonge so great varietie of considerations, everie one might
make his choise of such thinges, as might best serve his devotion"
(p. 49); and St. François de Sales urging the reader to "take this for
a generall rule, never to restraine, or with-hold thy affections once
inflamed with any devout motion, but let them have their free
course." (p. 138)

In accordance with this freedom of procedure we find that colloquies may be made not only at the end of the set sequence but
at any time during an exercise: indeed, the Jesuit Gibbons says "it
will be best, and almost needfull so to do" (§ 2, ¶ 25); and Puente
proves the point by scattering colloquies frequently throughout the
course of his meditations. In these colloquies of Puente we find
something very close to the tone and manner of Donne's religious
poetry: subtle theological analysis, punctuated with passionate questions and exclamations:

> O my soule, heare what this our Lord saieth: Which of you
> can dwell with devouring fier? O who shallbee able to dwell
> in these perpetuall ardours? If thou darest not touche the light
> fier of this life, why doest thou not tremble at the terrible fier of
> the other? Contemplate this fier with attention, that the feare
> thereof may consume the fier of thy insatiable desire, if thor-
> ough thy want of fervent zeale, the fier of God's love bee not
> sufficient to consume them. (1, 144)

> O God of vengeance, how is it that thou hast not revenged
> thy selfe on a man so wicked as I? How hast thou suffred mee
> so long a time? Who hath withhelde the rigour of thy justice,
> that it should not punish him, that hath deserve[d] so terrible
> punishment? O my Soule, how is it, that thou doest not feare,
> and tremble, considering the dreadefull judgement of God
> against his Angells? If with so great severitye hee punished
> creatures so noble, why should not so vile, and miserable a
> creature as thou, feare the like punishment? O most powerfull
> creator, seeing thou hast shewed thy selfe to mee not a God

of vengeance, but a father of mercye, continue towardes mee
this thy mercye, pardonning my sinnes, and delivering mee
from hell, which most justly for them I have deserved. (*1*, 55)

More specific similarities are found in the passage where Puente
urges that in addressing colloquies to God, or Christ, or the Trinity
we should offer "titles and reasons, that may move them to graunt
us what wee demaund." In Christ, he says, we may claim such titles
as his sufferings and his love,

> Sometimes speaking to the eternall Father, beseeching him to
> heare mee for the Love of his Sonne; for the Services hee did
> him; and the Paines that for his love hee endured. Other times
> speaking to the Sonne of God: alledging unto him the love
> that hee bare us, the Office that hee holdeth of our Redeemer,
> and Advocate; and the greate Price that wee cost him . . . .
>
> Other Titles there are on the part of our Necessitye, and
> Miserye, alledging before our Lord, like *David*, that wee were
> conceived in Sinne, that wee have disordered passions, strong
> enemies . . . and that without him wee are able to doe noth-
> ing. That we are his Creatures made according to his owne
> Image, and Likenesse, and that for this cause the devill perse-
> cuteth us to destroye us, and that therefore it appertayneth to
> him to protect us. (*1*, 4–5)

Donne's Sonnet 2 certainly looks like a colloquy stemming from
such advice as this:

> As due by many titles I resigne
> My selfe to thee, O God, first I was made
> By thee, and for thee, and when I was decay'd
> Thy blood bought that, the which before was thine;
> I am thy sonne, made with thy selfe to shine,
> Thy servant, whose paines thou hast still repaid,
> Thy sheepe, thine Image, and, till I betray'd
> My selfe, a temple of thy Spirit divine;
> Why doth the devill then usurpe on mee?
> Why doth he steale, nay ravish that's thy right?
> Except thou rise and for thine owne worke fight,
> Oh I shall soone despaire, when I doe see

That thou lov'st mankind well, yet wilt'not chuse me,
And Satan hates mee, yet is loth to lose mee.

Such general or fragmentary parallels between Donne's poetry and Jesuit methods of meditation are strongly supported by the fact that at least four of the "Holy Sonnets" appear to display, in their total movement, the method of a total exercise: they suggest the "premeditation" or the recapitulation, in miniature, of such an exercise; or, at least, a poetical structure modeled on the stages of a complete exercise. Such a threefold structure, of course, easily accords with the traditional 4-4-6 division of the Petrarchan sonnet, and thus provides a particularly interesting illustration of the way in which poetical tradition may be fertilized and developed by the meditative tradition. Perhaps the clearest example is found in Holy Sonnet 11, which suggests the traditional meditative procedure briefly described by Antonio de Molina: "Thus when we see our Saviour taken prisoner, and used so ill, whipped and nayled on the Crosse; we consider that we be there present amongst those villaines, and that our sinnes be they who so abuse him, and take away his life"; [1] and developed with dramatic detail by Puente:

> Then I am to set before mine eyes Christ Jesus crucified, beholding his heade crowned with thornes; his face spit upon; his eyes obscured; his armes disioincted; his tongue distasted with gall, and vineger; his handes, and feete peerced with nailes; his backe, and shoulders torne with whippes; and his side opened with a launce: and then pondering that hee suffereth all this for my sinnes, I will drawe sundrye affections from the inwardest parte of my heart, sometimes trembling at the rigour of God's iustice . . . sometimes bewailing my sinnes which were the cause of these dolours: and sometimes animating myselfe to suffer somewhat in satisfaction of myne offences, seeing Christ our Lord suffered so much to redeeme them. And finally I will beg pardon of him for them, alledging to him for a reason, all his troubles, and afflictions, saying unto him in amorous colloquie.
>
> O my most sweete Redeemer, which descendest from

1. Antonio de Molina, *A Treatise of Mental Prayer*, [trans. J. Sweetman], ([St. Omer], 1617), pp. 60–1. The original appeared in 1615.

heaven, and ascendest this Crosse to redeeme men, paying their sinnes with thy dolours, I present myselfe before thy Majestie, grieved that my grievous sinnes have been the cause of thy terrible paines. Upon mee, O Lord, these chastizements had been iustlie imployed, for I am hee that sinned, and not upon thee that never sinnedst. Let that love that moved thee to put thyselfe upon the Crosse for mee, move thee to pardon mee what I have committed against thee. (*1*, 59–60)

Similarly, in Donne's sonnet, the speaker has made himself vividly present at the scene, so dramatically conscious of his sins that he cries out to Christ's persecutors in lines that throw a colloquial emphasis on the words "my," "mee," and "I":

> Spit in my face you Jewes, and pierce my side,
> Buffet, and scoffe, scourge, and crucifie mee,
> For I have sinn'd, and sinn'd, and onely hee,
> Who could do no iniquitie hath dyed:

but after this passionate outcry the tone of the next quatrain shifts to one of tense, muted, intellectual brooding, as the understanding explores the theological significance of the scene:

> But by my death can not be satisfied
> My sinnes, which passe the Jewes impiety:
> They kill'd once an inglorious man, but I
> Crucifie him daily, being now glorified.

And then, with another marked shift in tone, the speaker turns to draw forth in himself the appropriate "affections," suffusing intellectual analysis with the emotions of love and wonder:

> Oh let me then, his strange love still admire:
> Kings pardon, but he bore our punishment.
> And *Iacob* came cloth'd in vile harsh attire
> But to supplant, and with gainfull intent:
> God cloth'd himselfe in vile mans flesh, that so
> Hee might be weake enough to suffer woe.

Likewise, in the first quatrain of Sonnet 7 we may see the dramatic operations of both imagination and memory, for here the speaker remembers the description of Doomsday in the book of Revelation, especially the opening of the seventh chapter: "I saw four angels standing on the four corners of the earth"; and he cries out, seeing them there in a vivid composition of place:

> At the round earths imagin'd corners, blow
> Your trumpets, Angells, and arise, arise
> From death, you numberlesse infinities
> Of soules, and to your scattred bodies goe . . . .

With the "matter" of the meditation thus "composed" and defined, the understanding then performs its analysis in the second quatrain, "discoursing" upon the causes of death throughout human history: a summary of sin and a reminder of its consequences:

> All whom the flood did, and fire shall o'erthrow,
> All whom warre, dearth, age, agues, tyrannies,
> Despaire, law, chance, hath slaine, and you whose eyes,
> Shall behold God, and never tast deaths woe.

Finally, in the sestet, the will expresses its "affections" and "petitions" in colloquy with God, "as one friend speaks to another, or as a servant to his master":

> But let them sleepe, Lord, and mee mourne a space,
> For, if above all these, my sinnes abound,
> 'Tis late to aske abundance of thy grace,
> When wee are there; here on this lowly ground,
> Teach mee how to repent; for that's as good
> As if thou'hadst seal'd my pardon, with thy blood.

"When wee are there"—those words which so puzzled I. A. Richards' students [2] may be explained if we realize that this is part of a

2. I. A. Richards, *Practical Criticism* (New York, Harcourt, Brace, 1935), pp. 44–5. Miss Gardner would interpret this sonnet as developing in accordance with the two preludes of the Ignatian method, the octave giving the "composition" and the sestet the petition "according to the subject-matter." This seems to me a valid interpretation: since the whole progress of the exercise would have been "premeditated" and foreseen, the action of the "three powers" would be anticipated in the preludes. See her excellent analysis of this and other "Holy Sonnets" in John Donne, *The Divine Poems*, ed. Helen Gardner (Oxford, Clarendon Press, 1952), pp. l–liv.

traditional colloquy with God after a visualization of the Day of Doom. "Wee," though no doubt including all sinners, suggests primarily God and the individual speaker's soul; "there" refers to the throne of Judgment in the heavens, as presented in the book of Revelation; "there" is thus in sharp contrast with the "lowly ground" where the soul now prays for grace, with theological overtones relating to the Catholic sacrament of Penance.

Somewhat the same procedure appears also to be operating in Holy Sonnet 9, where an example of Donne's besetting sin of intellectual pride is "proposed" in an audacious, blasphemous evasion of responsibility:

> If poysonous mineralls, and if that tree,
> Whose fruit threw death on else immortall us,
> If lecherous goats, if serpents envious
> Cannot be damn'd; Alas; why should I bee?

The problem thus set forth concretely is then pursued abstractly in the second quatrain, which reveals the speaker's knowledge of the proper theological answer to his question, but he continues the evasion and increases the blasphemy by first an implied ("borne in mee"), and then a direct, attack on God's justice:

> Why should intent or reason, borne in mee,
> Make sinnes, else equall, in mee more heinous?
> And mercy being easie, and glorious
> To God; in his sterne wrath, why threatens hee?

But at last, and very suddenly, the thin wall of this uneasy argument collapses and the poem concludes with one of Donne's most vehement colloquies, giving the answer that has been implicit and premeditated throughout:

> But who am I, that dare dispute with thee
> O God? Oh! of thine onely worthy blood,
> And my teares, make a heavenly Lethean flood,
> And drowne in it my sinnes blacke memorie;
> That thou remember them, some claime as debt,
> I thinke it mercy, if thou wilt forget.

And fourthly, with a slightly different division of lines, I believe that we can follow the same movement in Sonnet 5, which presents in its first four lines a "composition by similitude" defining precisely the "invisible" problem to be considered:

> I am a little world made cunningly
> Of Elements, and an Angelike spright,
> But black sinne hath betraid to endlesse night
> My worlds both parts, and (oh) both parts must die.

The next five lines form a unit overflowing the usual Petrarchan division; and appropriately, since the intellect is here using a mode of violent hyperbole:

> You which beyond that heaven which was most high
> Have found new sphears, and of new lands can write,
> Powre new seas in mine eyes, that so I might
> Drowne my world with my weeping earnestly,
> Or wash it, if it must be drown'd no more:

and then, inevitably, the last five lines, another firm unit, show the passionate outburst of the affections thus aroused, ending with a petition in colloquy with God:

> But oh it must be burnt! alas the fire
> Of lust and envie have burnt it heretofore,
> And made it fouler; Let their flames retire,
> And burne me ô Lord, with a fiery zeale
> Of thee and thy house, which doth in eating heale.[3]

We can see then why, as Grierson records, three manuscripts of the "Holy Sonnets" entitle them "Devine Meditations." [4] They are, in the most specific sense of the term, meditations, Ignatian meditations: providing strong evidence for the profound impact of early Jesuit training upon the later career of John Donne.

3. Cf. Puente, *1*, 88: "O most just judge, and most mercifull Father, I confesse that I am thorough my sinnes a blacke, and filthy cole, and halfe burnt with the fier of my passions, washe mee, o Lord, and whiten mee with the living water of thy grace, and therwith quenche this fier that burneth mee . . . ." Also Puente, *1*, 274: "in steede of drowning the worlde againe with another deluge; or burning it with fier like Sodom; hee [God] would drowne it with abundance of mercies, and burne it with the fier of his love . . . ."

4. *The Poems of John Donne*, ed. Herbert J. C. Grierson (2 vols., Oxford, Clarendon Press, 1912), *1*, 322.

Finally, let us turn to examine the adumbrations of this method of meditation in one of Donne's longest, greatest religious poems, one for which, unlike the "Holy Sonnets," we can give the precise date and occasion: "Goodfriday, 1613. Riding Westward." The manuscript headings recorded by Grierson fill out our information: "Riding to Sr Edward Harbert in Wales"; "Mr J. Dun goeing from Sir H. G. on good friday sent him back this meditation on the way." [5] The first ten lines of this meditation form an elaborate, deliberately evolved "composition by similitude":

> Let mans Soule be a Spheare, and then, in this,
> The intelligence that moves, devotion is,
> And as the other Spheares, by being growne
> Subject to forraigne motions, lose their owne,
> And being by others hurried every day,
> Scarce in a yeare their naturall forme obey:
> Pleasure or businesse, so, our Soules admit
> For their first mover, and are whirld by it.
> Hence is't, that I am carryed towards the West
> This day, when my Soules forme bends toward the East.

The composition has thus precisely set the problem: profane motives carry the soul away from God, while the soul's essence ("forme"), *devotion*, longs for another, greater object. The speaker then proceeds, by intellectual analysis, to develop (lines 11–32) this paradox of human perversity, by playing upon the idea that the speaker, in going West on human "pleasure or businesse," is turning his back upon the Cross. He is thus refusing to perform the devotion proper to the day; he is refusing, that is, to *see* the place and participate in its agony as if he were "really present":

> There I should see a Sunne, by rising set,
> And by that setting endlesse day beget;
> But that Christ on this Crosse, did rise and fall,
> Sinne had eternally benighted all.
> Yet dare I'almost be glad, I do not see
> That spectacle of too much weight for mee.
> Who sees Gods face, that is selfe life, must dye;
> What a death were it then to see God dye?

5. *Idem, 1, 336.*

Nevertheless, in the very act of saying that he does not see these things, he develops the traditional paradoxes of the scene in lines that echo the meditative treatises:

> Could I behold those hands which span the Poles,
> And turne all spheares at once, peirc'd with those holes?
> Could I behold that endlesse height which is
> Zenith to us, and our Antipodes,
> Humbled below us? or that blood which is
> The seat of all our Soules, if not of his,
> Made durt of dust, or that flesh which was worne
> By God, for his apparell, rag'd, and torne? [6]

And next, as we should expect of one reared in the Catholic meditative tradition, he considers the sorrows of the Virgin:

> If on these things I durst not looke, durst I
> Upon his miserable mother cast mine eye,
> Who was Gods partner here, and furnish'd thus
> Halfe of that Sacrifice, which ransom'd us?

And now, with the analysis completed, the speaker ends his meditation, with perfect symmetry, in a ten-line colloquy which accords with the directions of St. Ignatius Loyola:

> Imagining Christ our Lord before us and placed on the Cross, to make a colloquy with Him . . . Again, to look at myself, asking what I have done for Christ, what I am doing for Christ, what I ought to do for Christ; and then seeing Him that which

6. Cf. Luis de Granada, pp. 288–9: "Lift up thyne eies unto that holie roode, and consider all the woundes, and paines, that the Lorde of maiestie suffereth there for thy sake . . . . Beholde that divine face (which the Angels are desirous to beholde) how disfigured it is, and overflowed with streames of bloude . . . .

"That goodly cleare forhead, and those eies more bewtifull than the Sunne, are now dimmed and darkened with the bloude and presence of deathe. Those eares that are wonte to heare the songes of heaven, doe now heare the horrible blasphemies of synners. Those armes so well fashioned and so large that they embrace all the power of the worlde, are now disjoynted, and stretched out upon the crosse. Those handes that created the heavens, and were never injurious to anie man, are now nayled and clenched fast with harde and sharpe nayles."

He is, and thus fixed to the Cross, to give expression to what shall present itself to my mind. (p. 23)

Though these things, as I ride, be from mine eye,
They'are present yet unto my memory,
For that looks towards them; and thou look'st towards mee,
O Saviour, as thou hang'st upon the tree;
I turne my backe to thee, but to receive
Corrections, till thy mercies bid thee leave.
O thinke mee worth thine anger, punish mee,
Burne off my rusts, and my deformity,
Restore thine Image, so much, by thy grace,
That thou may'st know mee, and I'll turne my face.

Thus similitude, visualization, theological analysis and the eloquent motions of the will have all fused into one perfectly executed design —a meditation expressing the state of devotion which results from the integration of the threefold Image of God: memory, understanding, will. And thus once again the process of meditation appears to have made possible a poem which displays this "articulated structure," this "peculiar blend of passion and thought": [7] the perfect equipoise of a carefully regulated, arduously cultivated skill.

5

By the opening of the seventeenth century there appears to have developed on the Continent a marked reaction against the rigorous methods of meditation advocated by the Jesuits; and this reaction, we might suppose, would be reflected in England. The tendency is represented at its best in St. François de Sales, who admired the Jesuit exercises but preferred to develop his own method of meditation, deeply indebted to the Jesuits but less rigorous, less fearsome, less intellectual. St. François' spirited and frequently rash disciple, Jean Pierre Camus, makes explicit this tendency among the Devout Humanists of France: in his treatise *The Spiritual Combat* (1631) he displays his impatience with "so many actes of the understanding, Will, Memory, Preludes, Pointes, Affections, Resolutions, Thankes-

7. *Works of Herbert*, ed. Palmer, *1*, 140; *Metaphysical Lyrics and Poems*, ed. Grierson, p. xvi.

givings, oblations, demands, Preparations, Invocations, Compositions of Place, Representations, with all that great and combersome traine, whereof the instructions for Meditation are full." [1] This is all part of Camus' rather surprising argument that "it is easier to Contemplate, then to meditate; and that more doe contemplate, (though they reflect not of it) then do meditate." He is referring here to what he calls a "kind of simple contemplation in simple soules, which forerunns meditation," though he concedes that there is a higher kind of contemplation which follows after meditation, and that meditation is "in some sort a necessary meanes, considering the course of nature." (pp. 223–35) His main point is to avoid an excess of directions which may frustrate the achievement of devotion; and in the course of his argument he ridicules the intricate directions for meditation that some advisers are giving to simple folk incapable of performing such complicated exercises. As one reads through the following satirical account, it is impossible not to feel its application to the massive and intricate treatise of the Jesuit Puente:

Let's, for example, upon Christmas day, tell a soule that beleeves simply, and adores Jesus borne of the blessed Virgin, that she should place her selfe in the presence of the little Jesus; that she should frame in her imagination the manger of Bethlem together with the oxe, the Asse, haye, straw, the Blessed Virgin, S. Joseph, the night, the cold season, the stable open on every side to the winde and weather, the child quaking with cold, lying all along upon the litter, swadled in poor cloutes, adored by his holy mother, his foster-father, the angels, Pastors, etc. Tell her further, that she is to invoke the divine grace, to make her preludes, her preparatory prayers. From thence, make her passe on to her three points of Consideration. Shew her how she is to amplifie and enlarge her reasons and discourses, by looking upon, waighing and examining all; the causes, the effectes, the time, place, persons, all the circumstances, actions, words. etc. Then teache her, how she is to move herselfe to good affections out of her discourse and reasoning, affections of all sorts of love;

1. Jean Pierre Camus, *A Spirituall Combat: A Tryall of a Faithfull Soule or Consolation in Temptation*, [trans. Thomas Carre, i.e., Miles Pinkney], (Douay, 1632), p. 222.

Compassion, Feare, Joy, Greife, Mercy, Compunction, etc. Instruct her how out of these affections she is to forme Resolutions. Yet further, give her a modell of thankesgiving, unions and the rest. In fine speake to her touching attentions, Actuall, habituall, vertuall: of distractions, of want of guste, of lightes, visions, with a number of other tearmes. Doe you not plainly discover that in steede of giving her the wings of a dove to fly, you lay a loade upon her, under which she is not able to sturre . . . . (pp. 228–30)

We may imagine that such objections would strike a very sympathetic response in George Herbert, who, in writing of "The Parson preaching," objects that the common "way of crumbling a text into small parts, as, the Person speaking, or spoken to, the subject, and object, and the like, hath neither in it sweetnesse, nor gravity, nor variety." [2] And in fact, Herbert's *Temple*, as we shall show later, bears a marked affinity to the practices of Devout Humanism in France, as represented in St. François de Sales' *Introduction to the Devout Life*.

Nevertheless, in six or seven of Herbert's poems we can, I think, see reflections of the formal process of meditation which these French humanists never renounced but only qualified. Notice, for instance, the movement of Herbert's "Life." It begins in the way that we have found typical of meditative poetry, with a firm, direct statement of the topic to be considered:

> I made a posie, while the day ran by:

then the next two lines, in parenthetical fashion, announce the purpose of the meditation, the end to be achieved, and the method to be followed; the essential point lies in the implications of the phrase, "my remnant":

> Here will I smell my remnant out, and tie
> My life within this band.

The first stanza then concludes with a summary of the total situation:

> But Time did beckon to the flowers, and they
> By noon most cunningly did steal away,
> And wither'd in my hand.

2. *Works of Herbert,* ed. Hutchinson, p. 235.

Now, in Herbert's gentle manner, comes the process of the understanding, as the speaker quickly grasps the meaning of the incident, and brings it home to the affections:

> My hand was next to them, and then my heart:
> I took, without more thinking, in good part
>   Times gentle admonition:
> Who did so sweetly deaths sad taste convey,
> Making my minde to smell my fatall day;
>   Yet sugring the suspicion.

And the whole concludes in stanza 3 with affections and resolutions presented in a brief colloquy with the flowers (St. François de Sales, we recall, had suggested that colloquies might be held "even with insensible thinges"):

> Farewell deare flowers, sweetly your time ye spent,
> Fit, while ye liv'd for smell or ornament,
>   And after death for cures.
> I follow straight without complaints or grief,
> Since if my sent be good, I care not if
>   It be as short as yours.

In much the same deliberate, "articulated" way the longer poem, "Man," makes its progress. It opens, as several of Herbert's poems do, by remembering something the speaker has read or heard, in this case something like the following passage from Bellarmine's meditations on man:

> But now the external end of everything is that for which it is made. The end of a palace is the dweller therein; the end of a tree is the possessor thereof; the end of man is only his Lord God, for of himself and for himself he made man, and he keepeth, feedeth, and payeth him his wages . . . . But mark diligently, O my soul, the things which are made for man are profitable to man, and not to themselves; beasts labour for man and not for themselves, the fields, vineyards and orchards fill the granaries, cellars and purses of men; neither do servants labour, sweat and toil for themselves, but for the profit, ease and pleasure of their masters. But thy Lord God, who wanteth nothing,

would have man truly serve him, and yet the profit and reward of his service he will not have.[3]

In Herbert's poem the memory and the imagination establish the subject thus in the opening stanza:

> My God, I heard this day,
> That none doth build a stately habitation,
>   But he that means to dwell therein.
>   What house more stately hath there been,
> Or can be, then is Man? to whose creation
>   All things are in decay.

For the next five stanzas, the understanding performs an analysis of the wonders of man, in relation to the universal order of things:

> For us the windes do blow,
> The earth doth rest, heav'n move, and fountains flow.
>   Nothing we see, but means our good,
>   As our delight, or as our treasure:
> The whole is, either our cupboard of food,
>   Or cabinet of pleasure.

·   ·   ·   ·   ·

> All things unto our flesh are kinde
> In their descent and being; to our minde
>   In their ascent and cause.

In the seventh stanza, after the understanding has thus led the way, the affections begin to "kindle" into exclamations, first of wonder:

> Each thing is full of dutie:
> Waters united are our navigation;
>   Distinguished, our habitation;
>   Below, our drink; above, our meat;
> Both are our cleanlinesse. Hath one such beautie?
>   Then how are all things neat?

3. Robert Bellarmine, *The Ascent of the Mind to God by a Ladder of Things Created* . . . . *In the first English Translation, by T. B. Gent.* Published at *Doway, 1616,* with intro. by James Brodrick (London, Burns, Oates, and Washbourne, 1928), p. 18. The original appeared in 1615.

and next of love:

> More servants wait on Man,
> Then he'l take notice of: in ev'ry path
> He treads down that which doth befriend him,
> When sicknesse makes him pale and wan.
> Oh mightie love! Man is one world, and hath
> Another to attend him.

The ninth and final stanza then achieves the summation of the whole exercise, a colloquy in which God is petitioned to grant his favor:

> Since then, my God, thou hast
> So brave a Palace built; O dwell in it,
> That it may dwell with thee at last!
> Till then, afford us so much wit;
> That, as the world serves us, we may serve thee,
> And both thy servants be.

Other examples of this kind of "argumentative evolution" may be found in "Affliction" (5), "Confession," "Grieve not the Holy Spirit," and "The Crosse"; all of which, in their own flexible ways, first compose the problem, then analyze its parts, and end with resolutions and petitions in colloquy with God. But there is no need to belabor the point or to examine in detail the related procedure that is found, for example, in George Wither's meditation on the marigold,[4] in Andrew Marvell's "On a Drop of Dew," or in Henry King's "A Contemplation upon Flowers."

6

I should like to conclude the discussion of this aspect of meditative practice by considering briefly one poem by Richard Crashaw and one by Henry Vaughan; for these two poems display the medi-

4. George Wither, *A Collection of Emblemes* (London, 1635), p. 209. Quoted by Rosemary Freeman, *English Emblem Books* (London, Chatto and Windus, 1948), p. 26; an interesting example of the relationship between emblems and meditation. What Miss Freeman says (p. 173) of the English Catholic emblem-books will hold also for Wither and Quarles: "Their main purpose is the practice of meditation, and to this purpose the emblems are no more than contributory factors."

tative structure with a special clarity, occurring as they do amid
the works of two poets whose achievements do not usually lie in
the area of such construction. At the same time these poems represent, and will serve to emphasize, two particular kinds of meditation that deserve our notice.

Crashaw's hymn, "To the Name above Every Name, the Name
of Iesus," does not, at a first glance, declare its relationship to the
threefold movement which we have been discussing. Nevertheless,
it appears to derive its fundamental procedure from a prototype of
the central method of meditation practiced during the seventeenth
century: the *Scala Meditatoria* or *Scala Meditationis*, set forth originally by Johan Wessel Gansfort in the latter part of the fifteenth
century, popularized in the *Rosetum* of Joannes Mauburnus (1494),
and used as the basis for the very influential treatise by Joseph Hall,
The Arte of Divine Meditation (1606). The relationship of the
various forms of this *Scala* to each other and to Crashaw's hymn is
a complicated matter that requires presentation in tabular form; I
have therefore placed the details of analysis in an appendix. But
even a brief look at the *Scala* reproduced on the opposite page will
show that here is a process fundamentally the same as that presented in the Jesuit *Exercises:* preparatory steps; then a threefold
process involving the memory, understanding, and will; then terminal steps that are fundamentally colloquies.[1]

If we set Crashaw's hymn beside this *Scala* a total effect emerges
which is perfectly summed up in the poem's most brilliant phrase,
"the witt of love"; for it is a poem in which the most daring poetical
indulgences are firmly controlled by "wit"—in all the meanings of
that word. Wit in the sense of intellectual ingenuity, producing
a hundred surprises of word and phrase; wit in the sense of humor,
which plays delicately throughout the earlier part of the poem, in
Herbert's way; and above all, wit in the sense of intellectual power,
planning and executing a careful movement of the whole through
prologue, *mise en scène*, developing action, climax, and epilogue.
The building of this action, unique in Crashaw's poetry, creates the
pleasure of watching a mind mold its art upon an ancient model,
now following its lessons literally, now using it playfully and flexibly, but never losing sight of the fundamental process. The play

1. Cf. Watrigant, *Études*, 73, 210.

Scala meditatoria

p er gradus ascendebatur in templum.

Modus recolligendi

Questio — Qua sc; quisq; a se requirat — Quid cogito / Quid cogitandum — Exuscitatiua

Gradus preparatorij

Scrussio — Est repulsio cor; que minus cogitanda — Expediunt — Depulsiua obstantiu
Electio — magl.s.cogitador; puta q magl; Coferunt decent — Assumptiua coferentiu

Gradus processor; z mentis

Comemoratio — Est actualis electe z destinate rei cogitatio — Herer coduplicatioe penetrat
Cosideratio — Est sedula z iterato comemoratio z inhesio do nec proprie noscat comemoratu —
Attentio — Est fira z attenta cosideratio. vel pspectio rei csidrate z comemorate — Figit
Explanatio — Est queda, illustratio in attentione positor; — Illustrat
Tractatio — Est rer; comemorator; cosiderator; rc. ad alia qda extesio — Extendit

Gradus processor; et iudicij

Diiudicatio — Est q pro dignitate sua suscepta res estimatur. — Estimat
Causatio — Est stabilitio facte diiudicatiois sic cofirmatio oronis — Stabilit.
Ruminatio — est morosa supior; cu pratoe tractar; docc gustu attigat — Iterado inqrit.

Gradus processor; et affectus

Gustatio — est q sic supiorib; mocmur ac docemur. ira h nos affici setim; — Uidz; exclamatoe
Querela — Est qrentis ipacia vel denuciatio displicentis — Deplagit lametatioe
Optio — q qd dulce iudicat possidere desiderat. i e desiriu cplacet; — Esurit desideratione
Confessio — Est veritatis assensus z publica agnitio — Cogesta detegit.
Oratio — Est optionis ad deum insinuatio — Erigit
Mensio — Est oratorum collatio z orantium —
Obsecratio — Est cum sacre rei attestatione oratio — Animat / Extorquet
Confidentia — Est psense z agite boitat; argumtu ad ipetrada mones — Possidet

Gradus terminator;

Grarumactio — Perceptor; veror; bonor; gradis estimatio est — Refundit
Comendatio — Desideror; suor; in dei boitate fiducialis remissio — Custodit
Permissio — Est integ; ppe volutatis in dei volutate resignatio — Holocaustat

Modus comorandi

Coplexio — Est gradus silis cum gradu ruminatio. Hec coplexio est omnium gradnu sicut Ruminatio tantu intellectualium. vnde maximam copiam prestat.

The "Scala Meditatoria," from the *Rosetum* of Joannes Mauburnus, Zwolle, 1494

(*Pierpont Morgan Library*)

of wit is symbolized in the poem's very appearance on the page: long lines floating out, almost beyond control, but brought up sharply with some simple quatrain; just as, in the words themselves, the most flamboyant rhetoric is held in check by a sudden touch of common speech. It is a masterwork in the poetry of meditation, and one of the very last in its kind. The poets of the latter half of the seventeenth century did not often perform at their best in the eucharistic mode that this poem, basically, commemorates. The poetry of meditation continues, but in different directions indicated by the most explicit example of meditative structure to be found among the poems of Henry Vaughan.

It is the poem beginning "I walkt the other day (to spend my hour)"—that is, the speaker's regular, daily hour of meditation. This day he has, as in the action of Isaac frequently cited in meditative books, gone "out to meditate in the field" (Genesis 24.63); and as he walks he finds his image for analysis, which he composes in detail for three stanzas:

> I walkt the other day (to spend my hour,)
>   Into a field
> Where I sometimes had seen the soil to yield
>   A gallant flowre,
> But Winter now had ruffled all the bowre
>   And curious store
>   I knew there heretofore.

2.

> Yet I whose search lov'd not to peep and peer
>   I'th' face of things
> Thought with my self, there might be other springs
>   Besides this here
> Which, like cold friends, sees us but once a year,
>   And so the flowre
>   Might have some other bowre.

3.

> Then taking up what I could neerest spie
>   I digg'd about

That place where I had seen him to grow out,
        And by and by
I saw the warm Recluse alone to lie
        Where fresh and green
He lived of us unseen.

The process of the understanding occupies the next three stanzas, the central triad in this poem of nine stanzas, and begins thus in stanza 4 to discover the "verity":

  Many a question Intricate and rare
        Did I there strow,
  But all I could extort was, that he now
        Did there repair
  Such losses as befel him in this air
        And would e'r long
  Come forth most fair and young.

Now, in the fifth and middle stanza of the poem, comes the luminous moment, the revelation of its hidden theme: here the poem moves swiftly from the cool and objective to the passionate and personal. The earlier hints of personification are now intensified to endow the root with the appurtenances of the deathbed and the grave; and, with the easy, associative transition typical of Vaughan at his best, the speaker is openly meditating on the loved one he has lost:

  This past, I threw the Clothes quite o'r his head,
        And stung with fear
  Of my own frailty dropt down many a tear
        Upon his bed,
  Then sighing whisper'd, *Happy are the dead!*
        What peace doth now
  Rock him asleep below?

Yet we are still in the sequence of the understanding, and the sixth stanza reverts to the impersonal and objective, as the speaker quietly generalizes on the value of drawing "doctrine" from the creatures:

  And yet, how few believe such doctrine springs
        From a poor root
  Which all the Winter sleeps here under foot

> And hath no wings
> To raise it to the truth and light of things,
> But is stil trod
> By ev'ry wandring clod.

Now, with the doctrine fully understood, the poem moves to its final triad of stanzas: a colloquy with God, which presents in petition the essence of Vaughan's meditative quest, with specific reference to the personal loss that dominates the present poem and with overtones significant for Vaughan's total achievement as poet:

7.

> O thou! whose spirit did at first inflame
> And warm the dead,
> And by a sacred Incubation fed
> With life this frame
> Which once had neither being, forme, nor name,
> Grant I may so
> Thy steps track here below,

8.

> That in these Masques and shadows I may see
> Thy sacred way,
> And by those hid ascents climb to that day
> Which breaks from thee
> Who art in all things, though invisibly;
> Shew me thy peace,
> Thy mercy, love, and ease,

9.

> And from this Care, where dreams and sorrows raign
> Lead me above
> Where Light, Joy, Leisure, and true Comforts move
> Without all pain,
> There, hid in thee, shew me his life again
> At whose dumbe urn
> Thus all the year I mourn.

There is the essence of Bellarmine's popular treatise based on St. Bonaventure, *The Ascent of the Mind to God by a Ladder of Things Created*. It is a poem which draws its subject-matter from an ancient meditative tradition,[2] and which proceeds by methods fundamental to the century's devotional life. Yet its strong focus on the "creatures" moves away from the Cross that forms the center for the meditations of Southwell, Donne, Herbert, and Crashaw; its focus points the way toward Marvell's "Upon Appleton House," toward the *Centuries* of Thomas Traherne, toward the seventh book of *Paradise Lost*.

7

It is significant that this development of a poem according to the three powers of the soul should be reflected in some of the finest poems written by Southwell, Donne, Herbert, Crashaw, and Vaughan. But a greater significance lies beyond this. In the procedure reflected in these few poems we find, I believe, a fundamental discipline underlying many other poems by these writers in which this threefold process is not observable. For the art of meditation was a discipline of the kind which R. P. Blackmur has described in discussing the poetry of Yeats. "It is the very purpose of a supernaturally derived discipline, as used in poetry," says Blackmur, "to set the substance of natural life apart, to give it a form, a meaning, and a value which cannot be evaded . . . . for the poet the discipline, far from seeming secondary, had an extraordinary structural, seminal, and substantial importance to the degree that without it he could hardly have written at all." [1]

Meditation was a discipline directed toward creating the "act of pure attention" which D. H. Lawrence saw as essential to all significant discovery or decision: "you choose that object to concentrate upon which will best focus your consciousness." [2] It was a

2. For the background of this use of the "creatures" in meditation, see the recent work by Ruth Wallerstein, *Studies in Seventeenth-Century Poetic* (University of Wisconsin Press, 1950), chap. 8.

1. R. P. Blackmur, "The Later Poetry of W. B. Yeats," in *The Expense of Greatness* (New York, Arrow Editions, 1940), p. 75; reprinted in *Form and Value in Modern Poetry*, New York, Anchor Books, 1957.

2. D. H. Lawrence, *Etruscan Places* (London, Martin Secker, 1932), pp. 97–9.

discipline directed toward creating the kind of concentration which Wallace Stevens has described in a passage of his "Credences of Summer":

> Three times the concentred self takes hold, three times
> The thrice concentred self, having possessed
>
> The object, grips it in savage scrutiny,
> Once to make captive, once to subjugate
> Or yield to subjugation, once to proclaim
> The meaning of the capture, this hard prize,
> Fully made, fully apparent, fully found.[3]

It was a discipline devoted to developing exactly the state of mind which Coleridge described in that famous account of the Imagination which has become the foundation of modern literary criticism: without the alteration of a word Coleridge's account, in all its details, becomes a perfect definition of the soul in successful meditation:

> The poet, described in *ideal* perfection, brings the whole soul of man into activity, with the subordination of its faculties to each other, according to their relative worth and dignity. He diffuses a tone and spirit of unity, that blends, and (as it were) *fuses*, each into each, by that synthetic and magical power, to which we have exclusively appropriated the name of imagination. This power, first put in action by the will and understanding, and retained under their irremissive, though gentle and unnoticed, controul (*laxis effertur habenis*) reveals itself in the balance or reconciliation of opposite or discordant qualities: of sameness, with difference; of the general, with the concrete; the idea, with the image; the individual, with the representative; the sense of novelty and freshness, with old and familiar objects; a more than usual state of emotion, with more than usual order; judgement ever awake and steady self-possession, with enthusiasm and feeling profound or vehement . . . .

3. Wallace Stevens, *Transport to Summer* (New York, Alfred A. Knopf, 1947), pp. 109–10.

We are reminded that this analogy is more than coincidental when Coleridge concludes his account by adapting a description of the soul's activity from a poem of Elizabethan times:

'Doubtless,' as Sir John Davies observes of the soul (and his words may with slight alteration be applied, and even more appropriately, to the poetic IMAGINATION)

'Doubtless this could not be, but that she turns
    Bodies to spirit by sublimation strange,
As fire converts to fire the things it burns,
    As we our food into our nature change.

From their gross matter she abstracts their forms,
    And draws a kind of quintessence from things;
Which to her proper nature she transforms,
    To bear them light on her celestial wings.

Thus does she, when from individual states
    She doth abstract the universal kinds;
Which then re-clothed in divers names and fates
    Steal access through our senses to our minds.' [4]

It is no surprise, then, to find the Jesuit Puente describing the ultimate goal of meditation in terms of poetical kinds, adapting the passage of Ephesians (5.18-20) which our period constantly used to justify the writing of religious poetry: "Be filled with the spirit; speaking to yourselves in psalms and hymns and spiritual songs, singing and making melody in your heart to the Lord; giving thanks

4. Samuel Taylor Coleridge, *Biographia Literaria*, ed. J. Shawcross (2 vols., Oxford, Clarendon Press, 1907), 2, 12-13. Coleridge has drastically altered the third stanza here, which reads thus in the first edition of the *Nosce Teipsum* (London, 1599):

This doth she, when from things *particular*,
    She doth abstract the *universall kinds*,
Which bodilesse, and immateriall are,
    And can be lodg'd but onely in our minds . . . .

See *The Poems of Sir John Davies, Reproduced in Facsimile from the First Editions in the Henry E. Huntington Library and Art Gallery*, ed. Clare Howard (New York, Columbia University Press, 1941), p. 136.

always for all things unto God and the Father in the name of our
Lord Jesus Christ." There are, says Puente, four "divine affections,
wherewith wee may speake in our hartes to God" during those colloquies that arise from meditation. The first consists of "Interiour
Psalmes," which he defines as "actions of the love of God, with
effectuall desires, and determinations to serve, and obey him, offer-
ing our selves to keepe most perfectly his commandements, and
counsailes." The second, of hymns: "affections of the praises of God,
reckoning up all the excellencies, and perfections that hee hath,
and the workes that hee hath donne." The third, of "Spirituall Canticles": "affections of spirituall ioy, and alacritie, rejoicing that
God is who hee is." And the fourth, thanksgivings. Into these
"divine affections" all the faculties aroused by meditation pour
their strength: theology is suffused with emotion; concrete detail
is filled with sublime thought; until the soul in meditation becomes
a rich and delicate whole, displaying "the right use of the senses
and interior powers of the soule, reducing them all to union":

> For the memorie and the understanding only love when they
> remember, thinke and ponder the things that provoke to love.
> The imagination, and the appetites of the soule doe likewise
> love, when they budde forth imaginations and affections, which
> doe awaken and give life to love. The sences love, when the
> eyes, eares, toungue, and tast only desire to see, heare, tast, and
> speake of those things, which are directed to this love: and
> all the corporall members love, when they all serve in the
> workes of the love of God. And finallie, all our forces love,
> when all emploie them selves in loving God, with that inten-
> siveness which they can, and in overcoming the difficulties
> which oppose them selves, and in resisting the temptations
> which divert them from loving: that charitie may in such sort
> be rooted in the soule, that nothing created can separate it
> from the same, nor the waters of manie tribulations extinguish
> it . . . .[5]

The art of meditation thus underlies the *ars poetica:* in English religious poetry of the seventeenth century the two arts fuse, inseparably, for both are rooted in this charity.

5. Puente, *1*, 6–7, 430; *2*, 596.

CHAPTER 2

Meditations on the Life of Christ

. . . the interest is in the locked and inseparable combination, or rather it is in the person in whom the combination has its place. Therefore we speak of the events of Christ's life as the mystery of the Nativity, the mystery of the Crucifixion and so on of a host; the mystery being always the same, that the child in the manger is God, the culprit on the gallows God, and so on. Otherwise birth and death are not mysteries, nor is it any great mystery that a just man should be crucified, but that God should fascinates—with the interest of awe, of pity, of shame, of every harrowing feeling.

Gerard Manley Hopkins, Letter to Robert Bridges, Oct. 24, 1883

WE HAVE seen in the preceding chapter several ways in which meditation on the life of Christ played a significant part in the devotional life of our period. Yet such formal meditations as these only serve to point the way toward a central, habitual mode of thinking which, coming down from St. Bernard and St. Bonaventure, saturated the entire life of the devout individual. "Everything in the world," says the *Spiritual Combat*, can be related to the events of Christ's life and death; "everything about you will be a reminder of them":

> An humble cottage will represent the stable and manger where He was born. The rain falling on the earth will call to mind the bloody sweat with which He watered the Garden of Olives. The stones are figures of the rocks which split at His death. When you gaze at the sun or the earth, remember that when He died the earth trembled, and the sun grew dark. The sight of water will recall the water flowing from His

side. A thousand other objects will lend themselves to these considerations.[1]

Everywhere we turn in the meditative treatises of the time we find exhortations to cultivate this cast of mind, with various dramatic directions. Thus Southwell adds the suggestion that, on going to bed at night, "I may imagine to lie by the pillar, crosse, maunger, or some such place, where Christ was present, that when I wake in the morning, he may be the first, that shall come into my mind." [2] And St. François de Sales suggests, as a remedy for temptation, that one "hastely runne in spirit to the crosse . . . imagining thou seest him hanging theron before thy face, and embrace the foot of the crosse upon thy knees, laying fast hold upon it . . . ." (p. 466) Through all such practices the ordinary layman of the time was constantly encouraged to work toward the goal set forth by the *Stimulus Amoris:* a state of mind in which "*Christ crucified* appeares unto him in everie place, and at all times." [3]

In these practices, no doubt, lies the background for such meditation as we find in Donne's poem "The Crosse":

> Who can deny mee power, and liberty
> To stretch mine armes, and mine owne Crosse to be?
> Swimme, and at every stroake, thou art thy Crosse;
> The Mast and yard make one, where seas do tosse;
> Looke downe, thou spiest out Crosses in small things;
> Looke up, thou seest birds rais'd on crossed wings;

or for the utterly familiar way in which Herbert's poetry everywhere mingles memories of the Passion with homely images. But more specific relationships with poetry may be found in the ways of imagining the whole life of Christ set forth in the famous medieval *Meditations* attributed to St. Bonaventure.[4] Here is a book which

1. *The Spiritual Combat*, translation revised by William Lester and Robert Mohan (Westminster, Md., Newman Bookshop, 1947), pp. 69–70.

2. Robert Southwell, *A Short Rule of Good Life* [London? 1598?], p. 57.

3. *Stimulus Divini amoris: That is The Goade of Divine Love*, [trans. B. Lewis Augustine], (Douay, 1642), p. 65.

4. The work was probably composed or compiled by an unknown Franciscan of the early fourteenth century, who incorporated in the work a treatise on the Passion which may actually be the work of St. Bonaventure. For an excellent brief account of the problems of authorship see the *Diction-*

we must examine in some detail, for in it we find a prototype of the imaginative meditation cultivated by the Jesuits, and at the same time an immense difference which may help to delineate some of the characteristic qualities of religious poetry in the sixteenth and seventeenth centuries.

The central impact of the *Meditations on the Life of Christ* arises from its insistence that every detail of the story must be dramatized as if one were present. Over, and over, runs the refrain: "Be present, then, in spirit at all He does . . . . look at Him and at the disciples, and endeavour to reconstruct the scene . . . . For if you wish to gather fruit from these things, imagine that you are actually present when the Lord Jesus says or does them; as if you heard with your own ears, and saw with your own eyes, and attend with your whole mind and heart, intently and joyfully, putting aside for the moment all other cares and solicitudes." We must imagine the facial expressions, the gestures, the tone of voice of the actors before us, see the armed men approach at the Crucifixion, "with an air of great ferocity and determination . . . talking loudly," or watch Mary "on her knees, with her arms crossed on her breast, with tearful countenance and hoarse voice." Or at the Nativity we must see how Mary "blushed modestly at having to speak to so many strangers," how Joseph, "who was a carpenter by trade, may have constructed a shelter," and how he, "taking the saddle of the ass, and extracting from it the cushion of hair or wool, placed it beside the manger, that our Lady might sit upon it." [5] So, with delicate elaboration, we have the manger scene presented in the adaptation of the treatise made by Nicholas Love around the year 1400 and printed thus by Wynkyn de Worde in 1525:

and anone she devoutly enclynynge with soverayne Joye toke hym in her armes, and swetely clepynge and kyssynge layde hym in her lappe. and with a full pappe as she was taught of the holy ghost wasshed hym all aboute with her swete mylke and so wrapped hym in the kerchefe of her heed, and layde

---

naire de Spiritualité, ed. Marcel Viller et al. (Paris, Gabriel Beauchesne, 1932—), *1*, cols. 1,848–51.

5. *Meditations on the Life of Christ*, pp. 85, 303, ix, 359–60, 31–3.

hym in the cratche, and anone the oxe and the asse knelynge
downe layde downe theyr mouthes in the cratche, brethynge
at theyr noses upon ye chylde that they knewe by reason that
in that colde tyme ye childe so symply covered had nede to be
warmed in that maner.[6]

Not only are we thus to compose the scene but we are to move
onto the stage ourselves: "Take Him, then, into your arms, keep
Him there, earnestly look into His face, reverently kiss Him." Or
we may go to visit the child in Egypt: "I imagine that you will discover Him playing with other children, and that when He sees you,
He will run forward to welcome you." "Take up, then, the child
Jesus in your arms, put Him upon an ass, and carefully lead Him
along, and if He wishes at any time to get off, do you joyfully receive Him in your arms and hold Him lovingly there for a while,
at least until His Mother reaches you, for at times she may be tired
and walk more slowly." [7]

"I think it delightful to meditate thus," says the author, "whatever the facts may have been." For, as he has explained in his preface, "we are allowed to meditate on the Sacred Scripture, to set it
forth and to expound it in a variety of ways, as we judge best,
as long as we write nothing contrary to truth, justice, and sound
doctrine, or against faith or morals." Thus the meditations may
proceed with full dramatic freedom, "passing over no circumstance, however trivial." For, the author urges—and this is the
essential point of the treatise: "Such thoughts enkindle our devotion, increase our love, give us new fervour, lead us to compassion,
bestow on us purity and simplicity of heart, incline us to poverty
and humility." [8]

Seeking such affections with a simple directness, the meditations

6. *Vita Christi* (London, 1525), Pt. 1, chap. 6. The original form of Love's
version is available in the sumptuous edition: *The Mirrour of the blessed
lyf of Jesu Christ*, ed. L. F. Powell, Oxford, 1908. Love's version is better
called an adaptation than a translation, since it omits a great deal of material
which Love thinks may be tedious for the "simple folk" to whom his version
is addressed; for this reason I have quoted chiefly from the complete version
made by Sister M. Emmanuel.

7. *Meditations on the Life of Christ*, pp. 37, 69.

8. *Idem*, pp. 36, ix, 56, 61.

keep the "wise men and commentators" [9] at a great distance, often deliberately turning away from the worries of the intellect, as in this passage from the meditation on the Epiphany in the version of Nicholas Love:

> What these thre gyftes offred of the kynges betoken ghostly and many other thynges that the gospell telleth as it is expowned by holy doctours is suffycyently and fully wryten in other places. Wherfore we passe over all that here. But what hope ye was done with that golde of so grete pryce? Whether our lady reserved it and put it in treasour? Or elles bought therwith londes and rentes? Naye god forbede! For she that was a perfyte lover of poverte toke no hede of worldly goodes. But what[?] she lovynge poverte and understandynge her blyssed sones wyll, not onely thrugh his inspiracyon techynge her in soule withinforth, but also by shewynge his wyll withoutforth that he loved not suche rychesse, peraventure turnynge awaye ofte sythes his face fro ye golde, or spyttynge therupon. Within a fewe dayes and shorte tyme she gave it all to poore men, for ye kepynge therof that lytell tyme was to her but a grete burden and hevy charge.[10]

In these medieval meditations the pious affections and "good motions" thus arise directly from a vivid apprehension of the physical scene. When theology is present it is given in simple abstractions, never explored or elaborated: the understanding does not here intervene to make "discourses" on the theological significance of the scene.

2

We can see, then, the immense difference between this kind of purely affective meditation, and the method of meditation which I have described in Chapter 1. In these medieval meditations the humanity of Christ is dominant.[1] We are told in general terms, here

9. *Idem*, p. 338.
10. *Vita Christi*, Pt. 1, chap. 8.
1. It is important to note that the influential *Life of Christ*, written in the latter part of the fourteenth century by Ludolph the Carthusian, is a much

and there, to recall the fact of the Divinity and Godhead; but these aspects are understated, for it is the human details that will stir the desired feelings: "be moved to pity and compassion." "Consider and ponder each separate thing, for there are many points to be thought of, and all are inexpressibly sad and touching." [2] But Fray Luis de Granada takes special care to warn his reader that such meditation on the sufferings of Christ is only the "first maner of meditatinge upon his most bitter passion." This, he warns, "must not be the finall ende of this exercise, but rather it must be used as a meane to come to other endes":

> to witt, to understande hereby what a passhinge great love he bare unto thee, that woulde suffer so much for thee; and what a great benefite he did unto thee, in byeinge thee with so deare a price: and how much thou art bounde to doe for him, who hath done, and suffered so much for thee: and above all this, how greatlie thou oughtest to abhorre thy sinnes, and be greived with them, sith they were the cause of his so longe and painefull martiredome . . . . Whereby it appeareth, that this first maner of meditatinge (by waie of takinge compassion of the bitter paines of our Saviour) is as it were a meane, or a ladder unto all others. (p. 333)

The results of this increased emphasis on the works of the understanding are evident on every page of Fray Luis' meditations: the pity and compassion, the vivid imagination of the scene, are present, in fervent detail—but coalesced with, and developed by, intricate

---

more learned work, with greater emphasis upon the Divinity: this perhaps indicates the tendency of the times. But the emphasis of the *Meditations* of "Bonaventure" is supported by two other works of extraordinary popularity: the *Imitation of Christ*, and the *Meditations* attributed to St. Bernard. One sentence from the English version of the latter will indicate its temper: "Let thy heart be *wounded* with the *sword* of *sorrow*, and let thine eies be drowned with a flood of teares: let thy heavie *groanes* and sorrowfull sighes beginne in the morning, and let them not cease in the evening: Oh let the fervencie of thy *lamentation*, demonstrate the burning zeale of thy compassion, which thou doest beare to mine afflicted Iesus." (*Saint Bernard His Meditations*, Pt. 1, p. 264.)

2. *Meditations on the Life of Christ*, pp. 347, 343.

intellectual analysis which drives home the central Paradox of the God made man. Thus, in this passage based on the scene in Gethsemane, we find a careful development from visual imagination to impassioned paradox:

> Consider then now, o my soule, how much that highe and divine maiestie abased himselfe for thy sake . . . . Consider now, how they leade him, as one depryved of all authoritie, and put to open shame . . . . Consider our saviour well, how he goeth in this dolefull waie, abandoned of his owne disciples; accompanied with his enemies: his pase hastened and disordered; his breathe in a maner gone: his colour changed; his face chafed, and inflamed . . . . And yet in all this evile entreatinge of his person, beholde the modest behaviour of his countenance, the comelye gravitie of his eies, and that divine resemblance, which in the middest of all the discourtesies in the world coulde never be obscured. Ascende also yet a little higher, and consider diligentlie what he is, whom thou seest thus led, and caried awaye, with such great contumlie and dishonor. This is he, that is the worde of the father: the everlastinge wisdome: the infinite vertu: the cheefe goodnes: the perfet felicitie: the true glorie: and the cleare fountaine of all beawtie. Consider then, how for thy salvation and redemption, vertu is here tyed with bandes: innocencie is apprehended: wisdome flowted, and lawghed to scorne; honor contemned: glorie tormented: and the cleare welspringe of all bewtie trowbled with weepinge and sorrowe. (pp. 75–7)

This attempt to grasp, simultaneously, the Godhead and the manhood represents the central aim of meditations on the life of Christ during our period: "to knowe Christ Jesus our Lord, true God, and man, with so certaine, proper, entire, and perfect a knowledge, that it may arrive to understand, and penetrate the infinite dignitie of his person, and the inestimable riches, and treasures of his grace, with greate esteeme, and valuation thereof." [3]

It is in the Jesuit art of meditating on the life of Christ that these

---

3. Puente, *1*, 239. Cf. Louis de Blois, p. 32: "Nor should he think of Him as man only, but as God and man, the true Light. Let him conceive, I repeat, a supernatural image of the supersubstantial Lord Jesus." Also Antonio de

efforts to fuse understanding and will, theology and emotion, abstract and concrete, divine and human, reach a climax of intensity and intricacy. St. Ignatius developed for his meditations on the life of Christ a fivefold sequence of exercises which differed in several important respects from the procedure followed during his first (purgative) week. Here we have three preludes, instead of the two advised for the first week. The first, and additional, prelude ensures a vivid "composition of place" by directing the meditator "to call to mind the history of the matter which I have to contemplate." (p. 36) In the Nativity meditation, for example, this consists of thinking "how our Lady already with child for about nine months, as it may piously be thought, seated on an ass, left Nazareth, together with St. Joseph and a servant-girl, leading an ox, in order to go to Bethlehem . . . ." (p. 38) In the first four exercises the meditation proper is then performed by the "three powers," taking two different events for the first two exercises, and performing "repetitions" of these for the next two. The fifth exercise, however, is quite different, and represents the distinctive contribution of St. Ignatius to the art of meditation on the life of Christ. It is the famous "application of the senses" to the matter of the foregoing mysteries, in the following manner:

> The first point is to see the persons with the eyes of the imagination, meditating and contemplating in particular their circumstances, and deriving some fruit from the sight.
>
> The second is to hear what they are saying, or might say; and by reflecting on oneself, to take some fruit from this.
>
> The third is to smell and taste the infinite sweetness and delight of the Divinity, of the soul, and of its virtues, and all else, according to the character of the person contemplated, reflecting on oneself and deriving some fruit from this.
>
> The fourth is to feel with the touch; as, for example, to kiss and embrace the spots where such persons tread and sit, always endeavouring to draw fruit from this.[4]

Molina, pp. 55–6: "the Compassion which we ought to have of Christ our Saviour must not be as a naturall affect . . . but it must be as an affect of Faith . . . ."

4. St. Ignatius, pp. 40–1. This procedure is foreshadowed in the First Week by a similar application of the senses to the meditations on Hell which constitute the fifth exercise here.

It staggers the mind to ponder the effect that such a complex sequence would have upon a poet—"meaning by the poet any man of imagination," as Wallace Stevens would say. It should produce a hitherto unparalleled integration of feeling and thought, of sensuous detail and theological abstraction. Nor would such an effect be limited to the brief period of "retreat," for the Jesuits quickly adapted this method to the practice of daily meditation on the life of Christ. The procedure consists in a twofold meditation on each mystery: the first exercise being "more intellectual and more concerned with reasoning," and the second more concerned with "the sensible qualities of things, as sights, sounds, and the like." [5] Thus, after Puente has presented the meditations in which "the three Faculties of the soule (especially the understanding) are to exercize their actes" (*1, 12*), he recommends "a forme of praier, applying the interiour faculties of the soule, to the contemplation of the mysteries, that have been meditated." This, Puente explains, "is a forme rather of contemplation, then of meditation";

> for . . . meditation runneth from one thing to another, seeking out hidden verities, as hitherto hath been donne: but contemplation is a simple beholding of the truth without varietie of discourse, with greate affections of admiration, and love: and as regularly it is obtained after meditation, so after we have meditated these mysteries of our Saviour Christ, it shall not be amisse to runne over eache of them againe with this manner of affectuous contemplation, which wee call application of the faculties: for as the exteriour faculties doe very briefely without the windings of discourses perceive their obiects, and are delighted, and pleased in them: so in this contemplation, the interiour senses of the soule (which are her owne interiour faculties with the variety of their actes) without new discourses, presupposing those which have been donne at other times, perceive these verities, and collect from thence, mervailous affections of devotion . . . . (*1, 385–6*)

We can see, first of all, that this twofold process is quite in accord with the period's increased emphasis on the "understanding,"

5. I take the phrasing from the Jesuit *Directory* of 1599: see the translation by W. H. Longridge appended to his edition of the *Spiritual Exercises* (4th ed. London, A. R. Mowbray, 1950), p. 314.

and its insistence that the "point" must be thoroughly analyzed before the affections can be trusted to follow the right direction. Thus we find that Puente's first meditation on the Nativity presents a startling contrast with the manger scene which I have quoted from Nicholas Love's medieval version of "Bonaventure." Enough detail is given to compose the scene firmly, and then the mind is quickly drawn to consider the intellectual significance of the scene:

> [Mary] brought forth her only begotten Sonne, and forthwith she tooke him in her armes. O what content, and joy received she at that first viewe, not staying upon the outward beauty of the bodye, but passing to the beauty of the soule, and of the dietye! On the one side she embraced him and kissed him lovingly as her Sonne: and on the other side shee shruncke backe, and humbly retired, considering that he was almightie God: for with these two armes God desireth to bee embraced; with charity, and humility; with love, and reverence . . . .

> I will beholde the person of that childe, making a comparison betweene what he is, as he is almightie God, and betweene what he is there, as he is man; with an affection of admiration, and love the greatest that I am able: pondering how this childe is that God of majestie, whose seate is heaven . . . . And on the other side, he is layd in a maunger in the middest betweene two dull and lumpish beastes: And he that is the worde of the eternall Father, by whom he created all things . . . is become a childe not yet able to speake, his handes and feete beeing swathled, and he not able to stirre. And he whose vesture is the infinite light of the deity . . . he, even he, is wrapped up in poor mantles, and ragges . . . . (*1*, 343–4)

In this extreme contrast between Puente and "Bonaventure" we have the essential difference that one discovers in comparing Southwell's "New Prince, new pompe" with the fourteenth-century poems on the Nativity collected by Carleton Brown.[6] In Southwell's poem, as we have seen, the understanding has intervened to

6. *Religious Lyrics of the XIVth Century*, ed. Carleton Brown (Oxford, Clarendon Press, 1924): see especially poems 56, 57, 58, 75.

"enquire" into the "veritie," and it proceeds to develop the matter in a series of paradoxes much more elaborate and detailed than the medieval poems show. Now, with the matter thus thoroughly "understood," the Jesuit follows up this first method of meditation by the second method of "affectuous contemplation," to produce in Puente's treatise a second meditation on the manger-scene which bears a remarkable analogy to Southwell's most famous poem, "The burning Babe":

> Beholding the harte of the childe burning in love, and in desier of my salvation, shedding teares of sorrowe for my sinnes, and offring himselfe for them to the eternall Father, I will ioyne my harte unto his, that he may fasten unto it that love, and that sorrowe, entring into discourses with him, that he may ioyne me unto himselfe.
>
> . . . . .
>
> Then putting myselfe in the presence of the childe Iesus, I will with the eare of my soule hearken unto the wordes which he speaketh to his eternall Father, and unto the amorous colloquies he holdeth with him upon the businesse of our salvation . . . I will alsoe hearken unto the exteriour lamentations that he maketh, and will learne to lament my sinnes: I will heare what this childe would say unto mee, if he shoulde speake to me there where he was. (*1*, 385f.)

As I in hoarie Winters night stood shivering in the snowe,
Surpris'd I was with sodaine heate, which made my hart to glowe;
And lifting up a fearefull eye, to view what fire was neere,
A prettie Babe all burning bright did in the ayre appeare;
Who, scorched with excessive heate, such floods of teares did shed,
As though his floods should quench his flames, which with his teares
    were [fedd]:
Alas, (quoth he) but newly borne, in fierie heates I frie,
Yet none approach to warme their harts, or feele my fire but I;
My faultlesse breast the furnace is, the fuell wounding thornes:
Love is the fire, and sighes the smoake, the ashes shames and scornes;
The fewell Iustice layeth on, and Mercie blowes the coales,
The metall in this furnace wrought, are mens defiled soules:

For which, as now on fire I am to worke them to their good,
So will I melt into a bath, to wash them in my blood.
With this he vanisht out of sight, and swiftly shrunk away,
And straight I called unto minde, that it was Christmasse day.

I believe we can see what has happened to make possible the peculiar timbre of this poem: it looks like an "application of the
senses," following after, and gathering up the results of, ordinary
meditation by the three powers. Thus the author can give, in the
first six lines, a particularly vivid "composition," and can then both
see and hear the babe explaining the Incarnation and Passion in
such a way that the doctrine is inseparable from the concrete imagery which sets it forth. The parallel with Jesuit practices is driven
home if we also compare "The burning Babe" with the following
colloquies from Puente's meditation on the Passion:

> O that I could enter into his enflamed hart, and see the furnace
> of infinit fire that burneth therein, and melt in those flames,
> that issuing forth full of love, I might love as I am loved, and
> . . . suffer with love, for him who suffered for me, with so
> great love! From this interiour love burst forth such exterior
> signes and demonstrations, as was sufficient to mollifie a hart
> more frozen then yce it selfe, and more hard then any marble.
>
> O infinit love, and immense fire, which the waters of so im-
> mense tribulations could not extinguish, but was enkindled the
> more therewith ! (2, 25–6)

In "New Prince, new pompe" and "The burning Babe," which
are always placed thus, one after the other, in the early editions,[7]
we may see companion-meditations on the Nativity, after the two
methods advised by the Jesuits for such meditation. Their paired nature is somewhat obscured by the practice, found in the early editions as well as in modern ones, of printing the first in ballad stanza,
and the second, as above, in fourteeners. But after all the fourteener
is only another way of printing this stanza, and both might as well
be printed in the same visual form—preferably, I think, in ballad
stanza, which is for some reason less awkward to the modern eye. If

7. The manuscripts reverse this order: see McDonald, pp. 21, 24, 26, 28,
45–6.

printed in this way, one poem would have seven, and the other eight, stanzas; but it would, I think, be clear that these poems can justifiably be called companion-variations on the medieval nativity-ballad, done after the Jesuit manner. It is a manner which deliberately evolves a subtle fusion of passion and thought, of concrete imagery and theological abstraction, presented in a sequence of articulated, climactic structure: all arising from the central effort to comprehend the Godhead and the manhood of Christ simultaneously and without separation, to feel and know the fact of Incarnation with every faculty that man can muster. We have gone far beyond the simple affections of popular medieval piety: we are moving toward the complex texture of English religious poetry of the seventeenth century.

3

The results of this kind of complex meditation lie diffused throughout the seventeenth century; the most important effect lies in the general cast of mind which, we assume, such meditation would develop. But here and there, as in the case of meditation by the "three powers," we can find specific passages of poetry where the application of the senses to the life of Christ is manifest, especially the sense of sight, "which is commonly first begon withall." [1] The senses are strongly at work in two of Donne's meditations which we have discussed in Chapter 1: the sonnet, "Spit in my face, you Jews," and "Good Friday, 1613"; as well as in the brilliant octave of Holy Sonnet 13, where the speaker finds a refuge from his fear of Judgment by turning to the vision of the crucified Christ within his heart:

> What if this present were the worlds last night?
> Marke in my heart, O Soule, where thou dost dwell,
> The picture of Christ crucified, and tell
> Whether that countenance can thee affright . . . .

The "picture" is then analyzed in such a way as to keep constantly before the speaker imagery representing both the awful and the loving aspects of his Lord: the Day of Doom and the Day of Mercy; the Judge and the Redeemer; the God and the Man:

1. Gibbons, "Methode of Application of our five Senses," § 2, ¶ 2.

Teares in his eyes quench the amasing light,
Blood fills his frownes, which from his pierc'd head fell.
And can that tongue adjudge thee unto hell,
Which pray'd forgivenesse for his foes fierce spight?

The meditative mind of the speaker then boldly finds the answer to his soul's problem, by adapting one of the themes of his "idolatrie": as he once said to "all my profane mistresses," now he tells his soul, "This beauteous forme assures a pitious minde."

Far greater discretion is found in Herbert's "The Agonie," which operates through an application of the senses to the scenes of Gethsemane and Calvary. It begins, in Herbert's mild way, with a plain statement of purpose, and a light satirical touch against the "diviners" of line 3:

Philosophers have measur'd mountains,
Fathom'd the depths of seas, of states, and kings,
Walk'd with a staffe to heav'n, and traced fountains:
But there are two vast, spacious things,
The which to measure it doth more behove:
Yet few there are that sound them; Sinne and Love.

The meaning of sin is to be found by visualizing the scene in the Garden, for the reasons given by Antonio de Molina:

The affect of Contrition is an inward detestation of sinne, great sorrow for having offended Allmighty God, and a firme purpose to sinne no more. And for this it is a great motive to know the malice and turpitude that a sinne conteyneth in it selfe, the which no way is knowne better, then by seeing what Christ suffered to destroy the said sinne; for by the payne we discover the greatnes of the fault. (pp. 56–7)

Who would know Sinne, let him repair
Unto Mount Olivet; there shall he see
A man so wrung with pains, that all his hair,
His skinne, his garments bloudie be.
Sinne is that presse and vice, which forceth pain
To hunt his cruell food through ev'ry vein.

The method of meditation here is also especially close to that of Fray Luis de Granada, even down to the use of the traditional image of the wine press: "Yee that are desirous of wyne, to cure your woundes, this is that cluster of grapes, that was brought out of the lande of promise into this vale of teares, which is now crushed, and pressed upon the presse of the Crosse, for the remedie and redresse of our offences." (p. 141) Herbert develops this image in his last stanza by applying the sense of taste to the scene at the Cross, with consequent suggestions of the actual reception of the "Sacrament of Love":

> Who knows not Love, let him assay
> And taste that juice, which on the crosse a pike
> Did set again abroach; then let him say
> If ever he did taste the like.
> Love is that liquour sweet and most divine,
> Which my God feels as bloud; but I, as wine.

As the last stanza implies, such meditation on the life of Christ formed part of the usual preparation for the service of the Eucharist, and of succeeding meditation upon the benefits of the sacrament. This is made particularly clear in Henry Vaughan's devotional handbook, *The Mount of Olives* (1652), where, among his "Admonitions" regarding preparation for Communion, we find him recommending:

> let thy sleep that night be shorter then usual, be up with the day, or rather with thy Saviour, who rose up early, while it was yet dark. Meditate with thy self what miracles of mercy he hath done for thee. Consider how he left his Fathers bosome to be lodged in a manger, and laid by his robes of glory to take upon him the seed of *Abraham*, that he might cloath thee with Immortality. Call to minde his wearisome journeys, continual afflictions, the malice and scorne he underwent, the persecutions and reproaches laid upon him, his strong cries and teares in the days of his flesh, his spiritual agony and sweating of blood, with the Implacable fury of his Enemies, and his own unspeakable humility, humbling himself to the death of the Crosse . . . .[2]

2. *The Works of Henry Vaughan*, ed. Leonard Cyril Martin (2 vols., Oxford, Clarendon Press, 1914), *1*, 157-8. For other accounts see St. François de Sales, Pt. 2, chap. 14; and *Spiritual Combat*, chap. 55.

Then, in the "Meditation before the receiving of the holy Communion," we find the following dramatic example of these practices, based on the theme, "Thy life here was nothing else but a pilgrimage and laborious search after sinners, that thou mightst finde them out and make them whole."

> How many scorching and wearisome journeys didst thou undergo for our sakes! How many cold and tedious nights didst thou watch and spend abroad in prayer, when the birds of the aire lay warme in their nests, and thou hadst not a place to put thy head in! In the day time I finde thee preaching in the Temple, and all night praying in the Mount of *Olives;* a little after on thine own Sabbath travelling for me in the corne-field; Another time (wearied with thy journey) sitting on the Well of *Jacob,* and begging a draught of that cold water from the woman of *Samaria;* Now again I meet thee on the Asse, made infinitely happy by so glorious a rider . . . . But (Oh!) with what language shall I attempt thy passion? thy bloody sweat, thy deep and bitter agony, thy lingring peece-mealed death, with all the lively anguishments, and afflictions of thy martyr'd Spirit?

And again, among the "Admonitions after receiving the holy Communion" Vaughan advises: "You should meditate upon his birth, life, doctrine and passion, his death and buriall, resurrection and ascension, and his second coming to judgement." [3]

Such advice, coming as it does in a book published only two years after the first part of *Silex Scintillans*, and three years before the publication of the second part, holds deep implications for the meditative life that underlies the many poems on these topics which occur in both parts of *Silex Scintillans*. In particular such meditation appears to have a very close relationship with one of Vaughan's finest achievements, "The Search," which presents a highly original variation on the whole procedure of meditating on the life of Christ, from Nativity to Crucifixion. The opening lines are richly symbolical:

> 'Tis now cleare day: I see a Rose
> Bud in the bright East, and disclose
> The Pilgrim-Sunne . . . .

3. *Works of Vaughan, 1,* 161–4.

Literally, this is an admirable presentation of the dawn, using Vaughan's typical imagery from nature, and in accord with Vaughan's above advice: "be up with the day, or rather with thy Saviour, who rose up early . . . ." But the "Rose" is also the traditional symbol of the Virgin; and the "Pilgrim-Sunne" which she "discloses" is her Son, whose life, as Vaughan has said above, "was nothing else but a pilgrimage and laborious search after sinners." Simultaneously (for Vaughan's imagery works in this mode of melting association) the Rose could suggest Christ himself, who is twice referred to as the "Rose of Sharon" in Vaughan's Communion meditations.[4] The poem thus is built upon an irony made explicit in the close: the speaker has spent the night in far-extended search for a Savior who has already searched for and found him, as Vaughan's appended motto from Acts (17.27, 28) makes clear: "That they should seek the Lord, if happily they might feel after him, and finde him, though he be not far off from every one of us, for in him we live, and move, and have our being."

> all night have I
> Spent in a roving Extasie
> To find my Saviour; I have been
> As far as *Bethlem*, and have seen
> His Inne, and Cradle; Being there
> I met the *Wise-men*, askt them where
> He might be found, or what starre can
> Now point him out, grown up a Man?
> To *Egypt* hence I fled, ran o're
> All her parcht bosome to *Nile's* shore
> Her yearly nurse; came back, enquir'd
> Amongst the *Doctors*, and desir'd
> To see the *Temple*, but was shown
> A little dust, and for the Town
> A heap of ashes, where some sed
> A small bright sparkle was a bed,
> Which would one day (beneath the pole,)
> Awake, and then refine the whole.

Here is another clue to the variation Vaughan is working upon the practice of seeing Christ as actually present in the places of the

4. *Ibid.*, *1*, 156, 161.

Holy Land; for the "Temple" and the "Town" here suggest the graveyard ("dust" and "ashes") and the human body—St. Paul's "temple of the Spirit." The "small bright sparkle," then, would be this Spirit, which will at the Day of Doom achieve the resurrection of the body. It is within this "Temple" that the Savior will be found: not in the external places of his Incarnate manifestation—places where Vaughan now searches in the traditional way:

> Tyr'd here, I come to *Sychar;* thence
> To *Jacobs wel,* bequeathed since
> Unto his sonnes . . .
>   And here (O fate!)
> I sit, where once my Saviour sate;
> The angry Spring in bubbles swell'd
> Which broke in sighes still, as they fill'd,
> And whisper'd, *Jesus had been there*
> But *Jacobs children would not heare.*
> Loath hence to part, at last I rise
> But with the fountain in my Eyes,
> And here a fresh search is decreed
> He must be found, where he did bleed;
> I walke the garden, and there see
> *Idaea's* of his Agonie,
> And moving anguishments that set
> His blest face in a bloudy sweat;
> I climb'd the Hill, perus'd the Crosse
> Hung with my gaine, and his great losse,
> Never did tree beare fruit like this,
> *Balsam* of Soules, the bodyes blisse;
> But, O his grave! where I saw lent
> (For he had none,) a Monument,
> An undefil'd, and new-heaw'd one,
> But there was not the *Corner-stone* . . . .

Unable to find his Savior in these places, he decides that Christ must have retired to the Wilderness, leaving the cruelties of man:

> He liv'd there safe, 'twas his retreat
> From the fierce *Jew,* and *Herods* heat,

And forty dayes withstood the fell,
And high temptations of hell;
With Seraphins there talked he
His fathers flaming ministrie,
He heav'nd their *walks*, and with his eyes
Made those wild shades a Paradise,
Thus was the desert sanctified
To be the refuge of his bride . . . .

Christ's retirement to the Wilderness is usually taken by the meditative handbooks as a symbol of the retirement of the soul to solitude for prayer and meditation: either actual solitude or "spiritual retirement." [5] This seems to be the implication here: solitude, especially (for Vaughan) the solitude of nature, becomes a symbol for the spiritual retirement of the soul (the bride of Christ) in its devotions. Soon the one who so fervently seeks and asks will hear his answer:

But as I urg'd thus, and writ down
What pleasures should my Journey crown,
What silent paths, what shades, and Cells,
Faire, virgin-flowers, and hallow'd *Wells*
I should rove in, and rest my head
Where my deare Lord did often tread,
Sugring all dangers with successe,
Me thought I heard one singing thus;

1.

Leave, leave, thy gadding thoughts;
Who Pores
and spies
Still out of Doores
descries
Within them nought.

.   .   .   .   .

5. See *Meditations on the Life of Christ*, chap. 17; Francisco de Osuna, pp. 96–7; Puente, *1*, 458.

3.

To rack old Elements,
or Dust
and say
Sure here he must
needs stay
Is not the way,
nor just.

Search well another world; who studies this,
Travels in Clouds, seeks *Manna*, where none is.

The first stanza suggests that Christ is to be found within one's self;
hence the phrase "Search well another world" suggests the little
world of man, and the "Manna," the eucharistic elements which,
when received, make Christ fully present within this little world.
This interpretation would accord exactly with Vaughan's admonition, in his *Mount of Olives*, to engage in careful self-examination
as a preparation for reception of the Eucharist, for "such as our
pre-disposition is, such also shall our proportion be of this spiritual
Manna." [6]

4

All such meditations are based, fundamentally, on the ancient and
widespread practice of "mental" or "spiritual" communion, which
ranged from imaginative re-enactment of the eucharistic service, as
presented in the fourth book of the *Imitation of Christ*, down to
the simplest memorial of the Passion. These acts of mental communion, both the *Imitation* and the *Spiritual Combat* insist, "should
be practiced as often as possible":

> And verilie everie devout man maye everye daye, and everye
> houre go healthfullie, and without prohibition unto the spirit-
> uall Communion of Christe, that is to saye, in remembringe
> of his passion . . . . For so ofte a man is housled misticallye
> and invisibly, as he remembreth devoutly the misterie of the
> incarnation of Christ, and his passion, and is thereby kindled
> into his love.[1]

6. *Works of Vaughan, 1,* 155.
1. *Spiritual Combat,* pp. 157, 168; *Imitation of Christ,* Bk. 4, chap. 10; quoted

From this point of view, not only the specifically eucharistic poems but all the many references to the wounds of Christ that we find in the poetry of Southwell, Donne, Herbert, Crashaw, and Vaughan may be taken as brief acts of mental communion, along with the poems specifically devoted to the wound in Christ's side which we find in the works of Southwell, Herbert, and Crashaw.

Most important of all, this practice of mental communion will help to explain the significance of the four opening poems in Herbert's "Church": "The Altar," "The Sacrifice," "The Thanksgiving," and "The Reprisall," which re-enact, through meditation, the eucharistic service, with more than a few reminiscences of the ancient Mass. Miss Freeman and Miss Tuve [2] have both pointed out that the dramatic method of "The Sacrifice" is based fundamentally on the ancient tradition of the *Improperia*, the Reproaches of Christ spoken from the Cross, a portion of the service for Good Friday. Miss Tuve has gone on to point out the highly traditional nature of the paradoxes involved in this poem, as seen in other portions of the liturgy for Holy Week, and in medieval poetry related both to this liturgy and to the ancient tradition of the Pleading of Christ. But she has, I believe, gone too far in arguing that Herbert's "Sacrifice" displays "precisely the tone of the 'Reproaches' and of sundry medieval lyrics," that "Herbert's supposedly Metaphysical harshness or irony in the diction is quite native to the tradition," and that, in short, the "tension of ambiguities and serried meanings which Empson has commented on is precisely what Herbert owes" to the medieval tradition.[3] Empson, in his sly rejoinder,[4] concedes that it was "rather absurd of me to call so traditional a poem 'unique,'" but he also points out that none of Miss Tuve's examples provides a writer "who clashes in plain words, as Herbert does, the

---

from the version of Richard Whitford, *The Folowing of Christ,* [Rouen?], 1585.

2. Freeman, pp. 160–2; Rosemond Tuve, "On Herbert's 'Sacrifice,'" *KR,* *12* (1950), 51–75. A more elaborate treatment of the poem and its backgrounds will be found in Miss Tuve's recent book, *A Reading of George Herbert* (London, Faber and Faber, 1952), pp. 19–99.

3. *KR, 12,* 53, 58, 60. Miss Tuve is referring to the analysis of "The Sacrifice" given by William Empson in his *Seven Types of Ambiguity* (2d ed. London, Chatto and Windus, 1947), pp. 226–33.

4. *KR, 12,* 735–8.

idea of the mercy and yearning love of Christ against the idea of his terrible and inevitable revenge." The key to this matter is found in the statement which Empson pounces upon: Miss Tuve's assertion that the "ambiguity, density, and ambivalence of tone that we think of as so especially 'Metaphysical' are either explicit in the tradition, or implicit in the deliberate juxtaposition of concepts and images in the liturgy . . . ." [5] "Surely," Empson remarks, "the act of making 'explicit' these very remarkable parts of a tradition is worth notice; it might even be worth calling a new style."

It is a new style: for Herbert's "Sacrifice" is a *meditation* upon the liturgy, developing the events of Passion Week according to the intricate methods of the seventeenth century: visualization, intellectual analysis, profit drawn from the dual and simultaneous vision of the God made man. All the matters explored in meditative literature of the seventeenth century were either explicit or implicit in the medieval heritage; the central aim of the art of meditation was precisely to make explicit whatever remained implicit: to analyze, to understand, and then to feel and profit from the matter. This is exactly the difference that we feel between Herbert's subtle, packed, deft, explicit treatment of the paradoxes and the simple, implicit statement of the paradoxes which one finds in the liturgy and in the popular medieval poetry cited by Miss Tuve.

Consider, for example, the two following paradoxes from the Improperia, together with the corresponding passage from a fourteenth-century lyric cited by Miss Tuve:

> For thee I struck the kings of the Chananites: and thou hast struck My head with a reed.

> I gave thee a royal sceptre: and thou hast given to My head a crown of thorns.

>> Kynges of chanaan ich vor the boet;
>> And thou betest myn heved wyth roed.

>> Ich gaf the croune of kynedom;
>> And thou me gyfst a croune of thorn. [6]

5. *Ibid.*, p. 64.

6. *Daily Missal*, ed. Gaspar Lefebvre (2d ed., Bruges, 1927), pp. 819–21; *Religious Lyrics of the XIVth Century*, ed. Brown, p. 18 (spelling slightly modernized).

Now compare these simple oppositions with the elaboration they receive at the hands of Herbert:

> Then on my head a crown of thorns I wear:
> For thése are all the grapes *Sion* doth bear,
> Though I my vine planted and watred there:
> > Was ever grief like mine?

> So sits the earths great curse in *Adams* fall
> Upon my head: so I remove it all
> From th' earth unto my brows, and bear the thrall:
> > Was ever grief, &c.

> Then with the reed they gave to me before,
> They strike my head, the rock from whence all store
> Of heav'nly blessings issue evermore:
> > Was ever grief, &c.

> They bow their knees to me, and cry, *Hail king:*
> What ever scoffes & scornfulnesse can bring,
> I am the floore, the sink, where they it fling:
> > Was ever grief, &c.

> Yet since mans scepters are as frail as reeds,
> And thorny all their crowns, bloudie their weeds;
> I, who am *Truth*, turn into truth their deeds:
> > Was ever grief, &c.

The most striking aspect of this passage is the way in which the intellect manipulates these various ironies into one compact symbolical unit, satirizing the worldly rule of men. At the same time, it will perhaps be clear that the base from which these ironies are developed is considerably different from that of the Improperia. In the latter each paradox is developed from a central contrast between the favors which God has bestowed on the children of Israel in bringing them up out of Egypt and the disgrace they are now heaping on Christ. This contrast plays a part in Herbert's "Sacrifice," but it is not the central mode of development, which instead consists in the usual meditative procedure of pondering the events of Passion Week, in narrative sequence, from the scene in Gethsemane to the death on the Cross, and "drawing some profit from the matter." This is performed through a vivid apprehension of the scenes by the senses: seeing the places, watching the actors, hearing the words spoken, as in Gethsemane:

> Yet my Disciples sleep: I cannot gain
> One houre of watching; but their drowsie brain
> Comforts not me, and doth my doctrine stain:
> > Was ever grief, &c.

> Arise, arise, they come. Look how they runne!
> Alas! what haste they make to be undone!
> How with their lanterns do they seek the sunne!
> > Was ever grief, &c.

> .   .   .   .   .

> See, they lay hold on me, not with the hands
> Of faith, but furie: yet at their commands
> I suffer binding, who have loos'd their bands:
> > Was ever grief, &c.

And so throughout the events of Passion Week: "Heark how they crie aloud still, *Crucifie*"; "Ah! how they scourge me!" "Behold they spit on me."

Another aspect of the difference between this poem and the representative products of medieval piety may be seen if we will set the poem against some of the popular lyrics of the fifteenth century which manifest the kind of affective piety found in the *Meditations* of the pseudo-Bonaventure. Here, for instance, is a part of a popular carol by James Ryman (written c. 1492): it is especially interesting because Ryman is using a combination of monorime and refrain that suggests the traditional basis for Herbert's stanza-form:

> Haue myende, I was put on the rode
> And for thy sake shedde my hert blode.
> Beholde my payne; beholde my moode;
> > O synfull man, yeve me thyn hert.

> Beholde me, hede, hande, foote, and side;
> Beholde my woundes fyve so wyde;

> Beholde the payne that I abyde;
>   O synfull man, yeve me thyn hert.
>
> Haue myende, man, how fast I was bounde
> For thy sake to a pilloure rounde,
> Scorged till my bloode fell to grounde;
>   O synfull man, yeve me thyn hert.[7]

The carol develops simple emotions of pity and love: the whole emphasis falls upon the immense mercy of Christ; fear of judgment and of God's omnipotent power are excluded from consideration. But the central strength of Herbert's poem resides in its ability to keep constantly before the mind both the immensity of God's omnipotence and the immensity of God's love, the companion-powers of punishment and mercy: "A memory of the revengeful power of Jehovah gives resonance to the voice of the merciful power of Jesus," as Empson has said [8] in basing his analysis on this central ambiguity:

> They buffet him, and box him as they list,
> Who grasps the earth and heaven with his fist,
> And never yet, whom he would punish, miss'd:
>   Was ever grief, &c.
>
>   .   .   .   .   .
>
> Servants and abjects flout me; they are wittie:
> *Now prophesie who strikes thee*, is their dittie.
> So they in me denie themselves all pitie:
>   Was ever grief, &c.
>
>   .   .   .   .   .
>
> Weep not, deare friends, since I for both have wept
> When all my tears were bloud, the while you slept:
> Your tears for your own fortunes should be kept:
>   Was ever grief, &c.

7. *The Early English Carols*, ed. Richard Leighton Greene (Oxford, Clarendon Press, 1935), p. 192 (I have omitted the editor's brackets and italics).

8. *Seven Types*, p. 229.

Now this aspect of God the Punisher is of course not absent from popular medieval treatises and poems on the Passion. It occurs, even in the *Meditations* of the pseudo-Bonaventure: "O wretched men, how terrible will that Sacred Head which you now impiously strike one day appear to you!" "With bitterness of heart He wept over their eternal loss and danger, and at that moment He also foretold their temporal destruction." [9] But these aspects of the Godhead, as I have noted earlier, are underplayed: overwhelmed by pity and love for the manhood. Thus the paradoxes implicit in the Incarnation and Crucifixion tend to remain implicit, whereas in Herbert's poem they are consistently explored and explicated.

Is it wrong, then, to speak, as Empson does, of "Herbert's method" [10] in this poem? Miss Tuve is certainly right in arguing that fundamental aspects of this "method" are traditional in medieval song and liturgy; and we have argued that other aspects of the method are traditional ways of performing meditations on the Passion, especially as part of the exercise of mental communion. Herbert's method is to organize all these traditions into one powerful commemoration of the Sacrifice: the coalescence and reaffirmation of a score of traditional motifs in one magnificent union.

5

One highly significant aspect of meditations on the life of Christ remains for our consideration: the meditations fostered by devotion to the Virgin Mary, particularly those of the rosary, which, like other forms of methodical meditation, were assuming their modern form in the century preceding the birth of Donne. Devotion to the Virgin, especially encouraged by the Jesuits, was one of the strongest resources cultivated by the Counter Reformation. Since England had fully participated in this devotion during the fourteenth and fifteenth centuries, it seems that a fertile ground must have remained in this area for the emissaries of the Counter Reformation to work upon. There is abundant evidence in the literature of our period that this was indeed so.

One of the finest tributes to the reluctance of conservative Anglicans to give up this devotion is found, as we might expect, in George

9. *Meditations on the Life of Christ*, pp. 346, 313.
10. *Seven Types*, p. 231.

Herbert: in his remarkably ambiguous poem, "To All Angels and Saints." It is a poem which best displays its power, I think, if we can hear behind it the ringing exhortations of the *Spiritual Combat* or of St. François de Sales: "let no day pass without imploring the assistance of Our Lady, the queen of all the saints, your guardian angel, the glorious archangel St. Michael, or any other saint to whom you have any particular devotion." [1] To all such exhortations Herbert replies with a delicately tempered tribute, which, in the rising fervor that glows through its caution, shows the painful problem in a beautifully modulated tension:

> Oh glorious spirits, who after all your bands
> See the smooth face of God without a frown
> > Or strict commands;
> Where ev'ry one is king, and hath his crown,
> If not upon his head, yet in his hands:
>
> Not out of envie or maliciousnesse
> Do I forbear to crave your speciall aid:
> > I would addresse
> My vows to thee most gladly, Blessed Maid,
> And Mother of my God, in my distresse.
>
> Thou art the holy mine, whence came the gold,
> The great restorative for all decay
> > In young and old;
> Thou art the cabinet where the jewel lay:
> Chiefly to thee would I my soul unfold . . . .

Then, after that muted echo of the Virgin's Litanies, he explains why he must repress this willingness, in a stanza brimful of ambiguity:

> But now, alas, I dare not; for our King,
> Whom we do all joyntly adore and praise,
> > Bids no such thing:
> And where his pleasure no injunction layes,
> ('Tis your own case) ye never move a wing.

1. *Spiritual Combat*, p. 146; cf. St. François de Sales, Pt. 2, chap. 16.

"But *now, alas*, I dare not." Why *now?* Shouldn't the argument apply always? And doesn't the "alas" show a strange regret for God's failure to supply the required "injunction" that would make such devotion possible? For God, of course, is "our King" whom "we" —that is the Angels, Saints, Herbert, and other human beings— "do all joyntly adore and praise." Or is it as simple as this? Isn't there at the same time a lurking suggestion of another, earthly King, who *now, alas*, "bids no such thing" for the Anglican? It is hard to avoid the implication, though Herbert proceeds, with perfect tact, to develop his poem with explicit reference to God alone:

> All worship is prerogative, and a flower
> Of his rich crown, from whom lyes no appeal
> > At the last houre:
> Therefore we dare not from his garland steal,
> To make a posie for inferiour power.

It is convincing: a reasonable apology; and yet—in the last stanza— the uneasiness and regret return, along with a feeling of readiness, almost a hope, perhaps, that some way could yet be found to make these old devotions possible:

> Although then others court you, if ye know
> What's done on earth, we shall not fare the worse,
> > Who do not so;
> Since we are ever ready to disburse,
> If any one our Masters hand can show.

Henry Vaughan, amid the controversies of the Commonwealth, is not so tactful. In his poem "The Knot" he praises the Virgin in terms that openly defy the Puritan by expressing an essentially Catholic view of the Virgin's place in the scheme of things:

> Thou art the true Loves-knot; by thee
> > God is made our Allie.
> And mans inferior Essence he
> > With his did dignifie.
>
> For Coalescent by that Band
> > We are his body grown,

> Nourished with favors from his hand
> Whom for our head we own.

> And such a Knot, what arm dares loose,
> What life, what death can sever?
> Which us in him, and him in us
> United keeps for ever.

The echo of the Communion liturgy in the last stanza is especially daring: such an implicit equation with Christ is exactly the point against which the Reformers directed their attack on Maryolatry. But this is only a more defensive and vehement way of saying what Donne takes for granted in a stanza of his "Litany," adding in the last two lines the doctrine of intercession which Vaughan never quite expresses:

> For that faire blessed Mother-maid,
> Whose flesh redeem'd us; That she-Cherubin,
> Which unlock'd Paradise, and made
> One claime for innocence, and disseiz'd sinne,
> Whose wombe was a strange heav'n, for there
> God cloath'd himselfe, and grew,
> Our zealous thankes wee poure. As her deeds were
> Our helpes, so are her prayers; nor can she sue
> In vaine, who hath such titles unto you.

Certainly the Counter Reformation made vigorous attempts to appeal to such latent or overt sympathies in England. By the middle of the seventeenth century, as Miss Freeman has pointed out (pp. 180–3), sodalities of the Virgin seem to have been established in England: the Jesuit Henry Hawkins, who spent some twenty-five years in England during the first half of the century, wrote his book of meditations on the Virgin, *Partheneia Sacra* (1633), especially for the use of the members of the "Parthenian Sodalitie," as his title-page says. And his book had been preceded by a stream of earlier manuals, teaching the use of the rosary in meditation on the lives of Mary and Christ. These were usually books printed abroad and smuggled into England in what appear to have been great quantities,[2] for several of them went through more than one edition. One of the earliest seems to have been printed in London itself, somewhere around the year 1580: the translation of Gaspar Loarte's popular manual.[3] The handbooks of Luca Pinelli and Alexis de Salo were also translated; while other handbooks were composed in English specifically for the use of Catholics in England.[4] In addition to such treatises, elaborate directions for meditating with the rosary were included in some of the general treatises on meditation translated into English, such as those by Puente, Richeome, and Antonio de Molina.

The tendencies of all such works are summed up in one particularly bold attempt by an Anglican to encourage devotion to the Virgin: Anthony Stafford's *The Femall Glory: or, The Life, and Death of our Blessed Lady*, published in London with official permission in 1635. Fundamentally, the book presents a sequence of Catholic meditations on the combined lives of Mary and Christ, from Mary's birth to her Assumption, using all the methods that we have here discussed: seeing the place, imagining the speeches made, and taking the same liberties that the pseudo-Bonaventure encouraged: "what the Scripture omitteth, must be supplied by our charitable imagination." (p. 147) By guarding himself on all the more controversial issues, and by carefully avoiding any reference to the rosary, he may, as he says, "humbly submit this"

2. See White, *Devotional Literature*, p. 136, for discussion of the capture in 1626 of one consignment of "Popish Bookes," containing 74 copies of an *Angelicall Exercise to stirre up to the Love of the blessed Virgin*. I have not been able to identify this book.

3. See my Introduction, sec. 2; and Southern, pp. 216–19, 408–9. Southern also discusses (pp. 214–16, 449–50) an earlier English rosary-book published at Bruges in 1576. Loarte's treatise was reprinted at Rouen in 1613.

4. Luca Pinelli, *The Virgin Maries life*, trans. "R.G.," Douay, 1604; another issue seems to have appeared in the same year at Rouen; it was evidently combined with *The Societie of the Rosary* in an edition that appeared at St. Omer, 1624. Alexis de Salo, *An Admirable Method to Love, Serve and Honour the B. Virgin Mary*, trans. "R.F.," [Rouen], 1639. Thomas Worthington, *The Rosarie of our Ladie*, Antwerp, 1600. Sabin Chambers, *The Garden of our B. Lady. Or a devout manner, how to serve her in her Rosary*, [St. Omer], 1619. *The Societie of the Rosary. Newly Augmented* [St. Omer? c. 1600]; this is clearly a second edition, but I find no record of the first edition.

to the Censure and determination of the Church of *England*, whose not Connivence alone, but approbation I know I shall have in boldly affirming that she was a transcendent Creature, not to be ranked in respect of her worth, with any of her sexe, but to have a place assign'd her apart, and above them all; being not to be considered as a meere woman, but as a Type, or an Idaea of an Accomplisht piety. (p. 219)

If, then, this ancient devotion fought hard to maintain a place in England, we may reasonably expect to find it reflected in the poetry of the period, and even to find, in poets of Catholic rearing, some echoes of the methods of the rosary.

6

Meditation according to the rosary is a various and complicated matter: anyone who has read the above-mentioned treatises will at once agree with Thurston that there were indeed an "inconceivable variety of ways of saying the Rosary . . . even where Dominican influence was strong, and that too as late as the middle of the seventeenth century." [1] For our present purposes, however, we need to consider only the two most important of these varieties.

The first is meditation according to the divisions of the Dominican rosary—now the established rosary of the Catholic Church. This is a rosary of 150 "Aves," divided into fifteen "decades," which are, for meditation, subdivided into three parts of five decades each. Meditation according to this rosary, as described in Gaspar Loarte's treatise, is exactly the method which has come down to the present day: meditation on the five joyful, the five dolorous, and the five glorious mysteries.[2] Thus the central events in the lives of Mary and Christ were meditated in orderly sequence from beginning to end, including the legendary events of the life of Mary, both before the birth and after the death of Christ.[3]

1. Herbert Thurston, "Our Popular Devotions. II.—The Rosary. V.—The Fifteen Mysteries," *The Month*, 96 (1900), 620–37; see especially p. 631.

2. Annunciation, Visitation, Nativity, Presentation, Finding of Christ in the Temple; Gethsemane, Whipping of Christ, Crown of Thorns, Carrying of the Cross, Crucifixion; Resurrection, Ascension, Coming of the Holy Ghost, Assumption of the Virgin, Coronation of the Virgin.

3. For the elaborate use of legendary materials concerning the life of Mary

These meditations, as Loarte explains, are to be performed with the usual dramatic methods which we have already discussed—with the usual blending of concrete detail and abstract thinking. But there is one all-important difference between their method and the method of a full spiritual exercise, a difference emphasized by Loarte in discussing his division of each mystery into three points: "everye point," he says, "is so plainly distinguished a-part, as one hangeth not of an-other, but ech one is absolute in his owne conclusion." [4] This clearly is quite a different process from that of the full Ignatian exercise, where, as we have seen in Chapter 1, the points are not each "absolute in his owne conclusion" but play their part in an organic development, moving from composition, through analysis, to affections. Loarte's procedure here, as the meditations themselves show, does not lead to any such articulated, cumulative structure, but produces instead three self-contained, predominantly intellectual meditations upon a given mystery.

This is exactly what happens in certain of Southwell's poems dealing with the lives of Mary and Christ, poems all cast in three or four stanzas, with a clearly demarked topic for each stanza. There is no organic development; we have instead three or four witty, pious meditations on a given mystery. The stanzas on the Presentation are representative:

> To be redeemde the worlds Redeemer brough[t],
>   Two seely turtle doves for ransome paies,
> O wares with empires worthie to be bought,
>   This easie rate doth sound, not drowne thy praise,
> For sith no prise can to thy worth amount,
> A dove, yea love, due price thou doest account[.]
>
> Old *Simeon*, cheape pennie worth and sweete,
>   Obteind when thee in armes he did imbrace,

---

before the Annunciation see the very popular handbook by Alberto Castello, *Rosario della gloriosa vergine Maria*, Venice, 1522; I have used the edition of Venice, 1564. It is important to note that the whole of the combined lives of Mary and Christ might also be covered in reciting only five decades of this rosary; see Antonio de Molina, p. 161, and *Societie of the Rosary*, pp. 75–92.

4. Loarte, *Instructions*, f.9.

His weeping eies thy smiling lookes did meete,
  Thy love his heart, thy kisses blest his face,
O eies, O heart, meane sights and loves avoyde,
Base not your selves, your best you have enioyde[.]

O virgine pure thou dost those doves present,
  As due to law, not as an equall price,
To buy such ware thou wouldst thy selfe have spente,
  The world to reach his worth could not suffice,
If God were to be bought, not worldly pelfe,
But thou wert fittest price next God himselfe.

Each of the three ingenious stanzas is a self-contained unit, loosely
linked to the others by the general paradox of redeeming the Redeemer with so small a ransom; the poem simply ends when each
significant aspect of the scene has been covered. What we have here
seems to be a work in which the continental art of the sacred epigram
(as found in Crashaw's *Epigrammata Sacra*) is combined with meditation on the life of Christ after the manner suggested by Southwell's fellow-Jesuit for meditation by the rosary.

We may, at any rate, clearly distinguish the poems by Southwell
in this style from those which we have already discussed as resembling the development of a full Ignatian exercise. *Moeoniae* (1595),
in which most of these poems on Mary and Christ first appeared, begins with a clear sequence of ten poems, all but one presented in
three stanzas of the kind which we have just described: "The Virgine
Maries conception," "Her Nativitie," "Her Spousalls," "The virgins
salutation," "The Visitation," "His circumcision," "The Epiphanie"
(in four stanzas), "The Presentation," "The flight into Egypt," and
"Christs returne out of Egypt." In a prefatory note the publisher,
John Busby, speaking of the "Poems and divine Meditations" presented in *Moeoniae*, warns his readers "that having in this Treatise
read Maries visitation, the next that should folow is Christs nativity,
but being afore printed in the end of Peters Complaint, we have
heere of purpose omitted." He is referring to the edition of *Saint
Peters Complaint* that had appeared earlier in 1595, where, among
the miscellaneous poems that follow the long "Complaint," we find
a poem on Christ's Nativity, in four stanzas related in style to the

above ten poems of *Moeoniae*. Immediately after it comes a similar poem on "Christs Childhoode," in three stanzas, which looks as if it ought to follow after the poem on the return from Egypt. I cannot agree with Janelle's argument (pp. 161–2) that these two poems, in their development of paradoxes, display a different style from the above poems in *Moeoniae*. The one on Christ's childhood is in fact less paradoxical than some of the poems in *Moeoniae;* and although it is true that the poem on the Nativity displays an extreme use of paradox, this is exactly what we should expect would happen in dealing with this mystery. I can therefore see no reason to discount Busby's statement. The volume *Saint Peters Complaint* was posthumously published, and I can find no evidence to support Janelle's assumption (p. 157) that its contents were prepared by Southwell. On the contrary, the evidence provided by the volume itself—all the evidence we have—suggests that this is a compilation of materials made by another hand, probably by the publisher. Someone, as Busby's statement suggests, has simply plucked these two poems on Christ out of their place in the *Moeoniae* sequence, and put them in the *Complaint* volume in an appropriate place, just before Southwell's clumsy poem in fourteeners, "A Child my choice," with which they would accord in subject-matter:

> Alas, hee weepes, he sighes, he pants, yet doe his Angels sing,
> Out of his teares, his sighes and throbs, doth bud a ioyfull spring.

But if these two could be plucked out of the sequence, why not others? The answer probably lies in a certain caution with regard to a poetical sequence so obviously Roman in inspiration. We may attribute the greater boldness of *Moeoniae* to the success of the preceding publication, as Busby's preface suggests. But even here some caution is registered, for Busby did not print two more poems in this style which exist in manuscript and which seem obviously to conclude this sequence: "The Death of Our Ladie," and "The Assumption of our Lady"; these were not printed until the nineteenth century.[5] Anyone can see, I think, why they were not printed in the

5. First printed in *The Poetical Works of the Rev. Robert Southwell*, ed. William B. Turnbull, London, 1856. The following stanzas from "The Death of our Ladie" are taken from *The Complete Poems of Robert Southwell*, ed. Alexander B. Grosart, London, 1872.

early editions, for their hyperbolic praises of the Virgin go beyond anything allowed by even the most conservative Anglican orthodoxy:

> Weepe, living thinges, of life the mother dyes;
>   The world doth loose the summ of all her blisse,
> The quene of Earth, the empresse of the skyes;
>   By Marye's death mankind an orphan is:
> Lett Nature weepe, yea, lett all graces mone,
> Their glory, grace, and giftes dye all in one.
>
> Her face a heaven, two planettes were her eyes,
>   Whose gracious light did make our clearest day;
> But one such heaven there was and loe! it dyes,
>   Deathe's darke eclipse hath dymmed every ray:
> Sunne, hide thy light, thy beames untymely shine!
> Trew light sith wee have lost, we crave not thine.

We may note here a point which we shall discuss later: the way in which these hyperboles suggest Donne's treatment of Elizabeth Drury in the *Anniversaries*. But all I wish to stress here is that Southwell seems to have written a sequence of poems in this style which runs from Mary's Conception to her Assumption, and which appears to be related in some way to the meditations of the rosary. It is apparent that the fourteen poems which we have just described do not fit the sequence of fifteen meditations used with the Dominican rosary. One could conclude simply that a great many poems have been lost; yet it is not by any means necessary to assume that Southwell followed the normal topics set forth for this rosary. There was in Southwell's time another kind of rosary, now almost forgotten but then very widely used: it was known as the "*corona* of our Lady." Thurston has thoroughly described the use and the popularity of the corona, known among Catholic scholars as the Bridgettine rosary. "In the sixteenth and seventeenth centuries," he declares, "the *corona* of our Lady was almost, if not quite, as commonly recited by the faithful as the Rosary properly so called." [6] And he notes a point of special concern for students of Southwell and

6. Herbert Thurston, "Our Popular Devotions. VI.—The so-called Bridgettine Rosary," *The Month*, 100 (1902), 189–203; see esp. p. 202.

Donne: that the *Libellus Precum*, the manual of the Jesuit sodalities, "seems to contemplate nothing else but" the use of the corona. "It is obvious that the writer supposes that every Jesuit scholar" will possess this kind of rosary.[7]

The corona consisted of a set of beads numbering sixty-three Aves (according to the supposed years of the Virgin's life) and arranged in six decades, with a final appendage of three Aves and a Paternoster. Its use in meditation on the lives of Mary and Christ is fully set forth, along with directions for using the Dominican rosary, in three rosary-treatises written specifically for the use of English readers: *The Societie of the Rosary* (c. 1600), and the handbooks of Thomas Worthington (1600) and Sabin Chambers (1619).[8] It is clear from all three of these books that the usual procedure was to divide the materials for meditation into seven parts, either distributing the events considered into seven sections, or using the seventh part—the appendage of three Aves and the Pater —for some sort of concluding topic, such as the merits of Mary. The Jesuit Chambers also explains (pp. 61–76) how to use the six decades of the beads to meditate on the six feasts of the Virgin: her Conception, her Nativity, her Presentation, her Visitation, her Purification (i.e., Christ's Presentation), and her Assumption. Certainly, as Janelle has suggested (pp. 127, 273), the celebration of these feasts has a great deal to do with Southwell's cycle, which frequently echoes the liturgy. But most important is the fact that the corona was used to throw special emphasis on the life of the Virgin before and after the life of Christ, as we see from Worthington's preface, where he explains that the corona "is divided into seven partes," as follows:

> in the first part are proposed those things to be meditated, that belong to the preparations made for her coming, before she was borne. In the second, such as pertaine to her birth and education. In the third, how she cooperated with the B. Trinitie, in Christs incarnation and nativite. In the fourth, her par-

7. *Month, 96*, 633–5.
8. See *Societie of the Rosary*, pp. 58, 66–73; Worthington, preface; and Chambers, pp. 15, 261–72

ticipation with him, both in ioyes and afflictions, most part of his life in this world. In the fifth her singular compassion in the time of his Passion, and death. In the sixth, the rest of her life, with her death and assumption. And in the seventh and last part, her most glorious Coronation, and exaltation above al Saincts and Angels . . . .

It is interesting, at least, to conjecture that these fourteen poems by Southwell are related in some way to this mode of meditation by the corona.

7

We are on firmer ground when we turn to Donne's "La Corona" sonnets, where the title, the sevenfold division of materials, and the method of meditation followed all suggest very strongly that this cycle of sonnets is an adaptation of the popular practice of meditation according to the corona. Donne's sequence is, of course, addressed to Christ, and the life of the Virgin is very carefully subordinated; this is what we should expect in an Anglican adaptation of the corona. Moreover, the use of the term "corona" with reference to meditations focused on Christ would find a precedent in the popular practice, mentioned also in these English rosary-treatises, of using a "corona of our Lord"—a rosary of thirty-three Aves.[1] At the same time, Donne's title describes the continental practice of linking sonnets or stanzas in the form called the corona, where the last line of each sonnet or stanza forms the first line of the next, and the last line of the whole sequence repeats the line that began it. Annibal Caro in 1558 had published a famous "Corona" linking nine sonnets in this manner,[2] while Chapman, in his "Coronet for his Mistresse Philosophie" (1595), followed the mode by thus linking ten sonnets. The mode was also being used in Italy to celebrate the Virgin: I have run across a book by Curtio Verallo, *Corona di laudi a Maria Vergine* (Venice, 1617), in which there are sixteen sequences of five sonnets apiece, all linked according

1. See Worthington, preface; *Societie of the Rosary*, p. 59.

2. See Annibal Caro, *Opere*, ed. Vittorio Turri (Bari, 1912), *1*, 161–5. Cf. Tasso's *corona di madriali*, *Poesie*, ed. Flora (Milan, 1952), pp. 751–4. Gascoigne's *Hundreth Sundrie Flowres* (1575) has a series of seven linked sonnets.

to this form of the *corona di sonnetti*.[3] Donne, as usual, is not doing anything simple: his "La Corona" is a complex synthesis of methods and materials from both religious and profane poetry, from the liturgy of the Church, and from all the various ways of meditating on the life of Christ which we have discussed in this chapter.

But the fundamental impulse and outline of the sequence is found, I believe, in the meditations of the corona. The sevenfold division of materials, as given in the treatise of the Jesuit Chambers (pp. 261–72), is particularly suggestive. Chambers divides the combined lives of Mary and Christ into six parts (for the six decades of the corona), with a seventh, concluding, meditation on Mary's merits. The materials of his first part are of course not used by Donne, since this deals with the legendary life of the Virgin before the birth of Christ; in place of this Donne devotes his first sonnet to an introductory prayer to God. Sonnet 2 of "La Corona," however, accords with Part 2 of Chambers' division, for both are focused on the Annunciation. Part 3 in Chambers, compared with "La Corona" 3, presents the most striking parallel, for here Donne is following the method of the corona in running quickly over a great many events, from the Nativity to the flight into Egypt:

> *Immensitie cloysterd in thy deare wombe,*
> Now leaves his welbelov'd imprisonment,
> There he hath made himselfe to his intent
> Weake enough, now into our world to come;
> But Oh, for thee, for him, hath th'Inne no roome?
> Yet lay him in this stall, and from the Orient,
> Starres, and wisemen will travell to prevent
> Th'effect of *Herods* jealous generall doome.
> Seest thou, my Soule, with thy faiths eyes, how he
> Which fils all place, yet none holds him, doth lye?
> Was not his pity towards thee wondrous high,
> That would have need to be pittied by thee?

3. Six sequences repeat the last line entirely, as in Donne's sequence: see Verallo, Laude 48, 52, 70, 101, 119, 144; in the rest, however great the variation, the last line always rimes with the first: see Laude 19, 28, 71, 88, 100, 116, 117, 127, 130, 147.

> Kisse him, and with him into Egypt goe,
> *With his kinde mother, who partakes thy woe.*

Part 3 of Chambers' sequence covers exactly the same compass of events, though more events are included. More important than this parallel, however, are the many ways in which the sonnet displays Donne's mastery of the whole art of Catholic meditation on the life of Christ. We note the presence of the Virgin throughout, with strong emphasis on her sorrows, the technique of visualizing the scene by "thy faiths eyes," the address to the actors in the scene, the speaker's address to his own soul, the intellectual development of paradoxes from the visual scene, the affections of pity, and the exhortation to "kisse" the child and follow him to Egypt as though the speaker were actually present.

Part 4 of Chambers' sequence, along with other matters, includes the finding of Christ in the Temple, to which Donne devotes his entire Sonnet 4. Part 5 in Chambers, devoted to the Passion, includes the matters covered in Donne's Sonnet 5: the sentencing of Christ, his suffering, the carrying of the Cross, and the Crucifixion. In Sonnet 5 Donne is again running over a series of events rapidly, to produce this brilliant combination of theological paradox, visualization, pity, and colloquy:

> *By miracles exceeding power of man,*
> Hee faith in some, envie in some begat,
> For, what weake spirits admire, ambitious, hate;
> In both affections many to him ran,
> But Oh! the worst are most, they will and can,
> Alas, and do, unto the immaculate,
> Whose creature Fate is, now prescribe a Fate,
> Measuring selfe-lifes infinity to'a span,
> Nay to an inch. Loe, where condemned hee
> Beares his owne crosse, with paine, yet by and by
> When it beares him, he must beare more and die.
> Now thou art lifted up, draw mee to thee,
> And at thy death giving such liberall dole,
> *Moyst, with one drop of thy blood, my dry soule.*

And finally, Chambers' Part 6 includes the Resurrection and Ascension, to which Donne devotes, respectively, his last two sonnets.

Now this parallel with Chambers' procedure is a very general one: I am not attempting to show a close following of any particular series of meditations, but only to suggest how the meditations of the corona may have exerted a very strong formative influence on the construction, divisions, and general procedure of Donne's sequence. Adepts in meditation, as I have said, are expected to modify and vary in all directions, in accordance with their own needs and creative powers.

A good many critics have noticed the difference in quality and in poetic method between these "La Corona" sonnets and the "Holy Sonnets" proper, but the essential difference has not, I think, been adequately defined and evaluated. The "La Corona" sonnets seem generally to be regarded as inferior, because of their highly intellectual cast; and this difference is usually explained by the supposition that they were written earlier than the other sonnets—according to Grierson, sometime around the years 1607-9—at a time when Donne's religion was, presumably, still largely an intellectual concern.[4] But the present study will, I hope, suggest another solution: that the "La Corona" sonnets are different from the other "Holy Sonnets" because they are based upon a different kind of meditative tradition. There is no need to postulate any difference in the dating of their composition: whenever they were written, poems composed according to the meditative methods of the corona would tend to differ fundamentally from poems developing out of the *Spiritual Exercises* of St. Ignatius Loyola. We have already seen this kind of difference in Southwell's various poems on the lives of Mary and Christ; and, at a much higher level of poetic value, I think we can see essentially the same distinction in Donne's sonnets. I have argued in Chapter 1 that the finest of the "Holy Sonnets," proper, represent the carefully integrated work of all the powers of the soul within the borders of a single sonnet; and in particular that several of them show a powerful development from vivid composition of place, through devout analysis, to impassioned colloquy. It seems inevitable that such a procedure should result in a powerful union and compression of forces within an individual poem.

But no such process is operating within the individual sonnets of the "La Corona" sequence; for, properly speaking, there are no individual sonnets here. We have one poem, one corona, held to-

4. *Poems of Donne,* ed. Grierson, 2, lii, 225-9.

gether by its repetition of lines, by its consequently interlocking rimes, and by its unbreakable sequence of events. Its method, as announced in Sonnet 1, is the twining of an endless wreath of praise: the twining of a mind that winds its way from paradox to paradox, sometimes seeing the spot, sometimes crying out sharply, but always enveloping the scenes and the cries in a rich sinuosity of intellectual analysis. The metaphor of twining is carried out even in the rime: for the use of repeated lines leads to a linkage of rime between the couplet that concludes each sonnet and the whole octave (abba, abba) of the next: thus the "high, nigh" which concludes Sonnet 1 is echoed by the "nigh, die, lye, trie" of Sonnet 2, and so on in every sonnet, returning to the octave of the first. More than this, the rime-schemes of lines 9–12 in each sonnet show an intertwining alternation, except for the seventh, where the scheme is the same as in the sixth: in Sonnets 1, 3, 5 the rime is cddc; in 2, 4, 6 it is cdcd. These are small effects, but they play their subtle, half-realized part in weaving the whole corona.

We should not ask, then, that the sonnets that form the corona should display the compacted strength of "At the round earth's imagin'd corners" or "I am a little world made cunningly"; but we should, instead, base our judgment upon the interplay, the wreathing, of one sonnet with another into one larger, and in its own fashion, equally compacted whole. From this standpoint we may feel how the traditional paradoxes,[5] so intricately annunciated in Son-

5. See Loarte, *Instructions*, f.29, where he speaks of how the Virgin "offred up her wel-beloved Infant to the celestial Father, who had of his infinite favour geven him for her sonne; and did by that meanes make her his owne mother, who was her owne and natural Father." Also f.22v.: "O divine excellencie, and dignitie due to thee alone, to be the mother of God, and mother of thine owne Father and Creator!" See also Southwell, "The nativitie of Christ":

> Behold, the Father is his daughters sonne:
> The bird that built the nest is hatchd therein:
> The old of yeres, an howre hath not out-runne,
> Eternall life, to live doth nowe beginne.
> The Word is dum, the mirth of heaven doth weepe;
> Mighte feeble is, and force doth faintly creepe.

Miss Gardner, in the notes to her new edition of the *Divine Poems*, shows how strongly these first two sonnets of the sequence echo the liturgy: see her fine analysis of "La Corona," pp. xxii–iv, which views this as a "single poem"—"inspired by liturgical prayer and praise."

net 2, modulate into the visual details and passionate outcries of
Sonnet 3; how the matching but milder paradoxes of Sonnet 4 similarly blend into varied meditation on the Passion in Sonnet 5; and
how the whole fulfills its firmly executed round in the personal
confessions and prayers—the colloquies—that dominate the last
two sonnets, culminating in the ritual sestet of Sonnet 7:

> O strong Ramme, which hast batter'd heaven for mee,
> Mild Lambe, which with thy blood, hast mark'd the path;
> Bright Torch, which shin'st, that I the way may see,
> Oh, with thy owne blood quench thy owne just wrath,
> And if thy holy Spirit, my Muse did raise,
> *Deigne at my hands this crowne of prayer and praise.*

8

We have now, perhaps, reached a point in our discussion where
we may sketch a theory, based on a study of these meditative
treatises and kindled by the studies of Pourrat and Gilson: a theory
which may help to clarify the significance of English religious
poetry in the seventeenth century. During the later Middle Ages,
it appears, a fissure developed between the theologians and the
devotees of affective piety. The fissure was revealed, and symbolized, early in the medieval period by the famous controversy
between Abelard, the protoscholastic, and St. Bernard, the prime
exponent of affective piety; and it widened as the two quite different systems of St. Thomas Aquinas and St. Bonaventure grew to
simultaneous maturity during the thirteenth century: the first based
on Aristotle, the second continuing the Platonic tradition of St.
Augustine. During the late Middle Ages the scholastics threw a deep
shadow over the affective life, a shadow which led some, such as
Thomas à Kempis and his Brothers of the Common Life, to renounce scholastic subtleties as the brood of folly and the bitter fruit
of that *curiositas* which St. Bernard had denounced as the father
of sin. During the sixteenth century, as the speculations of the
schoolmen lost something of their dominance, the currents of devotion and mysticism represented by St. Bernard and St. Bonaventure increased their influence, which of course had always remained
strong among Franciscans and kindred spirits. Men turned to re-

cover the powers of meditation and contemplation which had from the beginning received their profoundest impulse from the line of theologians and preachers thus set down in Joseph Hall's *Arte* (chap. 16), as he lists the most notable masters in the art of meditation: Origen, Augustine, Bernard, Hugh of St. Victor, Bonaventure, Gerson.

The last name, for our purposes here, is the most significant, for the devotional and mystical treatises of Jean le Charlier de Gerson, Chancellor of the University of Paris (1363–1429), represent a powerful synthesis of these two diverse, and sometimes warring, elements in medieval religion. Gerson was both a brilliant scholastic thinker and a powerful contemplative spirit; in himself and in others he attempted to achieve what may be called a reconciliation of Abelard with Bernard, of Aquinas with Bonaventure: a reconciliation in the practice of the devout life. His masterpiece, *On the Mountain of Contemplation*, exerted a germinal influence upon all the most important meditative and mystical treatises of the sixteenth and seventeenth centuries: in England, the treatise is cited as an authoritative work on meditation both by the future Bishop Hall and by the Puritan Richard Baxter.[1] Gerson is the forerunner of a rapprochement of forces which is the most remarkable feature of the meditative treatises of the sixteenth and seventeenth centuries: they constantly clarify their theological points by citing the distinctions and definitions of St. Thomas Aquinas, while taking their exhortations to, and methods of, meditation from St. Bernard and St. Bonaventure. We may take as representative the first chapter of the *Treatise on Prayer and Meditation* (c. 1558) by the Franciscan, San Pedro de Alcántara, which opens with a skillful definition of devotion by St. Thomas, continues with a long and fervent exhortation to meditate taken from the treatise of the pseudo-Bonaventure, and concludes with a similar exhortation from the works of the Augustinian, St. Laurence Justinian.

Thus the meditative treatises of our period were attempting to develop the spiritual life through utilizing all the rich and various resources of medieval religion. The achievements of scholastic philosophy had developed the abstract issues and principles of the re-

1. Hall, chap. 5; Baxter, *The Saints Everlasting Rest* (4th ed., London, 1653), Pt. 4, pp. 103, 118, 171, 193.

ligious life with a subtlety and clarity never before known; and at the same time, under the current of devotion represented by St. Bernard, the devout and ecstatic experiences of the spiritual life had received profound and fervent cultivation. It remained for the sixteenth and seventeenth centuries to merge these mighty currents into one complex and potent whole. From this effort to fuse the intellectual and the affective in meditation arose a peculiar tension of forces, everywhere evident in meditative treatises and in religious poetry of the seventeenth century—not only in England but throughout Europe. It seems fair to say that the central aim of Catholic spirituality during this period was to teach the devout individual how to maintain a proper balance and proportion between these two aspects of his nature. In this effort—to absorb and amalgamate, in perfect union, the intellectual and affective heritage of the Middle Ages—resides, I believe, the central tension of English religious poetry of the seventeenth century. It was a tension exacerbated and deeply stimulated by the violent religious controversies of the age, by the growth of a "new philosophy" which implicitly threatened the foundations of medieval thought, and by the enormous ranges of secular and pagan interests opened up by the recoveries and discoveries of the period, whether literary or geographical. For the religious man a central and all-inclusive solution to these problems was insistent, urgent: he found that solution, if at all, in a union of the powers of his soul in the service of devotion. And hence we find the immense difference between medieval religious lyrics and the religious poetry of our period. Whether it be the theological "wit" of a medieval hymn, in which Walter Ong and Carleton Brown have rightly seen the seeds of later "metaphysical" wit,[2] or the paradoxes of the Improperia and the liturgy in general, or the simple affective piety of a nativity-carol: to all these aspects of medieval literature the mind of the seventeenth century turned its meditative powers, and developed them all into a new style which, at its best, displayed the union of the powers of the soul with extraordinary subtlety and intensity. Puente sums it up in his meditation on the words "Porro unum est necessarium" (Luke 10.42):

2. Walter J. Ong, "Wit and Mystery: a Revaluation in Mediaeval Latin Hymnody," *Speculum*, 22 (1947), 310–41; *Religious Lyrics of the XVth Century*, ed. Carleton Brown (Oxford, Clarendon Press, 1939), p. xxv.

Thou art troubled and perplexed with many thoughtes, affections, and cares, but the most necessary point is, that thy soule be one, that is to say, united and recollected within it selfe: one in hir sensuall affections, reducing them to union with the spirit . . . one in hir will, referring hir whole will, entirely to the will of almightie God . . . one in hir cares, abridging them all in one, to become agreable to the divine bounty . . . one in hir thoughtes, gathering them all together . . . one finally in love, placing it wholy in one only infinit good . . . . (*1*, 430)

No wonder, then, that James Smith, in the best definition of metaphysical poetry yet offered, should argue that the central impulse of such poetry "is given by an overwhelming concern . . . with problems either deriving from, or closely resembling in the nature of their difficulty, the problem of the Many and the One." [3]

A final instance of poetical meditation on the lives of Mary and Christ may be taken as the perfect symbol of these tendencies: Richard Crashaw's "Sancta Maria Dolorum or the Mother of Sorrows. A Patheticall descant upon the devout Plainsong of Stabat Mater Dolorosa." The old "plainsong" attributed to Jacopone da Todi consists of ten six-line stanzas;[4] Crashaw, using the various modes of meditation discussed in this chapter, has produced a "descant" in eleven ten-line stanzas: a poem twice the size of the original, making explicit the paradoxes, the dramatic situation, and the devotional application implicit in the medieval hymn. Where the hymn simply gives the clause, "dum videbat/Nati poenas inclyti," Crashaw makes us see the spot and simultaneously grasp the theological significance:

> Before her eyes
> Her's, & the whole world's ioyes,
> Hanging all torn she sees . . . .

So, throughout the poem, with a vividness never approached in the hymn, the mind is focused intensely through the eyes of the Mother:

3. James Smith, "On Metaphysical Poetry," in *Determinations*, ed. F. R. Leavis (London, Chatto and Windus, 1934), p. 24.

4. Text from *The Hymns of the Breviary and Missal*, ed. Matthew Britt (New York, Benziger, 1924), pp. 132–4.

> She sees her son, her GOD,
> Bow with a load
> Of borrowd sins; And swimme
> In woes that were not made for Him.
> Ah hard command
> Of loue! Here must she stand
> Charg'd to look on, & with a stedfast ey
> See her life dy . . . .

In the hymn this intensity of single focus is diffused throughout a simple, undramatic memorial of Passion Week:

> Pro peccatis suae gentis
> Vidit Jesum in tormentis,
> Et flagellis subditum.
> Vidit suum dulcem Natum
> Moriendo desolatum
> Dum emisit spiritum.

From this dramatic intensity of vision follows a passionate directness of colloquy, implicit, but unmatched, anywhere in the simple pleas of the hymn:

> Fac me tecum pie flere,
> Crucifixo condolere,
> Donec ego vixero.
> Juxta Crucem tecum stare,
> Et me tibi sociare
> In planctu desidero.

> Yea let my life & me
> Fix here with thee,
> And at the Humble foot
> Of this fair TREE take our eternall root.
> That so we may
> At least be in loues way;
> And in these chast warres while the wing'd wounds flee
> So fast 'twixt him & thee,
> My brest may catch the kisse of some kind dart,
> Though as at second hand, from either heart.

> Oh you, your own best Darts
> Dear, dolefull hearts!
> Hail; & strike home & make me see
> That wounded bosomes their own weapons be.
> Come wounds! come darts!
> Nail'd hands! & peirced hearts!
> Come your whole selues, sorrow's great son & mother!
> Nor grudge a yonger-Brother
> Of greifes his portion, who (had all their due)
> One single wound should not haue left for you.

In this interposition of the speaker between the mother and the son Crashaw presents his most elaborate cadenza: he has left the hymn far behind, and appears to be developing his variations according to the kind of procedure thus suggested in the treatise of Puente:

> consider the dolour that the most Blessed Virgin endured, at this her first beholding of her Sonne, for the eyes of our Lord Jesus, and of his Mother encountering one another, became both of them eclipsed and dazeled by the force of sorrowe; the mother remayned spiritually crucified with the sight of the Sonne, and the Sonne was tormented a new by beholding his mother, each of them holding their peace for very greefe and paine, the hart of the one emploied in feeling, the torments of the other, sorrowing much more for them, then for their owne. Putt then thy selfe (ô my soule) betweene those two crucified, and lift upp thine eyes to behold the Sonne crucified with great nailes of yron: then cast them downe to looke upon the mother, crucified with the sharpe stings of dolour and compassion. Beseech them both to devide their paines with thee in such sort, that thou maist be crucified with them by a true imitation.
> (2, 264)

In this manner, under the impulse of the art of meditation, religious poetry of the seventeenth century resembles a universal descant upon the devout plainsong of medieval piety.

CHAPTER 3

Self-Knowledge: the Spiritual Combat

We seek for truth in ourselves, in our neighbours, and in its essential nature. We find it first in ourselves by severe self scrutiny, then in our neighbours by compassionate indulgence, and, finally, in its essential nature by that direct vision which belongs to the pure in heart.

St. Bernard, *The Degrees of Humility and Pride*

SELF-EXAMINATION is not, properly speaking, meditation in the sense that dominates our present study; but it is in many ways inseparably related to the art of meditation. It is, first of all, an indispensable preparation for all exercises directed toward the love of God, whether devotional or mystical. In the terms of St. Bernard, self-scrutiny forms the first degree of Truth, because it leads away from curiosity and moves toward humility: "the characteristic virtue of those *who are disposed in their hearts to ascend by steps* from virtue to virtue, until they reach the summit of humility; where, standing on Sion as on a watch-tower, they may survey the truth." [1] Inevitably, then, in the popular *Meditations* attributed to St. Bernard, we find that the first "Motive to Mortification" is this:

Many know many things, and know not themselves: they pry into others, and leave themselves. They seeke God by those outward things, forsaking their inward things, to which God is neerer, and more inward. Therefore I will returne from outward things, to inward, and from the inward I will ascend to the Superiour: that I may know from whence I come, or whither I goe; who I am, and from whence I am: that so by the knowledge of my selfe, I may be the better able to attaine to the knowledge of God. For by how much more I profit, and goe

1. St. Bernard, *The Degrees of Humility and Pride*, pp. 10–11.

118

forward in the knowledge of my selfe, by so much the neerer I approach to the knowledge of God.[2]

In this way, and for these reasons, all the great popular treatises of the late Middle Ages insist on a "pitiless examination of conscience," as Pourrat has pointed out. (2, 291–302) Whether the treatise is attributed to St. Bernard or to Thomas à Kempis, the advice is the same—as we hear it resounding throughout the English translations of these treatises, immensely popular in the England of the sixteenth and seventeenth centuries.[3] "Examine thy life by a diligent and daily inquisition. Marke carefully how much thou doest profit and goe forward, or how much thou dost decay, and goe backewards." "Place all thy transgressions before thy eyes: place thy selfe before thy selfe, as it were before another, and so bewaile thy selfe." In the effort to achieve "inward peace," "inward devotion," "inward compunction," we must "set our axe depe to the roote of the tree, that we (purged from al passions,) may have a quiet minde." Every morning "thou shalt take a good purpose for that daye folowinge, and at night thou shalte discusse diligentlie, how thou hast behaved thee the daye before, in worde, in deede, and in thought."[4]

Such is the advice which Herbert is embracing in his "Church-Porch," that versified handbook on "good life":

> Salute thy self: see what thy soul doth wear.
> Dare to look in thy chest, for 'tis thine own:
> And tumble up and down what thou find'st there.
>
> Summe up at night, what thou hast done by day;
> And in the morning, what thou hast to do.
> Dresse and undresse thy soul: mark the decay
> And growth of it . . . .

2. *Saint Bernard His Meditations*, Pt. 2, pp. 1–2.
3. See White, *Devotional Literature*, pp. 76–86; Wright, pp. 240–4, 261–2.
4. *Saint Bernard His Meditations*, Pt. 2, pp. 47–8; *Imitation of Christ*, Bk. 1, chaps. 11, 19, 20, 21. See also *Meditations on the Life of Christ*, chap. 54; and *Certaine select Prayers, gathered out of S. Augustines Meditations*, London, 1577: e.g., Meditation 2, "Of the wretchednesse and frailtie of man": "What am I . . . . Agayne, what am I?"

"Even-song" shows Herbert carrying out this advice in a manner similar to that recommended by the handbooks, which suggest that the nightly examination of conscience be preceded by a reckoning of benefits received and a thanksgiving for them: [5]

> Blest be the God of love,
> Who gave me eyes, and light, and power this day,
>   Both to be busie, and to play.
> But much more blest be God above,
>   Who gave me sight alone,
>   Which to himself he did denie:
>   For when he sees my waies, I dy:
> But I have got his sonne, and he hath none.
>
>   What have I brought thee home
> For this thy love? have I discharg'd the debt,
>   Which this dayes favour did beget?
>   I ranne; but all I brought, was fome.
>   Thy diet, care, and cost
>   Do end in bubbles, balls of winde;
>   Of winde to thee whom I have crost,
> But balls of wilde-fire to my troubled minde.

Likewise his poem, "The Method," recalls the advice of the handbooks in regard to a proper "method" of succeeding in prayer: "Go search this thing,/Tumble thy breast, and turn thy book"—the book of conscience.[6] The "Parson's Library," he tells us in his *Country Parson*, is chiefly this inward book: "For the temptations with which a good man is beset, and the ways which he used to overcome them, being told to another, whether in private conference, or in the Church, are a Sermon." "So that the Parson having studied, and mastered all his lusts and affections within, and the whole Army of Temptations without, hath ever so many sermons ready penn'd, as he hath victories." [7] Fittingly, then, Herbert took as his

5. See St. François de Sales, Pt. 2, chap. 11; Puente, *1*, 195–9 (based on St. Ignatius, pp. 18–19).

6. Cf. St. François de Sales, Pt. 4, chap. 14; and *Spiritual Combat*, chaps. 44, 59.

7. *Works of Herbert*, ed. Hutchinson, p. 278.

text for his first sermon at Bemerton the biblical verse which sums up all these practices of self-examination: "Keep thy heart with all diligence." [8]

If we remember that such exhortations resound throughout the popular treatises of our period, whether Puritan, Catholic or Anglican, we may avoid a tendency to attribute the acute self-consciousness of English meditative poetry in this era chiefly to Donne's example, or to declare that "Herbert's extreme insistence on individual responsibility" is "rather Puritan than 'Churchly,' " [9] or to attribute to the influence of Epictetus the presence of such a consummately Christian view as that expressed by Donne in his significant lines to Rowland Woodward:

> Seeke wee then our selves in our selves; for as
> Men force the Sunne with much more force to passe,
> By gathering his beames with a christall glasse;
>
> So wee, If wee into our selves will turne,
> Blowing our sparkes of vertue, may outburne
> The straw, which doth about our hearts sojourne.

But may we not argue that the fierce inward scrutiny of Puritanism intensified this emphasis, put a "finer edge on the spiritual life" by pursuing methods of analysis that "called for more intelligence and more concentration than any of the Catholic techniques"? [10] I believe that the foregoing chapters will have shown that such a view represents a misapprehension of the devotional techniques of the Counter Reformation. Intense concentration on the "motions" of the self is not a peculiar tendency of Puritanism, though it has some peculiar aspects, deriving from Puritan theology, which will be discussed in the next chapter. But so far as self-examination is concerned the fact is that both Catholic and Puritan, while accusing each other bitterly of neglecting the inner life, were pursuing the art of self-knowledge by methods equally in-

8. Proverbs, 4.23. See Izaak Walton, "The Life of Mr. George Herbert," in *Lives,* World's Classics (London, Oxford University Press, 1936), p. 295.

9. *Works of Herbert,* ed. Palmer, *1,* 77.

10. M. M. Knappen, *Tudor Puritanism* (Chicago, University of Chicago Press, 1939), p. 399.

tense and effective—methods that had, on both hands, developed
a subtlety of self-awareness that went far beyond the popular
achievements of the Middle Ages.

Self-examination, in a variety of ways, was a prime quality of
Jesuit spirituality. The exhortations of the Middle Ages were developed by St. Ignatius into precise and rigorous methods of making both a "particular examen" (directed against some particular
sin) and a "general examen" of conscience. As soon as a man arises
in the morning, says the *Spiritual Exercises,* he must "resolve to
guard himself with diligence against that particular sin or defect
which he desires to correct and amend." Then at midday he makes
the first examination, "demanding an account from his soul concerning the particular fault in question . . . , reviewing the time
elapsed hour by hour, or period by period," marking on the first
line of a chart the number of times the sin has been committed. A
second examination is performed after supper in a similar manner,
"hour by hour, commencing from the first examination," and marking down the sins on the second line of the chart. Thus, by comparing the two lines, one can tell whether "any improvement has
taken place" during the day. (pp. 13–14) From day to day this "particular examen" proceeds, with increasing complexity, as explained
by Puente: "The same comparison I am to make betweene the sinnes
of one day, and those of another . . . and betweene those of one
weeke, and those of another . . . helping my memory by noting
them with two lines, or streakes for every day in the weeke."
(*1,* 199–203) The "general examen" is performed in the same way
every night, if not oftener, demanding "an account of my soul, first
of my thoughts, then of my words, lastly of my actions." [11]

Robert Southwell's *Short Rule of Good Life* shows vividly how
such practices were cultivated in England by the Jesuits. "I must
procure to foresee in every action, at the least in all the principall,
to fore-arme my selfe, against those occasions of sin, which shall
be offred in them." "I must have care of my senses, as the meanes

---

11. St. Ignatius, pp. 15–19; for a full explanation see the famous treatise by
Alphonsus Rodriguez, *Practice of Perfection and Christian Virtues,* trans.
Joseph Rickaby (3 vols., Chicago, Loyola University Press, 1929), Treatise
7, "On the Examen of Conscience," *1,* 421–64. Rodriguez' book originally appeared in 1609.

and entrance of temptations." "I must set downe with my selfe, some certayne order in spending my time, alotting to every hower in the day, some certaine thinge to be done in the same." "I must not think to get al vertues at once, or cut off all imperfections togither, but having a generall resolution to get vertue, and leave all vice, begin with some one, endeavouring to breake my selfe of some one faulte, which I am most inclined unto, and procuring to get the contrary vertue." (pp. 40–4)

Anyone familiar with Puritan exhortations to "good life" will notice striking similarities in these Jesuit practices. I am not concerned to argue for influence one way or another, but only to note how all these practices arose from a central preoccupation of the entire age, shared by Christians of every creed.

Of more particular interest for our present study is the fact that self-analysis went hand in hand with the entire process of meditation. St. Ignatius provides subtle "rules for the discernment of spirits": rules, that is, for "perceiving and knowing the various motions excited in the soul; the good, that they may be admitted; the bad, that they may be rejected"; together with another set of rules "for discerning and understanding scruples and the insinuations of our enemy." (pp. 106–14, 118–20) In making the repetitions of the exercises one selects, accordingly, those "motions" which are most advantageous to the soul, and focuses on them. After the whole exercise has been completed, St. Ignatius advises that "for the space of a quarter of an hour, sitting or walking, I will examine how I have succeeded in the contemplation or meditation" (p. 29)—advice repeated and expanded by his followers. Thus Richard Gibbons, in explaining "What is to be done after Meditation," sets down six points: first, we must examine carefully every step in the exercise just performed, from the preparations to the colloquy, to see where it went well or badly; second, "We may examine the distractions we have suffered, and the remedies we have used to reclaime our selves"; third, "We may examine the consolations we have felt, seeking the occasions of them"; fourth, "We may examine the desolations if we have had any, searching out their causes"; fifth, we may consider "whether we have had aboundance of matter for our discourse or scarcity, endeavoring to find the causes of both," or we may examine the affections and "good purposes" that have been aroused; and lastly—a practice that may suggest the origin of much religious poetry—"We may note in some little booke those thinges which have passed in our Meditation, or some part of them, if we think them worth the paynes." [12]

Meditation, in its turn, led back to self-analysis: the Ignatian exercises of the First Week—on sin and hell—are designed to arouse a sense of the fearful necessity of self-knowledge, a necessity which the early Jesuits drove home by including formal meditations on death, judgment, and the Prodigal Son as a part of the First Week.[13] Furthermore, St. Ignatius recommends an additional "method of prayer" which proceeds by detailed consideration of one's self in relation to the Ten Commandments, the seven deadly sins, the three powers of the soul, and the five senses; the method combines self-examination with the formal procedure of the full Ignatian exercise. (pp. 77–9)

Finally, as I have said earlier, in the usual course of daily meditation advised by such writers as Fray Luis de Granada or San Pedro de Alcántara, one whole sevenfold sequence is devoted to meditation on such matters as man's misery, sin, death, judgment, hell, and heaven, all aimed at achieving the knowledge thus described by Fray Diego de Estella:

> This singular saying (know thy selfe) is a worde descended from heaven above . . . know first who thou arte, whence thou camest, where thou arte, and whether thou arte going: thou arte a mortall man, a little earth, a vessell of corruption, and full of much miserie and necessitie: thou camest cryinge from thy mothers bellie, thou art conceyved in sinne, invironed aboute with all daungers, and going toward thy grave. (p. 209)

12. Gibbons, § 3; cf. Rodriguez, *1*, 387–8: "it will be a good plan for a man to note down what he gathers from the meditation, putting in writing, not at length, but briefly, the desires and purposes that he draws from it and also some truths and illustrations or discoveries of error which the Lord is wont to give therein, sometimes concerning certain virtues, sometimes concerning the mysteries meditated."

13. See the Jesuit *Directory*, chap. 14, par. 1; chap. 15, par. 4. *Exercitia Spiritualia* (Rome, 1609) adds a formal exercise on the Prodigal Son, as well as exercises on judgment and death.

2

All these efforts in pursuit of self-knowledge reached their culmination in a treatise of extraordinary popularity which we may take as the second great landmark in the development of spiritual exercises during the sixteenth century. It is the famous *Spiritual Combat* attributed to the Theatine writer, Lorenzo Scupoli, the supreme achievement in the "conquest of the self" cultivated by the Italian school of the sixteenth century. This remarkable book first appeared in 1589 in a version compact and unified in its total effect; but in the numerous editions that quickly followed it received elaborate additions that nearly doubled its size. By 1610, when all the materials now included in modern editions appear to have been in circulation, the book had become a rather jumbled repository for an immense variety of meditative practices.[1] It was especially popular in France through its recommendation by St. François de Sales, who kept it as his constant companion; and thus it came to play a formative part in the third great landmark among the meditative treatises of our period: St. François de Sales' *Introduction to the Devout Life* (1609). In Spain, too, it was popular, especially in a version made by Juan de Castaniza, to whom its authorship thus came to be frequently attributed. There were two different English translations: the first, following the original Italian version, was printed at Louvain in 1598 and reprinted at Rouen in 1613. In 1652 a completely independent English version appeared in Paris, taken from the Spanish and attributed to Juan de Castaniza.[2]

1. See the prefaces by Carlo di Palma in *Combattimento Spirituale*, 2 parts, Naples, 1837; this seems to be a reprint of an edition of 1657, since the preface to the second part is dated in that year. I refer only to the 66 chapters of the work proper: there are also "Additions" which amount to 38 more chapters. For an excellent contemporary view of the variant forms in which the *Combat* was circulating prior to 1650, and of its great popularity in all forms, including translations into Latin, French, Spanish, and German, see the translator's "Advertisement" prefixed to the English version of 1652.

2. The first version is entitled *The Spiritual Conflict*: its publication is assigned to Louvain, 1598, in the translator's "Advertisement" prefixed to the second version. The latter appeared in a volume bearing the general title,

From such evidence it appears certain that it must have been a book well known in England: Maycock (pp. 48–9) is surely right in asserting that Nicholas Ferrar must have come to know it during his long stay in Italy; and indeed, since we know that St. François de Sales' *Introduction* was a book especially cherished at Little Gidding, a knowledge of the *Combat* would seem to follow from this fact alone. It is, then, a book which may hold some significance for English literature of the seventeenth century and especially for the writing of any poet, such as Herbert, who was closely connected with the group at Little Gidding.

The center of the book is self-analysis, the prime weapon in the spiritual combat: "you must wage continual warfare against yourself and employ your entire strength in demolishing each vicious inclination, however trivial." (p. 6) One by one, the vicious tendencies of man must be attacked and diminished in power, little by little, with the aid of all the powers of the soul and all the powers of the universe:

> The first thing to do when you awake is to open the windows of your soul. Consider yourself as on the field of battle, facing the enemy and bound by the iron-clad law—either fight or die.
>
> Imagine the enemy before you, that particular vice or disorderly passion that you are trying to conquer—imagine this hideous opponent is about to overwhelm you. At the same time, picture at your right Jesus Christ, your Invincible Leader, accompanied by the Blessed Virgin, St. Joseph, whole companies of angels and saints, and particularly by the glorious Archangel Michael. At your left is Lucifer and his troops, ready to support the passion or vice you are fighting and resolved to do anything to cause your defeat.

．　　．　　．　　．　　．

The Christian Pilgrime in his Spirituall Conflict, and Conquest, Paris, 1652. This consists of two parts with separate title-pages: first, *The Spiritual Conflict*, attributed to Juan de Castaniza, described as "The Second Edition" and dated 1652; and second, an entirely separate treatise entitled *The Spirituall Conquest* and dated 1651

Begin to fight immediately in the name of the Lord, armed with distrust of yourself, with confidence in God, [with] prayer, and with the correct use of the faculties of your soul. With these weapons, attack the enemy, that predominant passion you want to conquer, either by courageous resistance, repeated acts of the contrary virtue, or any means that heaven gives you to drive it out of your heart. Do not rest until it is conquered. (pp. 46–7)

Self-analysis is thus dramatically related to the universal order of things: "the rational faculty is placed between the divine will above it and the sensitive appetite below it, and is attacked from both sides," God working upon the soul by grace, and the Devil by the fleshly appetites. (p. 33) "This is a battle from which we cannot escape . . . . The fight against passion will last a lifetime, and he who lays down his arms will be slain." (p. 184) Self-analysis, then, becomes a way of taking up arms on the side of God; it is a fundamental duty to God, and must be performed with all the perseverance and subtlety that one can muster.

The weapons set forth, as in the last paragraph above, are four in number: distrust of self, confidence in God, "exercise" [3]—that is, the proper use of the senses and the faculties of the soul in considerations directed toward the extirpating of vices and the planting of virtues—and prayer, which includes both petition and meditation. Still another weapon is mentioned at the close of the treatise, the Eucharist, whether received actually or mentally. No Puritan treatise could be more rigorous in condemning, and indeed ridiculing, reliance upon external forms and outward exercises: these are helps, says the *Combat*, if properly used, but improperly used, they lead to damnation. For the spiritual life consists in this, and in this only: "in knowing the infinite greatness and goodness of God, together with a true sense of our own weakness and tendency to evil, in loving God and hating ourselves, in humbling ourselves not only before Him, but, for His sake, before all men, in renouncing entirely our own will in order to follow His." (p. 5) The *Combat*,

3. I use the term of the first English version: see *The Spiritual Conflict* (Rouen, 1613), chap. 4.

indeed, represents what may very well be called a kind of Catholic Puritanism: free of predestination, Semi-Pelagian in its insistence that although without grace "we are incapable of one meritorious thought," nevertheless our "victory depends entirely on the diligent effort that is expended." (pp. 8, 89)

The subtlety of effort expended in this battle leaves no corner of the mind unexamined: the whole treatise is one astonishing tribute to the psychological penetration of the sixteenth-century masters of self-analysis. The central effort is directed toward developing a constant wariness and alertness with regard to the tendencies of the will, for reasons that will be familiar to everyone who recalls Milton's treatment of the Fall in *Paradise Lost*:

> As long as the understanding remains unbiased by the passions, it will easily distinguish between truth and falsehood, between real evil masquerading as good, and real good under the false appearance of evil. However, as soon as the will is moved either to love or hatred by the object, the understanding cannot form a true estimate of it, because the affection disguises it and imprints an incorrect idea. When this is again presented to the will which already is prepossessed, it redoubles its love or hatred, pushes beyond all limits, and is utterly deaf to the voice of reason.
>
> In this distorted confusion, the understanding plunges deeper and deeper into error and represents the object to the will in vivid colors of good and evil.
>
> Consequently . . . , the two noblest faculties of the soul are bewildered in a network of error, darkness and confusion. Happy are those who strip themselves of all attachment to creatures and then endeavor to discover the true nature of things before they permit their affections to be attached . . . .
>
> (pp. 21–2)

To avoid this recurrence of the Fall in every man, the *Combat* stresses the need for arduous consideration by the intellect of every situation that arises: "When an object presents itself, let the understanding weigh its merits with mature deliberation before the will is permitted to embrace it . . . ." "Do nothing rashly, therefore, since a single unobserved factor of time or place may ruin everything." (pp. 21–2) Above all, "Watch your senses carefully," and learn to regulate them in such a way that, "instead of embracing objects for the sake of false pleasure, they become accustomed to draw from the same objects great helps for the sanctification and perfection of the soul." This is done by training the mind to act in a manner that readers of seventeenth-century poetry will recognize:

> When an agreeable object is presented to the senses, do not become absorbed in its material elements, but let the understanding judge it. If there is anything in it that does please the senses, remember that this is not from the thing itself, but from God, Whose invisible hand created and endowed it with all its goodness and beauty.

> .   .   .   .   .

> When you behold the verdant trees or plants and the beauty of flowers, remember that they possess life only through the will of that divine Wisdom that, unseen by all, gives life to all things.

> .   .   .   .   .

> When the beauty of mankind impresses you, you should immediately distinguish what is apparent to the eye from what is seen only by the mind. You must remember that all corporeal beauty flows from an invisible principle, the uncreated beauty of God. You must discern in this an almost imperceptible drop issuing from an endless source, an immense ocean from which numberless perfections continually flow.

> (pp. 65–7)

Thus the concepts of Neoplatonic philosophy were brought home to the everyday life of every man. The result must have been, for those who fervently followed the advice, a universe and a daily life electrical with imagery, where every commonest event wore a glow of transcendent power.

In such training, I believe, we find the roots of the "peculiarity of the metaphysical poets" which Mrs. Bennett has accurately described: "that the relations they perceive are more often logical than sensuous or emotional, and that they constantly connect the abstract with the concrete, the remote with the near, and the sublime with the commonplace." [4] More generally, we may also see in these practices the roots of that power of detachment which enables the speaker in these poems to analyze a problem even while he participates in the dramatic action: the ability to hold the experience off at arm's length, inspect it, explore it, judge it—that ability which Eliot, in his essay on Andrew Marvell, has described as the essence of wit. It is an ability which displays itself in "an equipoise, a balance and proportion of tones," in "a constant inspection and criticism of experience," in "a recognition, implicit in the expression of every experience, of other kinds of experience which are possible": a kind of wisdom which "leads toward, and is only completed by, the religious comprehension." [5]

Certainly it is no accident that the opening work in the collection of Marvell's *Miscellaneous Poems* (1681) should be his "Dialogue between the Resolved Soul, and Created Pleasure," and that the opening words should be:

> Courage my Soul, now learn to wield
> The weight of thine immortal Shield.
> Close on thy Head thy Helmet bright.
> Ballance thy Sword against the Fight.
> See where an Army, strong as fair,
> With silken Banners spreads the air.
> Now, if thou bee'st that thing Divine,
> In this day's Combat let it shine:
> And shew that Nature wants an Art
> To conquer one resolved Heart.

It is not only a Puritan poem: this imagery from Ephesians is as much a part of the *Spiritual Combat* as it is of *Pilgrim's Progress*; the poem illustrates the aptness of Eliot's remark that Marvell was "more a man of the century than a Puritan." [6] The poem properly comes first in the volume because it represents, more than any other

4. Joan Bennett, *Four Metaphysical Poets* (Cambridge, University Press, 1934), p. 4.

5. T. S. Eliot, "Andrew Marvell," *Selected Essays*, pp. 261–2, 256.

6. *Idem*, p. 253.

poem by Marvell, the "monomachy of motives" [7] within man which absorbed the attention of the seventeenth century. And its assurance, its "internal equilibrium" [8] is, I believe, a testimony to the careful exercises in self-scrutiny which we are here discussing. Whatever the temptation offered, whatever change of tactics the change in verse-form may emphasize, the soul answers in unaltered couplets, with punning and with epigrammatic skill, basing its stand firmly on the view of St. Bernard pronounced in the soul's final couplet:

> None thither mounts by the degree
> Of Knowledge, but Humility.

This detached poise, this judicious quality, this critical awareness of all the implications of a scene was cultivated, "exercised," by continual practice in meeting situations of special danger to the individual. The *Combat* insists that everyone must begin by thoroughly understanding "what thoughts and desires usually occupy your mind." In this way one can discover that "dominant passion which must be singled out as your greatest enemy, the first to be attacked." (p. 49) Thus we move from virtue to virtue, we learn to "cultivate one firmly, then another." "For in the acquisition of a particular virtue, and in the focusing of thought upon its cultivation, the memory will be exercised more in this one line of endeavor; your understanding, enlightened by divine assistance, will find new means and stronger motives for attaining it, and the will itself will be invigorated with fresh ardor in the pursuit." "Such concentrated power of action," the *Combat* insists, "is not possible when the three faculties are divided, as it were, by different objects." (pp. 107–8) Thus the "whole soul" is focused upon a single end and aim, the whole man is mustered out and "exercised" in the "tactics" of meeting the assaults of temptation.

Here is the usual procedure, followed in meeting all attacks of "sensuality" except the attacks of sexual impulses: for these, special

7. See the compilation by Abraham Fleming, *A Monomachie of Motives in the mind of man: Or a Battell betweene Vertues and Vices of contrarie qualitie*, London, 1582.

8. Eliot, *Selected Essays*, p. 263.

methods of escape and flight to the Cross are to be used. (chap. 19)
First of all the initial "impulses of the sensual appetite that oppose
reason must be carefully checked, that the will should not give its
consent to them." But this is not enough; the enemy is wily, and
when he sees us resisting courageously he will for a time desist, in
an effort to prevent the formation of a virtuous habit, to lull us into
a false security. To avoid this, we must ourselves release these sensual
impulses "in order to give them a greater setback." We must deliberately bring to mind whatever moved us to a given vice. Then,
"when you recognize the same emotion rising in your lower appetite,
mobilize the entire force of your will to suppress it." But even then
we are not safe: we are never safe; and a "third trial" of this kind
may be needed "in order to steel ourselves" against these vicious impulses. Finally, of course, these actions must always be accompanied
by "acts of those virtues which are opposed to the vicious inclina-
tions we encounter." (pp. 36–7)

Such practices as these, I believe, are of the utmost importance for
the poetry we are considering. It is clear that Donne and Herbert,
for instance, are adept at singling out their dominant temptations,
and that their poetry is in part a record of their attempts to "exercise" themselves in defense against these temptations. In his religious
poetry Donne deals with two dominant vices: the "sinne of feare"
which he was still combating in one of his last hymns, and the sin
of intellectual pride, which he recognized in his famous allusion to
his "Hydroptique immoderate desire of humane learning and languages." [9] The way to deal with these, as we have seen, is to face
them squarely, arouse the sinful impulses deliberately, and then repel them by examining all situations in the light of one's ultimate
goal: conformity with the will of God. In Holy Sonnet 1 we watch
the speaker, in the octave of the poem, deliberately arouse sensations
of "despaire" and "terrour" at the thoughts of sin and death and hell,
and then, in the sestet, firmly repel them by confidence in God's
grace. Or in Holy Sonnet 9 we see him deliberately cultivate the
blasphemous thoughts of his unruly intellect that dares dispute with
God—and then repel these outrageous "motions" by casting himself
on God's mercy.

9. "A Hymne to God the Father"; *Letters to Severall Persons of Honour*,
ed. Charles Edmund Merrill, Jr. (New York, Sturgis and Walton, 1910), p. 44.

Similarly in Herbert's "The Collar" we can watch the deliberate cultivation of blasphemous thoughts: but, as in Donne's Sonnet 9, the speaker is at bottom in firm control throughout; he knows how foolish, how ridiculous, how childish, this outburst is, and he knows from the first line what the conclusion will be:

> But as I rav'd and grew more fierce and wilde
> > At every word,
> Me thoughts I heard one calling, *Child!*
> > And I reply'd *My Lord.*

Over and over again in Herbert's poetry we can see this perfectly executed movement, notably in poems such as "Affliction" (1) or "The Crosse," where Herbert's "cunning bosome-sinne" of discontent, due to the frustrations arising from his ill body, is explored in all its ramifications, with blasphemous murmurings and bitter accusations against God's justice; but all concluding, like "The Collar," in a whiplash of self-control and conformity with God's will. There is, indeed, in the *Spiritual Combat* much specific advice on exactly this subject of impatience arising from bad health: chapter 31 is largely devoted to the problems of the sick man who

> bears his illness with such resignation that the enemy fears he will acquire habitual patience, and suggests to the victim the many creditable works he might do were he in a state of health. The victim is persuaded that his would be a service to God, humanity, and to his own soul were he physically well, and soon the enemy contrives to make him desirous of health and uneasy under his burden. The more earnest the wish, the greater the disappointment, and patience at length gives way to impatience under a burden that is viewed as hindering the accomplishments of works most acceptable to God.
>
> Once the enemy has gained his point, the grand designs vanish gradually, and the patient is left with a gnawing dissatisfaction, and all the attendant evils arising from an impatient desire to cast off a yoke.

The solution, of course, lies in "the patient acceptance of the crosses of life which like a thread must be woven into the fabric of our spiritual lives."

Thus, in "The Crosse," the speaker complains:

> What is this strange and uncouth thing?
> To make me sigh, and seek, and faint, and die,
> Untill I had some place, where I might sing,
>   And serve thee; and not onely I,
> But all my wealth and familie might combine
> To set thy honour up, as our designe.

> And then when after much delay,
> Much wrastling, many a combate, this deare end,
> So much desir'd, is giv'n, to take away
>   My power to serve thee; to unbend
> All my abilities, my designes confound,
> And lay my threatnings bleeding on the ground.[10]

> One ague dwelleth in my bones,
> Another in my soul (the memorie
> What I would do for thee, if once my grones
>   Could be allow'd for harmonie):
> I am in all a weak disabled thing,
> Save in the sight thereof, where strength doth sting.

That is, his ability to see the Cross before him stings him into impatience with those infirmities which prevent him from carrying out the great designs he had planned for the glory of that Cross.[11] But already the poem is revealing the true source of the speaker's

10. I am puzzled by the use of the word "threatnings" here, which Herbert's editors do not explain. It is clearly not used with the normal implications, but appears to mean something like "offerings." The usage is perhaps related to the old verb "threap," as suggested by *OED:* "Threaten," 6: "*To threaten kindness (upon* a person): app. an altered form of the phrase *to threap kindness.*" *OED* gives examples from Holinshed and Lyly. Other implications of the verb "threap" are perhaps relevant: cf. "threap" v. 3: "To persist in asserting (something contradicted or doubted); to affirm positively or pertinaciously"; also 4a: "to lead or try to lead one to believe by persistent assertion." Cf. the use of "threatned" in the opening line of "The Holdfast."

11. *Works of Herbert,* ed. Hutchinson, p. 534: "I am altogether weak except when I contemplate the cross; but its strength spurs me to action."

trouble: there is far too much insistence on the "I" and the "my" and the "me"—fourteen times in three short stanzas: a note of personal willfulness emphasized by the scarcely covert pride in "all my wealth and familie"—think of how all this might have added to God's honor! And then the human willfulness comes out into the open in a tone of self-indulgent petulance, with an effect of deliberate ironic awareness:

> Besides, things sort not to my will,
> Ev'n when my will doth studie thy renown . . . .

But suddenly, in three lines at the close, the whole edifice of self-will collapses, as we have known it would:

> And yet since these thy contradictions
> Are properly a crosse felt by thy Sonne,
> With but foure words, my words, *Thy will be done.*

In these practices of self-analysis, then, we may find yet another reason why, in this meditative poetry, we feel the end so firmly implicit in the beginning: the poet understands the situation thoroughly; he has dealt with it repeatedly, and he knows from the outset how the rebellion must be, and will be, quelled. Here we appear to have a discipline essential—though not alone—in producing the peculiar, tense coexistence of conflicting elements under steady control, moving toward a predetermined end: the outstanding quality of all the finest achievements in English religious literature of the seventeenth century, from its shortest lyric to its grand epics in poetry and prose.

3

Among all these instruments to self-knowledge, the most widely and intensely cultivated remains to be considered: the meditation upon death, which Fray Luis de Granada presents to his readers with this recommendation:

the house of earth (which is our grave) is the schoole of true wisdome, where almighty God is wont to teach those that be his. There he teacheth them how great is the vanity of this world: There he sheweth unto them the misery of our flesh, and the shortnes of this life. And above all, there he teacheth them to know themselves, which is one of the most highest points of Philosophy that may be learned. (pp. 203–4)

Such meditation went far beyond the single weekly exercise which Fray Luis is here advising: ideally, the devout man attempted to keep the thought of death forever in his mind, as the *Imitation of Christ* and the whole great tradition of the *Ars Moriendi* had urged: "If thou diddest well, thou shouldest so behave thy selfe in every deede, and in every thought, as thou shouldest in this instant dye." "Blessed be those persons, that ever have the houre of death before their eyes, and that everie daye dispose themselves to die." [1] And this was not just a matter for beginners in the spiritual life: it was a mode of meditation which, as Puente says, "is very profitable for all those, that walke in any of the three wayes, Purgative, Illuminative, and Unitive; wherein all men ought often to exercize themselves, though with different endes." For "Principiants," the aim is "to purge themselves of their sinnes"; for "Proficients," "to make hast to store up vertues"; for the Perfect, "to despise all things created, with a desire to unite themselves by love with their Creator." (*1, 77*)

With such incentives the sixteenth and seventeenth centuries proceeded to develop the meditation on death into a brilliantly imaginative exercise. The Jesuit "composition of place" and "application of the senses" brought their intensifying beams to bear upon the deathbed scenes and wormy circumstance which the medieval *Ars Moriendi* had simply envisioned—with the vivid results thus suggested by Robert Persons:

> Imagine then (my friend,) even thou I saye, which art so fresh and froelicke at this instant, that the ten, twentie, or two yeres, (or perhaps two monethes or daies,) which thou hast yet to live, were now come to an ende, and that thou were even at this present, stretched out upon a bed; wearied and worne with dolour and paine; thy carnal frindes about the weepinge and howlinge and desiring thie goodes; the phisitions departed with their fees, as having gyven the over; and thou lyinge there alone

1. *Imitation of Christ*, Bk. 1, chap. 23. For the tradition see Sister Mary Catharine O'Connor, *The Art of Dying Well; the Development of the Ars Moriendi*, New York, Columbia University Press, 1942.

mute and dumme in most pitiful agonie, expecting from moment to moment, the last stroke of death to be gyven unto the.[2]

Puente, Fray Luis, San Pedro de Alcántara, St. François de Sales, and
dozens of others give essentially the same dramatic advice: consider
the hour of death, "not as thou wouldest of a thing that were to
come, but as it were even now present"; "which is not difficult to
perswade, for it is possible that while I am saying, or reading, or
thinking upon this, I may want no more but one daye of my life: and
seeing that one daye must bee the last daye, I may imagine that it is
this present daye"; "imagine yourself sometime all alone in the face
of the agonies of death, and consider the things that would most
likely trouble you at that hour . . . . For the blow that can be
struck but once should be well-rehearsed." [3]

The most striking aspect of all such meditations, whether by Persons, or by Donne, or by so different a spirit as Robert Herrick,[4] is
the full self-awareness of the vision: the eye of truth that cuts aside
all cant, looking with a grim, satirical humor upon all the follies of
the world, seeing the worst of life and death with the poise of a detached, judicious intellect: the very poise of Hamlet in the grave-
diggers' scene. Consider, for instance, the grim humor that plays
throughout these passages from Fray Luis de Granada (which, we recall, would have been available to Shakespeare in several editions):

> a time maie happen, when some buildinge maie be made neare
> unto thy grave, (be it never so gaie, and sumptuous,) and that
> they maie digge for some earthe out of the same to make morter
> for a walle, and so shall thy seelie bodie (beinge now changed
> into earth) become afterwardes an earthen walle, although it
> be at this present the most noble bodie and most delicately cher-
> ished of all bodies in the worlde. And how manie bodies of
> Kinges and Emperors trowest thou have come already to this
> promotion. (pp. 201–2)

> Then doe they make a hole in the earthe of seven or eight
> foote longe, (and no longer though it be for Alexander the

2. Robert Persons, *A Christian Directorie* ([Rouen], 1585), p. 437.
3. Luis de Granada, p. 198; Puente, *1*, 81; *Spiritual Combat*, p. 187.
4. See his "Litany."

great, whom the whole worlde coulde not holde) and with that smalle rowme onelie must his bodie be contente. There they appoint him his howse for ever. There he taketh up his perpetuall lodginge untill the last daye of generall Judgment, in companie with other dead bodies: There the wormes crawle out to geve him his interteinement: To be short, there they let him downe in a poore white sheete, his face beinge covered with a napkin, and his handes and feete fast bownde: which trewlie needeth not, for he is then sure enough for breakinge out of prison . . . . There the earthe receyveth him into her lappe: There the bones of dead men kisse, and welcome him: There the dust of his auncesters embraceth him, and invite him to that table, and howse, which is appointed for all men livinge . . . .

Then the grave maker taketh the spade, and pykeaxe into his hande, and beginneth to tumble downe bones upon bones, and to tread downe the earth verie harde upon him. Insomuch that the fairest face in all the worlde, the best trimmed, and most charily kepte from wynde, and sonne, shall lye there, and be stamped upon by the rude grave maker, who will not sticke to laie him on the face, and rappe him on the sculle, yea and to batter downe his eies and nose flatte to his face, that they maie lye well and even with the earth. And the fyne dapperde gentleman who whiles he lived might in no wise abide the wynde to blowe upon him, no nor so much as a litle haire or moote to falle upon his garmentes, but in all hast it must be brusshed of with great curiositie, here they laie and hurle upon him a donghill of filthines, and dirte. And that sweete mynion gentleman also that was wont forsooth to goe perfumed with Amber, and other odoriferous smelles, must be contented here to lye covered all over with earthe, and fowle crawlinge wormes, and maggottes. This is the ende of all the gaie braveries, and of all the pompes, and glorie of the worlde. (pp. 220–1)

Alas, poor Yorick, poor Osric!

Yet such considerations are comparatively mild: the dissolution of the body may be accepted with a wry resignation, as Donne accepts it in his *Devotions*:

Now all the parts built up, and knit by a lovely *soule*, *now* but a *statue* of *clay*, and *now*, these limbs melted off, as if that *clay* were but *snow;* and *now,* the whole *house* is but a *handfull* of *sand,* so much *dust,* and but a *pecke* of *rubbidge,* so much *bone.* If *he,* who, as this *Bell* tells mee, is gone now, were some *excellent Artificer,* who comes to him for a *clocke,* or for a *garment* now? or for *counsaile,* if hee were a *Lawyer?* If a *Magistrate,* for *Justice?* [5]

But there are, as Fray Luis says, "two voiages" to be made in this meditation, of which this voyage of the body to the grave is the less important. The other, toward which the major effort of the meditation should be directed, is to "followe after the soule: and consider what waie it taketh through that newe region: whither it goeth: what shall everlastinglie become of it for ever, and ever, and what jugement it shall have. Imagin that thou arte now present at this iudgement." (pp. 201–2) This, says Puente, is the moment "I am to have allwaies before mine eyes." (*1,* 89)

There is the point on which three of Donne's "Holy Sonnets" are centered:

> Oh my blacke Soule! now thou art summoned
> By sicknesse . . . . (4)

> And gluttonous death, will instantly unjoynt
> My body, and soule, and I shall sleepe a space,
> But my'ever-waking part shall see that face,
> Whose feare already shakes my every joynt . . . . (6)

> Thou hast made me, And shall thy worke decay?
> Repaire me now, for now mine end doth haste,
> I runne to death, and death meets me as fast,
> And all my pleasures are like yesterday;
> I dare not move my dimme eyes any way,
> Despaire behind, and death before doth cast
> Such terrour, and my feeble flesh doth waste
> By sinne in it, which it t'wards hell doth weigh . . . . (1)

Here is the primary horror, the grimmest terror, which Fray Luis sees besetting the soul in a mood very close, even in its wording, to this first of Donne's "Holy Sonnets":

5. John Donne, *Devotions upon Emergent Occasions,* ed. John Sparrow (Cambridge, University Press, 1923), p. 105.

Then is the soule in a merveilous great conflict, and agonie, not so much for her departure, as for feare of the howere of her dreadfull accompt, approaching so neare unto her. Then is the time of tremblinge, and quakinge, yea, even of such as be most stowte, and couragious . . . . he can tourne his eies on no syde, where he shall not see occasions of great terrour, and feare. If he looke upwarde, he seeth the terrible sworde of the justice of almightie God threateninge him: If he looke downwarde, he seeth the grave open ever gapinge, and tarienge for him: If he looke within himselfe, he seeth his owne conscience gnawinge, and bytinge him: If he looke about him, there be Angels, and devils, on both sides of him, watchinge and expectinge the ende of the sentence, whether of them shall have the praie . . . . if after all this he take a vewe of him selfe, and consider what he is inwardlie, he shalbe wonderfully amased, and afraide to see himselfe in such a daungerous and terrible state . . . . O how fonde and blynde are the sonnes of Adam, that will not provide in time for this terrible passage? (pp. 217–18)

And so we have John Donne carefully tying himself in his shroud, analyzing the outward and the inward conditions of the sickbed in his prose *Devotions*, and including in his *Second Anniversary* the traditional procedure for a "Contemplation of our state in our death-bed": "Thinke thy selfe labouring now with broken breath," "Thinke thee laid on thy death-bed, loose and slacke," "Thinke thy selfe parch'd with fevers violence," "Thinke that thou hear'st thy knell," "Thinke Satans Sergeants round about thee bee," "Thinke thy friends weeping round," "Thinke that they close thine eyes," "Thinke that they shroud thee up," "Thinke that thy body rots,"

> Thinke thee a Prince, who of themselves create
> Wormes which insensibly devoure their State.[6]

The occasion, then, may be one of actual sickness, as Holy Sonnet 4 suggests, but the ills of sin provide occasions for every moment.

6. See *Second Anniversary*, lines 85–120, and the marginal gloss of the first edition; cf. the meditation on death by San Pedro de Alcántara, with its repeated injunction, "piensa," "piensa," "considera": *Tratado de la Oracion*

Likewise we find Barnabas Oley paying tribute to George Herbert's "mortification of the body, his extemporary exercises thereof, at the sight or visit of a Charnell House . . . at the stroke of a passing bell . . . and at all occasions he could lay hold of possibly . . . ." [7] The effects of all this we may see not only in Herbert's rejected poem, "The Knell," [8] but scattered throughout *The Temple*, in "Church-monuments," "Vertue," "Life," "Mortification," "A Dialogue-Antheme," "Time," "Death." Scattered throughout—this is essential. Palmer's unfortunate attempt to provide a chronological arrangement for the poems in *The Temple* transferred four of these poems from positions earlier in the book to a special section at the very end, entitled "Death"; [9] but such a rearrangement violates the essential purpose and place of such meditations in the devout life and in its representation, *The Temple*. Death is a part of life, meditation on death only a part of man's daily meditation: four "Holy Sonnets" out of nineteen; thirty-five lines out of a whole *Anniversary*, seven songs in a whole temple of praise.

This is made especially clear in Herbert's "Church-monuments," where the "acquaintance" of the flesh with the grave is presented as a lesser, but nonetheless indispensable, discipline which accompanies the prayer of the essential "I":

> While that my soul repairs to her devotion,
> Here I intombe my flesh, that it betimes
> May take acquaintance of this heap of dust;
> To which the blast of deaths incessant motion,
> Fed with the exhalation of our crimes,
> Drives all at last. Therefore I gladly trust
> My bodie to this school, that it may learn
> To spell his elements, and finde his birth
> Written in dustie heraldrie and lines;
> Which dissolution sure doth best discern,
> Comparing dust with dust, and earth with earth.

Y Meditacion (Buenos Aires, Cursos de Cultura Catolica, 1938), pp. 30–1: the words resound throughout San Pedro's meditations.

7. Life of Herbert prefixed to *Herbert's Remains*, London, 1652.

8. *Works of Herbert*, ed. Hutchinson, p. 204.

9. *Works of Herbert*, ed. Palmer, 3, 311–43.

These laugh at Jeat and Marble put for signes,
To sever the good fellowship of dust,
And spoil the meeting. What shall point out them,
When they shall bow, and kneel, and fall down flat
To kisse those heaps, which now they have in trust?
Deare flesh, while I do pray, learn here thy stemme
And true descent; that when thou shalt grow fat,
And wanton in thy cravings, thou mayst know,
That flesh is but the glasse, which holds the dust
That measures all our time; which also shall
Be crumbled into dust. Mark here below
How tame these ashes are, how free from lust,
That thou mayst fit thy self against thy fall.

I have printed the poem here without the division into six-line stanzas which it bears in the printed versions of *The Temple;* for, as
Hutchinson notes, both the early and the late manuscripts of *The
Temple* present it as a unit. The stanza-divisions appear to be an
editorial change prompted by the fact that the rime-scheme "implies
a six-line stanza." [10] But the total effect of the poem implies a union
overriding any stanzaic scheme. The movement of thought and syn-
tax ignores stanzaic division; the key word "dust" occurs as an end-
rime in three of these six-line components, while at the same time the
word "dust" is used three times and the word "dustie" once within
the interior of the line, to provide a subtle union of internal rime. All
this, together with the steady beat of the abcabc rime, serves to reinforce the sense of "deaths incessant motion." Furthermore, the
steady, onward pulsation of the poem suggests an equanimity, a calm,
a measured poise that reaches its inevitable close in the balanced
phrasing and alliteration of the last two lines. It is a perfectly constructed, perfectly cadenced achievement, utilizing the insistent
memory of "dust" in a manner faintly reminiscent of Puente's meditations on "dust":

> So that dust, and durte may serve for *Alarums* to recall to my
> memory myne originall, and the matter whereof I was formed,
> imagining, when I see them, that they crye out to mee, and say:

10. *Works of Herbert,* ed. Hutchinson, pp. 64, 499.

Remember that thou art dust, humble thy selfe as dust, love, serve, and obey thy Creator that tooke thee from the dust. And when I waxe proude with the giftes that I have, I am to imagine, that they crie unto mee, repressing my vanitye, and saying unto mee: Of what art thou prowde dust, and ashes? (*1*, 102)

Here we have a prime example of the way in which Donne's influence may be overestimated: "In *Church-Monuments* the sensibility which Donne made available for poetry moulds one of Herbert's finest poems, and gives an eloquent witness to the way in which Donne modified the sensibility of his time." [11] But surely we should see here a witness to the ways in which two gifted poets developed meditative materials in which the entire age participated. It is hard to see how meditations on death could be farther apart in mood and tone than are the poetical meditations of Donne and Herbert on this subject. In all Herbert's poems on death there is no trace of fear or horror at the prospect, but a calm, mild acceptance of the inevitable, often approaching the whimsical and jesting in tone:

> Death, thou wast once an uncouth hideous thing,
> > Nothing but bones,
> > The sad effect of sadder grones:
> Thy mouth was open, but thou couldst not sing.
>
> .   .   .   .   .
>
> But since our Saviours death did put some bloud
> > Into thy face;
> > Thou art grown fair and full of grace,
> Much in request, much sought for as a good.
>
> For we do now behold thee gay and glad,
> > As at dooms-day;
> > When souls shall wear their new aray,
> And all thy bones with beautie shall be clad.

11. George Williamson, *The Donne Tradition* (Cambridge, Harvard University Press, 1930), p. 103. Merritt Hughes long ago pointed out the importance of the devotional handbooks in cultivating this preoccupation with death: see his article, "Kidnapping Donne," in *University of California Publications in English, 4* (1934), 61–89; see pp. 65–6.

> Therefore we can go die as sleep, and trust
>   Half that we have
>   Unto an honest faithfull grave;
> Making our pillows either down, or dust.

There is in Herbert no revulsion against the flesh: it is "deare flesh"
—a beloved, though quite junior, partner, who may be addressed
as a child who has not quite understood. But in Donne's "Holy
Sonnets" we feel the depravity of the "feeble flesh"—with a consequent fear and horror of judgment, deliberately evoked: even
in his "Death be not proud" there is a tone of stridency, almost of
truculence—a sense of daring to stand up to the terror. The treatment of death by these two poets is, I think, typical of the way in
which, whatever the topic of meditation may be, each poet develops the common tradition along lines suited to his own personality, his own spiritual needs, and also, perhaps, according to the different schools of spirituality in which each poet has been trained or
in which he has found his fundamental affinity. To this last point,
a matter of major importance for our understanding of Donne and
Herbert, we must now turn our attention in considerable detail;
for it is in the methods of cultivating self-knowledge that the difference between schools of spirituality is best discerned.

4

Everyone has noticed the agony, the turbulence, the strenuosity
of Donne, best described by Donne himself in Holy Sonnet 19:

> I durst not view heaven yesterday; and to day
> In prayers, and flattering speaches I court God:
> To morrow I quake with true feare of his rod.
> So my devout fitts come and go away
> Like a fantastique Ague: save that here
> Those are my best dayes, when I shake with feare.

—and the comparative calm, assurance and mildness of Herbert:

> Then weep mine eyes, the God of love doth grieve:
>   Weep foolish heart,
>   And weeping live:
> For death is drie as dust. Yet if ye part,

> End as the night, whose sable hue
> Your sinnes expresse; melt into dew.
> ("Grieve not the Holy Spirit")

It is a comparative mildness only; we damage the essential Herbert if we overlook the deep turmoil and conflict that lies within his masterful control. But the difference is there: the goal, the chief and distinctive direction of Herbert's poetry, is summed up for us in these lines from "Conscience":

> My thoughts must work, but like a noiselesse sphere;
> Harmonious peace must rock them all the day,

or in these stanzas from "The Familie":

> What doth this noise of thoughts within my heart,
>   As if they had a part?
> What do these loud complaints and puling fears,
>   As if there were no rule or eares?
>
> But, Lord, the house and familie are thine,
>   Though some of them repine.
> Turn out these wranglers, which defile thy seat:
>   For where thou dwellest all is neat.
>
> First Peace and Silence all disputes controll,
>   Then Order plaies the soul;
> And giving all things their set forms and houres,
>   Makes of wilde woods sweet walks and bowres.
>
>   .   .   .   .   .
>
> Joyes oft are there, and griefs as oft as joyes;
>   But griefs without a noise:
> Yet speak they louder then distemper'd fears.
>   What is so shrill as silent tears?

But in Donne the noise of thoughts is clamorous; the grief pours forth in anguished eruption; the central mood and tone is summed up in the violence and tumult of his famous "Batter my heart, three person'd God."

In this contrast we see represented, I believe, an essential difference between Jesuit meditation and another important current in

Catholic spirituality which may be described as Salesian—since in St. François de Sales we find one of its most significant representatives during the seventeenth century. There is a twofold distinction to be made: one in regard to emotional violence in meditation and self-analysis, and the other in regard to the extent of intellectual operations. Both of these we find carried, in the "Holy Sonnets," to the extreme limit compatible with unified control, and elsewhere in Donne quite frequently out of control, as in the *First Anniversary*. I do not wish to appear to overlook Donne's native disposition— that "mechanism of sensibility" which seems to have been remarkably unruly in all its tendencies: given to violent emotions, endowed with intellectual abilities of astonishing velocity, penetration and comprehension; his endowments, his range of interests and achievements, all make Donne tower above Herbert like some enormous statue of Laocoon. But it seems that such a disposition and mentality would find a fundamental affinity and satisfaction in the methods of the Jesuit exercises: and this, I believe, is why—as in the case of James Joyce later on—the imprint of Jesuit methods of meditation stayed with Donne throughout his life, despite his violent attacks on the Jesuit order.

There were, of course, Jesuits and Jesuits: some, like Southwell, were deeply imbued with Franciscan influence; and the Jesuit treatises on meditation are by no means all the same. Nevertheless, I believe that in the meditative literature of the period certain tendencies stand out sharply as characteristic of Jesuit spirituality in this time: tendencies summed up and amply demonstrated in the treatise of Luis de la Puente, probably the most popular and most influential of all the Jesuit books of meditation published during the seventeenth century.[1] First of all, the Jesuits appear to have placed special emphasis upon arousing that fear of God to which Donne gives such magnificent expression. The last "rule" in the *Spiritual Exercises* is, most significantly, this:

> Although it is above all things praiseworthy to greatly serve God our Lord out of pure love, yet we ought much to praise

1. One must recognize, however, the great popularity of Rodriguez' *Practice of Perfection;* this is not, properly speaking, a book of meditation, though it contains a section on the subject, where the general tendency is much milder than in Puente.

the fear of His Divine Majesty, because not only is filial fear a pious and most holy thing, but even servile fear, when a man does not rise to anything better and more useful, is of great help to him to escape from mortal sin; and after he has escaped from it, he easily attains to filial fear, which is altogether acceptable and pleasing to God our Lord, because it is inseparable from Divine love.

In evoking this blend of fear and love, of which the "Holy Sonnets" are compounded, the Jesuit of our period tends to cultivate a greater degree of emotional tumult, as well as a greater degree of intellectual "discourse" than writers of a Salesian tendency appear to allow. Puente's treatise stands as massive proof, with its intricate intellectual analysis and its equally intricate cultivation of the "method of affectuous contemplation." Certainly the Jesuit writers advise caution and moderation in these matters: the director of the exercises is expected to prevent dangerous excesses in either of these directions.[2] But the Jesuit conception of moderation appears to allow greater violence in both directions than the Salesian ideal would permit. One can feel this difference in reading the *Spiritual Combat*, where, with all the clear evidence of Jesuit influence and all the constant urging of strenuous effort, we are frequently warned that the Christian in combat must take care to avoid disturbing his "tranquillity of mind." Our sorrow "must be calm and moderate"; we must preserve "a calm and tranquil soul." "Any disquiet on our part is displeasing to God." If you realize that you have sinned, do not "become panic-stricken," but with "an unperturbed heart, indict your vicious passions," and trust yourself to the mercy of God. Moreover, "After you have done this, do not upset yourself by examining whether God has forgiven you or not. This is a complete loss of time, an outcropping of pride, a spiritual sickness . . . ." (chaps. 25, 26)

This tendency in the *Combat* is reinforced a hundredfold by the fact that it was sometimes accompanied in seventeenth-century editions, as in the present day, by the famous treatise *Pax Animae* (1580), frequently attributed to Scupoli. This treatise, probably the work of the Spanish Franciscan, Juan de Bonilla, exerted a pro-

2. See the Jesuit *Directory*, chap. 8, par. 3.

found influence upon the *Spiritual Combat*, upon St. François de Sales, and, I believe, directly or indirectly, upon George Herbert. It is a treatise devoted to "the art of quieting the turmoil of the spirit," the art of promoting a "tranquillity" of mind in which the spiritual combat is carried on, incessantly and vigorously, but "with a certain mildness and effortless ease." Self-examination consists in a "mild, peaceful, constant attention to the feelings of the heart"; "the principal effort of our lives should be the quieting of our hearts, and the prudent guidance of those hearts lest they go astray." In this way of "serenity" and "simplicity," says the treatise, in words that lead the way toward Herbert's "silent tears," "every action of our lives shall be performed in the repose of a heaven-sent peace in which even silence is eloquent." Avoid "impulsiveness or clamor," avoid "using force or violence on our hearts." Do not "dwell too long in sifting the various circumstances of your faults." "Anxiety and dejection of mind do no good, but only disturb and depress the spirit." "Instead of languishing in sorrow and dejection, the soul should bloom forth into acts of thanksgiving, establishing itself in peace and submission to the appointments of heaven."

Clearly, such a way of life throws much less emphasis on purgative meditations: on sin, death, hell, judgment, and the consequent horror and terror that such meditation tends to evoke. In fact, the treatise plainly sets the mind in an opposite direction: "Rather let us gradually accustom our souls to contemplate nothing but the love and goodness of God." [3] Herbert moves in exactly this direction: death, as we have seen, has no terror; judgment is faced with the gaiety of a love-song:

> Come away,
> Make no delay.

3. The whole treatise consists of only 15 very short chapters. The above quotations are taken from the translation of the *Pax Animae* appended to the Newman Press edition of the *Spiritual Combat*: see chaps. 1, 2, 4, 6, 7, 13, 14. Another translation easily available is appended to the Newman Press edition of San Pedro de Alcántara's *Treatise on Prayer and Meditation*, trans. Dominic Devas (Westminster, Md., 1949); the version of the *Pax Animae* here is based on the English version that appeared in Paris in 1665, attributing the treatise to San Pedro.

> Summon all the dust to rise,
> Till it stirre, and rubbe the eyes;
> While this member jogs the other,
> Each one whispering, *Live you brother?*

In short, sin loses its fearsomeness in the realization of God's over-whelming love, displayed in the Eucharist and all it represents. The result is indeed a "certain mildness and effortless ease," a poetry which perfectly accords with St. François de Sales' advice that all meditation and self-analysis should be performed "faire and softly" ("tout bellement et doucement"): a poetry of meditation nowhere better described than in this passage where St. François de Sales presents the essence of what I have called the Salesian tendency:

> When thou desirest earnestly to be freed from any evil, or to obtaine any good; the first thing thou must doe, is to repose thy mind, and quiet thy thoughts and affects from over-hastie poursuite of thy desire; and then faire and softly beginne to pourchase thy wishe, taking by order, and one after another, the meanes which thou judgest convenient to the attaining thereof . . . .
> *My soule is allway in my hands ô Lord and I have not forgotten thy law;* sayd David. Examin often every day, at least morning and evening, whether thy soule be in thy hands, or some passion of unquietnes hath robbed thee of it. Consider whether thou have thy hart at commandement, whether it be not es-caped and fled away from thee, to some unrulie affection of love, hatred, envie, covetousnes, feare, joye, sadnes: and if it be wandred astray, seek it out presently, and bring it back againe gentlie [*tout bellement*] to the presence of God, resign-ing it with all thy affections and desires unto the obedience and direction of his divine pleasure.[4]

4. St. François de Sales, pp. 479–80; the whole chapter "Of unquietnes of mind" bears an extraordinary similarity to Herbert's "The Familie": see Pt. 4, chap. 11; cf. *Introduction à la Vie dévote*, ed. Charles Florisoone (2 vols., Paris, Éditions Fernand Roches, 1930), 2, 148–9.

5

Whatever the methods by which self-knowledge is pursued, the ultimate goal remains the same: to move from Fear to Charity, from distrust of the self to confidence in God: by the intense exercise of self-analysis to purge the soul, and so make way for the "presence of God." In this "Sanctuary of the Soul," [1] deep within the self, one discovers, according to the tenets of St. Bernard and St. Bonaventure, the Image of God. Not an Image restored from without by special grace, but an Image that has always been, indestructibly, there: the creative presence of divinity within man; a power, defaced and weakened by sin, but still potential, and once discovered and recovered by self-scrutiny, capable of achieving, through Charity, a high degree of conformity with the will of its Maker. This principle finds a full and clear expression in Henry Vaughan's poem, "Vanity of Spirit," which, in its presentation of the processes and ultimate goal of self-analysis, provides a suitable conclusion for our present chapter.

In this poem the speaker, exhausted with study, as it seems, emerges from his room and lies down beside a spring to seek refreshment in nature. There, with admiration but without satisfaction, he seeks to find the Maker in the external creation; and then at last turns to search within himself, where he finds "traces" ("vestigia," in St. Bonaventure's terms) [2] of that creative power that moves the springs of all the world. And so the speaker gains, first, some apprehension of the unity of all creation, and then receives, at last, a glimpse of the defaced Image of God within himself; but the vision fades, for in this life the Image can never be fully restored:

> Quite spent with thoughts I left my Cell, and lay
> Where a shrill spring tun'd to the early day.
> I beg'd here long, and gron'd to know

1. Cf. Louis de Blois, chap. 3; and the title of the very popular book of meditations, devoted to self-knowledge and the life of Christ, by the English lawyer, Sir John Hayward, *The Sanctuarie of a Troubled Soule*, London, 1600.

2. See *Itinerarium Mentis in Deum*, chaps. 1, 2: St. Bonaventure, *Opera Omnia* (11 vols., Quaracchi, 1882–1902), 5, 296–303. Vaughan, of course, is adapting the term, not using it strictly; his transference of the term from external to internal serves to emphasize the discovery of a cosmic unity.

Who gave the Clouds so brave a bow,
Who bent the spheres, and circled in
Corruption with this glorious Ring,
What is his name, and how I might
Descry some part of his great light.
I summon'd nature: peirc'd through all her store,
Broke up some seales, which none had touch'd before,
Her wombe, her bosome, and her head
Where all her secrets lay a bed
I rifled quite, and having past
Through all the Creatures, came at last
To search my selfe, where I did find
Traces, and sounds of a strange kind.
Here of this mighty spring, I found some drills,
With Ecchoes beaten from th'eternall hills;
Weake beames, and fires flash'd to my sight,
Like a young East, or Moone-shine night,
Which shew'd me in a nook cast by
A peece of much antiquity,
With Hyerogliphicks quite dismembred,
And broken letters scarce remembred.
I tooke them up, and (much Joy'd,) went about
T'unite those peeces, hoping to find out
The mystery; but this neer done,
That little light I had was gone:
It griev'd me much. At last, said I,
Since in these veyls my Ecclips'd Eye
May not approach thee, (for at night
Who can have commerce with the light?)
I'le disapparell, and to buy
But one half glaunce, most gladly dye.

It is all remarkably close to the movements traced in St. Bonaventure's *Itinerarium Mentis in Deum*. There the first two stages in the soul's ascent consist in the effort to find God "mirrored in the external world" ("ducendo nos in Deum per *vestigia* sua, per quae in cunctis creaturis relucet").[3] But these stages, though holding

3. *Itinerarium*, chap. 3; *Opera Omnia*, 5, 303; *The Franciscan Vision*, p. 35.

greater satisfaction than Vaughan's speaker finds, are nevertheless only preliminary to the much more important movement which begins after these attempts to find God in the creatures "have guided us to the point where we experience the impulse to enter in within the sanctuary of our souls, there to see God reflected in His image." There, says St. Bonaventure, "we shall behold the reflection of God as in the light of some candelabrum which reveals the radiance of the Holy Trinity emanating from the surface of our souls." [4] And then, after explaining how the powers of the soul receive their knowledge, he concludes his account of the third stage of ascent with the imagery of light that dominates his treatise—imagery that, once again, reminds us that the fundamental inspiration for Vaughan's finest achievements does not lie in the occult but in the great, central meditative traditions:

> All these sciences are governed by fixed and infallible principles which are like so many lights or rays that reach our minds from the eternal law. So filled are we with this effulgence of light falling on us from God that, unless we are entirely blind, we shall be led from the contemplation of our souls and their natural powers to the contemplation of God's eternal light. This irradiation of light and its contemplation grips the wise and holds them in wonder and admiration, but it confounds the foolish and disturbs them in their failure to avail of faith so that their knowledge may be increased. And so the prophecy is fulfilled: "Wondrously flashed Thy light from the eternal hills; Dismayed were all the foolish of heart." [5]

Thus the process of self-scrutiny does not end in self-contempt, but moves beyond this to a recovery of self-esteem; self-contempt is only a half-knowledge: full self-knowledge demands a recognition of the incalculable value of the Image which lies beyond and beneath all deformity.

4. *Idem.*

5. *Idem*, p. 44. The "prophecy" is taken from the Vulgate version of Psalm 75.5–6: "Illuminans tu mirabiliter a montibus aeternis" (Psalm 76 in the English versions, which are here quite different in both the Prayer Book and the King James versions). Cf. St. Bonaventure's *Opera Omnia*, 5, 305–6.

CHAPTER 4

Problems in Puritan Meditation: Richard Baxter

What manner of men should they be, who are yet at such great uncertainties, whether they are Sanctified or Justified, or whether they are the Children of God or no, or what shall Everlastingly become of their Souls, as most of the godly that I meet with are? They that have discovered the excellencie of the Kingdom, and yet have not discovered their interest in it, but discern a danger of perishing and losing all, and have need of that advice, *Heb.* 4.1. and have so many doubts to wrestle with daily as we have; How should such men bestir themselves in time?

Sirs, if you never tried this Art, nor lived this life of heavenly contemplation, I never wonder that you walk uncomfortably, that you are all complaining, and live in sorrows, and know not what the Joy of the Saints means.

Richard Baxter, The Saints Everlasting Rest, 1650

BEFORE the more detailed study of the poets who constitute the major interest of this book, it seems essential to consider a question which may have troubled the reader since the outset: what were the Puritans doing all this time? The Puritans constantly speak of "meditation": didn't Puritanism play a fundamental part in the development of this art of meditation? But, as Baxter explains, "Meditation hath a large field to walk in, and hath as many objects to work upon, as there are matters, and lines, and words in the Scripture, as there are known Creatures in the whole Creation, and as there are particular discernable passages of Providence, in the Government of the persons and actions, through the world." [1] This

1. Richard Baxter, *The Saints Everlasting Rest* (4th ed., London, 1653),

kind of pondering, with its resultant "good thoughts," the Puritans practiced, but their typical usage of the term "meditation" does not, before the middle of the seventeenth century, refer to the kind of methodical exercises which we have discussed in the first two chapters here; and even their intense pursuit of self-examination has an aim considerably different from that which we have just discussed. The excellent studies of English Puritanism by Knappen and Haller [2] will explain the background for these differences; for the present purpose I shall rely chiefly upon the testimony of Richard Baxter in the year 1650, when he addressed to his fellow-Puritans the famous treatise, *The Saints Everlasting Rest,* the first Puritan treatise on the art of methodical meditation to appear in England, and one of the most popular Puritan books of the entire seventeenth century. Baxter's treatise has been prompted by the fact that he finds about him, in this year of the Commonwealth's victory, a distressing number of "forlorn, uncomfortable, despairing Christians." It is, he says, "a Truth too evident . . . That many of Gods Children do not enjoy that sweet Life, and blessed Estate in the World, which God their Father hath provided for them." He finds a "strange disagreement, between our Professions and Affections" —a disagreement which he traces partly to "some secret lurking Unbelief" and partly to the neglect of affective meditation: "that it is a duty constantly and conscionably practised even by the godly, so far as my acquaintance extends, I must, with sorrow, deny it: It [meditation] is in word confessed to be a Duty by all, but by the constant neglect denied by most." "And why so much preaching is lost among us, and professors can run from Sermon to Sermon, and are never weary of hearing or reading, and yet have such languishing, starved Souls; I know no truer nor greater cause then their ignorance, and unconscionable neglect of Meditation." [3] And so, in the fourth and last part of his treatise, he gives "a Directory for the getting and keeping of the Heart in Heaven: By the diligent

---

Pt. 4, p. 153. I refer to this for greater convenience, since the second, revised, edition of 1651 (the basic text) has a huge gap in its pagination. There were ten editions of the work between 1650 and 1670.

2. William Haller, *The Rise of Puritanism . . . 1570–1643,* New York, Columbia University Press, 1938.

3. Baxter, Pt. 4, pp. 61, 4–5, 147–8.

THE
SAINTS
Everlasting
REST.

The Fourth Part.

Containing a Directory for the getting
and keeping of the Heart in Heaven :

By the diligent practice of that Excellent unknown Duty of

Heavenly Meditation.

Being the main thing intended by the Author, in
the writing of this Book ; and to which all
the rest is but subservient.

And Isaac went out to meditate in the Field, at the Eventide, Gen. 24 63.
In the multitude of my Thoughts within me, thy Comforts delight my soul, Psal. 94. 19.
When I wake, I am still with thee, Psal. 139 18.
*For our Conversation is in Heaven ; from whence also we look for the Saviour, the Lord
Jesus Christ : Who shall change our vile body, that it may be fashioned like unto his
glorious Body ; according to the working whereby he is able, even to subdue all things to
himself,* Phil. 3. 20, 21.
For where your Treasure is, there will your Heart be also, Matth. 6. 21.
Master it is good for us to be here, Mark 9. 5.

London Printed by *Rob. White,* for *T. Underhill,* and *F. Tyton,* and are
to be fold at the sign of the Bible in great Woodstreet, and at
the three Daggers in Fleetstreet. 1649.

Title-page of the fourth part of Richard Baxter's *Saints Everlasting Rest*,
1649/50 (licensed January 15, 1649/50; general title-page dated 1650)

(Yale University Library)

155

practice of that Excellent unknown Duty of *Heavenly Meditation*. Being the main thing intended by the Author, in the writing of this Book; and to which all the rest [nearly 700 preceding pages] is but subservient."

Why has this art been neglected by the Puritans? Baxter makes the reasons abundantly clear, through his explicit analysis of the causes of neglect, and through his clear statement of the fundamental assumptions of Puritan spirituality. The reasons lie, inevitably, in the general Puritan acceptance of the Calvinistic doctrine of Grace. Not all Puritans, of course, accepted the Calvinistic doctrine in all its rigor: Milton is a notable exception. Nevertheless, it remains the dominant motif in English Puritanism, and even those who, like Milton, attempted to modify its stern and terrible outlines were deeply affected by its prevailing temper. And this temper was not at all conducive to the development of the art of meditation as we have been describing it.

First of all, Puritan doctrine made it plain that salvation could never, in any sense, be merited: the Grace of God, with its gift of "sincere, saving Faith," fell where it would; human efforts could not in any way affect the course of its operations. Where, then, is the motive for meditation? A Catholic writer could urge, with Fray Luis de Granada, that a man, by meditation, must do "on his parte so much as lieth in him" (p. 309); it is always within the power of man's free will to "cooperate" with the workings of Grace; there is no need to wait for special inspiration, as Puente explains with particular clarity:

> when the holy Spirit with speciall inspiration moveth us to pray, all is easie, and sweet: for that hee recollecteth the memory, reviveth the discourses, raineth showers of meditations, inkindleth the affections, accordeth the petitions, ordereth the colloquyes, and maketh perfect the whole worke of praier, our selves cooperating without trouble. But when this speciall succour is wanting, it is necessary that wee our selves, using our freewil with the assistaunce of grace, which never faileth us, apply our faculties to the exercise of their actes in the forme afore saide, whereby wee provoke the holy spirit to ayde us, with the speciall succour of his inspirations. (*1, 20*)

But Puritan doctrine insisted that the spiritual life depended entirely on special Grace, accorded the Elect even before the beginning of time. Devotion waited on the operations of the Spirit: without this Gift all efforts at prayer and meditation were doomed to fail. "Methods" of meditation, dependent on the efforts of the three powers of the human soul—what good were these? The Spirit would provide its own Method, and who would presume to "cooperate" with it, or to explain how its mysterious workings could be "provoked." This widespread attitude among Puritans is the most difficult obstacle which Baxter has to face in attempting to convert his people to the practice of methodical meditation. To the dispersion of this attitude he directs all his splendid powers of persuasion. Even for the mild and charitable Baxter, no words are too strong to use in denouncing "those Seducers who in their Ignorance mis-guide poor Souls" by persuading them "so to expect their comforts from the Spirit, as not to be any Authors of them themselves, not to raise up their own hearts by Argumentative means, telling them that such Comforts are but hammered by themselves, and not the genuine Comforts of the Spirit." (Pt. 3, p. 160)

> As the Papists have wronged the Merits of Christ, by their ascribing too much to our own Works; so it is almost incredible, how much they [Protestants] on the other extream, have wronged the safety and consolation of mens Souls, by telling them, that their own endeavours are onely for Obedience and Gratitude, but are not so much as Conditions of their Salvation, or Means of their increased Sanctification or Consolation. And while some tell them, that they must look at nothing in themselves, for Acceptation with God, or Comfort . . . And others tell them, That they must look at nothing in themselves, but onely as signes of their good Estates: This hath caused some to expect onely Enthusiastick Consolations; and others to spend their dayes in enquiring after signs of their sincerity . . . .

He then proceeds to explain what is needed, in terms that make it plain he is preparing to advise the kind of meditative exercises practiced by Catholics and Anglo-Catholics:

> Had these poor Souls well understood, that Gods way to perswade their wills, and to excite and actuate their Affections,

is by the Discourse, Reasoning, or Consideration of their Understandings, upon the Nature and Qualifications of the Objects which are presented to them: And had they bestowed but that time in exercising holy Affections, and in serious Thoughts of the promised Happiness, which they have spent in enquiring only after Signs; I am confident, according to the Ordinary Workings of God, they would have been better provided, both with Assurance, and with Joys. (Pt. 4, p. 5)

As these passages imply, another problem for Baxter resides in the Puritan view of Grace. Not only did Calvinistic theology discourage the Puritan from engaging in methodical meditation; it led him to turn his energies in quite a different direction. To clarify this we must explore a deeper distinction. One may say that the Christian concept of Deity comprehends a paradox summed up in the two words Charity and Omnipotence: Christian theology develops from the tension between these two poles. Catholic spirituality of the seventeenth century stresses the pole of Charity: Puritan spirituality stresses the pole of Omnipotence. The resultant contrast is summed up in the different treatment accorded the problem of predestination, especially the problem of reprobation. The solution of the problem adopted by the Counter Reformation is, I believe, fairly represented in the popular medieval treatise attributed to St. Bonaventure, the *Stimulus Amoris:* it lies in the conviction of the paramount place of Charity, the Love of God, in the theological system. Logically, the *Stimulus* concedes, it is true that some must be ordained to reprobation. Nevertheless, basing his stand on Charity, the writer advances this audacious solution: "But if I be ordained to reprobation, and shall not enioy God after this life, I will use all the meanes that possibly I can, that I may have him at least, and possesse him as much as may be, in this present life; to the end, I want not so great a good both *here* and *hereafter* too." But after thus meeting the possibility head on, he proceeds to treat it as in fact almost impossible. "But to what state and place soever God hath ordained me, it makes no matter: this I know, and am sure of, that he cannot deny himselfe. I will therefore embrace him with all my heart, and with all that is within me; and will hold him so fast and close unto me, as that, although *the breake of day appeare,*

I will not let him goe, unlesse he blesse me." Or if it seems impossible to do this, "I know what I will doe," says the writer—and here we find the core of his treatise: "I will goe and hide my selfe in the cavernes of his wounds, and there remaine quietly." "Neither will it be decent for himselfe to put me out from thence who saies: *Him that cometh to me, I will not cast forth.* And therefore he cannot damne me, unlesse he will condemne himselfe of falshood and iniustice." (pp. 476–83) Thus through the *stimulus amoris* the problem of reprobation comes to occupy only seven pages out of nearly six hundred: but in *The Saints Everlasting Rest* the problem, directly and implicitly, occupies the major portion of a treatise of nearly a thousand pages.

For the Puritan, basing his argument on God's Omnipotence, is forced to discard the advice of the *Stimulus:* as Baxter says, "we must not make his knowledge active, and his purpose idle; much less to contradict each other, as it must be, if from eternity he purposed salvation alike to all, and yet from eternity knew that only such and such should receive it." (Pt. 1, p. 4) This Rest of which he is speaking, says Baxter, "is the Saints proper and peculiar possession":

> It belongs to no other of all the sons of men; not that it would have detracted from the greatness or freeness of the gift, if God had so pleased, that all the world should have enjoyed it: But when God hath resolved otherwise, that it must be enjoyed but by few, to find our names among that number, must needs make us the more to value our enjoyment. (Pt. 1, p. 95)

"To find our names among that number"—there, for the Puritan, lay the overwhelming question: the question which must be answered before any other aspect of the spiritual life could be considered. "Seeing then that the case is so dangerous", says Baxter, "what wise man would not follow the search of his heart both night and day till he were assured of his safety?" (Pt. 3, p. 174)

Bunyan's example is exceptional only in the force and eloquence of its revelation; fundamentally, he reveals in *Grace Abounding* the terror that beset thousands of devout Puritans in his time: "for that the Elect only attained Eternal Life, that I, without scruple, did heartily close withal; but that my self was one of them, there lay

the question." Consequently, "for some years together" Bunyan
lay groaning under the burden of the question: "But how if you
want Faith indeed? But how can you tell you have Faith?" "How
can you tell you are elected? And what if you should not? How
then?" The result of this agony was that it made Bunyan turn to
his Bible and "with careful Heart, and watchful Eye, with great
fearfulness, to turn over every leaf, and with much diligence mixt
with trembling, to consider every Sentence, together with its natural
force and latitude." And sometimes after a period of such study,
the Scripture "would call, as running after me":

> Then would the text cry, *Return unto me;* it would cry
> aloud, with a very great voice, *Return unto me, for I have
> redeemed thee.* Indeed, this would make me make a little stop,
> and as it were look over my shoulder, behind me, to see if I
> could discern that the God of Grace did follow me with a par-
> don in his hand . . . .[4]

Thus the Puritan tended to concentrate upon two companion-forms
of thought, which are usually what the Puritan means when he
refers to his "meditation": scrutiny of Scripture and self-scrutiny,
both aimed at discerning the God of Grace approaching with a pardon in his hand. As Baxter says, with his usual perfect clarity:

> The great means to conquer this Uncertainty is Self-Examina-
> tion, or the serious and Diligent trying of a mans heart and
> state by the Rule of Scripture. This Scripture tells us plainly,
> who shall be saved, and who shall not: So that if men would but
> first search the Word to find out who be these men that shall
> have Rest, and what be their properties by which they may be
> known; and then next search carefully their own hearts, till
> they find whether they are those men or not; how could they
> chuse but come to some Certainty? (Pt. 3, p. 137)

But what if the certainty turned out to be reprobation? "How
then?" Again Bunyan shows the horror: how, in the fear of just
such a certainty, the curse of Esau sounded in his ears, and how
meditation on Christ, far from stirring up love and devotion,

4. John Bunyan, *Grace Abounding to the Chief of Sinners*, ed. John
Brown (Cambridge, University Press, 1907), pp. 22, 28, 19–20, 76, 52.

brought, perversely, only despair: "Behold, then, his Goodness, but your self to be no partaker of it." [5] The only hope is to find the "evidences" of salvation, and to this search the Puritan bent the best efforts of his mind, with the help of treatises, sermons, exemplary autobiographies, and the personal ministry of his preacher, as Baxter shows in a significant passage of autobiography:

> As I lay under seven years doubting and perplexity of spirit my self, much through my ignorance in the managing of this work, so was I very inquisitive still after signs of Sincerity, and I got all the Books that ever I could buy, which lay down Evidences and Marks of true Grace, and tended to discover the Difference betwixt the true Christian and the Hypocrite or Unsound: I liked no Sermon so well as that which contained most of these Marks: And afterward when I was called to the Ministry my self, I preached in this way as much as most. I have heard as many complaints of Doubting distressed Souls as most: and had as many that have opened their hearts to me in this point . . . . (Pt. 3, p. 195)

It is a revealing glimpse into the Puritan heart; no wonder, then, if meditation leading toward the love of God tended to wither away before the burning presence of this question. For the Marks were many and hard to estimate—too many, Baxter thought, and he attempted to show, with elaborate arguments, how all these could be reduced to one: "The Supremacy of God and the Mediator in the Soul, or the precedency and prevalency of his Interest in us, above the Interest of the flesh, or of inferiour good." (Pt. 3, p. 211) But this matter of "prevalency" is very hard to determine: Baxter's subtle mind seems to complicate, rather than simplify, the ready and easy way to establish certainty set forth by Arthur Dent in his extraordinarily popular treatise, *The Plaine Mans Path-way to Heaven. Wherein every man may clearely see, whether he shall be saved or damned* (1601)—one of the two books which Bunyan's wife brought with her as her dowry,[6] and a book from which Bunyan learned a great deal about the art of crisp, colloquial dialogue on matters of faith. Dent, at the beginning of his treatise, sets

5. *Idem*, p. 56.
6. *Idem*, p. 10. Dent's treatise saw 27 editions by 1648.

down what he calls "eight infallible notes and tokens of a regenerate minde"—"the eight signes of salvation":

> A love to the children of God.
> A delight in his word.
> Often and fervent prayer.
> Zeale of Gods glorie.
> Deniall of our selves.
> Patient bearing of the crosse, with profit, and comfort.
> Faithfulnesse in our calling.
> Honest, iust, and conscionable dealing in all our actions amongst men.[7]

One can see, as several students of Puritanism have observed,[8] that if a man searched hard for these Marks he was likely to find them: that is, "good life" would come to be cultivated as an essential "assurance" of election. Good life had no merit as a good work, but it was an "evidence," a sign, a mark that solaced the soul. Baxter himself makes this clear: "he that wants Assurance of the truth of his Graces, and the comfort of Assurance, must not stand still and say, *I am so doubtful and uncomfortable that I have no minde to duty;* but ply his duty, and exercise his Graces, till he finde his Doubts and Discomforts to vanish." (Pt. 3, p. 168) Through such psychological compulsion the Puritans defeated the assertions of Rome that their doctrine was subversive of morality. Good works played no part in salvation; but they were essential to preserve the sanity of the Elect.

Subtle preacher that he is, Baxter makes use of this inner compulsion of the Puritan to provide a motive for the kind of meditation that he is advocating in the *Saints Everlasting Rest:*

> Consider, A heart set upon heaven, will be one of the most unquestionable evidences of thy sincerity, and a clear discovery

7. Dent, pp. 31–2. "The contraries unto these, are manifest signes of damnation" (p. 32). Near the end of the treatise another discussion of signs occurs, with three different series given, one of nine, one of eight, and one of seven, signs (see pp. 249–52).

8. See Knappen, pp. 348, 393–5; Haller, pp. 88–91; Max Weber, *The Protestant Ethic and the Spirit of Capitalism,* trans. Talcott Parsons (London, Allen and Unwin, 1930), pp. 98–128; esp. pp. 114–15.

of a true work of saving grace upon thy soul. You are much
in enquiring after Marks of sincerity, and I blame you not,
it's dangerous mistaking when a mans salvation lies upon it:
You are oft asking, How shall I know that I am truly sanctified? Why, here is a mark that will not deceive you, if you
can truly say that you are possessed of it; Even, a heart set
upon Heaven. (Pt. 4, p. 55)

"A heart set upon Heaven": there, again, even in Baxter's exhortations to meditate, we find a fundamental difference between Puritan and Catholic, in the direction that their meditative vision takes.

2

Students of English Puritanism have often remarked upon the
small part which the person and humanity of Christ played in Puritan writings of the sixteenth and seventeenth centuries. Of Christ
the Redeemer and Mediator we hear much—"Christ as Mediator
is not the Ultimate End, but the Way to the Father" [1]—but of the
man, the babe in the manger, the suffering servant on the Cross, we
hear remarkably little, in comparison with the kinds of Catholic
devotion which have been discussed in Chapter 2. Miss White has
noted this tendency in the native English devotional books of our
period, where "concentration on the redemptive aspect of Christ's
life in this world inevitably resulted in more attention being paid
to his official role than to his personality." And thus, in consequence, the "continental writing of the time on the life and personality of Christ seems so much livelier, so much richer." It was
a tendency already evident in the reformed primers of the middle
of the sixteenth century, where Miss White has remarked upon
the attempt "to draw the pious reader's mind from the emotional
and imaginative contemplation of the Passion of Christ . . . and
direct it to a more systematic consideration of the lessons to be
drawn therefrom, with especial stress on satisfaction and redemption." [2]

Numerous reasons for this difference in emphasis at once spring

1. Baxter, Pt. 3, p. 207.
2. White, *Devotional Literature*, p. 195; *Tudor Books of Private Devotion*,
p. 111; see also pp. 97–8, 147–8; and Knappen, p. 376.

to mind. Even a moderate reformer might well object to the great liberties which the Roman writers took in such meditation, justifying all manner of nonbiblical excursions on the grounds that they aided in devotion. Such an argument would not only be theologically suspect, but the very "sighs and sobs" which proceeded from such meditation might seem to encumber and obscure the essential theological issues. Furthermore, the Puritan mistrust of all sensory aids to devotion would lead him away from anything like an Ignatian "application of the senses." Yet the fundamental reason surely lies in sacramental doctrine, in the emphasis on Incarnation which Catholic doctrine involves, and in the consequent sanctification of the sensory which flows from this. It was the doctrine of the "real presence" that made possible that delicate sense of "presence" which characterizes Catholic meditation on the life of Christ. The reverse, we may suppose, would tend to happen in the mind of one who denied the "real presence." Baxter makes the point as plainly and vehemently as we could wish, when, among various reasons for meditating on Heaven, he declares:

> Also there is Christ our Head, our Husband, our Life: and shall we not look towards him, and send to him, as oft as we can, till we come to see him face to face? If he were by Transubstant[iat]ion in the Sacraments or other ordinances, and that as gloriously as he is in Heaven, then there were some reason for our lower thoughts: But when the Heavens must receive him till the restitution of all things; let them also receive our hearts with him. (Pt. 4, pp. 87–8)

Thus in the first part of *Pilgrim's Progress*, Christian pauses only briefly at the place of the Cross, where his Burden falls off. His heart is set toward Heaven; Calvary is only a place where something important, never to be repeated, happened long ago. He looks earnestly and with tears at the Sign on the Hill, but there is no man there except himself. And then, after the "shining ones" have changed his raiment and given him his "mark" and "roll"—his "evidences"—he leaps for joy and pushes on, for his rest, his comfort, is not to be found in this deserted spot.

Thus, too, Milton found he could complete a great ode on the Nativity, which for most of its course deals with all the world except the manger scene, briefly mentioned in the first stanza, and almost visualized in the last:

> But see the Virgin blest,
> Hath laid her Babe to rest.
>   Time is our tedious Song should here have ending;
> Heav'ns youngest teemed Star
> Hath fixt her polisht Car,
>   Her sleeping Lord with Handmaid Lamp attending:
> And all about the Courtly Stable,
> Bright-harnest Angels sit in order serviceable.

Milton puts last the concrete scene which would normally begin a Catholic meditation on this subject. The Incarnation is not the essential point of his poem: it is the Redemption and its effects on the future course of human history. Even the briefest comparison with Crashaw's hymn on the Nativity, "Sung as by the Shepherds," provides us with a significant contrast between the spirituality of English Puritanism and the spirituality of the Counter Reformation. Crashaw, through the shepherds, makes himself intimately present at the manger-scene: "We saw," "I saw"—those repeated words provide the dramatic focus and create an intimate application of the senses to the scene:

> See see, how soon his new-bloom'd CHEEK
>   Twixt's mother's brests is gone to bed.
> Sweet choise, said we! no way but so
> Not to ly cold, yet sleep in snow.

At the same time, the theological emphasis lies on God's Love; though the paradoxical Power of this "Mighty Babe" is fully recognized, it is overpowered by the stress on "love's Noon" in the second line, on "Love's architecture" in the middle, and on the gentleness of his Kingship at the close:

> To thee, dread lamb! whose loue must keep
>   The shepheards, more then they the sheep.
> To THEE, meek Majesty! soft KING
>   Of simple GRACES & sweet LOVES.
> Each of vs his lamb will bring

> Each his pair of sylver Doues;
> Till burnt at last in fire of Thy fair eyes,
> Our selues become our own best SACRIFICE.

The eucharistic reference, occurring in a passage that echoes the motifs of popular love-poetry, reminds us forcibly that this poem is centered on the Incarnation:

> Great little one! whose all-embracing birth
> Lifts earth to heauen, stoopes heau'n to earth.

But Milton's poem in its opening lines announces the difference in theme:

> This is the Month, and this the happy morn
> Wherein the Son of Heav'ns eternal King,
> Of wedded Maid, and Virgin Mother born,
> Our great Redemption from above did bring . . . .

The Love of God is never mentioned in Milton's poem; it celebrates instead his wondrous Power, displayed throughout the universe, from the moment of its Creation to the moment of its ultimate Doom:

> Our Babe to shew his Godhead true,
> Can in his swadling bands controul the damned crew.

With the theme of Redemption comes an emphasis on the need for redemption: the "leprous sin" of man, the "scaly Horrour" of the Dragon, and the worship of false gods: an emphasis announced in the opening images of nature's depravity:

> Only with speeches fair
> She woo's the gentle Air
>   To hide her guilty front with innocent Snow,
> And on her naked shame,
> Pollute with sinfull blame,
>   The Saintly Veil of Maiden white to throw,
> Confounded, that her Makers eyes
> Should look so near upon her foul deformities.

But in Crashaw's poem the snowflakes move toward the manger in an effort to assist and pay tribute to the Infant:

> I saw the curl'd drops, soft & slow,
>   Come houering o're the place's head;
> Offring their whitest sheets of snow
>   To furnish the fair INFANT's bed[.]
> Forbear, said I; be not too bold.
> Your fleece is white But t'is too cold.

Crashaw, then, produces a ritual love-song; Milton, a hymn in praise of the Power and Glory. So, in English literature of the seventeenth century, we see the emphasis on Charity producing the religious love-lyric; while the emphasis on Omnipotence makes possible the creation of those two Puritan epics in poetry and prose.

But when Milton, shortly after this superb display of early poetical powers, turned to write a companion-poem on the Passion, he found himself, for some reason, utterly unable to complete it. Is it because he has tried to write a love-song?

> Me softer airs befit, and softer strings
> Of Lute, or Viol still, more apt for mournful things.

These are instruments for Herbert or Crashaw, but Milton cannot handle them. He follows the traditional themes and methods: he calls for tears, he transports himself to the scene, he tries to visualize it: the devices of Catholic meditation struggle to find a home in Spenserian poetic:

> See see the Chariot, and those rushing wheels,
> That whirl'd the Prophet up at *Chebar* flood,
> My spirit som transporting *Cherub* feels,
> To bear me where the Towers of *Salem* stood,
> Once glorious Towers, now sunk in guiltless blood;
>   There doth my soul in holy vision sit
> In pensive trance, and anguish, and ecstatick fit.

> Mine eye hath found that sad Sepulchral rock
> That was the Casket of Heav'ns richest store,
> And here through grief my feeble hands up lock,
> Yet on the softned Quarry would I score
> My plaining vers as lively as before;
>   For sure so well instructed are my tears,
> That they would fitly fall in order'd Characters.

> Or should I thence hurried on viewles wing,
> Take up a weeping on the Mountains wilde,
> The gentle neighbourhood of grove and spring
> Would soon unbosom all thir Echoes milde,
> And I (for grief is easily beguild)
>   Might think th'infection of my sorrows loud,
> Had got a race of mourners on som pregnant cloud.

There, with the worst line he ever wrote, Milton stops, and we have the appended explanation: "This Subject the Author finding to be above the yeers he had, when he wrote it, and nothing satisfi'd with what was begun, left it unfinisht." But was it a matter of his years? A deeper explanation seems more likely, perhaps the explanation provided by Haller, when he says that the Puritan preachers "made the atonement signify the appointment of the elect soul to join with Christ in the war against the eternal enemy":

> Thus the symbolism of the nativity and the passion came to mean little to the Puritan saints, and Christmas and Easter faded from their calendar. Their holy days were the days when they fasted and humiliated themselves for defeats they themselves had brought upon the spirit or the days when they gave thanks for the victories which had been vouchsafed to them by divine providence . . . . The Puritan saga did not cherish the memory of Christ in the manger or on the cross . . . . The mystic birth was the birth of the new man in men. The mystic passion was the crucifixion of the new man by the old . . . . (pp. 150–1)

3

Baxter deliberately sets out to recover for the Puritans some of these devotional practices which had fallen away as a result of Calvinist thinking. This is perfectly clear from his constant marginal references to St. Bernard, Gerson, Cardinal Nicholas of Cusa, the Jesuit Nieremberg, and, with special frequency, to Bishop Hall—who was himself engaged in exactly this kind of devotional recovery. But Baxter does not leave this purpose to implication. In an interesting passage where he is exhorting his people to labor in this work of meditation, and denouncing those who refuse the work, he gives an enormous marginal quotation from "Gerson. part. 3. fol. 386. De monte contemplationis, cap. 43." The passage from Gerson deals with the error of those who "refuse to give themselves to prayer or Meditation, except they feel themselves brought to it by devotion; and except it be when these duties delight them." To these men Gerson gives the traditional answer: "That if they strive as much as in them lieth," they will be "more accepted then if the heat of devotion had come to them suddenly, without any such conflict." The reason is, Gerson says, "Because they go to warfare for God, as it were, at their own cost and charges, and serve him with greater labour and pain." Baxter stresses the point by exclaiming, "Reade this you Libertines, and learn better the way of Devotion from a Papist." (Pt. 4, p. 118) And so the Puritan too is urged to "Set upon thy heart roundly; perswade it to the work; take no denial; chide it for its backwardness; use violence with it." (Pt. 4, p. 245) Or, with a metaphor and humor remarkably akin to Bunyan:

> If lying down at the foot of the Hill, and looking toward the top, and wishing we were there, would serve the turn, then we should have daily travellers for Heaven. But *the Kingdome of Heaven suffereth violence, and the violent take it by force:* There must be violence used to get these first fruits, as well as to get the full possession . . . . But as the sluggard that stretched himself on his bed, and cried, O that this were working! So dost thou talk and trifle, and live at thy ease, and say, O that I could get my heart to Heaven! (Pt. 4, pp. 116–17)

All these elaborate exhortations, "motives" and defenses are essential for Baxter's purpose, since he is about to explain a method of meditation fundamentally the same as that set forth by the Jesuits: "the set and solemn acting of all the powers of the soul." He emphasizes the *all* in this definition: the "whole soul," he declares, must be employed in this practice, and not simply the "understanding" so vigorously exercised by the preachers, who, he says, are especially prone to rest in "the meer studies of heavenly things, and the notions and thoughts of them in our brain." This kind of activity, so popular with all, "is but meer preparation: This is not the life we speak of." Many, he says, have been deceived by this: "They have thought that Meditation is nothing but the bare thinking on Truths, and the rolling of them in the understanding and memory, when every School-boy can do this, or persons that hate the things which they think on." But "the great task in hand" is this: "to get these truths from thy head to thy heart, and that all the Sermons which thou hast heard of Heaven, and all the notions that thou hast conceived of this Rest, may be turned into the bloud and spirits of Affection." (Pt. 4, pp. 146–52, 122)

He then proceeds to outline a careful sequence of operations in methodical meditation, with directions that we have heard before: "What Affections must be Acted, and by what Considerations and Objects, and in what Order." First, he explains, "you must by *cogitation* go to the Memory (which is the Magazine or Treasury of the Understanding) thence you must take forth those *heavenly doctrines*, which you intend to make the subject of your *Meditation*." The next step is "to present it to your *Judgment*: open there the case as fully as thou canst," to prove the truth and value of the joys of Heaven, including here the "*truth* of thy own *Interest* and *Title*." From these operations follow the usual "Affections": love, desire, hope, courage, joy, hatred of sin, "filial Fear," grief, shame, repentance, and so on. (Pt. 4, pp. 184–208) But most revealing is his detailed example of "how to excite the affection of Love," for here we see with particular clarity the amalgamation of Catholic and Puritan spirituality which Baxter is attempting to achieve. Baxter turns here to recover, in modified form, and in a special context, the ancient practices of the pseudo-Bonaventure: fervent visual meditation on the Passion. The Catholicity of this is stressed by a long marginal quotation on the Love of God from "Gerson. de monte Contemplationis in parte operum tertia fol. 382." Baxter begins by telling his reader, with typical Puritan emphasis, to view Christ in Heaven, but gradually the vision is transformed into something very close to such meditation on the Passion as we have seen in Herbert's "Sacrifice":

> Draw near and behold him: Dost thou not hear his voice?
> . . . . He that cals to them who pass by, to behold his Sorrow
> in the day of his Humiliation, doth call now to thee to behold
> his Glory in the day of his Exaltation: Look well upon him;

Dost thou not know him? why, it is he that brought thee up from the pit of hell: It is he that reversed the sentence of thy Damnation, that bore the Curse which thou shouldst have born . . . . And yet dost thou not know him! why, his Hands were pierced, his Head was pierced, his Sides were pierced, his Heart was pierced with the sting of thy sins, that by these marks thou mightest always know him . . . . Hast thou forgotten since he wounded himself to cure thy wounds, and let out his own blood to stop thy bleeding? Is not the passage to his heart yet standing open; If thou know him not by the face, the voice, the hands; if thou know him not by the tears and bloudy sweat, yet look nearer, thou maist know him by the Heart . . . . (Pt. 4, pp. 191–6)

Such use of the senses in devotion is suspect, as Baxter well knows; with his typical honesty he brings the problem out into the open and strives to overcome in his people their mistrust of such devotional methods. He argues that the right way to deal with these treacherous senses does not consist in pursuing only the "pure work of Faith." For this work of Faith, he says, in a revealing passage, "hath many disadvantages with us, in comparison of the work of *Sense*. Faith is imperfect, for we are renewed but in part; but *Sense* hath its strength, according to the strength of the flesh." And then he adds the point which the Catholic, with his devotion focused on the "real presence," never needed to utter: "The object of Faith is far off; we must go as far as Heavn for our Joyes: But the object of sense is close at hand." What, then, he asks, shall be done in this violent division of worlds? The suggestion he advances is exactly the one which the Counter Reformation had long been advocating; and Baxter advances it with a defensive tone that indicates the dangerous territory he is here entering:

Why sure it will be a point of our Spiritual prudence, and a singular help to the furthering of the work of Faith, to call in our Sense to its assistance: If we can make us friends of these usual enemies, and make them instruments of raising us to God, which are the usual means of drawing us from God, I think we shall perform a very excellent work. Sure it is both possible and lawful, yea, and necessary too, to do something in this

kind; for God would not have given us either our senses themselves, or their usual objects, if they might not have been serviceable to his own Praise, and helps to raise us up to the apprehension of higher things.

The Scripture, he adds, provides us with a justification for this
method, since it constantly conveys spiritual things by familiar
sensory objects; and indeed, in these concrete images of Scripture
we may find one of the best ways to "further our Affections in this
Heavenly work." (Pt. 4, pp. 216–21)

He thus gives what might be called a directory for John Bunyan
to follow:

> Thus take thy *heart* into the *Land of Promise;* shew it the
> pleasant hills, and fruitful valleys; Shew it the clusters of
> Grapes which thou hast gathered, and by those convince it
> that it is a blessed Land, flowing with better then milk and
> honey; enter the gates of the *holy City;* walk through the
> streets of the *New Jerusalem* . . . . (Pt. 4, p. 205)

> When thou settest thy self to meditate on the joyes above,
> think on them boldly as Scripture hath expressed them. Bring
> down thy conceivings to the reach of sense. Excellency with-
> out familiarity, doth more amaze then delight us: Both Love
> and Joy are promoted by familiar acquaintance . . . . Sup-
> pose thou were now beholding this City of God; and that thou
> hadst been companion with *John* in his Survey of its Glory;
> and hadst seen the Thrones, the Majesty, the Heavenly Hosts,
> the shining Splendor which he saw. Draw as strong supposi-
> tions as may be from thy sense for the helping of thy affections:
> It is lawful to suppose we did see for the present, that which
> God hath in Prophecies revealed, and which we must really
> see in more unspeakable brightness before long . . . . And
> the more seriously thou puttest this supposition to thy self, the
> more will the Meditation elevate thy heart. (Pt. 4, pp. 219–20)

Of course, he warns, "I would not have thee, as the Papists, draw
them in Pictures, nor use mysterious, significant Ceremonies to
represent them." Nevertheless, certain other Papist practices are
acceptable in meditation on such heavenly matters: "get the liveliest

Picture of them in thy minde that possibly thou canst; meditate of them, as if thou were all the while beholding them, and as if thou were even hearing the *Hallelujahs*, while thou art thinking of them." (Pt. 4, pp. 220–1) Moreover, we may certainly go beyond the details of scriptural text: in a passage especially prophetic of Bunyan he argues that "There is yet another way by which we may make our senses here serviceable to us; and that is, By comparing the objects of Sense with the objects of Faith; and so forcing Sense to afford us that *Medium*, from whence we may conclude the transcendent worth of Glory, By arguing from sensitive delights as from the less to the greater." Thus, for example,

> How delightful are pleasant odors to our smel? How delightful is perfect Musick to the ear? how delightful are beauteous sights to the eye? such as curious pictures; sumptuous, adorned, well-contrived buildings; handsome, necessary rooms, walks, prospects; Gardens stored with variety of beauteous and odoriferous flowers; or pleasant Medows which are natural gardens? O then think every time thou seest or remembrest these, what a fragrant smel hath the precious ointment which is poured on the head of our glorified Saviour, and which must be poured on the heads of all his Saints? . . . . How delightful is the Musick of the Heavenly Host? How pleasing will be those real beauties above? (Pt. 4, pp. 221–3)

In short, as he has said earlier, wherever we look, whatever we do, we will find about us "helps to a Heavenly Life":

> Make an advantage of every Object thou seest, and of every passage of Divine providence, and of every thing that befals in thy labour and calling, to mind thy soul of its approaching Rest. As all providences and creatures are means to our Rest, so do they point us to that as their end. Every creature hath the name of God and of our final Rest written upon it, which a considerate believer may as truly discern, as he can read upon a post or hand in a cross way, the name of the Town or City which it points to. This spiritual use of creatures and providences, is Gods great end in bestowing them on man . . . . O therefore that Christians were skilled in this Art!

He concludes this exhortation with a sentence which contains both the essence of the Puritan dilemma and the essence of Baxter's solution: "You can open your Bibles, and read there of God and of Glory: O learn to open the creatures, and to open the several passages of providence, to reade of God and glory there. Certainly by such a skilful industrious improvement, we might have a fuller taste of Christ and heaven, in every bit of bread that we eat, and in every draught of Beer that we drink, then most men have in the use of the Sacrament." (Pt. 4, pp. 135–6)

These considerations of the understanding, with their consequent affections, should be accompanied, Baxter adds, by "Soliloquy"—a colloquy with one's own soul—"to quicken thy own *heart:* Enter into a serious debate with it: Plead with it in the most moving and affecting language: Urge it with the most weighty and powerful *Arguments.*" But Baxter then gives this a curious and typical Puritan twist. Declaring that "*Soliloquy* is a Preaching to ones self," he says that "Therefore the very same *Method* which a *Minister* should use in his Preaching to others, should a *Christian* use in speaking to himself." That is, one should follow the usual divisions of a seventeenth-century sermon: Explication, Confirmation, Application, Use of Information, Use of Instruction, Use of Examination, and so on. (Pt. 4, pp. 209–13) And thus we find a Puritan sermon intercalated in the higher reaches of the method of meditation; nothing, I think, could pay higher tribute to Baxter's shrewdness and dexterity in bringing together the best that both sides could offer in the service of devotion. Finally, the whole process concludes in Prayer: "from this speaking to our selves to speak to God." (Pt. 4, p. 214)

It is, fundamentally, the sequence of St. Ignatius, of Fray Luis, of St. François de Sales, though these writers are not mentioned. We can hardly doubt that Baxter knew their methods, but he has wisely limited his overt references to less controversial figures, from whom, indeed, he could have gained the essentials of his method—especially from Gerson and Hall. And so the Puritan, too, through strenuous effort, might achieve that union of the powers of the soul which his dependence on Special Grace, his inward researches, and his mistrust of the senses had, for a time, disrupted. In Baxter's plea for an integration of the whole man in the service of devotion, we have a sign that English Puritanism is entering a new stage, symbolized by the publication of his treatise in the year 1650. With this greater breadth of vision, manifested also in Peter Sterry, Marvell, Milton, and Bunyan, the spirit of English Puritanism was soon to show itself in literary achievements that equaled, and in some respects surpassed, the achievements of the Catholic and Anglican poets that form the chief concern of the present study.[1]

To three of these poets we must now turn our attention, with a greater emphasis upon the poetry. The art of meditation can provide a basic structure, a basic outlook, a basic discipline; but to pass into poetry, meditation must be fused with the techniques, the traditions, distinctive of poetry—with forms of verse, modes of imagery, strategies of writing, inherited and stimulated by the poets of the Renaissance, both secular and religious. The second part of this study will therefore range beyond the strictly meditative; yet meditation remains, I believe, the vital center of this poetry.

1. For a helpful study of Puritan spirituality, written from a different standpoint, see Gordon Stevens Wakefield, *Puritan Devotion: Its Place in the Development of Christian Piety* (London, Epworth Press, 1957).

PART 2

Three Meditative Poets

My lute awake performe the last
Labour that thou and I shall waste:
And end that I have now begonne:
And when this song is song and past:
My lute be styll for I have done.

Sir Thomas Wyatt, "The lover complayneth
the unkindnes of his love"

Wilt thou forgive that sinne where I begunne,
  Which was my sin, though it were done before?
Wilt thou forgive that sinne; through which I runne,
  And do run still: though still I do deplore?
    When thou hast done, thou hast not done,
          For, I have more.

John Donne, "A Hymne to God the Father"

CHAPTER 5

Robert Southwell and the Seventeenth Century

Poets by abusing their talent, and making the follies and faygnings of love the customarie subiect of their base endevours, have so discredited this facultie, that a Poet, a Lover, and a Lyer, are by many reckoned but three words of one signification. But the vanitie of men, cannot counterpoyse the authoritie of God, who delivering many parts of Scripture in verse, and by his Apostle willing us to exercise our devotion in Hymnes and spiritual Sonnets, warranteth the Art to be good, and the use allowable . . . . But the devill as he affecteth Deitie, and seeketh to have all the complements of Divine honour applyed to his service, so hath he among the rest possessed also most Poets with his idle fansies. For in lieu of solemne and devout matter, to which in duety they owe their abilities, they now busie themselves in expressing such passions, as onely serve for testimonies to how unworthy affections they have wedded their wills. And because the best course to let them see the errour of their works, is to weave a new webbe in their owne ioome, I have heere laide a few course threds together, to invite some skilfuller wits to goe forward in the same, or to begin some finer peece: wherein it may be seene how well, verse and vertue sute together.

Southwell, epistle prefatory to *Saint Peters Complaint*, 1595

In the year 1586 Robert Southwell, missionary priest of the Jesuit order, landed on the shores of England after more than ten years' absence. Now a man of twenty-five, he had spent the last nine of his formative years in Rome, amid the origins of the great outpouring of baroque art nourished by the Counter Reformation. Looking about him, he might well lament the poor estate of English religious poetry, which hobbled along in worn-out garb, mumbling the same old tunes, while on every side one might see the results of experiment in the poetry of profane love. *Tottel's Miscellany*, with its overwhelming proportion of love-poems, was to see two editions shortly after Southwell's arrival (1587, 1589); and although these were in fact the last Elizabethan printings of that famous book, the impulses that it represented were now coming into full sway: the poetical techniques of Italian and French sonneteers, and the native tradition of the love-ballad. Sidney's supreme blending of these two traditions remained, of course, in manuscript, and there is no evidence that Southwell ever saw it. But he could have seen that formidable sequence of profane "passions," Thomas Watson's *Hekatompathia or Passionate Centurie of Love* (1582), where a broad range of Italian, French, Latin, and Greek poetry is rifled and the spoils doggedly set before the reader. Meanwhile, in the *Handfull of pleasant delites*, just published in 1584,[1] he might have seen how varied and skillful the strains of the popular love-ballad had come to be. True, in the soberest of all the miscellanies, *The Paradyse of daynty devises* (1576), only a third of the poems dealt with the woes of the lover; but these were, alas, the better poems in the volume.

The *Paradise*, indeed, illustrated the case with particular clarity. Here was a miscellany that was rapidly surpassing Tottel's in popularity, running through six editions between 1576 and 1590 (with only two for Tottel's in that period); and four more editions were to follow between 1596 and 1606; it was by far the most popular of all the miscellanies published during Elizabeth's reign.[2] In some respects this fact might at first seem encouraging to anyone interested in repressing the follies of profane love, for its love-poetry is remarkably tepid, tending rather to deplore than to praise the fancies of lovers; while two-thirds of its poems are devoted to ethical and religious matters. Certainly the popularity of the *Paradise* reveals an audience eager for religious poetry; but it does not represent any-

1. An earlier edition of this miscellany seems to have appeared in 1566: see *A Handful of Pleasant Delights*, ed. Hyder Rollins (Cambridge, Harvard University Press, 1924), pp. x–xv.

2. See *The Paradise of Dainty Devices (1576–1606)*, ed. Hyder Rollins (Cambridge, Harvard University Press, 1927), pp. xiii–xxxi.

thing like a renaissance of devotional verse. As the elegiac note of the Dedication indicates, most of its poetry, in all editions, comes from an earlier age: the first edition appears to represent a collection of poems gathered "for his private use" by Richard Edwards, who died in 1566.[3] The three chief poets, with at least a dozen poems apiece, are Edwards himself, the second Baron Vaux, who died in 1556, and William Hunnis, said to be in the "winter" of his age in 1578.[4] The tone and tenor of the volume are very well set by the piece that opens it in all editions: "The Translation of the blessed Saint Barnards verses, conteynyng the unstable felicitie of this way-faring worlde." [5] Given in its Latin original, together with old-fashioned English hexameters, it testifies both to the appeal of medieval attitudes and themes in late Elizabethan days, and to the kind of solemn English verse that passed for religious poetry in Southwell's time:

> The pompe of worldly prayse, which worldlinges hold so deere,
> In holy sacred booke, is likened to a flowre:
> Whose date dooth not conteyne, a weeke, a moonth, or yeere,
> But springing nowe, dooth fade againe within an houre.
> And as the lightest leafe, with winde about is throwne,
> So lyght is lyfe of man, and lightly hence is blowne.

This, the best stanza of the translation, is not without a mild felicity; it represents the modest achievement that the *Paradise* can offer in its better pieces. Yet, when all is said, most of the verse in the *Paradise* is moral, not religious: there are proverbs and precepts aplenty, didactic tales, praises of the "mean estate," exhortations to "Vertue"; but hardly a dozen pieces can fairly be said to strike a religious note. The degree of religious fervor achieved in the volume of 1576 may be fairly suggested by this sample from Lord Vaux, on the whole the best poet of the volume:

> And nowe since I, with faith and doubtlesse minde,
> Doo fly to thee by prayer, to appease thy yre:
> And since that thee, I onely seeke to finde,

3. This conclusion is based on the publisher's dedication, together with the special prominence of Edwards' name on the title-page: see *Paradise*, ed. Rollins, pp. xiii, xlix, 180.

4. *Idem*, p. liii.

5. The authorship of the original poem is uncertain: cf. *idem*, p. 181.

> And hope by faith, to attayne my iust desyre.
> Lorde, minde no more youthes error and vnskill,
> And able age, to doo thy holy wyll.[6]

What could be done to shake devotional verse out of this stupor? A way is suggested by Donne's uncle, Jasper Heywood, in two poems added to the 1585 edition of the *Paradise:* one, "The complaint of a sorrowful Soule," is a "meditation on sins" evoked by reminding the soul of the coming Day of Doom; and the other is a meditation applying the case of the Prodigal Son to the self.[7] Both these poems are utterly different from the five assigned to Heywood in the first two editions of the *Paradise* (1576, 1578).[8] These poems published earlier must, it seems, have been written before Heywood left England as a recusant exile in 1561 or 1562—to become, shortly afterwards, a Jesuit. The two poems added later seem almost certainly to be the product of Heywood's later years; at least, one line in the poem on the Prodigal Son seems to point to a late date: "My lustes left me, when strength with age was worne." The addition of these two poems in 1585 may be traced to Heywood's return to England as a missionary priest in 1581, and to the notoriety of his arrest and imprisonment in 1583–84. It may be significant, then, to note that of the first five poems mentioned, one is the labored lament of a lover, one is an Easter hymn that makes no effort toward an intimate grasp of the mystery, and the other three are merely collections of proverbs and precepts. But the two poems of 1585 display the meditative sequence of the three powers of the soul, with an effort toward intensity of self-analysis, toward intimate self-address and colloquy with God, unmatched by any other poems in the *Paradise:*

> O Soueraigne salue of sinne, who doest my soule behold,
> That seekes her selfe from tangling faultes, by striuing to vnfold,
> What plea shall I put in, when thou doest Summons send . . . .

6. *Idem*, poem 17.

7. *Idem*, poems 126, 127; these are assigned to "I. Heiwood"; another poem (124) added in 1585 is initialed "I. H."; this may be by Heywood, but it is simply a collection of aphorisms.

8. *Idem*, poems 10, 12, 95, 96, 100 (the last being added in the second edition). All these are assigned at their first appearance to "Iasper Heywood"; except for poem 95, which is only initialed "I. H." in 1576; 1578 assigns it to "I. Haiwood." See Rollins' chart after p. xiv.

Whereon whils I do muse, in my amazed minde,
Froward thoughts, familiar foes, most fiers assaults I finde:
My conscience to my face, doth flatlie me accuse,
My secret thoughts within my eares, do whisper still these newes.

Now to come home with him [Prodigal Son], and pardon pray,
My God I say, against the heauens and thee,
I am not worthy, that my lippes should say:
Behold thy handie worke, and pitie me,
Of mercy yet my soule, from faultes set free
To serue thee here, till thou appoint the time,
Through Christ, vnto thy blessed ioyes to climbe.

In these two poems, clumsy as they are, we may sense the impact
of the Counter Reformation on English poetry; we may see the
way in which Southwell was soon to follow, with his various "Sinners' Complaints" and "The prodigall childs soule wracke"; we
may even catch a glimpse of the way in which Heywood's nephew,
John Donne, would ultimately utilize in poetry those Jesuit exercises which this very uncle may have taught him.

But first came Robert Southwell, seeking to reform English
poetry by bringing to it certain arts that he had found flourishing
on the Continent: the practice of religious meditation, and the
conversion of the methods of profane poetry to the service of God.
In establishing these arts on English soil, Southwell became the
first significant writer of a new kind of English poetry, a kind which
at its best blended religious meditation with Elizabethan lyric. He
is a pioneer experimenting with an unstable compound of old and
new, producing only eight or nine poems without some grievous
flaw. But these few are among the best religious lyrics of the sixteenth century in England; and of those that are flawed, fully half
show here and there some iridescence of poetry that we may value.
Southwell is a poet, not a mere example of a trend; and our interest in his work must be twofold.

Looking over the whole range of his work, good and bad, poetry
and prose, we may distinguish five strands by which he is firmly tied
to the religious poets of the following century. First, his poetical
meditations on the lives of Christ and Mary discussed in the first
two chapters; second, his campaign, by precept and example, to

translate the devices of profane poetry into the service of religious devotion; third (largely a consequence, I think, of the second), the kinship between his poetry and George Herbert's; fourth, his importance in introducing to England the continental "literature of tears," especially of "Mary Magdalen's tears"; and finally, the tendency toward self-analysis in his poetry, together with the methods of self-analysis set forth in his popular prose treatise, *A Short Rule of Good Life*. Since the first of these strands has already been treated, let us turn now to the second.

2

Southwell's campaign to convert the poetry of profane love into poetry of divine love had, it seems, a strong impact upon the seventeenth century. His volume *Saint Peters Complaint*, with the eloquent prefatory letter cited at the head of this chapter, was printed in London no less than eleven times between 1595 and 1636, to say nothing of two continental and two Edinburgh editions during the same period. The volume contained, besides this significant preface, two introductory poems addressed to the reader, in which the same aim is urged, and the same castigation given to love-poetry; while, both in the long title-poem and in a dozen of the shorter pieces, the volume gave explicit examples of how the devices of profane love-poetry might be adapted to the service of religion.

With this volume we must also link Southwell's popular prose work, *Marie Magdalens Funeral Teares* (which saw eight editions in London and two on the Continent between 1591 and 1636), for here the Magdalen is presented as the pattern of the "perfect lover," with frequent echoes of devices familiar in love-poetry.[1] Both in his "Epistle Dedicatorie" and in his preface to this work Southwell sets forth his attack on profane literature, regretting "that the finest wittes loose themselves in the vainest follies," and expressing the

---

1. *Marie Magdalens Funeral Teares* (London, 1591), f.37v. Cf. f.12: "In true lovers every part is an eie, and every thought a looke, and therefore so sweet an obiect among so many eies, and in so great a light, could never lie so hidden but love would espie it." Also f.34: "so lovers in the vehemency of their passion, can neither thinke nor speake but of that they love, and if that be once missing, every part is both an eie to watch, and an eare to listen, what hope or newes may be had of it."

hope that his attempt here "may wooe some skilfuller pennes from unworthy labours."

> For as passion, and especially this of love, is in these daies the chiefe commaunder of moste mens actions, and the Idol to which both tongues and pennes doe sacrifice their ill bestowed labours: so is there nothing nowe more needefull to bee intreated, then how to direct these humors unto their due courses, and to draw this floud of affections into the righte chanel. Passions I allow, and loves I approve, onely I would wishe that men would alter their object and better their intent. For passions being sequels of our nature, and allotted unto us as the handmaides of reason: there can be no doubt, but that as their author is good, and their end godly: so ther use tempered in the meane, implieth no offence. Love is but the infancy of true charity, yet sucking natures teate, and swathed in her bandes, which then groweth to perfection, when faith besides naturall motives proposeth higher and nobler groundes of amitye . . . .

> Finally, ther is no passion but hath a serviceable use eyther in the pursuite of good, or avoydance of evill, and they are all benefites of God and helpes of nature, so long as they are kept under vertues correction.

With those words the aesthetic of the Counter Reformation establishes itself on English soil: how firmly may be suggested by the way in which the passage foreshadows the words of Henry Vaughan in the preface to *Silex Scintillans*, speaking of Herbert as "the first that with any effectual success attempted the diversion of this foul and overflowing stream." It seems clear that we have here a tradition running from Southwell, through Herbert, to Vaughan; for, as Herbert's editors have pointed out,[2] those sonnets which Herbert wrote to his mother when he was nearly seventeen, announcing his resolve to pursue religious poetry, are similar in sentiment to the above pronouncements by Southwell—although the style of these sonnets is highly imitative of Donne. From those

2. *Works of Herbert,* ed. Palmer, *1,* 95; *Works of Herbert,* ed. Hutchinson, p. 549.

youthful productions to the time when he laments his graying hair, this aim remained central to Herbert's poetry:

> Let foolish lovers, if they will love dung,
> With canvas, not with arras, clothe their shame:
> Let follie speak in her own native tongue.
> True beautie dwells on high: ours is a flame
>   But borrow'd thence to light us thither.
> Beautie and beauteous words should go together.
>
> ("The Forerunners")

> Where are my lines then? my approaches? views?
>   Where are my window-songs?
> Lovers are still pretending, & ev'n wrongs
>   Sharpen their Muse . . . .
>
> ("Dulnesse")

It is surprising that Herbert's use of the devices and situations of popular love-poetry has not been more strongly stressed in recent criticism of Herbert. Surely there is no need to exercise more restraint in this matter than did Herbert and Southwell themselves. Sacred parody [3] of love-poetry plays an essential part in much of Herbert's best work, and points the way to a fundamental relation between these two poets.

In much of Herbert's best work, yes; but the same cannot be said of Southwell. His efforts to convert these devices to the service of religion are not often successful: indeed they usually result in his worst pieces. Sufficient examples of this may be found in stanzas 55–75 of "Saint Peters Complaint," the address to the eyes of Christ, where Southwell indulges in all the worst extravagancies of Petrarchan poetry; in the incredibly bad "Josephs Amazement"; and in some of the pieces at the end of the volume *Saint Peters Complaint* (1595), where Janelle (pp. 215–23, 261–7) has shown Southwell's use of certain devices and themes found, for example, in Gascoigne and Breton. The quality of most of these efforts is all too well rep-

3. I use the word in the neutral sense illustrated by Herbert when he gives the title "A Parodie" to his transformation of Pembroke's love-poem. See below, pp. 315–16. Rosemond Tuve has shown that this usage of the term "parody" has a basis in musical tradition (*Studies in the Renaissance*, 8 [1961], 249–90).

resented by the opening stanza of "What ioy to live," where, as Janelle has pointed out (pp. 215–16), the first four lines appear to be a rough translation from the first quatrain of Petrarch's *Rime*, 134:

> I wage no warre, yet peace I none enioy,
>   I hope, I feare, I frie in freezing cold,
> I mount in mirth still prostrate in annoy,
>   I all the world imbrace, yet nothing hold.
> All wealth is want where chiefest wishes faile,
> Yea life is loath'd, where love may not prevaile.

The fourth line here certainly suggests that Southwell is translating from the original ("e nulla stringo, e tutto 'l mondo abbraccio"); but his choice of these lines, and his manner of adapting them to English verse, are perhaps guided by the fact that they had already appeared in English guise, not only in Wyatt's famous sonnet, but more recently in Watson's *Hekatompathia* and in a poem (79) of the *Paradise*—in both cases adapted to the six-line stanza used by Southwell.[4]

Southwell, in short, is not giving much more than he has promised to "his loving Cosin" in that letter published as a preface to the volume *Saint Peters Complaint:* a "few course threds" showing how the poetry currently in vogue might be adapted to better uses. The inferiority of Southwell's sacred parodies is largely inherent in the popular English modes that he is choosing to follow: modes, for the most part, summed up in the *Paradise*. Janelle points out (pp. 56–7, 255) how Southwell, through his intimacy with the old Catholic families of Vaux and Howard, would have found "a literary tradition alive"—the tradition of the "courtly makers," as represented in the works of the second Baron Vaux. It may well be that Southwell's connection with these conservative families, who were cut off from the court by religious differences, will explain why he shows no traces of knowing the poetry of Sidney or Spenser, why in many respects his poetry seems stiffly old-fashioned, despite

4. See *Tottel's Miscellany, 1557–1587*, ed. Hyder Rollins (2 vols., Cambridge, Harvard University Press, 1928), *1*, 37; *2*, 168; Thomas Watson, *Poems*, ed. Edward Arber (London, 1870), p. 76 (*Hekatompathia*, poem 40).

the fact that he is writing relatively late in the century. But the *Paradise* reminds us that these courtly makers and their imitators maintained a broad popularity in late Elizabethan days; Southwell is not working in an isolated eddy, but in a popular tradition that continued to exert its force in the early seventeenth century, and left its traces, as we shall see, in the poetry of George Herbert.

The fact remains, however, that there was very little left to be done with this thin and overworked vein; Southwell does not rise above the poetry of the *Paradise* unless he enriches this tradition by drawing upon either or both of two sources: the art of religious meditation, or the art of the later Elizabethan lyric. This may be seen in three of his parodies which rise above the level of his other attempts in this kind.

"At home in Heaven," following the meditative method, defines the theme tightly with the kind of dramatic, exclamatory opening that we may tend to associate with Donne or Herbert:

> Faire soule, how long shal veiles thy graces shroud?
>   How long shall this exile with-hold thy right?
> When will thy sunne disperse this mortall cloud,
>   And give thy glories scope to blaze their light?
> O that a starre more fit for Angels eyes,
> Should pyne in earth, not shine above the skyes!

With the theme firmly established, the "understanding" pursues for three stanzas its proof of the soul's surpassing beauty: proof found in the love that God bears the soul, and in the Sacrifice he made to save it:

> Thy ghostly beautie offered force to God,
>   It chayn'd him in the linkes of tender love . . . .

> This lull'd our heavenly Sampson fast asleepe,
>   And laid him in our feeble natures lap;
> This made him under mortall loade to creepe,
>   And in our flesh his god-head to enwrap . . . .

The paradoxes and ambiguities here, with simple diction, biblical allusion, theological reference, and love-convention, struggle for a complex chord that Donne and Herbert were soon to perfect.

Note especially the blending of Matthew (11.12) with love-convention in the first two lines ("regnum caelorum vim patitur, et violenti rapiunt illud"); and the compact implications of the next two lines, where the meaning of the Incarnation is suggested by superimposing the image of Madonna and child upon that of Samson and Delilah; together with the way in which the word "creepe" is made to suggest both the child, and the man bearing the Cross. With this proof of God's redeeming love before us, the fifth stanza then presents the cry of the "affections" and the will in bold and simple phrases that provide a striking instance of how love-conventions may be turned into colloquy:

> O soule, doe not thy noble thoughts abase,
>> To lose thy love in any mortall wight,
> Content thine eye at home with native grace,
>> Sith God himselfe is ravisht with thy sight.
> If on thy beautie God enamoured bee,
> Base is thy love of any lesse then hee.

The poem should end here, but unfortunately Southwell chooses to belabor the point for two additional and inferior stanzas; in fact he has already given one too many stanzas, for the sequence of the "understanding" goes on too long.

The second of these superior parodies is one not included in the first four editions of *Saint Peters Complaint*, but added in the "augmented" edition of 1602: "A Phansie turned to a sinners complaint," where, stanza for stanza, Southwell converts Sir Edward Dyer's popular lyric into a meditative analysis of sin and its cure.[5] Dyer's poem is not, strictly speaking, a love-poem: it seems to be a lament on his fall from Elizabeth's favor. But it uses the imagery and themes of a lover's complaint. On the whole Dyer's poem, though not distinguished, is better than the love-poetry of the *Paradise*: it is less wooden in its artifice, more logical in structure,

5. See the collection of Dyer's poems appended to the study by Ralph M. Sargent, *At the Court of Queen Elizabeth: The Life and Lyrics of Sir Edward Dyer* (London, Oxford University Press, 1935), pp. 184–7. Southwell omits the last three stanzas of Dyer's poem, which form a personal signature with a pun on Dyer's name. Sargent prints the poem in couplets; I have arranged my quotations in four-line stanzas, to match the form in which the early editions print Southwell's parody.

more melodious—much closer, in short, to the later Elizabethan lyric. Here is material worth retouching. Southwell takes it up with deft fingers, smooths out a breach of rhythm here, adds a bright verb for a pale one there, tightens up the use of balanced phrasing, gives emphasis and unity at certain points through careful alliteration, deepens the thought by use of religious paradoxes, and, above all, creates a fairly tight unity through his theme of the sinner's penitence. One may catch a glimpse of his typical procedure by comparing the first stanzas of each poem:

Dyer:
> Hee that his mirth hath loste,
> Whose comfort is dismaid,
> Whose hope is vaine, whose faith is scornd,
> Whose trust is all betraid . . . .

Southwell:
> Hee that his mirth hath lost,
> Whose comfort is to rue,
> Whose hope is fallen, whose faith is cras'd,
> Whose trust is found untrue . . . .

Southwell's Christian paradox, "Whose comfort is to rue," sets up the theme of his poem, and at once begins to strengthen continuity, by linking with the "rue" of stanza 2, which he leaves unchanged. The theme is continued throughout the poem by such changes as the addition of "teares" and "ruth" in stanza 4, and is summed up near the end in this revision:

Dyer:
> Mine Exercise naught ells
> But raginge agonies,
> My bookes of spightfull fortunes foiles
> And drerye tragedies . . . .

Southwell:
> My exercise remorse,
> And dolefull sinners layes,
> My booke remembrance of my crimes,
> And faults of former dayes.

Thus throughout the poem the classical theme of "fortune" is removed and the theme of Christian sorrow developed; in keeping with this, Dyer's frequent classical references are all removed and Christian themes and images substituted. Dyer's line, "My wine of

Niobe," becomes "My teares shall be my wine"; "Sisiphus and all his pheres" becomes "Iudas and his cursed crue"; and one whole stanza is thus changed:

Dyer:　　　　　My sense my passions spie,
　　　　　　　My thoughts like ruins old
　　　　　　　Of famous Carthage or the town
　　　　　　　That Sinon bought and sold . . . .

Southwell:　　My sense is passions spie,
　　　　　　　My thoughts like ruines olde,
　　　　　　　Which shew how faire the building was,
　　　　　　　While grace did it upholde.

It is sometimes said that Herbert's avoidance of classical imagery is a mark of Donne's influence; but Southwell's example here may suggest another precedent. Moreover, viewing Southwell's whole revision of Dyer, we may say that in neatness of pattern and deftness of point, in the blending of theological concepts with the simple language and movement of Elizabethan song, the poem develops a texture something like that which Herbert achieves in poems that, adopting a brief, four-line stanza, seek the guise of utter simplicity: poems such as "Submission" or "The Elixir."

Lastly we come to the third and best example of Southwell's skill in parody: "Marie Magdalens complaint at Christes death." Here is a blending of all the best devices of the later Elizabethan love-song with clear echoes of the meditative technique found in Southwell's prose meditation, *Marie Magdalens Funeral Teares*, and in other laments of the Magdalen that appear in popular treatises of meditation.[6] The poem draws power from its position in the original volume, *Saint Peters Complaint*, where it follows the crude verses, "Marie Magdalens Blush," written in the older style of the *Paradise*. No two poems could enforce more vividly the distance between Southwell's worst and best. After wading through such lines as

　　　　O sense, ô soule, ô had, ô hoped blisse,
　　　　You wooe, you weane, you draw, you drive me back,

6. See, for example, *Saint Bernard His Meditations*, Pt. 1, pp. 354–56; Loarte, *Instructions*, f. 77–9.

one can hardly believe that the opening stanzas of the next poem
could have been composed by the same man:

> Sith my life from life is parted:
>   Death come take thy portion,
> Who survives, when life is murdred,
>   Lives by meere extortion.
> All that live, and not in God,
> Couch their life in deaths abod.
>
> Seely starres must needs leave shining,
>   When the sunne is shadowed.
> Borrowed streames refraine their running,
>   When head springs are hindered.
> One that lives by others breath,
> Dyeth also by his death.

Southwell has here mastered the best that the popular love-lyric of
the time could offer, as Thomas Morley recognized by setting
three stanzas of the poem to one of his finest airs.[7] But the intellectual texture, the control of imagery and paradox, may be attributed
to Southwell's mastery of the art of meditation, as these parallels
with *Marie Magdalens Funeral Teares* may indicate: "The murder-
ing in his one death, the life of all lifes, left a general death in all
living creatures . . . ." "And sith he is to me so deare a life that
without him, all life is death . . . ." "Alas saith she, small is the
light that a starre can yield when the Sun is downe . . . ." "But sith
I can neither die as he died, nor live where he lieth dead, I will live
out my living death by his grave, and die on my dying life by his
sweete tombe." (f.4, 40v., 14v., 17)

After the first five stanzas of the poem have been developed in
this intellectual fashion, the poem rises to an effective close in two

7. See his *First Booke of Ayres* (London, 1600), ed. E. H. Fellowes (London, Stainer and Bell, 1932), pp. 18–19. The music is set to the fifth stanza
of Southwell's poem: "With my love my life was nestled"; stanzas 4 and
3 are also printed, in this order. The stanzas are not included in Fellowes'
English Madrigal Verse, 1588–1632 (2d ed., Oxford, Clarendon Press, 1929),
because this volume by Morley was not then available. The fine soprano
voice of my friend Margaret Hutchinson first drew my attention to this
"air" and its "ditty," which has not been hitherto identified.

stanzas which show more clearly than any others the impact of the art of meditation; for the first is a passionate self-address by Mary, and the next a traditional address to the spear that pierced Christ's side. In these stanzas, freighted with theological paradoxes, yet maintaining still the movement and conventions of the love-song, we have the strongest possible evidence for Southwell's position as a precursor of the meditative line, and especially of Herbert:

> O my soule, what did unloose thee
>   From thy sweet captivitie?
> God, not I, did still possesse thee:
>   His, not mine thy libertie.
> O, too happie thrall thou wart,
> When thy prison was his hart.
>
> Spightfull speare, that break'st this prison,
>   Seat of all felicitie,
> Working th[u]s, with double treason,
>   Loves and lives deliverie:
> Though my life thou drav'st away,
> Maugre thee my love shall stay.

3

Such general resemblances to Herbert will not, perhaps, be enough to strike a firm connection; but more specific links with Herbert's technique can be found. Many of these appear in what may seem the most unlikely place, the unwieldy poem in 132 stanzas entitled "Saint Peters Complaint." Certainly the total effect of this work is not close to Herbert. In the first place, the poem does not display impressive powers of construction: Southwell, in general, shows little of Herbert's ability to build a whole poem, except in a few cases, chiefly where the art of meditation has guided the poem's movement. Mrs. Nancy Brown (see above, p. xxiv) has shown that "Saint Peters Complaint" develops according to a significant meditative structure; but this effect is overlaid by Southwell's way of composing his stanzas with excessive parallelism and antithesis:

> How can I live, that thus my life deni'd?
> What can I hope, that lost my hope in feare?

> What trust to one, that truth it selfe defi'd?
> What good in him that did his God forsweare?
> O sinne of sinnes! of evils the very worst:
> O matchlesse wretch! ô catiffe most accurst! [1]

Nevertheless, if we persevere in reading this often tedious work, we can see how it might appeal to a young writer in search of models for religious verse. It has, despite its mannerisms, a more personal and intimate tone than one finds in the pious verse of the miscellanies. One might attribute this in part to the example of Tansillo's popular poem, "Le Lagrime di San Pietro," which strongly influenced Southwell here, as Praz and Janelle have shown.[2] On the other hand, Janelle has made it plain that Southwell is not following the general method of Tansillo's poem, which attempts to present a narrative and moves from place to place, whereas Southwell's work is a long lament spoken by Peter on one occasion. "It is not a narrative, but a meditation," Janelle acutely says, and in that fact, I think, we have the essential key to the intimate tone that the poem sometimes achieves, especially toward the end, where the supposed speaker is almost forgotten and the work becomes a personal confession. Southwell has apparently modified the procedure of Tansillo by following the tradition found in the treatises on meditation, where Peter's lament is taken as an occasion for a personal outpouring of grief. Thus the Jesuit Puente advises:

> Consider . . . the bitter teares of saint Peter, which did not proceed from a feare of punishment, but from a love unto his Master; For calling to mynd the favors and benefitts he had receaved of him, together with the ingratitude he had shewed in denying him in such an occasion, his eyes did convert themselves into two fountaynes of teares, with an extreame bitternes and greefe of hart . . . . Alas, (said he to himselfe) how canne I live, having renownced the author of life? Why doth not the earth open to swallowe me up, I having iniuryed the Creator of the same? O mouth most abhominable, how durst thou open thy selfe to sweare that thou knewest not him, who hath done

1. Stanza 10. The stanzas are numbered in Grosart's edition, but not in the early editions.

2. See Janelle, pp. 205–15; Mario Praz, "Robert Southwell's 'Saint Peter's Complaint' and its Italian Source," *MLR*, 19 (1924), 273–90.

unto thee so great good? O most cursed tounge, how wast thou lett loose to accuse thy selfe, if thou knewest him who had shewed unto thee so great love?

.   .   .   .   .

O my soule, as thou dost behould in S. Peter thy frailtie to comitt sinne, so likewise behould in him the force of divine grace, to convert thee from synne; and as he wept, so weepe thou likewise for thy synnes, to the end thou maist obtayne full pardon of them . . . . (2, 185–7)

Under the impulse of such meditative methods, the latter part of the poem rises to a level considerably above the rest, as in stanza 106:

> *Christ*, as my God, was templed in my thought,
> As man, he lent mine eyes their dearest light,
> But sinne his temple hath to ruine brought:
> And now, he lightneth terrour from his sight,
> Now of my lay unconsecrate desires,
> Profaned wretch I taste the earned hires.

The "Temple" imagery here is no doubt fortuitous, but in this combination of biblical imagery, personal confession, colloquial accent, logical movement, restrained parallelism, subdued alliteration and assonance—in all this we seem to have a pattern for much in Herbert. Indeed this final portion of the work is crammed with analogues to Herbert.

Immediately after the above stanza comes a sequence of four stanzas defining sin by exactly the technique of packed analogy used by Herbert in his poems of definition, "Prayer" (1) and "Dotage," as well as in the opening stanza of "Sunday," and to some extent in "Sinne" (1):

> Ah sinne, the nothing that doth all things file;
> Out-cast from heaven, earths curse, the cause of hell:
> Parent of death, author of our exile,
> The wrecke of soules, the wares that fiends doe sell,
> That men to monsters; Angels turnes to devils:
> Wrong, of all rights; selfe ruine; roote of evils.

.   .   .   .   .

> O forfeiture of heaven; eternall debt,
> A moments ioy; ending in endlesse fires;
> Our natures scum; the worlds entangling Net:
> Night of our thoughts; death of all good desires.
> Worse then al this: worse then all tongues can say,
> Which man could owe, but onely God defray.

Herbert could have found this method elsewhere in Elizabethan poetry: as usual Southwell is working in devices that had already become a part of popular English poetry; but the method is especially prominent in "Saint Peters Complaint," occurring in three other stanzas of this final section and in five stanzas earlier in the poem.[3] Only three stanzas beyond this definition of sin, we come upon a stanza (113) which, as Herbert's editors have noted,[4] uses the popular device that Herbert follows in the first part of "Justice" (1) and in the whole of "A Wreath":

> My eye, reades mournfull lessons to my hart,
> My hart, doth to my thought the greefes expound,
> My thought, the same doth to my tongue impart,
> My tongue the message in the eares doth sound;
> My eares, back to my hart their sorrowes send,
> Thus circling griefes runne round without an end.

Four stanzas after this, we come to the stanza (118) which Hutchinson has pointed out[5] as a striking parallel with one of Herbert's perfect achievements, the dialogue-lyric that closes the "Church":

3. Stanzas 5, 12, 35, 50, 87, 121, 123, 126; see also the last stanza of "Lewd love is losse" and the fourth stanza of "What ioy to live." Janelle (p. 165) remarks upon the frequency of these "definition stanzas" in "Saint Peters Complaint." For examples of this method see *Paradise*, ed. Rollins, poem 118; Watson, *Hekatompathia*, poem 18; *English Madrigal Verse*, ed. Fellowes, Pt. 1, p. 43: a poem by Deloney from Byrd's collection of 1588.

4. *Works of Herbert*, ed. Hutchinson, p. 542 (Hutchinson here refers to st. 103 of the "Complaint"; this must be a misprint). Palmer (*Works of Herbert*, 3, 142) cites the stanza as a parallel to Herbert's "Sinne's Round," which does not, however, use this mode of linkage but the mode of Donne's "La Corona." Southwell also uses the device in the last stanza of "Looke home," and very briefly in st. 114 of the "Complaint." For the device ("reduplicatio") see Watson, *Hekatompathia*, poem 41.

5. *Works of Herbert*, ed. Hutchinson, p. 543.

"Love" (3). The parallel is reinforced if we consider also the last
three lines of the succeeding stanza:

> At sorrowes dore I knockt, they crav'd my name:
> I aunswered one, unworthy to be knowne;
> What one, say they? one worthiest of blame.
> But who? a wretch, not Gods, nor yet his owne.
> A man? O no[;] a beast[?] much worse: what creature?
> A rocke: how cald? the rocke of scandale, Peter.

> From whence? from Caiphas house: ah dwell you there?
> Sinnes farme I rented there, but now would leave it:
> What rent? my soule; what gaine? unrest, and feare.
> Deare purchase. Ah too deare, will you receive it?
> What shall we give? fit teares, and times to plaine mee,
> Come in, say they; thus griefes did entertaine me.

Of Herbert's "Love" (3) it has been said that "No poem better
represents the way in which Herbert assimilated and modified
Donne's style." [6] Would it not be more accurate to say that this
poem represents the way in which Herbert assimilated and modified Southwell's style? Or at least that Herbert is adapting to religious uses the kind of love-dialogue that Southwell is here imitat-
ing—a kind that may be found in the *Paradise* and in many of the
"Books of Airs"? [7]

4

Let us turn now briefly to another aspect of Southwell's use of
the poetry of his time: his gnomic verses. One of these poems, "For-
tunes falshood," is completely in the old miscellany tradition of

6. Bennett, p. 71.
7. See especially *Paradise*, ed. Rollins, poem 43, which begins:

> I sigh? why so? for sorrowe of her smart.
> I morne? wherfore? for greefe that shee complaines.
> I pitie? what? her ouerpressed hart.
> I dread? what harme? the daunger shee sustaines,
> I greeue? where at? at her oppressing paines.
> I feele? what forse? the fittes of her disease,
> Whose harme doth me and her, alike displease.

And so on for nine more stanzas.

"fortune" poems, without any explicitly Christian touches. In his other poems of this type, as Janelle says (p. 257), Southwell modifies the "stoical" vein that dominates this wisdom-poetry of *Tottel's Miscellany;* yet I think Southwell is not in most cases adding more of a Christian note than can be found in the wisdom-poetry of the *Paradise.* What Southwell usually does is to take over the general type as found in the *Paradise,* smooth out the rhythms, tighten the grip of the phrasing, and in every way produce a neater, more compact stanza of aphorisms than the *Paradise* can offer. The best examples of Southwell's considerable skill here will be found in "Losse in delayes" or in "Times goe by turnes"; the latter would be a remarkably good poem of its type if Southwell, instead of adding a feeble fourth stanza, had stopped with the third:

> Not alwaies fall of leafe, nor ever spring,
> No endlesse night, yet not eternall day:
> The saddest Birds a season find to sing,
> The roughest storme a calme may soone allay.
> Thus with succeeding turnes God tempereth all:
> That man may hope to rise, yet feare to fal.

In these gnomic poems by Southwell, and in the poems of the *Paradise* which they resemble, we have the strand of Elizabethan poetry from which Herbert developed his "Church-porch," with its seventy-seven gnomic stanzas in the six-line form of the last example. That stanza-form, indeed, is the favorite of both Southwell and the poets in the *Paradise*—for any subject—and was of course widely used throughout Elizabethan poetry. When that form includes a blend of colloquial speech, proverb, homely imagery, and mild, wry humor, we have nearly all that is needed to make up the essential components of the "Church-porch"—as the following stanza from Southwell may show:

> While Pike doth range, the silly Tench doth flie,
> And crouch in privie creekes, with smaller fish:
> Yet Pikes are caught when little fish goe by,
> These fleete aflote, while those doe fill the dish;
> There is a time even for the wormes to creepe,
> And sucke the deaw while all their foes doe sleepe.
>
> ("Scorne not the least")

But Southwell's most elaborate effort in wisdom-poetry is a parody of the genre: the poem "Content and rich." Janelle suggests (p. 257) that this is an adaptation of Dyer's famous lyric, "My mind to me a kingdom is"; and certainly it echoes Dyer's poem in a number of places, as in the line, "My mind to me an Empire is." Yet this is not an exact parody such as Southwell performed upon Dyer's "Phancy." Whereas Dyer's poem here is in a six-line stanza, Southwell's is in poulter's measure, the measure of Lord Vaux's poem "Of a contented mynde" in the *Paradise* (poem 89), which has a strong general resemblance to Southwell's. Southwell is here gathering together echoes of the whole tradition of miscellany poetry dealing with the content found in the "mean estate," and transmuting all this into a thoroughly Christian attitude. Horace's famous poem on the subject had been translated or adapted in three different poems of *Tottel's Miscellany*,[1] notably by Surrey in his "Praise of meane and constant estate"; and it is from Horace's poem, directly or indirectly, that Southwell draws many of his generalizations and the specific imagery of the ship with the small sail in stanza 9. At the same time he is drawing upon Martial's famous epigram on the "happy life"—this time almost certainly from Surrey's version in *Tottel:* for Southwell's line, "Spare dyet is my fare," seems to echo Surrey's "meane diet, no delicate fare."[2] In general this is what Herbert also does in his poems "Constancie" and "Content," where he too participates in the widespread poetical practice of giving a Christian interpretation to the themes of pagan wisdom.

5

We come now to that literature of tears which flooded Europe during the sixteenth and seventeenth centuries, and in which most of our English meditative poets participated. Janelle has given an excellent account of this literature of remorse that accompanied the Counter Reformation, showing in particular how devotion to the tears of the Magdalen had become a literary cult.[1] Southwell

1. *Tottel's Miscellany*, ed. Rollins, *1*, 26, 150, 244; *2*, 152–3; cf. Horace, *Odes*, Bk. 2, Ode 10.

2. *Tottel's Miscellany*, ed. Rollins, *1*, 26; *2*, 150–2; cf. Martial, *Epigrams*, Bk. 10, Epigram 47.

1. Janelle, pp. 189–90, 205, 308, 313–14. See also Warren, pp. 134–6.

brings the tradition into England in many forms: in "Saint Peters Complaint," in his two short poems on Peter's remorse, in his prose meditation on the Magdalen, and in his two lyrics that present (so differently) her sorrows. I have mentioned in my Introduction the immediate influence of Southwell's example in this kind of writing; I should like to stress here two points in regard to *Marie Magdalens Funeral Teares:* its quality as a meditation, and its relation to seventeenth-century English poetry.

It is essential to notice that this prose work, like his lyric lament discussed earlier, is not a sentimental effusion but a highly intellectual meditation, exploring the significance of the Magdalen's grief at Christ's tomb and of her meeting with the risen Christ. Though evidently based on an Italian meditation attributed to St. Bonaventure,[2] the work displays the Jesuit art of meditation at the full, as applied to every word in the Gospel account of Mary's visit to the tomb. The meditator imagines himself present at the tomb, watching the actors in the scene; he engages in colloquies with Mary, the angels, and Christ, puts long speeches in their mouths, and debates with them in legal and theological fashion:

> Are not those thy wordes? *I love those that love mee, and who watcheth earely for me shall finde mee.* Why then doth not this woman finde thee, that was up so early to watch for thee? Why doest thou not with like repay her, that bestoweth uppon thee her whole love, sith thy word is her warrant, and thy promise her due debt? Art thou lesse moved with these tears that shee sheddeth for thee her onely Maister, then thou wert with those that shee shed before thee for her deceased brother? Or doth her love to thy servaunt more please thee then her love to thy selfe? Our love to others must not be to them but to thee in them. For he loveth thee so much the lesse, that loveth any thing with thee, that he loveth not for thee. If therefore shee then deserved wel for loving thee in an other, shee deserveth better now for loving thee in thy selfe, and if

2. See Janelle's discussion of the *Teares,* pp. 184–97; the account of Southwell's expansion of materials in this Italian manuscript provides further illustration of the differences between medieval and 16th-century ways of meditation, which have been discussed in Chap. 2 above.

in deede thou lovest those that love thee, make thy worde
good to her, that is so far in love with thee. (f. 10v.–11)

The style is highly formal, filled with rhetorical devices, and yet
it maintains a vigorous play of thought; throughout we feel ourselves in the presence of a subtle mind, rigorously trained in logical
analysis and argument. But the relation of this work to English
poetry lies chiefly in passages where this intellectual method is
suffused with emotion and directed toward the analysis of imagery.
Thus in the following eulogy of the Magdalen's tears we find, as
early as 1591, the appearance in English literature of those hyper-
bolical analogies later to be expended on "Eyes and Tears" by Herbert, Crashaw, Vaughan, and Marvell:

But feare not *Mary* for thy teares will obtaine. They are too
mighty oratours, to let any suite fall, and though they pleaded
at the most rigorous bar, yet have they so perswading a silence,
and so conquering a complaint, that by yeelding they overcome, and by intreating they commaund . . . . Repentant eies
are the Cellers of Angels, and penitent teares their sweetest
wines, which the savor of life perfumeth, the taste of grace
sweetneth, and the purest colours of returning innocency
highly beautifieth. This dew of devotion never falleth, but the
sunne of justice draweth it up, and upon what face soever it
droppeth, it maketh it amiable in Gods eie. For this water hath
thy heart beene long a limbecke, sometimes distilling it out of
the weedes of thy owne offences with the fire of true contrition. Sometimes out of the flowers of spirituall comforts, with
the flames of contemplation, and now out of the bitter hearbs
of thy Maisters miseries, with the heate of a tender compassion.
This water hath better graced thy lookes, then thy former
alluring glaunces . . . . Heaven would weepe at the losse of
so pretious a water, and earth lament the absence of so fruite-
full showers. No no, the Angels must still bathe them selves
in the pure streams of thy eies, and thy face shall still bee set
with this liquid pearle that as out of thy teares, were stroken
the first sparkes of thy Lordes love, so thy teares may be the
oyle, to nourishe and feede his flame. Till death damme up the
springes, they shall never cease running: and then shal thy

soule be ferried in them to the harbour of life, that as by them it was first passed from sinne to grace, so in them it may be wafted from grace to glorie. (f. 55v.–56v.)

Such a manner is certainly as close to Crashaw's "Weeper" as it is far from Herbert's usual style; yet, since Herbert shows a tendency to absorb in his poetry every significant tradition in devotional literature, we might expect even such extravagance to be represented, as it surely is in these stanzas from "Praise" (3):

> I have not lost one single tear:
> But when mine eyes
> Did weep to heav'n, they found a bottle there
> (As we have boxes for the poore)
> Readie to take them in; yet of a size
> That would contain much more.
>
> But after thou [Christ] hadst slipt a drop
> From thy right eye,
> (Which there did hang like streamers neare the top
> Of some fair church, to show the sore
> And bloudie battell which thou once didst trie)
> The glasse was full and more.

In the first stanza Herbert restrains the imagery by speaking in his usual matter-of-fact way, by referring to the "bottle" in Psalm 56.8, and by using the bland comparison with the poor box; but the extravagant development of the imagery in the second stanza reminds us that there is more in common between Herbert and Crashaw than is ordinarily conceded, and that even the violent conceits Southwell uses to address the eyes of Christ are not utterly without parallel in Herbert.

It may well be that the extravagance allowed—one might almost say, demanded—in this literature of tears will account for the violent imagery that Herbert uses in certain poems where he impinges upon this tradition of excess. Thus in "Grief" he combines a lover's sorrow with a sinner's remorse in lines that would not appear out of place in the more mannered portions of "Saint Peters Complaint":

> O who will give me tears? Come all ye springs,
> Dwell in my head & eyes: come clouds, & rain:

> My grief hath need of all the watry things,
> That nature hath produc'd. Let ev'ry vein
> Suck up a river to supply mine eyes,
> My weary weeping eyes . . . .

Similarly, in his one specific contribution to the theme of the Weeper, his poem "Marie Magdalene," Herbert opens with a conceit that seems to announce the poem's participation in a time-honored line of hyperbole:

> When blessed Marie wip'd her Saviours feet,
> (Whose precepts she had trampled on before)
> And wore them for a jewell on her head . . . .

And he continues in a vein of questioning and paradox similar to Southwell's method of developing the meaning of the Magdalen's "funeral tears":

> She being stain'd her self, why did she strive
> To make him clean, who could not be defil'd?
> Why kept she not her tears for her own faults,
> And not his feet? Though we could dive
> In tears like seas, our sinnes are pil'd
> Deeper then they, in words, and works, and thoughts.

To see how the tradition of tears is carried on beyond Herbert and Crashaw, we need only turn to Henry Vaughan's poem on the Magdalen; to Andrew Marvell's "Eyes and Tears," where the key to the whole is given in one stanza adapted from a Latin epigram on the Magdalen; to Marvell's superb "On a Drop of Dew"—"its own Tear"—with its unmistakable echoes of Crashaw's poem, "The Teare."

6

Finally, we come to the example of self-analysis and introspection set by the works of Southwell, both in poetry and in prose. In many aspects of his writing Southwell reveals the wellsprings of that self-awareness displayed in Donne and Herbert. Southwell's Latin prose devotions, based on the Jesuit exercises, show us the fervent and dramatic quality of his struggles in the spiritual combat, and serve to suggest the kind of devotional training any young

Catholic, such as John Donne, might have received from the Jesuits in England.

More important, we have available, in six editions published between 1598 (?) and 1636, a prose treatise that echoes these Latin remains: Southwell's *A Short Rule of Good Life*.[1] We have here a detailed introduction to the devout life which, like the later work of St. François de Sales, gives directions for regulating nearly every aspect of existence—dress, speech, smiles and tears, work and play. Its counsels are subtle and arduous, demanding the utmost perseverance in attempting to perform every action in the service of, and in the presence of, God. Hence the writer of the preface, fearing that these counsels may be too difficult for the reader at first, advises "that before thou begin to practise these Rules, contayning in them greate perfection, thou acquaint thy selfe with another Booke, entituled, *The exercise of a christian life* or such other like, least thou attempt to build a great house with a slender foundation, and climing to the toppe of a high ladder, without passing by the middle steps, at unwares, thou receave a fall."[2]

The basis of the book is found, as we might expect, in the Jesuit *Exercises*, *Directory*, and *Rules*.[3] At the same time, anyone who reads both the *Spiritual Combat* and Southwell's *Rule* can hardly fail to be impressed with the kinship between the two—a kinship that, I suspect, is due not only to the strong impact of Jesuit prac-

1. The treatise circulated in two quite different versions. One, printed under Catholic auspices, exists in two editions without place or date, under the title, *A Short Rule of Good Life*; McDonald (p. 113) conjectures that one of these may date from about 1598, since the work was registered for John Wolfe in this year. Another edition of this version appeared under the imprint: St. Omer, 1622. In the collected edition of Southwell's works published in London in 1620, a different version appeared under the title, *Short Rules of Good Life*; this adds ten pages of prefatory matter, and 25 pages of concluding matter, all evidently authentic, since it includes a dedication and two sets of prefatory verses, all signed "R.S." At the same time, this version omits the preface to the Catholic version, and through excision reduces the body of the work from 146 pages to 94 pages of comparable size. The latter edition was reprinted in the collected London editions of 1630 and 1636. My references are to the 1598(?) version, in the Bodleian copy.

2. The reference seems to indicate Loarte's treatise, though it could indicate Persons' *Directory*.

3. See Janelle, pp. 152, 248; and the *Regulae Societatis Iesu*, Rome, 1590.

tices upon the *Combat*, but may also be traced to Southwell's long residence in Italy. He was living in Rome from about 1577 until 1586, at exactly the time when the spiritual forces that produced the *Combat* (in 1589) were coming to maturity; and this may be the reason why Southwell, both in his *Rule* and in his other works, displays in places something of that mild, moderate, and cheerful temper that distinguished Italian spirituality in Southwell's time— a Franciscan temper, we might say, remembering that Southwell translated Fray Diego de Estella's *Meditations on the Love of God*.[4] The *Short Rule* lies somewhere between Donne and Herbert in temper: with a far greater effect of severity and violent effort than one usually finds in Herbert, but less than one usually finds in Donne.

The *Short Rule*, then, is a brief synthesis of all the methods of self-analysis and self-control which I have discussed in the third chapter of this study; and hence its popularity may be taken as a tribute to the impact upon England of these spiritual weapons of the Counter Reformation. Above all, it stresses the view of life as a "continuall combate" with the powers of evil, a "perpetual warfare" in which "I must alwaies stand upon my guarde, and be verie watchfull in every action." (pp. 6–7)

> Wherfore he that entreth into the way of life, must remember, that he is not come to a play, pastime, or pleasure, but to a continual rough battaile and fight, against most unplacable and spightfull enemies: and let him resolve him selfe, never in this worlde to looke for quiet and peace, no not so much as for any truce for a time, but arme him selfe for a perpetuall combat, and rather thinke of a multitude of happie victories, (which by Gods grace hee may obtaine) then of any repose or quietnes from the rage and assaulte of his enemies.
>
> (pp. 103–4)

There speaks the voice of Donne; yet elsewhere, when Southwell comes to deal with the details of everyday behavior, we feel a

4. The translation was not printed until the 19th century, when it was presented as an original treatise by Southwell in *A Hundred Meditations on the Love of God*, ed. John Morris, London, 1873. For Franciscan elements in Southwell, see Janelle, pp. 109–12, 173–84.

close similarity to the ideals of conduct set forth by George Herbert, particularly in his *Country Parson*. Southwell and Herbert are alike in their concern with "externall decencie," in their attention to "decent and comely" apparel, "handsome and clean, and as much as may bee without singularity, that therein the staidnes, and seemely estate of my soule may bee perceived"; in advice "to goe about the roomes of the house, and see that they be kept cleane and hansome, thinking that God is delighted in cleanlines, both bodily and ghostly, and detesteth sluttishnesse." They are alike in their cultivation of a "temperate modesty" in manner, "rather composed to mirth, then melancholy," "rather bent to smiling, then heavines, and free from frowning, and such like unseemly distemper." In short, they agree that the virtues necessary in social behavior are "modesty, decency, affability, meekenes, civility, and curtesie, shew of compassion to others miseries, and of joy at their welfare, and of readines to pleasure all, and unwillingnes to displease any." [5]

But to what extent does the advice found in the *Rule* leave its traces in Southwell's poetry? Certainly the Jesuit insistence upon the close inspection of every slightest motion of the mind inspires that excellent gnomic poem, "Losse in delayes"; certainly the conception of life as an interior combat lies at the core of "Mans civill warre," stirring it to considerable subtlety of imagery and thought; and the central aim of all Catholic self-analysis—to discover the image of God within man—lies behind the poem "Looke home," with its foreshadowing of certain lines in Marvell's "Garden":

> Retyred thoughts enioy their owne delights,
> As beautie doth in selfe-beholding eye:
> Mans mind a mirrour is of heavenly sights,
> A briefe wherein all mervailes summed lye:
> Of fairest formes, and sweetest shapes the store,
> Most gracefull all, yet thought may grace them more.
>
> The minde a creature is, yet can create,
> To Natures patterns adding higher skill . . . .

5. *Short Rule*, pp. 32–9, 52; the basis of such advice will be found in the "Regulae Modestiae" of the Jesuits: see *Regulae*, pp. 118–19; e.g., "Tota facies hilaritatem potius prae se ferat, quam tristitiam, aut alium minus

Yet these poems only describe the need for self-analysis: they do not present, with quivering intensity, the very act of analysis, as the poems of Donne and Herbert do. Southwell, we must concede, never shows in his poetry the introspective power that he reveals in his Latin prose remains. Only here and there, usually under the dramatic guise of Peter, the Magdalen, the Prodigal Son, or King David, do we catch some hints of an intense self-awareness—and these hints do not bear any great resemblance to the introspective manner of Donne and Herbert. Even Southwell's meditation "Upon the Image of death" remains very largely within the tradition of the poems in the *Paradise* on this theme; it plainly echoes "Saint Barnard's" famous poem, while its stanza-form, with the use of refrain, is exactly that of "Respice finem" (poem 22). Nevertheless, Southwell's meditation on death shows a much greater concentration on specific details, and a much stronger personal note, than one can find in the general precepts of these two poems. We may say, then, that his poems in general show a greater tendency toward the analysis and representation of inner states than one can find in the religious and didactic poetry of the miscellanies. His poems point the direction which religious poetry is soon to take; but they remain on the rim of the mind.

All this may be found in the one poem by Southwell where specifically Ignatian methods of self-analysis can be clearly seen at work. It is the poem "A vale of teares," a poetical representation of the two "preludes" advised by St. Ignatius (pp. 23–4) for the second spiritual exercise of the First Week: a "meditation upon sins." At the same time, it represents a vivid application of the senses of sight and hearing, and displays a threefold movement in accordance with the workings of the three powers of the soul: the preludes, as we might expect, anticipate the development of a full exercise.

In creating the first prelude, the composition of place, Southwell follows the directions, "to see with the eyes of the imagination and to consider that my soul is imprisoned in this corruptible body, and my whole self in this vale of misery." The imagery suggests some Alpine scene:

---

moderatum affectum." Cf. *Works of Herbert*, ed. Hutchinson, pp. 228, 241, 246, 267–8.

> A Vale there is enwrapt with dreadfull shades,
> Which thicke of mourning pines shrouds from the sunne[,]
> Where hanging clifts yeld short and dumpish glades,
> And snowy flouds with broken streames do runne . . . .

This is no romantic landscape: it is an allegorical setting for a meditation. The objects of nature are turned into symbols of the griefstricken, conscience-ridden soul: everywhere he looks the speaker finds badges of his woe. This is not made obvious from the outset, for Southwell is quite skillful in managing suspended implications. The first five stanzas are given over to apprehending the physical scene through the senses of sight and hearing, while subjective and personifying terms here and there gradually suggest a spiritual meaning. Looking back, one can see how the first stanza signals the poetic method: "mourning," "shrouds," "dumpish"—these words warn us not to take the scene as mere description, for these "broken streames" are tears, and the hissing, howling, roaring of the wind in stanza 3 is the sound of conscience in the ear of the soul:

> And in the horror of this fearefull quier,
> Consists the musicke of this dolefull place:
> All pleasant birds their tunes from thence retire,
> Where none but heavy notes have any grace.

"Grace": with the play on that word the religious meaning at last emerges, and the prologue of the poem reaches an effective end.

Now, in ten stanzas that form the heart of the poem, the understanding analyzes the imagery, beginning with four stanzas in which the meaning of the scene for the soul is brought forward through the introduction of human figures:

> Resort there is of none but pilgrim wights,
> That passe with trembling foote and panting heart . . . .

Yet the scene is never allowed to lose its objective existence: it is an image of the state of the penitent soul, but it is also a spectacle of "natures work" that pays tribute to the Creator's power—that power that makes the sinner tremble:

> who it viewes must needes remaine agast,
> Much at the worke, more at the makers might . . . .

In this ability to keep the external scene firmly before the senses, yet all the while drawing spiritual implications from it—in this lies the peculiar power of the poem, and of all poetry written under the impulse of the art of meditation. Here, then, is a "place for mated mindes"—for like minds—and also, in the old sense of the word, for minds confounded, rendered "helpless by terror, shame, or discouragement." [6] Once the external and the internal have been thus "mated," the poem may, in the next four stanzas, present the fluctuations of the spirit by details more specific than any thus far given, while the suggestions that arise from them are more complex:

> The strugling floud betweene the marble grones,
> Then roaring beates upon the craggie sides,
> A little off a midst the pibble stones,
> With bubling streams [and] purling noise it glides.

Then, with two summary stanzas, the first prelude ends, and the second prelude occupies the last four stanzas of the poem: "to ask for what I desire; it will be here to beg great and intense grief, and tears for my sins":

> [Sett] here my soule, [mayn]streames of teares afloate,[7]
> Here all thy sinfull foyles alone recount . . . .

> When *Eccho* doth repeate thy painefull cries,
> Thinke that the verie stones thy sinnes bewray,
> And now accuse thee with their sad replies,
> As heaven and earth shall in the latter day . . . .

These lines anticipate ("according to the subject-matter") the first point of the meditation that is to follow: "to recall to memory all the sins of my life, looking at them from year to year or from period to period." At the same time the lines, like the rest of the poem, hold fast to the advice of St. Ignatius in his additional directions for performing the exercises of the First Week: "not to desire to think

6. *OED*, "mate," v. 4.
7. I follow the reading of the manuscripts here (McDonald, p. 104), though the reading of the early editions is not impossible: "Sit here my soule, mourne streames of teares afloate."

on pleasant and joyful subjects . . . . because any consideration of joy and delight hinders the feeling of pain, grief, and tears for our sins; but rather to keep before my mind my wish to grieve and to feel pain, for that purpose rather calling to mind death and judgment." (pp. 29–30)

Meanwhile that line, "When *Eccho* doth repeate thy painefull cries," reminds us that Southwell is still at his task of converting the devices of love-poetry to religious uses: he is throughout the poem taking over the convention of the lover's "dumpish mood," which regards the objects of nature as signs of the sorrow that comes from his lady's disdain, as in stanza 15: "sorrow springs from water, stone, and tree." [8] The poem is a blending of the lover's and the sinner's tears, after the manner of his meditations on the tears of the Magdalen, as we may see from this stanza (the second from the end), which follows closely one portion of a passage cited earlier: "For this water hath thy heart beene long a limbecke, sometimes distilling it out of the weedes of thy owne offences with the fire of true contrition":

> Let former faults be fuell of the fire,
> For greife in Limbecke of thy heart to still
> Thy pensive thoughts, and dumps of thy desire,
> And vapour teares up to thy eies at will.

It is a very uneven poem, stumbling and crude in places, but in spite of all this, a remarkable achievement: a successful, though unsteady, experiment in something far beyond the ordinary range of Elizabethan religious poetry. It is not a poem in the style of the seventeenth century, but in its meditative methods, in its theme of tears, in its use of conventions from profane poetry, we may see in it the seeds of the poetry of meditation soon to follow.

8. See, for example, Wyatt's poem in *Tottel's Miscellany*, ed. Rollins, *1*, 42:

> Resownde my voyce ye woodes, that heare me plaine:
> Both hilles and vales causyng reflexion,
> And riuers eke, record ye of my paine . . . .

CHAPTER 6

John Donne in Meditation: the Anniversaries

Beare not therefore with her losses, for shee is won for ever, but with the momentary absence of your most happy sister: yea it can not iustly bee called an absence, many thoghts being daily in parlee with her, onely mens eyes and eares unwoorthy to enioy so sweet an obiect, have resigned their interest, and interested this treasure in their hearts, being the fittest shrines for so pure a Saint, whome, as none did know but did love, so none can nowe remember [but] with devotion. Men may behold hir with shame of their former life, seeing one of the weaker sexe honour her weaknesse wyth such a trayne of perfections. Ladies may admire her as a glorie to their degree, in whom honour was portraied in her full likenesse, grace having perfited Natures first draught with all the due colours of an absolute vertue: all women accept her as a patterne to immitate her gifts and her good partes.

Robert Southwell, The Triumphs over Death (in memory of Margaret Sackville), 1595

FROM the early days of Donne's Satire 3, where meditation struggles to convert the methods of Roman satire, down to the late days of his "Hymne to God the Father," where he seems to transform the refrain of Wyatt's love-lament,[1] the distinctive note of Donne is always his ground-tone of religious quest, even when the overt mode of the poem is one of mockery. His search for the One underlies and explains his discontent with the fluctuations of transitory passion, as he makes clear in the *Second Anniversary*:

1. See p. 177. For this view see *Mass. Rev., 1* (1960), 326-42.

> But pause, my soule; And study, ere thou fall
> On accidentall joyes, th'essentiall.
> Still before Accessories doe abide
> A triall, must the principall be tride.
> And what essentiall joy can'st thou expect
> Here upon earth? what permanent effect
> Of transitory causes? Dost thou love
> Beauty? (And beauty worthy'st is to move)
> Poore cousened cousenor, *that* she, and *that* thou,
> Which did begin to love, are neither now;
> You are both fluid, chang'd since yesterday;
> Next day repaires, (but ill) last dayes decay.
> Nor are, (although the river keepe the name)
> Yesterdaies waters, and to daies the same.
> So flowes her face, and thine eyes, neither now
> That Saint, nor Pilgrime, which your loving vow
> Concern'd, remaines; but whil'st you thinke you bee
> Constant, you'are hourely in inconstancie. (383–400)

Consequently, in his "Songs and Sonets" the central power arises from the way in which, along with his insistence on the physical, he grips the thin Petrarchan affirmation of spiritual love, and builds it up on every side with theological proofs and profound religious images.

Thus readers have disagreed over whether "The Extasie" is a poem of seduction or a deep theological and philosophical exploration of the relationship between body and soul: [2] for it is all these things, simultaneously. The wit of the title depends upon the double reference to "sensuall Extasie" and mystical *extasis;* the whole poem develops from the physical desires implied in the curious "composition of place" with which the poem opens:

2. See the controversy stirred up by Pierre Legouis' remarks in *Donne the Craftsman* (Paris, Henri Didier, 1928), pp. 61–9: cf. Merritt Hughes, "The Lineage of 'The Extasie,'" *MLR*, 27 (1932), 1–5; Frank A. Doggett, "Donne's Platonism," *Sewanee Review*, 42 (1934), 274–92; George Reuben Potter, "Donne's *Extasie*, Contra Legouis," *PQ*, 15 (1936), 247–53. For a striking treatment of the contrast between "sensuall Extasie" and spiritual ecstasy see St. François de Sales, *Love of God*, Bk. 7, chap. 4.

> Where, like a pillow on a bed,
>   A Pregnant banke swel'd up . . . .

Those desires, then, after long intellectual analysis of human love, are finally reconciled with the spiritual in an exhortation that involves the theological concepts of incarnation and revelation:

> To'our bodies turne wee then, that so
>   Weake men on love reveal'd may looke;
> Loves mysteries in soules doe grow,
>   But yet the body is his booke.

Likewise, the somber tradition of meditation on death lies behind "The Funerall," with its half-mocking transformation of a symbol of physical lust into a religious "mystery":

> Who ever comes to shroud me, do not harme
>   Nor question much
> That subtile wreath of haire, which crowns my arme;
> The mystery, the signe you must not touch,
>   For 'tis my outward Soule,
> Viceroy to that, which then to heaven being gone,
>   Will leave this to controule,
> And keepe these limbes, her Provinces, from dissolution.

Or, more violently, in "Twicknam garden" the tears and sighs of the traditional lover are converted into agony by a bitter play upon religious images:

> But O, selfe traytor, I do bring
> The spider love, which transubstantiates all,
>   And can convert Manna to gall,
> And that this place may thoroughly be thought
>   True Paradise, I have the serpent brought.

In his love-poems, then, the central wit consists in this: in taking up the religious motifs conventionally displayed in Petrarchan verse, and stressing them so heavily that any one of three results may be achieved. Sometimes the effect is one of witty blasphemy, as in "The Dreame," where he deifies his lady by attributing her arrival in his bedroom to her Godlike power of reading his mind.

Sometimes, as in "The Extasie," the poem maintains a complex tone in which the playful and the solemn, the profane and the sacred, are held in a perilous poise:

> As 'twixt two equall Armies, Fate
>   Suspends uncertaine victorie . . . .

And at other times human love is exalted to the religious level, notably in "A nocturnall upon S. Lucies day," where, in accordance with the ancient ecclesiastical usage of the term "nocturnal," or "nocturne," Donne presents a midnight service, a "Vigill," commemorating the death of his beloved—his saint. He recalls the passionate fluctuations of their worldly career, in terms that suggest a long period of frustrated spiritual devotion:

> Oft a flood
> Have wee two wept, and so
> Drownd the whole world, us two; oft did we grow
> To be two Chaosses, when we did show
> Care to ought else; and often absences
> Withdrew our soules, and made us carcasses.

But with her death his physical life has died, and he is "re-begot Of absence, darkenesse, death": in him love has "wrought new Alchimie" by expressing "A quintessence even from nothingnesse." His only life now lies in the spiritual realm where she now lives:

> You lovers, for whose sake, the lesser Sunne
>   At this time to the Goat is runne
>   To fetch new lust, and give it you,
>   Enjoy your summer all;
> Since shee enjoyes her long nights festivall,
> Let mee prepare towards her, and let mee call
> This houre her Vigill, and her Eve, since this
> Both the yeares, and the dayes deep midnight is.

Surely Mr. Murray is right in arguing that this poem deals with Donne's love for his wife;[3] its conclusion seems to point the way toward the opening lines of Holy Sonnet 17:

3. W. A. Murray, "Donne and Paracelsus: An Essay in Interpretation," *RES*, 25 (1949), 115–23. One must, I think, discard Grierson's hesitant sug-

Since she whom I lov'd hath payd her last debt
To Nature, and to hers, and my good is dead,
And her Soule early into heaven ravished,
Wholly on heavenly things my mind is sett.

It seems to me quite possible that Donne wrote the "Nocturnall" after his wife's death in 1617; though it might have been composed on some occasion of severe illness, such as one recorded in a letter by Donne (1606?), where he speaks of a certain "paper" written during a night of his wife's severe labor:

> It is (I cannot say the waightyest, but truly) the saddest lucubration and nights passage that ever I had. For it exercised those hours, which, with extreme danger to her, whom I should hardly have abstained from recompensing for her company in this world, with accompanying her out of it, encreased my poor family with a son. Though her anguish, and my fears, and hopes, seem divers and wild distractions from this small businesse of your papers, yet because they all narrowed themselves, and met in *Via regia*, which is the consideration of our selves, and God, I thought it time not unfit for this despatch.[4]

In any case, the "Nocturnall" vividly illustrates the way in which Donne's poetry, throughout his career, moves along a Great Divide between the sacred and the profane, now facing one way, now another, but always remaining intensely aware of both sides. In his

gestion (*Poems of Donne*, 2, xxii, 10) that the poem may have been addressed to Lucy, Countess of Bedford; for the imagery of the "Saint Lucies night," which occurs also in the *Second Anniversary* (line 120), provides its own metaphorical occasion (St. Lucy's Day, Dec. 13, "being the shortest day," according to the old calendar). See the interesting discussion of this problem by J. B. Leishman, *The Monarch of Wit* (London, Hutchinson's University Library, 1951), pp. 170–3. Leishman tends to feel that the "Nocturnall" deals with Donne's wife, but finds it hard to believe that Donne wrote the poem "after the actual death of his wife in 1617, when he had been two years in orders." But if the poem is fundamentally religious, the difficulty seems to lessen.

4. Donne, *Letters*, pp. 126–7; cf. Edmund Gosse, *The Life and Letters of John Donne* (2 vols., London, Heinemann, 1899), *1*, 154. Gosse says the letter "seems to refer to the birth of Francis Donne, baptized at Mitcham on the 8th of January 1607."

love-poetry the religious aspects are frequently so strong that they seem to overwhelm the fainter religious themes of Petrarchan poetry; while in six of the "Holy Sonnets" (3, 13, 14, 17, 18, 19) the memories and images of profane love are deliberately used in love-sonnets of sacred parody. One must observe, then, the greatest possible caution in considering the relation between the "profane" and the "religious" in Donne's work: individual poems will not fall easily into such categories; nor can the poems be safely dated by assumptions about the more religious, and the less religious, periods of his life.

2

Donne may well have written some of his love-songs and some of his "Holy Sonnets" during the same periods of his life: one of the most dubious assumptions in modern studies of Donne has been the universal acceptance of Gosse's dating of all the "Holy Sonnets" in 1617 or after, simply because one of the sonnets refers to the death of Donne's wife.[1] Grierson accepted this dating, and thereby gave it currency, along with the view that Donne's religious poems "fall into two groups": those written before his ordination, which are marked by a more intellectual style, and those written after his ordination and after the death of his wife, which are of a more passionate quality. But such distinctions are at best hazardous with a personality so paradoxical as Donne's; moreover, as I have suggested in the case of "La Corona," differences in style may also be explained by differences in the meditative traditions which Donne is following in certain poems. Grierson's examination of the manuscripts does not support the above dating of the "Holy Sonnets." He points out, for example, that in the Harleian manuscript they bear the heading: "Holy Sonnets: written 20 yeares since." After this general heading the manuscript then

1. Gosse, 2, 106. This assumption has now been effectively questioned by Miss Helen Gardner, in her recent edition of the *Divine Poems*. Her discussion of the dating of the "Holy Sonnets" (pp. xxxvii–l) seems to me absolutely convincing. She dates six of the sonnets between February and August, 1609, and most of the others shortly after; her printing of the sonnets in groups of twelve, four, and three is surely the right way to present them.

gives, under the special heading "La Corona," the seven sonnets properly belonging to that sequence. "Thereafter follow," Grierson adds, "without any fresh heading, twelve of the sonnets belonging to the second group, generally entitled *Holy Sonnets*." Noting that the date 1629 is given to other poems in this manuscript, Grierson remarks that this would bring us back to the year 1609, a dating which he is inclined to accept for "La Corona." But, as Grierson says, "the question is, did the copyist [of this manuscript] intend that the note should apply to all the sonnets he transcribed or only to the *La Corona* group?" Having already accepted Gosse's dating, he is forced to rule out the second group; yet the sonnet on Donne's wife is not among these twelve, and indeed the fact that only twelve of the sonnets occur here may suggest that the nineteen "Holy Sonnets" were not necessarily all written in the same period, as Gosse assumes. Grierson himself notes that he "cannot find a definite significance in any order," and that "each sonnet is a separate meditation"; this would seem to destroy the basis for Gosse's dating.[2]

Furthermore, it is a curious fact that Donne's "Elegie on Mistris Boulstred," who died on August 4, 1609,[3] seems unquestionably to represent a recantation of his famous sonnet:

> Death be not proud, though some have called thee
> Mighty and dreadfull, for, thou art not soe,
> For, those, whom thou think'st, thou dost overthrow,
> Die not, poore death, nor yet canst thou kill mee.

The opening lines of the elegy seem explicitly to answer this opening of the sonnet:

2. *Poems of Donne*, ed. Grierson, *2*, 225–9, 231; and the textual notes for the sonnets, *1*, 317–31. Miss Helen Gardner has called my attention to the fact that Grierson's description of the appearance of the "La Corona" sonnets in the Harleian manuscript is not quite accurate. He says (*2*, 227) that the general heading "is followed at once by 'Deign at my hands,' and then the title *La Corona* is given to the six sonnets which ensue." But all seven sonnets appear under this title, as I have since observed.

3. *Idem*, *2*, 212. Miss Gardner (*Divine Poems*, pp. xlvii–xlviii) also discusses the significance of this recantation; she points out that E. K. Chambers, in his pioneer edition of Donne's poems (1896), had observed the relationship between this Elegy and Holy Sonnet 10 and suggested the priority of the sonnet.

> Death I recant, and say, unsaid by mee
>> What ere hath slip'd, that might diminish thee.
> Spirituall treason, atheisme 'tis, to say,
>> That any can thy Summons disobey.

Lines 9–10 appear to reinterpret lines 7–8 of the sonnet:

>> And soonest our best men with thee doe goe,
>> Rest of their bones, and soules deliverie.

>> Now hee will seeme to spare, and doth more wast,
>> Eating the best first, well preserv'd to last.

And indeed all the first half of the elegy (1–34) amounts to a denial of the sonnet's ending, "death, thou shalt die." We have the parenthesis, "were Death dead" (15); and the exclamations, "O strong and long-liv'd death" (21), "How could I thinke thee nothing" (25), "O mighty bird of prey" (31). The conclusion seems inevitable that Holy Sonnet 10 must have been written before August 4, 1609. If this is so, could it not also be true of other "Holy Sonnets"?

The conjecture is supported by the evidence of Donne's painful letters from Mitcham, where he frequently speaks of his "meditation," [4] and by Grierson's dating of "La Corona" (1607–9), "The Annuntiation and Passion" (March 25, 1608), and "The Litanie" (1609–10).[5] Everything that we know of Donne indicates that, during the years from his marriage in 1601 down through the time

---

4. See Gosse, *1*, 174, 190, 195.

5. *Poems of Donne*, ed. Grierson, *2*, 225–9, 238–9; Rhodes Dunlap [*Modern Language Notes*, *63* (1948), 258–9] has shown that the occasion of the second of these poems must be March 25, 1608, the first day of the year, old style. To all such evidence of Donne's meditation during this period we should add the verse-letter to Rowland Woodward cited in Chap. 3 above, for Grierson (*Poems of Donne*, *2*, 146–8) conjectures that this was written between 1602–8. Donne's advice here with regard to "Blowing our sparkes of vertue" reminds one of similar references to Donne's exercises in self-analysis that occur in a letter printed by Evelyn Simpson in *A Study of the Prose Works of John Donne* (2d ed., Oxford, Clarendon Press, 1948), pp. 313–14; the letter seems to date from sometime around 1600. For the importance of such introspection in Donne's middle years see George Reuben Potter, "John Donne's Discovery of Himself," *University of California Publications in English*, *4* (1934), 3–23.

of his ordination in 1615, he was engaging in the most fervent and painful self-analysis, directed toward the problem of his vocation. The crisis and culmination of these efforts, I believe, is represented in the two *Anniversaries*, both of which, surprisingly enough, may have been written in the year 1611. (See Appendix 2.) Thus they seem to come immediately before the first clear announcement by Donne, in his letter of c. 1612, that he has decided to enter the ministry: "having obeyed at last, after much debatement within me, the Inspirations (as I hope) of the Spirit of God, and resolved to make my Profession Divinitie . . . ." [6] The relationship of the *Anniversaries* to these "debatements" is reinforced by the very close verbal and thematic similarities, pointed out by Mrs. Simpson, between these poems and Donne's *Essayes in Divinity:* those "Several Disquisitions, Interwoven with Meditations and Prayers," which "were the voluntary sacrifices of severall hours, when he had many debates betwixt God and himself, whether he were worthy, and competently learned to enter into Holy Orders." [7]

The *Anniversaries*, along with his other meditations of this period —including, perhaps, many of the "Holy Sonnets"—may be seen as part of the spiritual exercises which Donne was performing in the effort to determine his problem of "election": the term which St. Ignatius Loyola gave to that crucial portion of his *Exercises* of the Second Week (pp. 54–60), where the exercitant is faced with the problem of deciding upon a way of life, "as for example an office or benefice to be accepted or left." One of the problems here described by the *Exercises* is one that, according to Walton, troubled Donne when Morton in the year 1607 urged Donne to accept an office in the Church: "there are others that first desire to possess benefices and then to serve God in them. So these do not go straight to God, but wish God to come straight to their inordinate affections; thus they make of the end a means, and of the means an end; so that what they ought to take first they take last." [8] Among

6. Gosse, *2*, 20; Simpson, *Prose Works*, p. 29.

7. John Donne, *Essayes in Divinity*, London, 1651: title-page and note "To the Reader." See the excellent edition of this work by Evelyn Simpson (Oxford, Clarendon Press, 1952), pp. xiii–xvii; and Simpson, *Prose Works*, pp. 207–11.

8. Cf. Walton, *Lives*, p. 34: " 'And besides, whereas it is determined by the

the Jesuit methods for "making a sound and good election" in such matters, it is interesting—with the "Holy Sonnets" in mind—to notice that meditations on the love of God, on death ("as if I were at the point of death"), and on the Day of Judgment are especially recommended, along with another method that may have some relation to the poem which Donne later wrote "To Mr Tilman after he had taken orders": "The second rule is to place before my eyes a man whom I have never seen or known, and to consider what I, desiring all perfection for him, would tell him to do and choose for the greater glory of God our Lord, and the greater perfection of his soul; and acting so, to keep the rule which I lay down for another." For these methods of "election" might be used to confirm a decision made, as well as to make the original decision. Finally, it is worth noting that among the various "methods of prayer" recommended in the *Spiritual Exercises*, there is one that is similar to the method followed by Donne in "The Litanie": it consists "in considering the signification of each word" in a public, liturgical prayer, and in dwelling "on the consideration of this word, so long as he finds meanings, comparisons, relish, and consolation in thoughts about this word." (p. 80)

The *Anniversaries*, then, were composed during a period when Donne appears to have been utilizing all the modes of meditation and self-analysis that he knew, in the effort to make the crucial decision of his life. It was a period when his weighing of the sacred and profane tendencies within himself must have reached a climax of intensity; and this, I believe, is why the two poems represent Donne's most elaborate examples of the art of sacred parody and his most extensive efforts in the art of poetical meditation.

Yet the *Anniversaries* are not usually treated as whole poems. For one thing, the biographical facts underlying these poems lead readers to approach them with suspicion, since they were written in

----

best of *Casuists*, that *Gods Glory should be the first end, and a maintenance the second motive to embrace that calling;* and though each man may propose to himself both together; yet the first may not be put last without a violation of Conscience, which he that searches the heart will judge. And truly my present condition is such, that if I ask my own Conscience, whether it be reconcileable to that rule, it is at this time so perplexed about it, that I can neither give my self nor you an answer.' " See Gosse, *1*, 157–62.

memory of the daughter of Donne's generous patron, Sir Robert Drury—a girl who died in her fifteenth year, and whom Donne admits he never saw.[9] As a result, the elaborate eulogies of Elizabeth Drury are frequently dismissed as venal and insincere, while interest in the poems centers on those passages which reflect Donne's awareness of the "new philosophy," on explicitly religious portions, or on any portions which provide illustrative quotations for special studies of Donne and his period.

Such fragmentary appreciation of the poems has, I think, hampered an understanding of their full significance. For each poem is carefully designed as a whole, and the full meaning of each grows out of a deliberately articulated structure. Furthermore, a close reading of each poem shows that the two *Anniversaries* are significantly different in structure and in the handling of Petrarchan imagery, and are consequently different in value. The *First Anniversary*, despite its careful structure, is, it must be admitted, successful only in brilliant patches; but I think it can be shown that the *Second Anniversary*, despite some flaws, is as a whole one of the great religious poems of the seventeenth century.

3

Let us look at the structure of the *First Anniversary: An Anatomie of the World. Wherein, By occasion of the untimely death of Mistris Elizabeth Drury, the frailty and the decay of this whole World is represented*. The poem is divided into an Introduction, a Conclusion, and five distinct sections which form the body of the work. Each of these five sections is subdivided into three sections: first, a meditation on some aspect of "the frailty and the decay of this whole world"; second, a eulogy of Elizabeth Drury as the "Idea" of human perfection and the source of hope, now lost, for the world; third, a refrain introducing a moral:

> Shee, shee is dead; shee's dead: when thou knowest this,
> Thou knowest how poore a trifling thing man is.
> And learn'st thus much by our Anatomie . . . .

9. Donne, *Letters*, p. 219. For the interpretations of the *Anniversaries* recently advanced by Majorie Nicolson and Marius Bewley, see my Appendix 2.

In each section the second line of this refrain is modified so as to summarize the theme of the whole section; in the following outline of the poem I use part of the second line of each refrain as the heading for each section:

Introduction, 1–90. The world is sick, "yea, dead, yea putrified," since she, its "intrinsique balme" and "preserva-tive," its prime example of Virtue, is dead.

Section I, 91–190: "how poore a trifling thing man is."
 1. Meditation, 91–170. Because of Original Sin man has decayed in length of life, in physical size, in mental capacity.
 2. Eulogy, 171–82. The girl was perfect virtue; she purified her-self and had a purifying power over all.
 3. Refrain and Moral, 183–90. Our only hope is in religion.

Section II, 191–246: "how lame a cripple this world is."
 1. Meditation, 191–218. The "universall frame" has received in-jury from the sin of the Angels, and now in universe, in state, in family, " 'Tis all in peeces, all cohaerence gone."
 2. Eulogy, 219–36. Only this girl possessed the power which might have unified the world.
 3. Refrain and Moral, 237–46. Contemn and avoid this sick world.

Section III, 247–338: "how ugly a monster this world is."
 1. Meditation, 247–304. Proportion, the prime ingredient of beauty, no longer exists in the universe.
 2. Eulogy, 305–24. The girl was the "measure of all Symmetrie" and harmony.
 3. Refrain and Moral, 325–38. Human acts must be "done fitly and in proportion."

Section IV, 339–76: "how wan a Ghost this our world is."
 1. Meditation, 339–58. "Beauties other second Element, Colour, and lustre now, is as neere spent."
 2. Eulogy, 359–68. The girl had the perfection of color and gave color to the world.
 3. Refrain and Moral, 369–76. There is no pleasure in an ugly world; it is wicked to use false colors.

Section V, 377–434: "how drie a Cinder this world is."
1. Meditation, 377–98. Physical "influence" of the heavens upon the earth has been weakened.
2. Eulogy, 399–426. The girl's virtue has little effect on us now because of this weakened "correspondence" between heavens and earth; in fact the world's corruption weakened her effect while she lived.
3. Refrain and Moral, 427–34. Nothing "Is worth our travaile, griefe, or perishing," except the joys of religious virtue.

Conclusion, 435–74.

It seems clear that the religious motifs in Petrarchan lament, found at their best in Petrarch's poems "To Laura in Death," have here combined with strictly religious meditation to produce a poem which derives its form, fundamentally, from the tradition of spiritual exercises. The Jesuit exercises, we recall, normally involve a series of five exercises daily for a period of about a month, each meditation being precisely divided into points, usually into three points.

At the same time it is important to recall the ways of celebrating the Ideal Woman—the "Type, or an Idaea of an Accomplisht piety" [1]—represented in the meditations of the rosary which have been discussed in Chapter 2. The divisions of the Dominican rosary fall into three series of five meditations each, while, in Loarte's *Instructions*, every meditation "is distinguished into three pointes." (f.6v.) Meditation on only five of these mysteries at a time was quite common: the name "rosary," says Worthington, is "used sometimes largely, and sometimes strictly"; "largely" it contains fifteen mysteries; "strictly" it contains five, "as it is commonly ment, when one is appointed for penance, or for pardon, or for other like cause to say a Rosarie." (preface) Thus the number five becomes associated with the celebration of the Virgin: the five-petaled Rose becomes her flower. [2] This, evidently, is what lies be-

1. Stafford, p. 219; see above, Chap. 2, sec. 5.
2. See also the use of the number five in Ben Jonson's "Ghyrlond of the blessed Virgin Marie": "Here, are five letters in this blessed Name, Which, chang'd, a five-fold mysterie designe . . . ." (*Ben Jonson*, ed. C. H.

hind Donne's treatment of the five-petaled flower in his poem, "The Primrose":

> Live Primrose then, and thrive
> With thy true number five;
> And women, whom this flower doth represent,
> With this mysterious number be content . . . .

With this symbolic number in mind, it is even more suggestive to consider the Jesuit Puente's directions for using the rosary to meditate upon the virtues of Mary. "The principall thing wherein wee are to manifest our devotion, towards the Virgin," says Puente, is "the imitation of her heroicall virtues, wherunto it will greatly ayd, to meditate them in the recitall of the Rosarie, in every tenne Ave Maries, one virtue." And in doing this, we are to follow a threefold procedure: "fixing the eyes and intention upon three things."

> 1. Upon the heroicall acts which the Virgin exercised about that virtue . . . admiring her sanctitie, reioycing therin, glorifying God, who gave it unto her, and exulting for the reward which he hath given for such a virtu. 2. To fixe mine eyes upon the wante which I have of that virtu, and upon the contrary faults and defects wherinto I fall, sorrowing for them with great confusion and humiliation . . . . 3. To make some stedfast purposes, with the greatest stabilitie that I can, to imitate the B. Virgin in these acts of virtue, assigning to this effect some particular virtue, trusting in the favor of this pious Mother, that shee will assist me to performe the same. (2, 587)

Such a threefold division of meditation, within a larger fivefold structure, has a long tradition, as Wilmart has shown by his publication of the meditations of Stephen of Salley, an English Cistercian of the early thirteenth century.[3] Stephen gives fifteen meditations on the Joys of the Virgin, divided into three series of fives; the most interesting aspect of them here is the subdivision of each meditation

---

Herford, Percy and Evelyn Simpson [11 vols., Oxford, Clarendon Press, 1925–52], 8, 412). The poem was first published in Stafford's *Femall Glory*.

3. A. Wilmart, *Auteurs Spirituels et Textes Dévots du Moyen Age Latin*, (Paris, 1932), pp. 317–60.

The five-petaled Rose of Mary, from the *Rosario della gloriosa vergine Maria* of Alberto Castello, Venice, 1564

(*Pierpont Morgan Library*)

into three parts: (1) *Meditatio*, on the mystery itself; (2) *Gaudium*, a summary of the "Joy"; (3) *Peticio*, prayer to the Virgin invoking her assistance in the achievement of Christian perfection—the whole meditation ending with the refrain of an Ave Maria.

Meditation on the Virgin might easily influence Petrarchan eulogy; in fact Petrarch himself suggests such an influence by concluding his sequence to Laura with a *canzone* to the Virgin Mary. His previous treatment of Laura is different only in degree, not in kind. Thus in a poem describing what Donne calls "the Idea of a Woman," some connotations of Mary would appear to be almost inevitable for a poet of Donne's background. At any rate, in Donne's Introduction to his *Anatomie*, along with Petrarchan hyperbole, we find Elizabeth Drury treated in terms which seem to adumbrate the practice of meditating on Mary: she is a "Queene" ascended to Heaven, attended by Saints; her Name has a mysterious power: [4]

Her name defin'd thee [the world], gave thee forme, and frame,
And thou forgett'st to celebrate thy name.

She is "A strong example gone, equall to law," she was "The Cyment which did faithfully compact, And glue all vertues." Nothing remains for us, in this dying world, but to arouse our souls to imitate her; such memory of her

> Creates a new world, and new creatures bee
> Produc'd: the matter and the stuffe of this,
> Her vertue, and the forme our practice is.

Yet we cannot sustain ourselves in this new "dignitie" without some defense against the assaults of the world upon us, and against that presumption which destroys the self-righteous:

> Yet, because outward stormes the strongest breake,
> And strength it selfe by confidence growes weake,
> This new world may be safer, being told
> The dangers and diseases of the old:
> For with due temper men doe then forgoe,
> Or covet things, when they their true worth know.

4. For devotion to the Name of Mary see Puente, *1*, 263–4.

The twofold aim of religious meditation is suggested in the last two lines. Meditation on the sinfulness of the "old man" and on the corruption of the world will teach men to "forgoe" the things of this world; and, conversely, meditation on the Example of Virtue will lead men to "covet" the imitation of the perfect soul.

In this twofold purpose of meditation lies another aspect of spiritual exercises which deserves consideration: the practice of dividing meditations into two sequences according to the seven days of the week, with two kinds of meditation each day.[5] Thus, in general, the exercitant alternates meditation leading to contempt of the world and of self with consolatory and uplifting meditation on Christ. As Juan de Ávila explains,

> They who are much exercised in the *knowledge* of themselves, (in respect that they are continually viewing their defects so neer at hand) are wont to fall into great sadnes, and disconfidence, and pusillanimity; for which reason, it is necessary that they do exercise themselves also in another *knowledge*, which giveth comfort, and strength, much more then the other gave discouragement . . . .
>
> It is therefore fit for thee, after the exercise of the *knowledge of thy selfe* to imploy thy mind, upon the *knowledge of Christ Iesus our Lord.*[6]

This widespread use of contrasting meditations is also given thorough development in an English work contemporary with the *Anniversaries:* Nicholas Breton's *Divine Considerations of the Soule* (1608). Breton gives two series of seven meditations, one on "the excellencie of God," the other on "the vilenesse of man," to be used in this manner:

> Looke then upon the greatnes of God and the smalnesse of man; the goodnes of God, and the vilenesse of man; the wisdome of God, and the folly of man; the love of God, and the hate of man; the grace of God, and the disgrace of man; the mercy of God, and the tyranny of man; and the glory of God,

5. See above, Chap. 1, sec. 1.
6. Juan de Ávila, *Audi Filia* ([St. Omer], 1620), pp. 336–8; the translation is attributed to Donne's friend, Sir Tobie Matthew.

and the infamy of man: and fixing the eye of the heart upon
the one and the other, how canst thou but to the glory of God,
and shame of thy selfe . . . cry with the Prophet David, *Oh
Lord what is man that thou doest visit him?* [7]

Donne's *Anatomie* seems clearly to fall into such a mold, with its
alternation of contempt (Meditation) and glorification (Eulogy);
Donne's Moral merely serves to draw a brief conclusion from this
contrast.

These examples are, I hope, sufficient to suggest the various and
flexible relationships that exist between Donne's *Anatomie* and the
tradition of methodical meditation. In particular, his fivefold sequence and his alternation of contempt and praise within each section mark the poem as a spiritual exercise. But the ultimate question
remains and has no doubt already been suggested by the above
parallels: is it valid to write in such a tradition when the pattern of
virtue is, literally taken, only a girl? Certainly the chief problem in
evaluating the poem has been very shrewdly put in the blunt ob-
jection of Ben Jonson: "That Donne's Anniversary was profane
and full of blasphemies; that he told Mr. Donne, if it had been written of the Virgin Mary it had been something; to which he answered that he described the Idea of a Woman and not as she
was." [8]

4

When does laudation of an Ideal Woman become thus objectionable in poetry with a strong religious note? It has not been generally considered so in Dante and Petrarch. Is it objectionable in
Donne? An answer, so far as this poem is concerned, may be suggested by noting Petrarch's general treatment of Laura in Death.
Petrarch has successfully combined eulogy with religious themes
by keeping his sequence always focused on his central symbol of
perfection: the *contemptus mundi*, the hyperbole of the world's
destruction, the praise of Laura in Heaven, are all justified by main-

7. Nicholas Breton, *Works*, ed. A. B. Grosart (2 vols., Edinburgh, 1879),
2, 23.

8. "Conversations with Drummond," *Ben Jonson*, ed. Herford and Simpson, *1*, 133 (modernized).

taining Laura as the origin and end of the poems' emotions, and thus making her the First Cause of the sequence.

> The chosen angels, and the spirits blest,
> Celestial tenants, on that glorious day
> My Lady join'd them, throng'd in bright array
> Around her, with amaze and awe imprest.
> "What splendour, what new beauty stands confest
> Unto our sight?"—among themselves they say;
> "No soul, in this vile age, from sinful clay
> To our high realms has risen so fair a guest."
> Delighted to have changed her mortal state,
> She ranks amid the purest of her kind;
> And ever and anon she looks behind,
> To mark my progress and my coming wait;
> Now my whole thought, my wish to heaven I cast;
> 'Tis Laura's voice I hear, and hence she bids me haste.[1]

Donne's *Anatomie* has no such focus: it has instead a central inconsistency which defeats all Donne's efforts to bring its diverse materials under control. For it is not correct to say, as Empson says, that "the complete decay of the universe" is presented as having been caused by the death of Elizabeth Drury. If this were so, the poem might achieve unity through supporting a dominant symbol of virtue's power, and one might be able to agree with Empson that the "only way to make the poem sensible is to accept Elizabeth Drury as the Logos." [2] But, after the Introduction has elaborately presented this hyperbole, one discovers in the first Meditation that Elizabeth Drury has, basically, nothing to do with the sense of decay in the poem. The whole first Meditation is strictly in the religi-

1. *Rime* 346 in the translation by John Nott: *The Sonnets, Triumphs and other poems of Petrarch*, trans. "various hands," London, G. Bell and Sons, 1907 (there printed as Sonnet 75 of the sequence "To Laura in Death"). For Petrarch's use of the hyperbole of the world's destruction see *Rime* 268, 326, 338, 352; by Donne's time this had evidently become a convention of compliment, as in Donne's love-poem, "A Feaver," and in a sonnet by Sannazaro pointed out by Mario Praz: see *A Garland for John Donne*, ed. Theodore Spencer (Cambridge, Harvard University Press, 1931), pp. 66–9.

2. William Empson, *English Pastoral Poetry* (New York, W. W. Norton, 1938), p. 84.

ous tradition; it meditates the decline of man through sin from God's
original creation:

> There is no health; Physitians say that wee,
> At best, enjoy but a neutralitie.
> And can there bee worse sicknesse, then to know
> That we are never well, nor can be so?
> Wee are borne ruinous . . . .
> For that first marriage was our funerall:
> One woman at one blow, then kill'd us all . . . .
>
> (91–106)

The meditation opens with an echo of the general confession in the
Book of Common Prayer—"there is no health in us"—a theme developed by St. Bernard and countless others:

> Engendered in sin, we engender sinners; born debtors, we give
> birth to debtors; corrupted, to the corrupt . . . . We are
> crippled souls from the moment when we enter into this world,
> and as long as we live there, and we shall still be so when we
> leave it; from the sole of our foot to the crown of our head there
> is no health in us.[3]

Continuing with a descant on traditional conceptions of the decay
of man from his first grandeur,[4] the meditation comes to a full climactic close as (in St. Bernard's terminology) the indestructible
Image of God within man makes its traditional judgment of the
ruined Likeness:

> Thus man, this worlds Vice-Emperour, in whom
> All faculties, all graces are at home . . .
> This man, so great, that all that is, is his,
> Oh what a trifle, and poore thing he is! (161–70)

3. St. Bernard, *Sermones de Diversis*, 42. 2; *Patrologiae cursus completus
. . . Series [latina]*, ed. Jacques Paul Migne (221 vols., Paris, 1844–65), *183*,
662. I quote the translation by Downes in Gilson's study of St. Bernard, p.
46 (see below, sec. 5, n. 2).

4. See St. Cyprian, *Liber ad Demetrianum*, secs. 3, 4; *Patrologiae cursus
completus*, 4, 564–7. One finds here the germ of many of Donne's comments on the world's decay throughout the *Anatomie*.

The first Meditation thus forms a unit in itself; it strikes one as having no fundamental relation to the preceding account of the destruction of the world by the girl's death.

Then, clumsily and evasively, the poem comes back to the girl and to the Petrarchan hyperbole of the world's death:

> If man were any thing, he's nothing now:
> Helpe, or at least some time to wast, allow
> T'his other wants, yet when he did depart
> With her whom we lament, hee lost his heart.
> (171–4)

The Eulogy is being tacked on; and soon the difficulty of including this hyperbole in the poem becomes embarrassingly obvious:

> shee that could drive
> The poysonous tincture, and the staine of *Eve*,
> Out of her thoughts, and deeds; and purifie
> All, by a true religious Alchymie;
> Shee, shee is dead; shee's dead: when thou knowest this,
> Thou knowest how poore a trifling thing man is.
> (179–84)

But we have known it before, and not for these reasons; thus the section comes to a flat and forced conclusion. We pause, and begin the second section almost as if the Eulogy and Moral had never intervened:

> Then, as mankinde, so is the worlds whole frame
> Quite out of Joynt, almost created lame:
> For, before God had made up all the rest,
> Corruption entred, and deprav'd the best:
> It seis'd the Angels, and then first of all
> The world did in her cradle take a fall . . . .
> (191–6)

This second Meditation includes the famous passage beginning "And new Philosophy calls all in doubt," where Donne sardonically turns the optimism of the scientists into proof of pessimism:

> And freely men confesse that this world's spent,
> When in the Planets, and the Firmament
> They seeke so many new; they see that this
> Is crumbled out againe to his Atomies. (209–12)

But this is not related to "the untimely death of Mistris Elizabeth Drury." The passage on the new philosophy is an integral part of a meditation on the effects of sin; the effects of the new philosophy represent the final stages in a long and universal sequence of decay.

The second Eulogy reveals an even further split in the poem. Instead of pursuing the explicitly religious imagery of the first Eulogy, Donne here attempts to secularize the compliments, at the same time using images traditionally associated with Mary: [5]

> She whom wise nature had invented then
> When she observ'd that every sort of men
> Did in their voyage in this worlds Sea stray,
> And needed a new compasse for their way;
> She that was best, and first originall
> Of all faire copies, and the generall
> Steward to Fate; she whose rich eyes, and brest
> Guilt the West Indies, and perfum'd the East . . . .
>
> (223–30)

The traditional religious feelings which have thus far been growing in the poem are here balked, particularly by the references to "wise nature" and "Fate." The poem has broken apart, and the break is not mended by the blurred imagery one finds in the following Moral and in the transition to Section III (lines 237–50). Here Donne presents the imagery of "this worlds generall sickenesse" with an imprecise and damaging ambiguity. What is the "feaver," the "consuming wound?" Is it that conventional one

5. Cf. Southwell's poem on the Virgin's Nativity: "Load-starre of all inclosed in worldly waves,/The car[d] and compasse that from ship-wracke saves." The imagery is based, of course, on the "Ave maris stella" and the interpretation of the name Mary as meaning "Star of the Sea": cf. Puente, *1*, 263: "Shee is the Starre of the sea, for that shee is the light, consolation, and guide of those, that sayle in the sea of this worlde, tossed with the greate waves, and tempestes of temptations . . . ." Cf. also Southwell's poem on the death of the Virgin, cited earlier, Chap. 2, sec. 6.

described in the Introduction as the result of the girl's death? Or is it the infection of Original Sin? The vague and general imagery tries to include both elements, but it will not do. The last words of the transition—"ages darts"—tell us clearly that the third and fourth Meditations, on loss of proportion and color, deal with the results of sin, not with emotions related to the poem's alleged protagonist.

The remaining Eulogies and the Conclusion try desperately to maintain something of the introductory hyperbole, but it cannot be done. The poem does not justify the elaborate imagery with which Donne attempts to transmute the girl into a symbol of virtue's power. The imagery seems extravagant—even blasphemous—not because of what we know about the circumstances of the poem's composition, but because the imagery is not supported by the poem as a whole.

The very fact that the poem is rigidly divided into sections and subsections gives us another aspect of its failure. Nearly all the joints between sections and subsections are marked by strong pauses or by clumsy transitions; while the Morals are strained in an attempt to bring Meditation and Eulogy into some sort of unity. The parts will not fuse into an imaginative organism. One can omit all the rest of the poem and simply read through the Meditations consecutively; the sequence is consistent and, with a brief conclusion, would form a complete—and a rather good—poem.

We should not leave the *Anatomie* without noticing in some detail the richness with which Donne develops these strictly religious aspects of the work. Let us look for a moment at the third Meditation, as complex a passage as Donne ever wrote. It works by a fusion of two main ideas. Astronomical observations seem to prove that the universe is decaying as a result of sin, for it seems to have lost its spherical, circular nature, the sign of immutable perfection. At the same time the passage mocks the vanity and presumption of man in attempting to understand and control God's mysterious universe. The irony of such attempts is that they only reveal—in two ways—the corruption of all things. Nevertheless man persists in the intellectual, Abelardian effort to comprehend the unknowable or inessential, persists in the *curiositas* which St. Bernard denounced as the father of pride.

Donne begins (251 ff.):

> We thinke the heavens enjoy their Sphericall,
> Their round proportion embracing all.
> But yet their various and perplexed course,
> Observ'd in divers ages, doth enforce
> Men to finde out so many Eccentrique parts,
> Such divers downe-right lines, such overthwarts,
> As disproportion that pure forme:

"Perplexed" is the central word here. The course of the heavenly bodies is so involved, so tangled, that man cannot follow it and is "enforced" to discover, or to invent ("finde out"),[6] a fantastically complicated scheme of the universe which serves to "disproportion that pure forme," but never surely hits the truth of things. We may also take "perplexed" in another sense: the heavenly bodies themselves seemed to be confused about their course.

> It teares
> The Firmament in eight and forty sheires,
> And in these Constellations then arise
> New starres, and old doe vanish from our eyes:
> As though heav'n suffered earthquakes, peace or war,
> When new Towers rise, and old demolish't are.

"It," grammatically, seems to refer to the heavens' "perplexed course." But in this context "It" may also refer by implication to the science of Astronomy which invented the forty-eight constellations; thus, when man's "knowledge" has settled things by violence ("teares"), erratic heaven refuses to conform. Nevertheless, presumptuous men

> have impal'd within a Zodiake
> The free-borne Sun, and keepe twelve Signes awake
> To watch his steps; the Goat and Crab controule,
> And fright him backe, who else to either Pole
> (Did not these Tropiques fetter him) might runne:

6. See *OED*, "find," *v.*, 2, 15; 4, 20. Charles Monroe Coffin gives an interesting discussion of this whole Meditation in a different context: *John Donne and the New Philosophy* (New York, Columbia University Press, 1937), pp. 181-2.

The Goat and Crab are ugly symbols of sensuality, and will the Sun obey such commanders? Apparently so; yet the Sun is full of guile that may deceive us:

> For his course is not round; nor can the Sunne
> Perfit a Circle, or maintaine his way
> One inch direct; but where he rose to-day
> He comes no more, but with a couzening line,
> Steales by that point, and so is Serpentine:
> And seeming weary with his reeling thus,
> He meanes to sleepe, being now falne nearer us.

The sun is degenerate, having fallen nearer to the sphere of corruption—serpentine in his winding and in his wiliness, and, like a drunken man, reeling toward a "lethargy" like that which has overtaken earth.

> So, of the Starres which boast that they doe runne
> In Circle still, none ends where he begun.
> All their proportion's lame, it sinkes, it swels.
> For of Meridians, and Parallels,
> Man hath weav'd out a net, and this net throwne
> Upon the Heavens, and now they are his owne.
> Loth to goe up the hill, or labour thus
> To goe to heaven, we make heaven come to us.
> We spur, we reine the starres, and in their race
> They're diversly content t'obey our pace.

Here the complex feelings of the Meditation reach a climax. All man's hubristic attempts have resulted only in a deceptive "mastery" of corruption. Man's claims to worldly power and knowledge mean only that he refuses to undergo the spiritual discipline necessary for his salvation.

The remainder of this third Meditation is not of such sustained power, and indeed goes to pieces in its last ten lines. A discussion of the earth's solidity interrupts the theme of proportion, and a shift to abstract morality at the close is too abrupt. The best of the poem is over.

5

The full title of Donne's *Second Anniversary* itself suggests the possibilities of a unity not achieved in the earlier poem: *Of the Progresse of the Soule. Wherein, By occasion of the Religious death of Mistris Elizabeth Drury, the incommodities of the Soule in this life, and her exaltation in the next, are contemplated.* Here, clearly, is an "occasion" to use Mistress Drury as a symbol naturally integrated with the traditional matter of religious meditation: a "Religious death" (not the "untimely death" of the *Anatomie's* title) is the ultimate aim in this life for all the devout. The poem's structure indicates that Donne is indeed moving throughout with the imaginative ease that marks the management of a truly unified conception.

The *Progresse* consists of an Introduction, only half as long as the Introduction to the preceding poem; a Conclusion, less than half as long; and seven sections which constitute the body of the work. These proportions, in a poem over fifty lines longer, indicate an important shift in emphasis. The Introduction and Conclusion to the *Anatomie,* with their emphasis on hyperbolic praise of the dead girl, make up a quarter of that poem; whereas these portions make up only about an eighth of the *Progresse.* Each section of the *Progresse* is subdivided in a manner reminiscent of the *Anatomie.* The first section contains (1) a Meditation on contempt of the world and one's self; (2) a Eulogy of the girl as the pattern of Virtue; (3) a Moral, introduced by lines which recall the refrain of the preceding poem:

> Shee, shee is gone; she is gone; when thou knowest this,
> What fragmentary rubbidge this world is
> Thou knowest, and that it is not worth a thought;
> He honors it too much that thinkes it nought.

But, as the following outline shows, the "refrain" does not appear hereafter, and of the remaining sections, only the second concludes with a distinct Moral; in the rest the moral is absorbed into the Eulogy:

Introduction, 1–44.
Section I, 45–84.
    1. Meditation, 45–64.
    2. Eulogy, 65–80.
    3. Refrain and Moral, 81–4.
Section II, 85–156.
    1. Meditation, 85–120.
    2. Eulogy, 121–46.
    3. Moral, 147–56.
Section III, 157–250.
    1. Meditation, 157–219.
    2. Eulogy, 220–50.
Section IV, 251–320.
    1. Meditation, 251–300.
    2. Eulogy, 301–20.
Section V, 321–82.
    1. Meditation, 321–55.
    2. Eulogy, 356–82.
Section VI, 383–470.
    1. Meditation, 383–446.
    2. Eulogy, 447–70.
Section VII, 471–510.
    1. Meditation, 471–96.
    2. Eulogy, 497–510.
Conclusion, 511–28.

This gradual modification of the strict mold which marked the sections of the *Anatomie* suggests a creative freedom that absorbs and transcends formal divisions. The first striking indication that this is true is found in the ease of the reader's movement from part to part. We are freed from the heavy pauses that marked the close of each section in the *Anatomie:* omission of the refrain and, above all, omission of the flat, prosy Morals, makes possible an easy transition from section to section; the only heavy pause occurs at the close of the long Moral in Section II. We are always aware that a new sequence is beginning: it is essential that we feel the form of the poem beneath us. But each new sequence, with the above ex-

ception, follows inevitably from the close of the preceding one, as
at the close of the first section, where the words of the very brief
Moral, "thought" and "thinkes," lead directly to the dominant command of the second Meditation: "Thinke then, my soule, that death
is but a Groome . . . Thinke thee laid on thy death-bed . . .
Thinke . . . Thinke . . ."; the traditional self-address of religious
meditation.

The transition within each section from Meditation to Eulogy is
even more fluent; we do not find here the sharp division of meaning
which marked these two elements in the *Anatomie*. In the previous
poem every Meditation was strictly a scourging of the world and
of man, every Eulogy the picture of a lost hope. But in the *Progresse* every Meditation, together with this scourging, includes
the hope of salvation which is imaged in the Eulogy, and in every
Meditation except the first, this hope, this upward look, is stressed
in the latter part of the Meditation, with the result that the reader is
carried easily into the realm where the symbol of perfect virtue
now lives.

In Sections III and V the distinction between Meditation and
Eulogy is even further modified, for the Meditation itself falls into
two contrasting parts. In Section III we have first (157–78) a meditation on the loathsomeness of the body, which "could, beyond escape
or helpe," infect the soul with Original Sin. But Donne does not
dwell long on this; he lifts his eyes from these "ordures" to meditate,
in a passage twice as long (179–219), his soul's flight to heaven after
death—a flight that leads directly to the Eulogy. Likewise, in
Section V, after meditating the corrupt company kept on earth
(321–38), Donne lifts his eyes to meditate (339–55) the soul's
"conversation" with the inhabitants of Heaven—a theme which
leads naturally into the Eulogy of Heaven's new inhabitant.

Fundamentally, the union of Meditation with Eulogy is due to
a difference in Donne's treatment of the Eulogies in this poem. Here
he has avoided a clash between eulogy and religious meditation by
giving up, except in the brief Introduction and first Eulogy, the
Petrarchan hyperbole which in parts of the *Anatomie* attributed
the decay of the world to the girl's death. This hyperbole, together
with the single reminder of the refrain, appears to be brought in at
the beginning of the *Progresse* to link this poem with its predecessor,

in line with Donne's original plan of writing a poem in the girl's memory every year for an indefinite period. The labored Introduction to the *Progresse* is certainly a blemish on the poem; yet it may be said that the reminiscences of the *Anatomie* are functional: they suggest that the negative "anatomizing" of the other poem may be taken as a preparation for the positive spiritual progress to be imaged in the second poem. At any rate, Donne does not use this hyperbole in the six later Eulogies, nor in the brief Conclusion, of the second poem. Instead, he consistently attempts to transmute the girl into a symbol of virtue that may fitly represent the Image and Likeness of God in man, recognition of which is, according to St. Bernard, the chief end and aim of religious meditation.

Thus Juan de Avila's *Audi Filia* begins its section on self-knowledge with a chapter (57) summarizing the command to "know thyself" which St. Bernard found in the famous verse of his beloved *Canticle:* "Si ignoras te, O pulchra inter mulieres, egredere, et abi post greges sodalium tuorum . . . ." [1] If the soul, the intended Bride, does not know herself—that is, does not know whence she comes, where she is, and whither she is going—she will live forever in the "Land of Unlikeness," that land of sin and disorder in which man forgets that he was made in God's Image and Likeness, and thus lives in a state of exile where the Image is defaced and the Likeness lost. As Gilson explains, "Man is made to the image of God in his free-will, and he will never lose it; he was made to the likeness of God in respect of certain virtues, enabling him to choose well, and to do the good thing chosen; now these he has lost" by sin. But the central fact is that the Image—free will—is indestructible; and hence "to know ourselves is essentially," in St. Bernard's view, "to recognize that we are defaced images of God." [2] Take care, says St. Bernard, "now thou art sunk into the slime of the abyss, not to forget that thou art the image of God, and blush to have covered it over with an alien likeness. Remember thy nobility and take

1. This quotation from the *Canticle* (1.7) is given in the version cited by St. Bernard in his *Sermones in Cantica Canticorum*, 34. 1; *Patrologiae cursus completus, 183,* 959; it differs from the modern Vulgate reading.

2. Étienne Gilson, *The Mystical Theology of Saint Bernard*, trans. A. H. C. Downes (New York, Sheed and Ward, 1940), pp. 225 (n. 45), 70.

shame of such a defection. Forget not thy beauty, to be the more confounded at thy hideous aspect." [3]

In accordance with the twofold aim of meditation implied in the last sentence, Donne's *Second Anniversary* presents seven Meditations which may be called, for the most part, a description of the "defaced image," the Land of Unlikeness; while the seven Eulogies, for the most part, create a symbol of the original Image and Likeness, the lost beauty and nobility that must not be forgotten. That is not to say that Donne gives up Petrarchan imagery; not at all—but this imagery is now attuned to the religious aims of the poem. The Eulogies are sometimes too ingenious; yet the excessive ingenuity remains a minor flaw: it does not destroy the poem's unity.

The fifth Eulogy is a good example:

> Shee, who being to her selfe a State, injoy'd
> All royalties which any State employ'd;
> For shee made warres, and triumph'd; reason still
> Did not o'rthrow, but rectifie her will:
> And she made peace, for no peace is like this,
> That beauty, and chastity together kisse:
> She did high justice, for she crucified
> Every first motion of rebellious pride:
> And she gave pardons, and was liberall,
> For, onely her selfe except, she pardon'd all . . . .
>
> (359–68)

The hyperbole is here so tempered, so controlled, by interpretation in terms of the virtue essential to a restored Likeness, that the more extravagant images which follow become acceptably symbolic of the importance of such virtue in the world: it is the one thing needful:

> Shee coy'nd, in this, that her impressions gave
> To all our actions all the worth they have:
> She gave protections; the thoughts of her brest
> Satans rude Officers could ne'r arrest.
> As these prerogatives being met in one,

3. St. Bernard, *Sermones de Diversis*, 12. 2; *Patrologiae cursus completus*, *183*, 571. I quote the translation by Downes in Gilson's above study, p. 71.

> Made her a soveraigne State; religion
> Made her a Church; and these two made her all.
>
> (369–75)

Thus throughout the *Progresse* Meditation and Eulogy combine to present its central theme: the true end of man.

Let us look now at the whole movement of the poem; we can then see that this central theme is clearly introduced at the beginning of the first Meditation, carried to a climax in the fourth and fifth sections, and resolved in the Eulogy of Section VI. There is no flagging of power in this poem: it is a true progress. After the labored Introduction, Donne strikes at once into the heart of his theme:

> These Hymnes, thy issue, may encrease so long,
> As till Gods great *Venite* change the song. [end of Intro.]
> Thirst for that time, O my insatiate soule,
> And serve thy thirst, with Gods safe-sealing Bowle.
> Be thirstie still, and drinke still till thou goe
> To th' only Health, to be Hydroptique so. (43–8)

The "Bowle" is the Eucharist, a "seale of Grace," as Donne calls it in his sermons.[4] One thinks of the "Anima sitiens Deum" in St. Bernard—the Soul, the Bride, which thirsts for God, desiring a union of will between herself and God, that union which at last results in Perfect Likeness after death.[5] This imagery is then supported in Section II by the line, "And trust th' immaculate blood to wash thy score" (106); as well as by the lines of Section III (214–15) where Donne refers to death as the soul's "third birth," with the very significant parenthesis, "Creation gave her one, a second, grace." One needs to recall that at the close of the *Anatomie* Donne has said that he

> Will yearely celebrate thy second birth,
> That is, thy death; for though the soule of man
> Be got when man is made, 'tis borne but than
> When man doth die. (450–3)

4. See Itrat Husain, *The Dogmatic and Mystical Theology of John Donne* (London, S.P.C.K., 1938), pp. 30–1.
5. Gilson, *Saint Bernard*, pp. 111–12.

The omission of Grace may be said to indicate the fundamental flaw of the *First Anniversary:* it lacks the firm religious center of the *Progresse.*

This promise of salvation is the positive aspect of the soul's progress; but, as Gilson says, "By this thirst for God we must further understand an absolute contempt for all that is not God." [6] This complementary negative aspect is consequently introduced immediately after the above lines on the Eucharist:

> Forget this rotten world; And unto thee
> Let thine owne times as an old storie bee.
> Be not concern'd: studie not why, nor when;
> Doe not so much as not beleeve a man. (49–52)

Donne is taking as his prime example of vanity that curiosity which forms the first downward step in St. Bernard's Twelve Degrees of Pride—curiosity, which occurs, St. Bernard tells us, "when a man allows his sight and other senses to stray after things which do not concern him."

> So since it [the soul] takes no heed to itself it is sent out of doors to feed the kids. And as these are the types of sin, I may quite correctly give the title of 'kids' to the eyes and the ears, since as death comes into the world through sin, so does sin enter the mind through these apertures. The curious man, therefore, busies himself with feeding them, though he takes no trouble to ascertain the state in which he has left himself. Yet if, O man, you look carefully into yourself, it is indeed a wonder that you can ever look at anything else. [7]

This theme of curiosity remains dormant until Section III of the poem, where it emerges gradually from Donne's magnificent view of his own soul's flight to Heaven after death. It is important to note that this is not, strictly speaking, "the flight of Elizabeth Drury's

6. *Idem,* p. 238, n. 161.
7. St. Bernard, *The Twelve Degrees of Humility and Pride,* pp. 6, 55–6. See Gilson, *Saint Bernard,* Appendix I, on the importance of *curiositas* in St. Bernard's thought, where "kids" is shown to be another reference to the *Canticle,* 1. 7: "Si ignoras te . . . ."

soul to Heaven," as most commentators describe it.[8] It is Donne's own soul which here is made a symbol of release, not only from physical bondage, but also from that mental bondage which is the deepest agony of the greatest souls:

> she stayes not in the ayre,
> To looke what Meteors there themselves prepare;
> She carries no desire to know, nor sense,
> Whether th' ayres middle region be intense;
> For th' Element of fire, she doth not know,
> Whether she past by such a place or no;
> She baits not at the Moone, nor cares to trie
> Whether in that new world, men live, and die.
> *Venus* retards her not, to 'enquire, how shee
> Can, (being one starre) *Hesper*, and *Vesper* bee.
> (189–98)

In the last two lines Donne is renouncing one of his own witty *Paradoxes and Problems;* in the earlier part he is renouncing the astronomical curiosity which had drawn his scorn in the greatest passage of the *Anatomie*. Here, however, as Coffin has well shown (pp. 171, 185–92), there is a much stronger emphasis on problems such as "fire" and the moon which were being debated in Donne's own day. From all such vain controversies the soul is now freed and

> ere she can consider how she went,
> At once is at, and through the Firmament.
> (205–6)

It is not until Section IV that this theme reaches its full, explicit development. Turning here from the heavens, Donne scourges the search for physical understanding of earth and its creatures; yet, as before, the very flagellation suggests an almost indomitable curi-

8. Charles Monroe Coffin has made some helpful comments on this passage in a letter which he kindly allows me to quote: "in the imagined progress of his own soul, he has implied the felicitous passage of hers . . . . There is, to me at least, a rather certain ambiguity in the situation, as I think there should be, and the momentary assimilation of the vision of his own progress into that which has 'exalted' E.D. into heaven seems appropriate and, I should say, inevitable."

osity, and shows a mind that has ranged through all the reaches of human learning:

> Wee see in Authors, too stiffe to recant,
> A hundred controversies of an Ant;
> And yet one watches, starves, freeses, and sweats,
> To know but Catechismes and Alphabets
> Of unconcerning things, matters of fact—
>
> (281–85)

matters which do not concern the true end of man, as implied in the following lines:

> When wilt thou shake off this Pedantery,
> Of being taught by sense, and Fantasie?
> Thou look'st through spectacles; small things seeme great
> Below; But up unto the watch-towre get,
> And see all things despoyl'd of fallacies: [9]
> Thou shalt not peepe through lattices of eyes,
> Nor heare through Labyrinths of eares, nor learne
> By circuit, or collections to discerne.
> In heaven thou straight know'st all, concerning it,
> And what concernes it not, shalt straight forget.
>
> (291–300)

All worldly philosophy is vain, for essential truth, says Donne, cannot be learned through sense-impressions of external things, nor through that "Fantasie" which transmits sense-impressions to the intellect. Such philosophy is the way of pride; true knowledge comes only through humility, as Donne, echoing St. Bernard, declares in a significant passage of his *Essayes*:

> It is then humility to study God, and a strange miraculous one; for it is an ascending humility, which the Divel, which emulates even Gods excellency in his goodnesse, and labours to be as ill, as he is good, hath corrupted in us by a pride, as much against reason; for he hath fill'd us with a descending pride, to forsake

9. Cf. Francisco de Osuna, p. 201: "Sion means 'a watchtower,' that is, the grace received by the heart during its recollection, whence much knowledge of God can be discerned."

God, for the study and love of things worse then our selves.

(pp. 3–4)

True knowledge lies within and leads to virtue, the fourth Eulogy explains:

> Shee who all libraries had throughly read
> At home in her owne thoughts, and practised
> So much good as would make as many more:
> Shee whose example they must all implore,
> Who would or doe, or thinke well . . .
> She who in th' art of knowing Heaven, was growne
> Here upon earth, to such perfection,
> That she hath, ever since to Heaven she came,
> (In a far fairer print,) but read the same . . . .
>
> (303–14)

Religious virtue creates, or rather *is*, the restored Likeness which, according to St. Bernard, makes possible some knowledge of God; with St. Bernard, as Gilson says, "the resemblance of subject and object is the indispensable condition of any knowledge of the one by the other." [10] This is made plain in the sixth Eulogy, which provides the resolution of the whole poem by obliterating all traces of Petrarchan compliment and giving explicitly in the terms of St. Bernard a definition of the soul's perfection on earth. The sixth Meditation leads the way into this Eulogy by an abstract definition of "essential joy":

> Double on heaven thy thoughts on earth emploid;
> All will not serve; Only who have enjoy'd
> The sight of God, in fulnesse, can thinke it;
> For it is both the object, and the wit.
> This is essentiall joy, where neither hee
> Can suffer diminution, nor wee. (439–44)

God is both the object of knowledge and the means of knowing; though this full knowledge and joy can never be achieved on earth, we can, the Eulogy explains, come closest to it by striving to restore the Divine Likeness, as did she,

10. Gilson, *Saint Bernard*, p. 148.

Who kept by diligent devotion,
Gods Image, in such reparation,
Within her heart, that what decay was growne,
Was her first Parents fault, and not her owne:
Who being solicited to any act,
Still heard God pleading his safe precontract;
Who by a faithfull confidence, was here
Betroth'd to God, and now is married there . . .
Who being here fil'd with grace, yet strove to bee,
Both where more grace, and more capacitie
At once is given . . . . (455–67)

Compare the words of St. Bernard, speaking of that conformity between the soul's will and God's which leads to mystic ecstasy:

It is that conformity which makes, as it were, a marriage between the soul and the Word, when, being already like unto Him by its nature, it endeavours to show itself like unto Him by its will, and loves Him as it is loved by Him. And if this love is perfected, the soul is wedded to the Word. What can be more full of happiness and joy than this conformity? what more to be desired than this love? which makes thee, O soul, no longer content with human guidance, to draw near with confidence thyself to the Word, to attach thyself with constancy to Him, to address Him with confidence, and consult Him upon all subjects, to become as receptive in thy intelligence, as fearless in thy desires. This is the contract of a marriage truly spiritual and sacred. And to say this is to say too little; it is more than a contract, it is a communion, an identification with the Beloved, in which the perfect correspondence of will makes of two, one spirit.[11]

The "faithfull confidence" of Donne's poem is akin to the "confidence" (*fiducia*) of St. Bernard, an attribute of the soul which has passed beyond fear of divine punishment and stands on the threshold of mystic ecstasy.[12] This recognition of the end of man

11. St. Bernard, *Sermons on the Song of Songs*, 83. 3; *Life and Works of Saint Bernard*, trans. Samuel J. Eales (London, 1889–96), 4, 508.
12. Gilson, *Saint Bernard*, pp. 24, 113, 138n.

on earth and in Heaven is the fulfillment of the poem; the brief remainder is summary and epilogue.

In such a poem of religious devotion the sevenfold division of sections assumes a significance beyond that of the fivefold division of the *Anatomie*. Seven is the favorite number for dividing religious meditations: into those *semaines* and *septaines* that were characteristic of the "New Devotion" in the Low Countries; [13] or into the contrasting meditations for each day of the week that formed the basis of popular daily exercises throughout Europe. A glance at the summary of the latter exercises, as presented by Fray Luis (see above, Chap. 1, sec. 1), will show that Donne is following closely their general tenor and development: from thoughts of sin, death, and the miseries of this life, to thoughts of happy "conversation" with the blessed in Heaven, of "essentiall joy" and "accidentall joyes." [14] But the sevenfold division of this poem suggests more than a relation to the practice of methodical meditation. As Donne says in his *Essayes*, "*Seven* is ever used to express infinite." (p. 129) It is the mystic's traditional division of the soul's progress toward ecstasy and union with the Divine. St. Augustine thus divides the progress of the soul into seven stages,[15] and anyone

13. See Debongnie, pp. 168, 170–1, 184–7, 209–11; and H. Watrigant, "La Méditation Méthodique et l'École des Frères de la Vie Commune," *Revue d'Ascétique et de Mystique*, *3* (1922), 134–55. See also Puente, *1*, 43 f.

14. With the latter part of the *Second Anniversary* compare Loarte, *Exercise*, pp. 92–3:

> Secondly, ponder what a comfort and sweete delight it shal-be, to be in that blessed societie of so many Angels, Saintes, Apostles, Martyrs, Confessors, Virgins, al of them being so bright and beautiful? what shal it be to see the sacred humanitie of Christ, and of his blessed mother? howe shal a man be ravished with the hearing of the sweet harmonie and melodious musicke that shal be there, and to enioye so sweete a conversation everlastingly.
>
> Thirdly consider howe yet besides these, ther shal be another glorye muche more excellent, and surpassinge all humane capacitie: which shal be, to see God face to face, wherin consisteth our essential beatitude. For that al other thinges, what soever may be imagined, be but accidental glorie: which being so exceeding great and incomparable, what shal the essential be?

15. See St. Augustine, *De Quantitate Animae*, with trans. by F. E. Tourscher (Philadelphia, Peter Reilly, 1933), chaps. 33–5.

familiar with mystical writings will realize how often the division has been used by later mystics, as in St. Teresa's *Interior Castle.* Thus Donne's *Progresse* uses both mystical structure and mystical imagery to express a goal: the Infinite, the One.

This does not mean that Donne's *Progresse* is, properly speaking, a mystical poem, even though he uses in his title the mystical term "contemplate," and in the poem cries, "Returne not, my Soule, from this extasie" (321). The next line after this—"And meditation of what thou shalt bee"—indicates that the ecstasy is metaphorical only. "Meditation" is always discursive, always works through the understanding; it is only the preparation for ascent to the truly mystical state now generally understood in the term "contemplation," which St. Bernard defines as "the soul's true unerring intuition," "the unhesitating apprehension of truth." [16] Donne's use of the word "contemplate" in the title of his *Progresse* may indicate a higher spiritual aim than the "represent" of the *Anatomie's* title, but his *Progresse* remains a spiritual exercise of the purgative, ascetic life. It represents an attempt to achieve the state of conversion best described by Donne himself in a prayer at the close of his *Essayes in Divinity:*

> Begin in us here in this life an angelicall purity, an angelicall chastity, an angelicall integrity to thy service, an Angelical acknowledgment that we alwaies stand in thy presence, and should direct al our actions to thy glory. Rebuke us not, O Lord, in thine anger, that we have not done so till now; but enable us now to begin that great work; and imprint in us an assurance that thou receivest us now graciously, as reconciled, though enemies; and fatherly, as children, though prodigals; and powerfully, as the God of our salvation, though our own consciences testifie against us.

16. St. Bernard, *On Consideration,* trans. George Lewis (Oxford, Clarendon Press, 1908), p. 41.

Engraved portrait of St. François de Sales by Martinus Baes,
from the English translation of St. François' *Treatise of the Love
of God*, Douay, 1630

(*Yale University Library*)

CHAPTER 7

George Herbert: in the Presence
of a Friend

Enfin, comme ceux qui sont amoureux d'un amour humain et naturel ont presque tousjours leurs pensees tournees du costé de la chose aymee, leur coeur plein d'affection envers elle, leur bouche remplie de ses louanges, et qu'en son absence ilz ne perdent point d'occasion de tesmoigner leurs passions par lettres, et ne treuvent point d'arbre sur l'escorce duquel ilz n'escrivent le nom de ce qu'ils ayment; ainsy ceux qui ayment Dieu ne peuvent cesser de penser en luy, respirer pour luy, aspirer à luy et parler de luy, et voudroyent, s'il estoit possible, graver sur la poitrine de toutes les personnes du monde le saint et sacré nom de Jesus. A quoy mesme toutes choses les invitent, et n'y a creature qui ne leur annonce la loüange de leur Bienaymé . . . .

St. François de Sales, *Introduction à la Vie dévote,* 1609

At the outset of his great study of Devout Humanism, Bremond notes with regret that he has left "untouched sundry chapters of Anglican history which would have illustrated that of France"; for he would like to have shown "how among the Anglicans of the first half of the seventeenth century was produced a temper analogous to French Devout Humanism . . . thus showing also that the influence of French writers, and notably of François de Sales, was felt across the Channel." My aim here is to examine this analogous temper in Herbert; to suggest some of the forces, both in devotional literature and in poetry, that may have shaped this temper; and, in particular, to develop the affinities between Herbert and St. François de Sales that have been briefly described in the fourth section of my third chapter.

The present chapter will deal with many writers besides St. François, but it begins with him, because his temper, his prose style, and his meditative practices seem closer to Herbert than anything else among the popular treatises of this or the medieval period. Furthermore, Herbert had a strong admiration for French culture, as we see from a letter that he sent to his brother in Paris in the year 1618: "You live in a brave nation, where, except you wink, you cannot but see many brave examples. Bee covetous, then, of all good which you see in Frenchmen, whether it be in knowledge, or in fashion, or in words; for I would have you, even in speeches, to observe so much, as when you meet with a witty French speech, try to speak the like in English: so shall you play a good marchant, by transporting French commodities to your own country." [1] It seems likely, then, that Herbert would have known and admired the writings of St. François de Sales, though it is not by any means necessary to assume a direct influence. Herbert could surely have been guided by the same forces that helped St. François create his spirituality; the *Imitation of Christ*, the *Pax Animae*, the *Spiritual Combat*, the works of the Jesuit humanists, the works of Fray Diego de Estella—to name only a few of the possibilities. For the essence of the devout life, as summed up in the second part of St. François' *Introduction*, lies in what the seventeenth century called "the practice of the presence of God"; and this was a "practice" shared in some degree by meditative writers of every order and creed: it was summed up also in a section of the Jesuit Rodriguez' treatise on *Perfection*, and was recommended by other Jesuit writers as an important part of preparation for meditation.[2]

Yet in the *Introduction* of St. François de Sales this sense of presence receives a special emphasis. Here we find set forth in detail four ways of placing oneself in the presence of God, as the first point in preparation for meditation. His first way is an abstract one, consisting "in a livelie and feeling apprehension of the omnipresence of God." The second moves toward a greater intimacy and concreteness, for it consists in thinking "that God is not only in the place

1. *Works of Herbert*, ed. Hutchinson, p. 366. In another letter of the same year he speaks of "a parcel of Books" which his brother is sending over to him, evidently from Paris (*idem*).

2. Rodriguez, Treatise 6; see also Puente, *1*, 16–18; Gibbons, § 2, ¶ 1–3.

where thou art: but that he is by a most particular and peculiar manner in thy hart, and in the verie bottom of thy spirit, which he quickeneth and animateth with his divine presence, being there as the hart of thy hart, and the spirit of thy spirit." In the third, the imagination is brought vividly into action, as we "consider and behold our blessed Saviour, who in his sacred humanitie, beholdeth from heaven all persons in the world, but especially all Christians, who are his children, and most particularlie, such as be in prayer: whose actions and be-haviour, he marketh most lovingly." And this, St. François adds, "is not a simple imagination of our phantasie, but an infaillable veritie: for although we see not him, yet he from thence above considereth and looketh upon us." The fourth "manner of presence"—the most intimate and dramatic method of all —"consisteth in helping our selves with a simple imagination, by representing to our thoughts, our Saviour in his sacred humanitie, as if he were hard by us, according as we are accustomed to represent our friends to our fancie, and to say, me thinks I see such a one doing this or that, it seemes unto me that I behold him thus or thus attired, and such like." But, St. François concludes, in a comment of the utmost significance: "if the venerable sacrament of the altar were present, then this presence were reall, and not by meere imagination, for the species and appearance of bread, should be as a tapistrie, behind which our Lord being really present, seeth and marketh our actions, although we see not him in his owne likenes." (pp. 120–3)

Such a "livelie" apprehension of this presence—"as the hart of thy hart," or as the father beholding his "children" "most lovingly," or as the "friend" present in every daily occasion—pervades not only the set periods of meditation and colloquy, but, ideally, penetrates every waking moment of one's life, through the constant cultivation of an extraordinary variety of devotional practices. Foremost among these is the practice of concluding each formal exercise of meditation with a "nosegay of devotion"—"a spirituall posy":

> Such as have delighted them selves walking in a pleasant garden, goe not ordinarily from thence, without taking in their hands, four or five flowers to smell on, and keepe in theire hands

all the daye after. Even so, when our mind hath spirituallie recreated it self, by affective discourcing and meditation of some sacred mysterie, we should cull out, one or two points which we have found most pleasing to our tast, and most agreeable to our understanding, upon which we might busie our mind, and as it were mentally smell theron all the rest of the day. (pp. 132–4)

Along with this result of meditation, one is advised to cultivate "five other sorts of shorter prayers, which be as it were helpes, and braunches of the other principall exercise." (p. 142) These, in order of importance, consist in: (1) a morning exercise of prayer, forecasting the events of the day; (2) an evening exercise, including examination of conscience; (3) spiritual retirement; (4) the use of "aspirations," short prayers, and good thoughts; (5) prayer in relation to the Mass. (Pt. 2, chaps. 10–14) In maintaining the effects of formal meditation, and increasing the sense of presence, the evening exercise is of great importance, since here one is advised to take time "to recollect thy spirit, before thy Lord Iesus Christ crucified (whome thou mayst represent unto thy selfe, by a simple consideration and an inward view of thy mind)," and to "kindle againe the fire of thy morning meditation, by a dozen of livelie aspirations, humiliations, and loving glaunces . . . Or els by repeating the points of thy meditation, in which thou feelest most savour; or by stirring up thy devotion by some new spirituall obiect . . . ." (p. 146) But with the third and fourth of these practices, which really form one practice, we come to two of the most important chapters in the entire *Introduction*, and discover methods of devotion that are, I believe, very close to the essential Herbert.

The practice of "the spiritual retyring of the soule" consists in this: "As often as thou canst in the day time, recall thy soule home to her with-drawing chamber, there to appeer in the presence of God, by one of those fower meanes" which he has earlier prescribed for use in the daily meditation:

and consider what God doeth, and what thou doest: and thou shalt find his eies turned to thee wardes, and perpetuallie fastned upon thee, by an incomparable love. O my God (mayest thou say) wherfore do not I look alwayes upon thee, as thou alwayes lookest upon me? wherefore thinckest thou so much upon me, ô my Lord? and wherefore think I so little upon thee? where be wee, whether wander wee ô my soule?

(p. 148)

This has the very accent of Herbert:

> My God, what is a heart,
> That thou shouldst it so eye, and wooe,
> Powring upon it all thy art,
> As if that thou hadst nothing els to do?
>
> ("Mattens")

An accent, an attitude, reinforced a hundredfold, when we remember Herbert's devotion to the wounds of Christ, and then read the passage that immediately follows the above in the *Introduction*:

> As birds have their nests upon trees, to retire themselves unto, when they stand in need; and deers have bushes and thickets to hide and shroude themselves, and to take the coolenes and shadowe in the summer heat: even so, my Philotheus, should our harts choose out everie day some place, either upon the mount of Calvary, or in the wounds of our redeemer, there to make our spirituall retreat at every occasion; there to re-create and refreshe our selves amidst the turmoile of exteriour affaires; there to be as in a fortresse, to deffend our selves against the poursuit of ghostlie temptations. (p. 149)

The ease and familiarity with which this imagery from ordinary life occurs is in itself akin to Herbert: for reasons made clear in the next chapter of the *Introduction*, which describes the practice of the "aspirations, iaculatory prayers, and good thoughtes," which occupy the soul in this "spirituall retreat":

> We retire our selves into God, because we aspire unto him: and we aspire unto him, to retire us into him: so that the aspiring of the soule unto God, and the spirituall retreat, do mutuallie entertaine one another, and both of them proceed and issue from holy thoughts.
>
> Aspire then verie often from the bottom of thy hart unto

God (ô my Philotheus) through briefe and short, yet burning and inflamed desires, darted from thy soule: admire his beautie; call upon him for his assistance; cast thy selfe in spirit at the foote of the crosse; adore his goodnes; question with him often about thy salvation; give thy soule unto him a thousand times a day, fasten the inward view of thy soule upon his inestimable sweetnes, stretch foorth thy hand unto him, as a little child doth to his Father, that he may conduct thee: place him in thy bosome like a sweet-smelling posie, plant him in thy soule like an encouraging standart: finally make a thousand sorts and diversities of motions in thy hart, to enkindle the love of God within thee . . . .

For thus, he explains, "are iaculatory prayers made"—through "ferverous desires and darts of devout love"; and as a consequence "our spirit once giving it self entirelie to the companie, hant, and familiaritie of his God, must needs be all perfumed, with the odoriferous ayre of his perfections." (pp. 152–4)

All this seems precisely a description of Herbert's *Temple:* "The Posie," "The Glance," "The Odour":

> My joy, my life, my crown!
> My heart was meaning all the day,
>   Somewhat it fain would say:
> And still it runneth mutt'ring up and down
> With onely this, *My joy, my life, my crown.*
>   ("A true Hymne")

> Of what an easie quick accesse,
> My blessed Lord, art thou! how suddenly
>   May our requests thine eare invade!
> To shew that state dislikes not easinesse,
> If I but lift mine eyes, my suit is made:
> Thou canst no more not heare, then thou canst die.
>   ("Prayer" 2)

These are the moments of success; but we may see, with even greater clarity, the essence of the life that lies deep within the poetry, in those poems which rehearse "the glimpse" denied, the times of dryness, "When my devotions could not pierce/Thy silent eares":

> My bent thoughts, like a brittle bow,
> Did flie asunder:
> Each took his way; some would to pleasures go,
> Some to the warres and thunder
> Of alarms.
>
> As good go any where, they say,
> As to benumme
> Both knees and heart, in crying night and day,
> *Come, come, my God, O come,*
> But no hearing.
>
> O that thou shouldst give dust a tongue
> To crie to thee,
> And then not heare it crying! all day long
> My heart was in my knee,
> But no hearing.
>
> ("Deniall")

In the service of these "bent thoughts" all creatures play their part, after the manner described in the passage of sacred parody that serves as an epigraph for this chapter—a passage in which the English translation preserves the delicate wit of the Salesian style:

> To conclude, as they that be enamoured with humane and natural love, have almost alway their thoughts fixed upon the parson beloved, their hart full of affection towards her, their mouth flowing with her praises; when their beloved is absent they leese no occasion to testifie their passions by kind letters, and not a tree do they meet with all, but in the barck of it, they engrave the name of their darling: even so such as love God fervently, can never cease thincking upon him, they draw their breath only for him, they sigh and sorrow for their absence from him, all their talk is of him and if it were possible, they would grave the sacred name of our Lord Iesus, upon the brest of all the men in the world.

"And certainly," St. François adds, "al creatures doe invite them to this, and not one but in its kind, declareth unto them the praises of their beloved . . . . all things provoke us and give us occasion of good and godlie thoughts, from whence afterward doe arise many motions and aspirations of our soule to God." (pp. 155–6) All things, all creatures, will remind us of this presence, as in the three chapters where St. François de Sales' favorite treatise, the *Spiritual Combat*, had taught the proper control of the senses, by using "everything in the world" to produce the "bonnes pensees" which the *Introduction* thus illustrates:

> S. Francisca considering and viewing attentively a pleasant brooke, upon the banck wherof she kneeled to pour foorth her prayers, was rapt into an exstasie, repeating oft times to her self these words: thus sweetly, and pleasantly floweth the grace of my God unto our harts, as this riverett danceth downe his channell. Another looking upon the fruit trees of an orchard, which were all bedecked with their timely blossoms, sighed and sayd, ay me wretch that I·am, wherfore am I alone without blossom or budd in the orchard of holy churche?
>
> (pp. 160–1)

Analogies in Herbert's poetry to these commonplaces at once spring to mind, in "Vertue," "The Rose," "Life," or in such lines as:

> Oh that I were an Orenge-tree,
>   That busie plant!
> Then should I ever laden be,
>   And never want
> Some fruit for him that dressed me.
>   ("Employment" 2)

> All things are busie; onely I
>   Neither bring hony with the bees,
> Nor flowres to make that, nor the husbandrie
>   To water these.
>   ("Employment" 1)

> Heark, how the birds do sing,
>   And woods do ring.
> All creatures have their joy: and man hath his.
>   ("Mans medley")

Or in the entire poem "Providence," where for 150 lines Herbert
develops the theme:

> All things that are, though they have sev'rall wayes,
> Yet in their being joyn with one advise
> To honour thee: and so I give thee praise
> In all my other hymnes, but in this twice.

Such "good thoughts" arising from the creatures are of course
related to, and reinforced by, the methods of analogy which Herbert recommends, and justifies by biblical precedent, in several well-
known passages of his *Country Parson*, particularly where he speaks
of using the "familiar illustration" in catechism: "This is the skill,
and doubtlesse the Holy Scripture intends thus much, when it con-
descends to the naming of a plough, a hatchet, a bushell, leaven,
boyes piping and dancing; shewing that things of ordinary use are
not only to serve in the way of drudgery, but to be washed, and
cleansed, and serve for lights even of Heavenly Truths." [3] It was
a method long used by the preachers, given profound theological
justification in the works of Hugh of St. Victor and St. Bonaventure, and popularized in the emblem-books which Miss Freeman
has treated in her valuable study. Herbert's subtlety, delicacy, and
daring in the use of common imagery is but another instance of the
way in which ancient modes of thought have been renewed and fertilized through the concentrated devotional methods of the seventeenth century. Through the search for the presence of God in
spiritual retirement all the day long, the poet of the *Temple* has
achieved the masterful use of familiar, simple imagery, summed up
in his famous poem "The Elixir," which, read from this point of
view, may be regarded as the key to his entire *Temple:*

> All may of thee partake:
> Nothing can be so mean,
> Which with his tincture (for thy sake)
> Will not grow bright and clean.
>
> A servant with this clause
> Makes drudgerie divine:
> Who sweeps a room, as for thy laws,
> Makes that and th'action fine.

3. *Works of Herbert*, ed. Hutchinson, p. 257.

This is the famous stone
That turneth all to gold:
For that which God doth touch and own
Cannot for lesse be told.

"Well then," St. François de Sales concludes, "in this exercise of spirituall retyring" and in this practice of "iaculatorie prayers, fervently darted from an enflamed desire"—in this "consisteth the great work of devotion";

> this exercise may supplie the want of al other prayers: but the want of it, can not almost be repayred by any other exercise: without it, we cannot well lead a contemplative life, and but badly performe the active life; without it, repose is but idlenes, and labour is but drudgerie: therefore I charge and coniure thee of all love to embrace this exercise from thy hart, and never to omitt it, or leave it of. (pp. 162-3)

Such a way of life must display itself in every utterance of the man who follows it. How should one speak in the presence of such a "friend"? The directions for colloquy discussed in my opening chapter show the way: this should be "familiar talke," "as one friend speaketh unto another." Thus it seems fair to apply in this case some of the advice that St. François gives in the third part of his *Introduction*, with regard to the proper ways of speaking in daily life— and here we must leave the English translation, for in these matters of style the exact nuance of the French is needed. True and false friendship may be distinguished, he says, in their ways of speaking: "l'amitié mondaine produit ordinairement un grand amas de paroles emmiellees . . . mais l'amitié sacree a un langage simple et franc . . . ." "En toutes conversations [that is, social relations in general, including speech], la naifveté, simplicité, douceur et modestie sont tous-jours preferees." "Que vostre langage soit doux, franc, sincere, rond, naif et fidelle." "Il n'y a nulle si bonne et desirable finesse que la simplicité." But such "simplicity" does not at all require a severity, a bareness, of style. St. Romuald and St. Anthony, the *Introduction* points out, were greatly praised because, in spite of their austerities, "ilz avoient la face et les paroles ornees de joye, gayeté et civilité." "Jeux de paroles" may play a part in "bonne conversation," though of course these ways must be pursued with "une modeste gayeté et joyeuseté." (2, 50, 67, 87, 74) And the style of St. François himself shows everywhere that witty conceits may be used, though always "bellement et douce-ment"—as in the passage of sacred parody that heads this chapter. Simplicity, in the Salesian spirit, implies a unity, a wholeness of mind that enables a man to speak naturally, as he really is. If he is witty, educated, courtly, these qualities may be expressed, for everything that a man is or has may be converted to the service of this friendly presence—only, as Southwell would say, these things must be "tempered in the meane."

2

All creation, then, including all poetical creation, should be "washed and cleansed," turned to gold, made worthy of this presence. This is the theme of the "Jordan" poems, where, as Nicholas Ferrar seems to indicate in the preface to the *Temple*, Jordan, river of Grace, is implicitly opposed to Helicon. Hutchinson has pointed out [1] that Herbert's way of suggesting this need for a poetical baptism bears a strong resemblance to the way in which Thomas Lodge announces a similar transformation in the preface to his prose meditation on the sorrows of the Virgin: *Prosopopeia, Containing the Teares of the holy, blessed, and sanctified Marie, the Mother of God* (1596). Here Lodge, now a convert to Catholicism, concludes his exhortation to the reader with a prayer based on the advice to bathe in Jordan ("Wash and be clean"), given by Elisha to Naaman (2 Kings 5.10–14): "our Lord send a plentifull harvest of teares by this meditation, that the devout heereby may wax more confident, the incredulous beleeving: the indifferent, more zealous, that now at last after I have wounded the world with too much surfet of vanitie, I maye bee by the true Helizeus, cleansed from the leprosie of my lewd lines, and beeing washed in the Iordan of grace, imploy my labour to the comfort of the faithfull." Now this work by Lodge, as Thurston has pointed out,[2] is modeled upon

1. *Idem*, p. 495. See also the discussion of the significance of "Jordan" in Miss Tuve's *Reading of Herbert*, pp. 182f.

2. Thurston, *Month*, *83*, 391–2; cf. N. Burton Paradise, *Thomas Lodge* (New Haven, Yale University Press, 1931), pp. 125–6.

Southwell's prose meditation on the tears of Mary Magdalen, and contains in the preface a clear reference to Southwell's writings in this genre of tears. We may thus see in it one of the first results of Southwell's campaign to "wooe some skilfuller pennes from unworthy labours," as well as a sign of the way in which the stream of English devotional literature was passing from Southwell to Herbert, whose "skilfuller wit" took up the "few coarse threads" that Southwell had "laid together" and combined them with many others to produce the "finer piece" for which Southwell had hoped.[3]

The "Jordan" poems point the way, though the first of these, taken alone, may seem to advocate a simplicity of bareness. But Herbert here is only denying the necessity—not the possibility—of using such elaborate "artificial" modes of poetry as Spenserian allegory, the pastoral convention, or the ways of riddling wit:

> Is it no verse, except enchanted groves
> And sudden arbours shadow course-spunne lines?
> Must purling streams refresh a lovers loves?
> Must all be vail'd, while he that reades, divines,
>   Catching the sense at two removes?

Those who wish may use such ways; but there is, for this writer, another way, which he announces with all the exaggeration of a convert:

> Shepherds are honest people; let them sing:
> Riddle who list, for me, and pull for Prime:
> I envie no mans nightingale or spring;
> Nor let them punish me with losse of rime,
>   Who plainly say, *My God, My King.*

3. Lodge's meditation in places bears some resemblance to Herbert's "Sacrifice." Mary sees the wounds of Christ on the Cross, remembers his earlier sufferings, and cries out in passionate paradoxes: "O you that passe this waie and beholde this bodie, you that looke on these wounds, and see these lims; tell me, Is not beautie oppressed? Majestie imbased? Innocencie martired? Come neere and iudge if anie griefe may be compared with mine?" And later she hears him speak from the Cross: "O man see what I suffer for thee, there is no griefe like to mine . . . ." A long series of paradoxes follows. See *Prosopopeia* (London, 1596: Hunterian Club reprint, 1880), pp. 30, 43-4.

The other "Jordan" poem considerably qualifies that emphasis, and is the more revealing, for it records the history of Herbert's progress in poetry: a movement from elaboration to restraint. In view of the echoes of *Astrophel and Stella* here—not only of the famous opening sonnet, but of eight or nine others as well— [4] this movement might be seen as a poetical development from the ways of Donne (among other intricate poets) to the ways of Sidney (among other simpler poets). At the same time the echoes of *Astrophel* create a superb example of the art of sacred parody:

> When first my lines of heav'nly joyes made mention,
> Such was their lustre, they did so excell,
> That I sought out quaint words, and trim invention;
> My thoughts began to burnish, sprout, and swell,
> Curling with metaphors a plain intention,
> Decking the sense, as if it were to sell.
>
> Thousands of notions in my brain did runne,
> Off'ring their service, if I were not sped:
> I often blotted what I had begunne;
> This was not quick enough, and that was dead.
> Nothing could seem too rich to clothe the sunne,
> Much lesse those joyes which trample on his head.
>
> As flames do work and winde, when they ascend,
> So did I weave my self into the sense.
> But while I bustled, I might heare a friend
> Whisper, *How wide is all this long pretence!*
> *There is in love a sweetnesse readie penn'd:*
> *Copie out onely that, and save expense.*

4. The resemblance to Sidney's opening sonnet does not consist only in the turn of the last line: "Foole, said my Muse to me, looke in thy heart and write." Herbert also echoes the middle lines: "I sought fit words to paint the blackest face of woe,/Studying inventions fine . . . ." Since Sidney uses the term "Invention" three times in this one sonnet, it is worth noting that Herbert originally entitled the poem "Invention" (*Works of Herbert*, ed. Hutchinson, p. 102). Herbert's last line, however, is verbally modeled more closely on the ending of Sidney's Sonnet 3: see the subsequent discussion for this and other parallels with Herbert.

One of my students, well versed in modern criticism of seventeenth-century poetry, suggested to me that the "friend" was probably Donne. But it is a much closer "friend" than either Donne or Sidney whose presence has guided Herbert toward these ways of poetical thrift.

Nevertheless, without attempting to argue that the busy 'weaving" thus renounced in the poem refers specifically to Donne, or to find another "master" in Sidney—I believe there is considerable truth in the suggestion that Herbert as poet developed away from an early enthusiasm for Donne's manner toward a style much closer to Sidney's. Evidence of this may be seen in some of the differences between the final and the early versions of certain poems, as recorded in Hutchinson's admirable edition. Thus, at the outset of the "Church-porch" we come upon this early version of the second stanza, which seems highly Donnean in its abrupt exclamations, its colloquial rush, its rude diction, its elliptical phrasing:

> Beware of Lust (startle not) o beware
> It makes thy soule a blott: it is a rodd
> Whose twigs are pleasures, & they whip thee bare,
> It spoils an Angel: robs thee of thy God.[5]

But in the final version the movement of the lines is smooth and graceful; the whole is tempered in keeping with the sacramental imagery which has here been introduced:

> Beware of lust: it doth pollute and foul
> Whom God in Baptisme washt with his own blood.
> It blots thy lesson written in thy soul;
> The holy lines cannot be understood.

But the most striking and sure evidence is found in those two sonnets which Herbert, in his seventeenth year, sent to his mother along with a letter reproving, like Southwell, "the vanity of those many Love-poems, that are daily writ and consecrated to *Venus*," and announcing his own firm "resolution to be, that my poor Abilities in *Poetry*, shall be all, and ever consecrated to Gods glory." [6] It

5. *Works of Herbert*, ed. Hutchinson, p. 6; for other examples see Hutchinson's textual notes, pp. 21, 43–4, 55, 61, 65.

6. Walton, *Lives*, pp. 268–9; *Works of Herbert*, ed. Hutchinson, pp. 206, 363.

has frequently been pointed out that these sonnets are strongly reminiscent of Donne's style. But we must also note the significant fact that these sonnets were not included in either the early or the final version of the *Temple;* both in the Williams manuscript and in the published version we find instead the paired sonnets entitled "Love," which take over the theme and some of the imagery of the early sonnets, but develop these materials in an utterly different way. The contrast is so crucial for the understanding of Herbert's development that it seems essential to quote both pairs and ask the reader to consider the differences very closely. Here are the early sonnets as Isaak Walton gives them to us; they seem to represent exactly the poetical methods described in "Jordan" (2)—weaving and winding in imitation of the breathless wit of Donne, and concluding, in each case, with the kind of macabre image typical of Donne but quite untypical of Herbert's mature achievements:

> My God, where is that ancient heat towards thee,
>   Wherewith whole showls of *Martyrs* once did burn,
>   Besides their other flames? Doth Poetry
> Wear *Venus* Livery? only serve her turn?
> Why are not *Sonnets* made of thee? and layes
>   Upon thine Altar burnt? Cannot thy love
>   Heighten a spirit to sound out thy praise
> As well as any she? Cannot thy *Dove*
> Out-strip their *Cupid* easily in flight?
>   Or, since thy wayes are deep, and still the same,
>   Will not a verse run smooth that bears thy name?
> Why doth that fire, which by thy power and might
>   Each breast does feel, no braver fuel choose
>   Than that, which one day Worms may chance refuse?

> Sure, Lord, there is enough in thee to dry
>   Oceans of *Ink;* for, as the Deluge did
>   Cover the Earth, so doth thy Majesty:
> Each Cloud distills thy praise, and doth forbid
> *Poets* to turn it to another use.
>   *Roses* and *Lillies* speak thee; and to make
>   A pair of Cheeks of them, is thy abuse.

Why should I *Womens eyes* for Chrystal take?
Such poor invention burns in their low mind
   Whose fire is wild, and doth not upward go
    To praise, and on thee, Lord, some *Ink* bestow.
Open the bones, and you shall nothing find
   In the best *face* but *filth*, when, Lord, in thee
   The *beauty* lies in the *discovery*.

When we turn to the two sonnets in the *Temple*, we find that the crowded imagery has been drastically pruned, and that the materials have been completely recast in such a way as to produce two carefully matched patterns. In particular, the charnel-house imagery which occurs in the final lines of both the early poems is removed, and instead we have simply the word "dust" in each of the later poems:

Immortall Love, authour of this great frame,
   Sprung from that beautie which can never fade;
   How hath man parcel'd out thy glorious name,
And thrown it on that dust which thou hast made,
While mortall love doth all the title gain!
   Which siding with invention, they together
   Bear all the sway, possessing heart and brain,
(Thy workmanship) and give thee share in neither.
Wit fancies beautie, beautie raiseth wit:
   The world is theirs; they two play out the game,
   Thou standing by: and though thy glorious name
Wrought our deliverance from th' infernall pit,
   Who sings thy praise? onely a skarf or glove
   Doth warm our hands, and make them write of love.

Immortall Heat, O let thy greater flame
   Attract the lesser to it: let those fires,
   Which shall consume the world, first make it tame;
And kindle in our hearts such true desires,
As may consume our lusts, and make thee way.
   Then shall our hearts pant thee; then shall our brain
   All her invention on thine Altar lay,

And there in hymnes send back thy fire again:
Our eies shall see thee, which before saw dust;
   Dust blown by wit, till that they both were blinde:
   Thou shalt recover all thy goods in kinde,
Who wert disseized by usurping lust:
   All knees shall bow to thee; all wits shall rise,
   And praise him who did make and mend our eies.

The devices which create the symmetry are skillfully managed: the parallel phrasing of each opening line; the clear division into octave and sestet (unlike the earlier sonnets), with the first line of the sestet in each case marked by antithetical phrasing in half-lines; the use of the term "wit" in each sestet, and of the terms "invention," "heart," and "brain" in the middle of each poem; and the interlocking rimes, "-ame," "-ain." At the same time the reference to placing poems on the "Altar," which occurs casually in the first of the early sonnets, is now placed directly in the center of the second poem, in such a way as to bind together with dramatic force the repeated usage of the terms "invention," "heart," and "brain." The neglect of the "glorious name," twice mentioned in the first sonnet of the *Temple,* is answered in the last two lines of the second, with a reminiscence of the lines in Philippians (2.9–10) on which Crashaw based his hymn: "Wherefore God also hath highly exalted him, and given him a name which is above every name: That at the name of Jesus every knee should bow, of things in heaven, and things in earth, and things under the earth."

The two sonnets of the *Temple* thus remind us, as the earlier sonnets do not, of the theme, and the images, and the measured symmetry of Sidney's famous palinode, with its use of the word "dust," its allusion to the light "That doth both shine, and give us sight to see," and its address to "Eternall Love":

      Leave me ô Love, which reachest but to dust,
      And thou my mind aspire to higher things:
      Grow rich in that which never taketh rust:
      What ever fades, but fading pleasure brings.

      Draw in thy beames, and humble all thy might,
      To that sweet yoke, where lasting freedomes be:

Which breakes the clowdes and opens forth the light
That doth both shine and give us sight to see.

O take fast hold, let that light be thy guide,
In this small course which birth drawes out to death,
And thinke how evill becommeth him to slide,
Who seeketh heav'n, and comes of heav'nly breath.
    Then farewell world, thy uttermost I see,
    Eternall Love maintaine thy life in me.[7]

It is in this effect of explicit, precise *building* that Herbert's kinship with Sidney declares itself most clearly; both poets, at their
best, create by setting together materials block by block, piece by
piece: the whole is *fitted* together, and though the construction
has a flexible rhythm, a fluent curve and sweep, we never lose sight
of the blocks which are thus neatly set together. We feel the difference from Donne's way in the opening of the second sonnet in
the *Temple*, where the imagery bears some resemblance to the conclusion of Holy Sonnet 5:

But oh it must be burnt! alas the fire
Of lust and envie have burnt it heretofore,
And made it fouler; Let their flames retire,
And burne me ô Lord, with a fiery zeale
Of thee and thy house, which doth in eating heale.

It is all one passionate unit: lines melt and fuse in the heat. In Herbert and Sidney the effect is quite different from this: as in the above
sonnets of the *Temple*, each line tends to maintain its identity, and
yet the mind slips over the edge, easily, deftly, into a half-line

7. Text from *The Countesse of Pembrokes Arcadia* (London, 1598), p.
490; I have omitted an erroneous period at end of line 7. See also Sidney's
Defence of Poesie: "Other sort of *Poetrie*, almost have we none, but that
Lyricall kind of Songs and Sonets; which Lord, if he gave us so good mindes,
how well it might be employed, and with howe heavenly fruites, both private and publike, in singing the praises of the immortall bewtie, the immortall goodnes of that God, who giveth us hands to write, and wits to conceive: of which we might wel want words, but never matter, of which we
could turne our eyes to nothing, but we should ever have new budding occasions." (*The Complete Works of Sir Philip Sidney*, ed. Albert Feuillerat
[4 vols., Cambridge, University Press, 1912–26], *3*, 41.)

which thus receives a subtle, not a pounding emphasis: "(Thy workmanship)"; "Thou standing by"; "Who sings thy praise?"

These similarities between Herbert and Sidney may perhaps be seen more clearly in Sidney's Sonnet 28, which, carrying on the theme of Sidney's opening sonnet, reminds us that praise of simplicity is one of the recurrent, dominant themes of *Astrophel and Stella*:

> You that with allegories curious frame,
>   Of others children changelings use to make,
>   With me those paines for Gods sake do not take:
>   I list not dig so deepe for brasen fame.
>
> When I say, *Stella*, I do meane the same
>   Princesse of Beautie, for whose only sake,
>   The raines of *Love* I love, though never slake,
>   And ioy therein, though Nations count it shame.
>
> I beg no subiect to use eloquence,
>   Nor in hid wayes do guide Philosophie:
>   Looke at my hands for no such quintessence;
>
> But know that I in pure simplicitie,
>   Breathe out the flames which burne within my heart,
>   *Love* onely reading unto me this art.[8]

This sonnet may also serve to remind us, in passing, that there was at least one poet before Donne who could combine an irritated "for God's sake" with philosophical imagery, and present all in a tone of conversation. But of course the conversation is quite unlike Donne's. The division into verse paragraphs, thus given in the 1598 folio, shows clearly the measured, tempered way in which this sonnet, in keeping with its theme, is built. In Herbert and Sidney there is time to pause, to balance, to watch the "keeping of accent," to bring the tone of courtly, cultivated conversation into a neatly modeled unit. *Neatness* is the word; Herbert's own word, as used

8. All quotations from *Astrophel and Stella* are also taken from the above edition of 1598.

in "The Familie": "For where thou dwellest all is neat." Neatness
of a kind that includes the qualities described in a passage of the
Country Parson where Herbert deals with the "Parson praying":
"his voyce is humble, his words treatable, and slow; yet not so slow
neither, as to let the fervency of the supplicant hang and dy between
speaking, but with a grave livelinesse, between fear and zeal, paus-
ing yet pressing." [9] *Treatable;* that is to say, "gentle, easy, moderate,
deliberate, not violent"; or, "distinct, clear, intelligible." [10] It is the
essential manner of Sidney and Herbert—and of St. François de
Sales; but far from the intricate, uneasy, immoderate talk of Donne.
When we speak of Donne's style as "conversational" we must distinguish:

> But if this medicine, love, which cures all sorrow
> With more, not only bee no quintessence,
> But mixt of all stuffes, paining soule, or sense,
> And of the Sunne his working vigour borrow,
> Love's not so pure, and abstract, as they use
> To say, which have no Mistresse but their Muse,
> But as all else, being elemented too,
> Love sometimes would contemplate, sometimes do.
> ("Loves growth")

This is not the manner of the cultivated, witty courtier: it is the
talk of a brilliant dialectician who takes all knowledge for his prov-
ince, comprehending in one long and dazzling sentence the worlds
of poetry, philosophy, religion, and carnal love: drawing all together by the power of one of the subtlest intellects that ever turned
its powers toward poetic expression. It is not the conversational
mode cultivated by Sidney and Herbert, or by Wyatt, Ben Jonson,
and the Elizabethan song-writers. It develops away from them in
accordance with the extraordinary powers with which Donne was
gifted, and in accordance also, I believe, with the way in which his
early education had trained those powers. Thus the dramatic stance

9. *Works of Herbert,* ed. Hutchinson, p. 231.
10. *OED,* "Treatable," 1, c, d. Cf. *OED,* "Neat," 7: "Characterized by
elegance of form or arrangement, with freedom from all unnecessary additions or embellishments; of agreeable but simple appearance; nicely made or
proportioned."

of Donne in his poetry, whether religious or profane, is seldom that of one who seeks simplicity. It is rather the stance of the teacher of "loves philosophy": the analytic dialectician, the learned diagnostician, the theological casuist.

But both in the *Temple* and in *Astrophel and Stella*, the search for simplicity is a constant element, the central stance of the dramatic speaker, permeating his remarks on theory of poetry, his attitude toward his mistress or Master, and, fundamentally, his attitude toward himself. This is most obvious in the remarks of Herbert and Sidney on poetry, their condemnation of elaborate modes of art, their insistence on the values of simple truth, as in Sidney's Sonnet 3, where he snubs the efforts of the "daintie wits," with their "phrases fine" and "strange similies," and concludes:

> in *Stellas* face I reed,
> What Love and Beautie be, then all my deed
> But Copying is, what in her Nature writes.

Or in Sonnet 55, which relates how he has often invoked the Muses to provide his speech with "choisest flowers":

> But now I meane no more your helpe to trie,
> Nor other sugring of my speech to prove,
> But on her name incessantly to crie:
> For let me but name her whom I do love,
> So sweete sounds straight mine eare and heart do hit,
> That I well find no eloquence like it.

Or in Sonnet 90, which perhaps expresses most clearly of all this central theme of both Sidney and Herbert:

> For nothing from my wit or will doth flow,
> Since all my words thy beauty doth endite,
> And love doth hold my hand, and makes me write.[11]

As the last passage indicates, this insistence on the manner of simplicity sometimes leads to the presentation of the speaker as love's

11. For further examples see *Astrophel and Stella*, sonnets 6, 15, 54, 70, 74. For an excellent treatment of this pose of the *naïf* in Sidney see the study by Richard B. Young, "English Petrarke," in *Three Studies in the Renaissance*, New Haven, Yale University Press, 1958.

simpleton, and is thus related to a striking device of total structure
that occurs several times in both Herbert and Sidney. It is the device
of "The Collar," where the speaker, for most of the poem, laments
that all his powers are "vainely spent" in the pursuit of this impossible love; yet in the end the apparent rebellion is easily quelled
by a word or a look, as in Sidney's sonnets 18 and 19, which conclude:

> I see my course to loose my selfe doth bend:
>   I see and yet no greater sorow take,
>   Then that I loose no more for *Stellas* sake.
>
> O let me prop my mind yet in his growth,
>   And not in Nature, for best fruits unfit:
>   Scholler, saith *Love*, bend hitherward your wit.

Perhaps the most striking of all, in relation to "The Collar," is Sidney's Sonnet 47, which opens with a tirade:

> What have I thus betrayed my libertie?
>   Can those blacke beames such burning markes engrave
>   In my free side? or am I borne a slave,
>   Whose necke becomes such yoke of tyranny?

But it concludes:

> Let her [go]: soft, but here she comes, go to,
>   Unkind, I love you not: O me, that eye
>   Doth make my heart give to my tongue the lie.

The similarity in technique is underlined by the fact that one of
Herbert's poems which best displays this device—"Affliction" (1)
—demolishes the rebellion with words highly reminiscent of the
technique used in the crushing last lines in at least three of Sidney's
sonnets:

> Well, I will change the service, and go seek
>   Some other master out.
>   Ah my deare God! though I am clean forgot,
>   Let me not love thee, if I love thee not.

Empson's interpretation of the last line is certainly right: "he has no
worse imprecation than the first part of the line, and it is used to

give force to the statement of purpose in the second"; [12] an interpretation reinforced by the fact that the preceding line suggests the
words of Psalm 31 in the Coverdale version: "I am cleane forgotten
as a dead man out of mind: I am become like a broken vessel." [13]
The echo reminds us that the middle of the poem also resembles
the complaints of this particular psalm of affliction:

> Have mercy upon me, O Lorde, for I am in trouble: and
> myne eye is consumed for very heavinesse, yea, my soule
> and my body.
> For my lyfe is waxen olde with heavinesse: and my
> yeeres with mourning.
> My strength fayleth me because of myne iniquitie: and
> my bones are consumed.

We are thus prepared to accept the sudden submission at the end.
Yet the lash of verbal play comes with a sharp surprise, as in the
close of Sidney's sonnets 61, 62, and 87:

> That I love not, without I leave to love.
> Deare, love me not, that ye may love me more.
> I had bene vext, if vext I had not beene.

Once one has been conditioned by these similarities, many more
spring to mind, both in general and in detail. Herbert's sonnet, "The
Holdfast," works in the mode of rapid internal dialogue used by
Sidney in Sonnet 34; the "Wreath" uses the method of line-by-line
repetition found in Sidney's Sonnet 44; the technique of definition
by a rapid sequence of analogies, found in Herbert's sonnets "Sinne"
and "Prayer," sounds almost like an answer to Sidney's identical
way of defining "kiss" and "lip" in sonnets 79 and 80. But these
are devices which Herbert would have found elsewhere in Elizabethan poetry, and especially in Southwell; they are more symptomatic of Herbert's all-pervasive art of sacred parody than of particular indebtedness to Sidney. More important than these details
is the general similarity in tone: the playful tenderness, the respect-
ful frivolity, the constant gleam of humor through the sighs; the

---

12. *Seven Types*, p. 184.
13. Quotations from the Coverdale Psalms throughout this chapter are
given from *The Psalter or Psalmes of David, after the translation of the great
Byble*, London, 1575.

tone which Leishman has very well described as "this peculiar humour of Herbert's, which runs through almost all his poetry, giving a rare human tenderness to his adoration and a saving sincerity to his abnegation, in somewhat the same way as Sidney's humour colours many of his finest sonnets to Stella." [14]

But I do not wish to overemphasize the example of Sidney. It would be more accurate to say that the evidence of Herbert's poetry points toward this hypothesis: that as Herbert developed in spirituality he found that the mode of Donne did not accord with the ideal of simplicity that he set for himself under the guidance of those spiritual masters in whom he found his own center of being. Consequently, he turned toward modes of poetry which accorded with this ideal: and where, more appropriately, than toward that love-poet who had himself spoken as one who sought simplicity?

Meanwhile, Herbert's love and mastery of music would have led him to those airs and madrigals which everyone was singing, and which developed a neatly patterned simplicity based on the fact that they were designed to be sung. Echoes of Elizabethan lute-songs ring throughout the *Temple*, in such motifs as the lover's address to his heart or his lute, and in the similarity between Herbert's handling of stanza-form and that found in E. H. Fellowes' superb collection, *English Madrigal Verse, 1588–1632*. It is important to notice how closely those dates, which represent the period of the flourishing of English song, accord with the dates of Herbert's birth and death (1593–1633); the *Temple*, appearing in 1633, may be seen as a culmination, a fulfillment, of the greatest era of English music: these poems are full of sounds and sweet airs plucked from the surrounding atmosphere. But we must leave this to the students of Fellowes' monumental work, and of Bruce Pattison's useful study of the song-writers of this period,[15] noting only that the poetry of the *Temple* belongs much more to the realm of the air than of the madrigal. For, as Fellowes points out in his preface, "the true madrigal was seldom set to more than one stanza of poetry," whereas "the Airs of the lutenists usually took the form

14. J. B. Leishman, *The Metaphysical Poets* (Oxford, Clarendon Press, 1934), p. 116.

15. Bruce Pattison, *Music and Poetry of the English Renaissance*, London, Methuen, 1948.

of solo-songs with several stanzas of words, for each of which, as a general rule, the same music was repeated." Hence the neat, simple, usually end-stopped pattern of these several stanzas, fulfilling Sidney's own account of the ideal poet: "Hee beginneth not with obscure definitions, which must blurre the margent with interpretations, and loade the memorie with doubtfulnesse: but hee commeth to you with words set in delightfull proportion, either accompanied with, or prepared for the well enchanting skill of *Musicke.*"[16]

It is exactly this pattern that Donne's poetry, in the main, breaks. Only a few of Donne's poems were set to music: only a few could be so set; they are not often written in this mode, but rather in the passionate tyranny of a spoken argument. Here, then, is another reason why the course of Herbert's development seems to move away from Donne toward that greater simplicity of Sidney and song, which accorded with Herbert's spiritual center. But there remains one more, all-important kind of poetry which we must not neglect; and here again, we find a link with Sidney.

3

Sidney's translation of the Psalms (1–43) represents, I believe, the closest approximation to the poetry of Herbert's *Temple* that can be found anywhere in preceding English poetry. Simplicity of phrasing, based on both the Coverdale and the Geneva versions, is here combined with frequent "wit" and constant metrical ingenuity, to produce what Hallett Smith has accurately called "a School of English versification."[1] Theodore Spencer, too, has called attention to the rich combination of "metrical experiment and simplicity of diction" in these translations, noting that out of Sidney's forty-three Psalms all but two are in different stanza-forms (7 and 12 are both in *terza rima*).[2] Yet in themselves the stanza-forms are not elaborate: unlike the extravagant intricacy of the forms attempted in the *Arcadia* poems, we find here that nearly all the Psalms are

16. "The Defence of Poesie," *Works*, ed. Feuillerat, 3, 19–20.
1. Hallett Smith, "English Metrical Psalms in the Sixteenth Century and their Literary Significance," *HLQ, 9* (1946), 249–71; see especially pp. 269–70.
2. Theodore Spencer, "The Poetry of Sir Philip Sidney," *ELH, A Journal of English Literary History, 12* (1945), 251–78; see especially pp. 254–5.

translated into stanzas of four, five, and six lines; and that the effect of variety is achieved by simple variations in rime or line-length. This is exactly the effect of subdued and controlled variety achieved in the *Temple*, where, though Palmer finds 116 different meters among the 169 poems,[3] one must add that three-fourths of the poems are written in four, five, and six-line stanzas—fifty of them in six-line stanzas—with variation achieved by slight changes in line-length and rime.[4] Only twice does Herbert attempt anything like the virtuosity in the long stanza which Donne so often displays in his "Songs and Sonets" and Sidney in his *Arcadia* experiments. Simplicity, as in Sidney's Psalms, includes a rich variety, but held within a strict control. The similarity in effect depends upon a whole reading of both works, but the kinship in idiom may be suggested by a few examples.

Let us take first one of the psalms of affliction—Psalm 6, where Sidney's translation is based chiefly on Coverdale:

> O Lord rebuke me not in thyne indignation: neyther chasten me in thy displeasure.
> Have mercie uppon me, O Lorde, for I am weake: O Lorde heale me, for my bones are vexed.
> My soule is also sore troubled: but Lord howe long wylt thou punyshe me?
> Turn thee, O Lorde, and delyver my soule: oh save me for thy mercies sake.
> For in death no man remembreth thee: and who wyl geve thee thankes in the pyt?
> I am weery of my groning, every night washe I my bed: and water my coutche with my teares.
> My beautie is gone for very trouble; and worne away because of al myne enimies.
> Away from me all ye that woorke vanitie: for the Lorde hath hearde the voyce of my weepyng.

3. *Works of Herbert*, ed. Palmer, *1*, 136–7.

4. Cf. the tabulation of Herbert's stanzaic forms in the interesting article by Albert M. Hayes, "Counterpoint in Herbert," *Studies in Philology, 35* (1938), 43–60; the tabulation of Sidney's metrics here, however, is invalidated by a failure to consider Sidney's Psalms and *Arcadia* poems.

The Lorde hath hearde my petition: the Lorde wyll receyve
my prayer.

All myne enimies shalbe confounded and sore vexed: they
shalbe turned backe, and put to shame sodainely.

Lord lett not mee a worm by thee be shent
    While thou art in the heate of thy displeasure:
    Ne let thy rage of my due punnishment
        Become the measure.

But mercy Lord, lett mercy thine descend,
    For I am weake, and in my weaknes languish:
    Lord help, for ev'n my bones their marrow spend
        With cruell anguish.

Nay ev'n my soule fell troubles do appall.
    Alas how long my God wilt thou delay me?
    Turn thee, sweete Lord, and from this ougly fall
        My deere God stay me.

Mercy, ô mercy Lord, for mercies sake,
    For death doth kill the wittnes of thy glory,
    Can of thy praise the tongues entombed make
        A heav'nly story?

Loe I am tir'd while still I sigh and grone:
    My moistned bed proofes of my sorrow showeth:
    My bed (while I with black night moorn alone)
        With my teares floweth.

Woe, like a Moth, my faces beutie eates,
    And age pul'd on with paines all freshnes fretteth;
    The while a swarm of foes with vexing feates
        My life besetteth.

Gett hence you evill, who in my ill rejoice,
    In all whose works vainenesse is ever raigning:

> For God hath heard the weeping sobbing voice
>   Of my complayning.

> The Lord my suite did heare, and gently heare
>   They shall be sham'd and vext, that breed my cryeng:
> And turn their backs, and straight on backs appeare
>   Their shamfull flyeng.[5]

The total effect of Sidney's version is to change a ritual poem into a poem of intimate, personal lament. The formal "O Lord" is changed to the simple "Lord," and the third stanza moves toward a closer intimacy with the added cries, "Alas," "my God," "sweete Lord," and "my deere God." In stanza 4 the poem throws, through repetition, much greater emphasis on the cries for mercy and the tears. At the same time the diction and the phrasing throughout the earlier part of the poem become much more colloquial and idiomatic than Coverdale's. But in the last four stanzas the poem builds toward complication, first by expanding the image of the tearful bed, next by adding the imagery of "Moth" and "swarm," and, in the last two stanzas, by developing a careful balance and symmetry of phrasing: the play on "Evill" (pronounced E'il) and "ill"; the assonantal balance of "vainenesse" and "raigning"; the effective repetition, "The Lord my suite did heare, and gently heare"; and finally, the labored play on "backs" by which he attempts to conclude with the kind of balanced turn used frequently in *Astrophel and Stella*. Throughout, the poem displays a more logical movement, as evidenced in the increased number of connectives.

   Thus Sidney's Psalms frequently achieve a sense of familiar presence, expressed in the simple, yet artful verse of Elizabethan song. In the ending of his version of Psalm 13, for example, the lumbering phrases of Coverdale are changed to a graceful lightness, with perhaps a touch of the art of sacred parody in the use of a favorite lover's rime:

5. For quotations from Sidney's Psalms, see Sidney's *Works*, ed. Feuillerat, 3, 187–246. The evidence that Sidney translated only the first 43 Psalms is summed up by Feuillerat, *idem*, 3, ix; the remainder were translated in a similar style by the Countess of Pembroke. The version was not printed until 1823; but the extant mss. indicate that it circulated widely in Herbert's time: see Feuillerat, *idem*, 3, 408–10.

But my trust is in thy mercie: and my hart is ioyful in thy salvation.

I wyl syng of the Lorde, because he hath dealt so lovingly with me: yea, I wyl prayse the name of the Lorde moste hyghest.

> Noe, noe, I trust on thee, and joy in thy
> Greate pitty:
> Still therefore of thy graces shalbe my
> Songs ditty.

In still other places even the great simplicity which marks the Geneva version has been further pruned by Sidney, with results that we may see in the stanzas of Psalm 38, with their contrapuntal riming:

O Lord, rebuke me not in thine anger, neither chastise me in thy wrath.

For thine arrowes have light upon me, and thine hand lyeth upon me.

> Lord, while that thy rage doth bide
> Do not chide:
> Nor in anger chastise me,
> For thy shafts have peirc'd me sore;
> And yet more
> Still thy hands upon me be.

For on thee, O Lord, doe I waite: thou wilt heare me, my Lord, my God.

For I said, Heare me, least they reioyce over me: for when my foote slippeth, they extoll themselves against me.[6]

> For on the, Lord, without end
> I attend:
> My God, thou wilt heare my voice.
> For I said, heare, least they be

6. I have used the edition of the Geneva Bible published by Christopher Barker, London, 1578; this prints the Geneva and the Coverdale versions of the Psalms in parallel columns.

> Gladd on me,
> Whome my fall doth make rejoyce.

Thus, amid a good deal of the clumsiness and uncertainty that seems characteristic of English metrical Psalms, we find stanzas of a simple dexterity that seem to point directly toward the achievement of Herbert:

> O tremble then with awfull will:
>   Sinne from all rule in you depose,
>   Talk with your harts and yet be still:
>   And when your chamber you do close,
>   Your selves, yet to your selves disclose.
>
> (Psalm 4)

> God my only portion is,
>   And of my childes part the blisse:
>   He then shall maintaine my lott.
>   Say then is not my lott found
>   In a goodly pleasant ground?
>   Have I not faire partage gott?
>
> (Psalm 16)

I should not wish to appear to be arguing only for a strong direct influence of Sidney's Psalms upon Herbert, though indeed this may be so. Sidney's version was not available in print in Herbert's time, but Donne knew the Sidney-Pembroke version well, as we see from his poem in praise of this translation; if Donne had seen these poems we may well believe that Herbert had seen them too, especially since Herbert was related to, and well known by, the Pembroke family. But the important thing is what is represented in Sidney's Psalms: the attempt to bring the art of Elizabethan lyric into the service of psalmody, and to perform this in a way that makes the psalm an intimate, personal cry of the soul to God—an effort in which, later, dozens of poets were to play their part; poets as different as Wither, Carew, Crashaw, Vaughan, or Milton. Here in the Psalms lay for the poet a challenge and an example which, as Hallett Smith has said, exerted its force even in the awkward version of Sternhold and Hopkins: "it cannot be overlooked by the historian of Elizabethan poetry as a force working for that direct, plain, 'mere English' quality against the lavish, ornamental, stylized manners." [7]

Moreover, one ought to note the significant fact that the word "meditation" occurs six times in the King James version of the Psalms, and nowhere else in this version of the Bible, while the word "meditate" occurs here nine times in the Psalms, and only once apiece in each of five other books. In the Psalms lay the prime models for the soul in meditation: here, above all places, lay a precedent for what I have called the poetry of meditation. This is especially clear in the *Introduction* of St. François de Sales, who constantly uses the Psalms as examples and precedents in urging his reader to the practice of meditation and the presence of God; and other meditative writers do the same. Similarly, the Song of Solomon provided poets with their prime justification for attempting to utilize the arts of profane love in the service of religious devotion. The history of English religious poetry in the sixteenth and seventeenth centuries can never be accurately recorded without remembering that for the devout poet of the time the greatest examples of religious poetry lay in the Bible.

Thus it is that hundreds of phrases from the Psalms, especially in the Coverdale (Prayer-Book) version, [8] echo throughout the *Temple*, as Herbert's editors have extensively—though by no means completely—recorded. These echoes of the Psalms permeate the *Temple* in a remarkable variety of ways. In "The Quip," for instance, the refrain, "But thou shalt answer, Lord, for me," comes from the Coverdale version of Psalm 38; [9] while the central situation of the jeering world is strongly reminiscent of a portion of Psalm 35: "But in mine adversitie they reioyced and geathered them togeather; yea the very abiectes came togeather against me unawares, making mowes at me, and ceassed not. With the flatterers were busie mockers." (Coverdale) The whole poem "Providence" suggests an individual psalm of praise modeled upon Psalm 104, which is subtitled in the King James version: "A meditation upon the mighty power

7. *HLQ*, 9, 266.
8. See the frequent parallels with this version recorded in Hutchinson's notes to his *Works of Herbert;* especially p. 537.
9. Cf. *idem*, p. 110.

and wonderful providence of God." [10] "Praise" (2) bears a strong resemblance to Psalm 116; [11] and yet it is not so much an imitation of any one psalm, as a blending of motifs from many psalms of praise: a resemblance reinforced here, as elsewhere, by the persistent parallelism of the phrasing. Most important of all are the psalms of affliction, for this word, which gives a title to five poems in the *Temple* and occurs in nine more, is used (including verbal forms) thirty-five times in the King James version of the Psalms, more often than in any other book of the Bible: Psalm 102, for instance, is described in the King James version as "A prayer of the afflicted, when he is overwhelmed, and poureth out his complaint before the Lord." The sighs and groans and tears of the afflicted lover form the ground-tone of the Psalms, as of the *Temple*. It is hardly too much to say, then, that the "Church" is a book of seventeenth-century psalmody, as the motto from the Coverdale Psalms (29) suggests on Herbert's title-page: "In his Temple doth every man speak of his Honour." The temple is both macrocosm and microcosm: the universe that praises God in Psalm 29, or the man, who, as Herbert says in "Providence," "doth present/ The sacrifice for all";

> while they below
> Unto the service mutter an assent,
> Such as springs use that fall, and windes that blow.

In this new book of personal psalms we can see, I think, the proper and honorable place of Donne's poetic mode within the total fabric: important, but not dominant; simply present along with all the other modes of poetry in his time which Herbert included in his *Temple:* the modes of Sidney and of Southwell, the gnomic style of the *Paradyse of daynty devises*, the lyric style of Dowland's or Campion's *Book of Ayres*, the pattern-poetry described by Puttenham,[12] the anagram, the acrostic, the ring, the wreath, the riddle, the charm,

10. Cf. *idem*, p. 518.

11. Cf. *Works of Herbert*, ed. Palmer, 2, 396.

12. See George Puttenham, *The Arte of English Poesie*, ed. Gladys Doidge Willcock and Alice Walker (Cambridge, University Press, 1936), pp. 91–7; the examples of the "Triquet" on p. 95 provide a precedent for the form of "Easter-wings," while the examples of the "Piller" on p. 97 suggest "The Altar." A closer parallel with the latter has been pointed out by Hutchinson

the animal fable, the narrative allegory; for all things, all creation, must play a part in this service and sacrifice. A total reading of the *Temple* leaves one with the impression that the writer has taken special pains to include at least one example of every kind of short poem popular in his day, along with at least one example of every kind of devotional practice. Thus we find one translation of a Psalm, one poem to the Magdalen, one poem "To all Angels and Saints," one echo-song, one anagram, one poem in the emblem-book tradition of the *Schola Cordis*,[13] one specific "Parodie" of a popular love-song, one "Posie," one "rose-song," one poem based on a classical myth,[14] one explicit parody of *Astrophel and Stella*, and one poem, "Vanitie" (1), which in theme, in imagery, in elaborate stanza-form acts as an explicit reminder of the intricacies of Donne. Yet amid all this variety, a dominant, central, personal idiom emerges, resembling that of Donne in places, but for the most part working in a conversational idiom and "neat" stanza-form that blends a biblical simplicity of phrase, a Sidneian, Salesian, courtly wit, and the delicate craftsmanship so often found among the English "Airs." This writer knows the art of poetry in all its areas; knows, certainly, and loves, the art of music; and knows the pictorial arts also, in some degree, as his frequent use of emblematic imagery testifies.[15] And all this is subdued and transformed in accord with a central, controlling ideal of

---

(*Works of Herbert*, pp. 484–5) in *A Poetical Rapsody*, London, 1602: see the edition by Hyder Rollins (2 vols., Cambridge, Harvard University Press, 1931–2), *1*, 180: "An Altare and Sacrifice to Disdaine, for freeing him from love." This is indeed so very similar to Herbert's poem, both in shape and in some of its wording (cf. the rime of "reares" and "teares" in the opening of both, and the word "sacrifice" in the conclusion of both), that it looks as though Herbert had performed a deliberate parody of this love-poem. The *Rapsody* was very popular in Herbert's day, with four editions between 1602 and 1621. For other precedents see Rollins' edition, *2*, 158–9.

13. "Love unknown": see Freeman, pp. 164–7.

14. "The Pulley," which combines the story of Pandora (cf. *Works of Herbert*, ed. Hutchinson, p. 533) with such advice on "rest" as may be found in the *Imitation of Christ*, Bk. 3, chap. 21.

15. See Miss Freeman's excellent chapter on Herbert. Miss Tuve's recent book thoroughly explores the relations between Herbert's leading images and iconography.

Christian Simplicity: an ideal that results in a poetic style proper
to the man, and hence fitly used in the practice of the presence of
God.

4

Finally, to clarify this ideal—and to suggest how it controls the
poetical traditions that enter into the *Temple*—it seems essential to
examine two other treatises that bear a close relation to Herbert's
spirituality. One is the *Imitation of Christ;* the other is Savonarola's
treatise, *De Simplicitate Christianae Vitae* (1496). Among the *Ferrar Papers* is a letter from Arthur Woodnoth to Nicholas Ferrar,
dated October 13, 1631, in which Woodnoth, speaking of Herbert,
remarks, "Savonarola in Latine he hath of the Simplicity of Chr:
Religion and is of great esteme with him." [1] Since this book does not
appear to be well known, it may be helpful to examine its principles
in some detail and to translate a few passages that seem clearly to display a fundamental kinship with the spirituality of the *Temple*. For
it may be that we have here an important key to Herbert's mature
way of life and to his ultimate poetical achievement.

Savonarola's treatise advises the constant cultivation of an ideal of
simplicity much broader and richer than his reputation as a reformer
might lead one to expect. The Christian, says Savonarola, "makes use
of riches, glory, dignities, honors, and other good things of the body,
for the necessity of either temporal or spiritual life, but not for pride,
or luxury, or avarice." [2] Things of this world are to be used in accordance with the needs of one's station in life, used, as this station itself is to be used: in the service of God, whatever the vocation. All
depends upon that "simplicity of heart," or "interior simplicity,"
which constitutes the center of Herbert's spirituality: "Christian
simplicity consists in this: that man through grace is made like unto
God: and that a uniformity appears in his words, thoughts, and
deeds." A man will achieve this condition

> if all things which his intellect knows or contemplates are God,
> or related to God. If all things which the will loves and desires

1. *The Ferrar Papers*, ed. B. Blackstone (Cambridge, University Press,
1938), p. 268.

2. Girolamo Savonarola, *De Simplicitate Christianae Vitae* (Strassburg,
1615), *Liber* 1, *Conclusio* 1.

are God himself, or are loved and desired because of God: and likewise those things held in hate which are deserving of hate. If he holds always in his memory God and his benefits. If his imagination [*phanthasia*] holds always before his eyes Christ Crucified and those things which pertain to him . . . . Thus the whole Christian life strives toward this end, that it may be purified from all earthly infection, both in the intellect and the will, and in the senses and the whole body: that the whole man, made clean, may become the sanctified temple of God . . . . (*Lib.* 2, *Concl.* 7)

Not that sensory experiences are to be scorned; quite the contrary, since man is so created that the intellect must work through the medium of corporal and sensory things.

And therefore we know by experience that when spiritual things are represented through corporal similitudes, they are better understood by men, and are held more firmly in the memory . . . . Consequently the sacred scriptures make use of similitudes and parables: because God provides for every creature in accordance with the condition of his own peculiar nature. Therefore let us begin with corporal things, in order to understand more easily spiritual things. (*Lib.* 2, *Concl.* 1)

This is not, then, a simplicity of abnegation; it is, like that of St. François de Sales, a simplicity of fullness, able to utilize exterior things in accord with their proper ends. *Simple* in the full Latin sense of *simplex*: open, frank, direct, sincere, pure, whole.

It is this concept of *simplicitas* which motivates Savonarola's ridicule of those who cultivate exterior ceremonies to the destruction of the inward man, and who value the intricacies of worldly learning above the simple truth of the Bible:

They never, or rarely, read the Scriptures, or reading they do not understand, or understanding, they do not taste: therefore they say, our mind is disgusted with this trivial fare. Who will let us hear the eloquence of Cicero, and the resonant words of the poets, and the sweet speech of Plato, and the subtleties of Aristotle? For this Scripture is simple, and food for mere women: preach to us subtle things. (*Lib.* 1, *Concl.* 11)

The way is thus prepared for a long discussion of the difference between the natural and the artificial, explaining how interior simplicity manifests itself in exterior simplicity, including simplicity of speech: "We call those exterior things simple which proceed from an interior principle [*forma*] conferred by God, either naturally or supernaturally, and which do not display the invention of art." And conversely,

> We call those things artificial, which proceed from human invention. Therefore we say that the motions of the human body and the senses are natural, since they follow the natural inclination of man. And likewise we say that speech is natural, when a man speaks according to the usage of other men, with whom he has associated from his boyhood: because that usage has become natural. When he follows this nature in speaking, he is said to speak naturally, not artificially. When, however, he does not follow the usage and custom of others, nor his own, according as he learned to speak in boyhood, but strives to imitate the discourse or eloquence of another, he is said to speak according to art. Likewise he who is full of the grace of God and Charity, if he utters his words as they are suggested by that principle, that is, by grace and charity: he is said to speak by the spirit of God, not artificially. (*Lib.* 3, *Concl.* 1)

All this struggle to achieve interior and exterior simplicity is not, of course, an end in itself; its purpose is to prepare the way for what Savonarola calls the "principal work of Christians": "prayer and meditation or contemplation of Divine things." If a man does not possess this simplicity he will not be free to pray and meditate successfully, and hence he will not possess the familiar presence of God, as did the ancient Fathers:

> Therefore our Fathers, both in the Old and in the New Testament, both secular and religious, loved simplicity: and sought this simplicity in their work. And thus being free for prayer and contemplation, they became godly and sanctified men, familiar with the Angels and Saints . . . . But we, quite the contrary, in these times are not free for prayer and contem-

plation, because we are too much occupied with exterior affairs, not loving simplicity of life. And thus today the man does not appear who possesses an intimate friendship with God: indeed it seems incredible that anyone should be illuminated in his deeds by God in that familiar way in which the holy fathers were illuminated. (*Lib.* 3, *Concl.* 4)

The whole treatise thus is designed to make way for that familiar presence which will be known only to the pure in heart, and known chiefly through two inseparable forms of "contemplation": the contemplation of Christ Crucified and the contemplation of the Scriptures. And thus we have his ultimate statement of the meaning and the purpose of this simplicity:

Simplicity of heart requires purgation from earthly affections, in order that the whole spirit and the whole soul may be directed toward God, and may become like unto God, that the whole man may be made simple in the likeness of God . . . . For the contemplation of Divine things requires the greatest tranquillity of heart: and therefore he who wishes to enjoy Divine illuminations must remove himself as far as possible from the clamor of this world . . . . Thus the holy Fathers, desiring the contemplative life, left behind all things, and retired to solitude, content with little, in order to have greater freedom for contemplation. Therefore, the more each man shall strive to achieve simplicity in his proper degree, the greater the consolations he shall receive from Christ.

(*Lib.* 5, *Concl.* 16)

It is evident how close the spirit and aim of Savonarola's treatise is to the *Introduction* of St. François de Sales, and also to that greatest treatise of all: the *Imitation of Christ*. I have not, thus far in this study, spoken much of the *Imitation*, partly because it is so well known, and partly because it is not, strictly speaking, a treatise on the art of meditation, but rather a book of precepts and examples leading toward a life maintained in the intimate presence and "familiar friendship" of Christ: "if through negligence of thy selfe thou loose him, what freende shalte thou then have? Without a freende thou mayest not long endure, and if Jesu be not thy freende moste before all other, thou shalt be verie heavye and desolate, and be lefte without all perfect frendship." (Bk. 2, chap. 8) That way of life is dramatically revealed in the great series of colloquies and dialogues which constitute the third and fourth books, where we read of "the inwarde speakinge of Christ to a faythfull soule," and see the fulfillment of the promise made earlier in the treatise that "There is betwixt almightie God and a devout soule manye ghostly visitinges, sweete inwarde speaking, great giftes of grace, many consolations, muche heavenly peace, and wonderous familiaritie of the blessed presence of God." (Bk. 2, chap. 1) Here the questioning of Christ "as a lover is wont to speake to his beloved, and a freende with his beloved freende" (Bk. 4, chap. 13), Christ's gentle answers to his "son" and the soul's fervent self-addresses are all intermingled in a style of the utmost simpleness and suppleness, compact with the biblical phrase, the homely proverb, the commonplace image.

One will best grasp the kinship of all this with Herbert through a reading of the great translation made about the year 1530 by Richard Whitford; a translation which, as Edward Klein has shown, enjoyed great popularity during the sixteenth century, and formed the basis of translations that were popular in the seventeenth century.[3] Since Klein's modernized version of Whitford's masterpiece is so easily available, there is no need to attempt a description of the extraordinary sense of "presence" which this translation conveys. In any case, brief quotations will not convey the effect, which resides in the thousands of familiar, intimate phrases, the hundred repetitions of the words "friend" and "son." Anyone who reads will see at once that here is the prime model for those familiar colloquies which the Jesuits and all the other meditative writers place at the apex of their exercises; and here too one finds a model for the way in which Herbert transformed the popular love-dialogue of

---

3. *The Imitation of Christ, From the First Edition of an English Translation Made c. 1530 by Richard Whitford,* ed. (in modernized form) Edward J. Klein, New York, Harper, 1941; see Klein's introduction to this edition for the popularity and influence of this translation. Klein's edition was issued in smaller format in 1943, with a very brief introduction.

Elizabethan poetry into the "inward speaking" of Christ and the faithful soul.

But we will not realize this fully without grasping the significance of the fourth, the eucharistic book, which contains the most intimate dialogues of all, and reveals the fundamental basis of that subtle, almost intangible sense of unity which pervades the interior of Herbert's *Temple*.

CHAPTER 8

George Herbert: the Unity of The Temple

Si, par quelque force forcee, vous ne pouves pas vous rendre presente a la celebration de ce souverain Sacrifice, d'une presence reelle, au moins faut-il que vous y porties vostre coeur pour y assister d'une presence spirituelle. A quelque heure donq du matin, allés en esprit, si vous ne pouves autrement, en l'église; unisses vostre intention a celle de tous les Chrestiens, et faites les mesmes actions intérieures au lieu ou vous estes, que vous feries si vous esties reellement presente . . . .

St. François de Sales, *Introduction à la Vie dévote*, 1609

HERBERT'S *Temple* displays a structure built upon the art of mental communion, and so designed, beyond any doubt, by George Herbert himself. The early Williams manuscript contains the skeleton of the same structure which the published *Temple* displays; [1] Walton gives, from Duncon's own testimony, the picture of Herbert handing to Duncon his book of "spiritual Conflicts" for delivery to Nicholas Ferrar; [2] and Ferrar himself, in his preface to the *Temple*, explains the lack of the usual introductory matter by his desire to present the work to the world "in that naked simplicitie, with which he left it." But the best evidence lies within the *Temple* itself.

Consider first the structure in the large. Is there any significance in the tripartite arrangement of "Church-porch," "Church," and

1. See *Works of Herbert*, ed. Hutchinson, pp. liv–v. I have studied a film of this manuscript, now in Dr. Williams's Library, London, and have used the Harvard transcript of the Bodleian manuscript of the *Temple*.

2. Walton, *Lives*, p. 314; cf. *Works of Herbert*, ed. Hutchinson, p. lxx.

"Church Militant"? Certainly the first two parts are much more closely related than the last two. And certainly the "Church Militant," in many respects, may seem to represent a rather desperate effort to salvage, if only by way of appendix, a very early poem. It has undergone careful revision, and it is deeply influenced by the themes, the idiom, and the management of pentameter couplet, found in Donne's *Anniversaries;* indeed the division of the poem into five parts by means of a refrain very strongly suggests the example of the *First Anniversary.* Yet it has, I believe, a function in the whole volume.

Among the meditations of the pseudo-Bonaventure there is a significant passage which, in its threefold division of the Christian life, may help to clarify the relationship which these three parts of Herbert's *Temple* bear to one another. "As I gather from Blessed Bernard's teaching," says this unknown Franciscan, "there are in the active life two parts":

> The first part is that in which a soul exercises herself chiefly in correcting herself, purging herself from vices, and acquiring virtues. And the same life is lived also, secondly, by helping our neighbour in doing good works and deeds of piety and charity. The second part of the active life is spent in doing good actively to the neighbour, to one's great merit, as in ruling, teaching, and helping in the salvation of souls.

But "between these two parts of the active life," says the writer, "there is the contemplative life." And hence, he adds, "we have this order":

> To begin with, one is exercised in prayer, sacred studies, service and conversation, occupied, as it were, in correcting one's faults and acquiring virtue. Then the soul rests in contemplation, seeking solitude and trying with all its might to please God alone. Thirdly, when it has been penetrated and illuminated by the aforesaid two exercises, by virtues and true wisdom, it gives itself up to the salvation of its neighbour.

"In the first part of the active life," he concludes, "it behooves the soul to be purified, corrected, and strengthened by the practice of virtues," as Herbert explains in the "Church-porch." Next, "in the contemplative life it has to be informed, illuminated, instructed, and trained," as in Herbert's "Church." "After that it can confidently go forth to help others and work at their perfection," as does "Religion" in the "Church Militant." "It can be proved," adds the Franciscan, "from reliable authorities that this is the right order of proceeding."[3]

The "Church-porch," with its precepts for "good life," provides in general what Southwell called "A Preparative to Prayer";[4] or, more specifically, a preparation for spiritual communion in prayer and meditation. This is suggested by the word "Perirrhanterium," the name of the "instrument for sprinkling holy water,"[5] which occurs as subtitle to the "Porch"; and more emphatically by the stanzas immediately following the "Porch," on the lintel of the "Church": "Superliminare":

> Thou, whom the former precepts have
> Sprinkled and taught, how to behave
> Thy self in church; approach, and taste
> The churches mysticall repast.

> Avoid, Profanenesse; come not here:
> Nothing but holy, pure, and cleare,
> Or that which groneth to be so,
> May at his perill further go.

The "Church-porch," from this standpoint, represents a versified elaboration of the methods of preparation for Communion thus advised by the *Imitation:*

> weepe and sorowe, that thou art yet so carnall and worldly, so unmortified from thy passions, so full of motions of concupiscences, so unware, and so evill ordred in thy outward wits, so oft wrapped in vayne phantasies, so muche inclined to outwarde and worldlie thinges, so negligent to inwarde thinges, so redie to laughinge and dissolution, so harde to weepinge and compunction, so readie to easie thinges, and to that that is likinge to the fleshe: so slowe to penance and fervor of spirite,

3. *Meditations on the Life of Christ*, pp. 219–20.
4. See the verses introductory to his *Short Rules of Good Life*, 1630.
5. *Works of Herbert*, ed. Hutchinson, pp. 476–7.

so curious to heare newe thinges, and to see fayre thinges, so lothe to meeke and abiect thinges, so covetous to have muche, so scarse to geve, so glad to holde, so unadvised in speakinge, so incontinent to be still, so evill ordred in maners, so importune in deedes, so greedie upon meate, so deafe to the word of God . . . . (Bk. 4, chap. 7)

Thus the "Church-porch" covers a world of error, and seeks to reform it by precepts that fall, despite some eddying and repetition, into three general divisions: sins related to individual conduct (stanzas 1–34); sins related to social behavior (35–62); and finally, sins related to specifically religious duties (63–77). It is a typical Herbertian touch that these stanzas, after undergoing drastic revision, should at last emerge with the "perfect number," seventy-seven: [6] signifying, no doubt, that the man thus regulated has at last reached a degree of perfection sufficient to permit him to partake of the "mysticall repast" which we have glimpsed from the very first stanza:

> A verse may finde him, who a sermon flies,
> And turn delight into a sacrifice.

As we pass under the lintel, "The Altar" stands before us, and the service proceeds in accordance with the advice of the *Imitation:*

then with a full resigninge and a wholle will offer thy selfe into the honour of my name in the Aulter of thy hart, as sacrifice to me, that is to saye, faythfullie committinge to me both thy bodie and soule, so that thou mayest be worthye to offer to me this high sacrifice . . . . (Bk. 4, chap. 7)

The sacrifice is not only the explicit service of mental communion represented in the long meditation on the Passion and the two poems of Thanksgiving that immediately follow: the sacrifice is all the poetry of the "Church"; the "frame" is both this particular

6. Cf. Chambers, p. 21, where he points out that in "vulgar languages" the Creed contains 77 words, and goes on to show that it was common to make "pious conceits" upon the significance of this number. The stanzas are numbered in the Bodleian ms., but not in the Williams ms., which contains 78 stanzas: see *Works of Herbert,* ed. Hutchinson, pp. 6, 10.

emblem-poem, and the structure of the "Church" which holds together the parts, the poems, of the "heart."

The first four poems of the "Church," then, form an inseparable sequence: "Altar," "Sacrifice," "Thanksgiving," and "Reprisall" —originally entitled, "The Second Thanks-giving": [7] for it solves the dilemma of gratitude for the Passion with which the first Thanksgiving, with a witty inconclusion, ends. Now in the next eleven poems the unity of the *Temple* begins to display its diversity, while maintaining a ritual, liturgical focus so strongly that this whole opening group of fifteen poems forms what may be called a sacramental introduction to the work: setting forth the basic problems and premises of the Christian life, before launching forth into the spiritual combat. With one exception, "The Sinner" (which appropriately follows the definition of sin in "The Agonie"), all of the eleven poems that follow "The Reprisall" are ritual and sacramental in theme, focusing attention on the Sacrifice, moving from "The Agonie" in Gethsemane to "Good Friday," "Redemption," "Sepulchre," Resurrection ("Easter," "Easter-wings"), and finally to the two poems on Baptism, the first of which speaks of the "blessed streams" that flowed from the "pierced side," thus linking tightly with the lines near the end of "The Sacrifice":

> For they will pierce my side, I full well know;
> That as sinne came, so Sacraments might flow . . . .

This links also with the last stanza of "The Agonie," and with the many other references to the wounds and blood of Christ that dominate the poems of this section. It is most appropriate, too, that this sacramental introduction should end with poems on the sacrament which represents the whole process of Death and Resurrection, both in Christ and in the individual Christian (Romans 6): the Baptism that makes possible the spiritual combat with "Nature"—fallen nature—described in the poem that follows these two poems on Baptism. "Nature" thus appropriately marks the beginning of those conflicts and questionings which constitute the main body of the *Temple*.

7. See *Works of Herbert*, ed. Hutchinson, p. 36. With the following analysis of unity compare the commentary of Joseph H. Summers in his excellent book, *George Herbert*, Cambridge, Harvard Univ. Press, 1954.

The Altar.

A broken A L T A R, Lord, thy servant reares,
Made of a heart, and cemented with teares:
    Whose parts are as thy hand did frame;
    No workmans tool hath touch'd the same.
        A H E A R T alone
        Is such a stone,
        As nothing but
        Thy power doth cut.
        Wherefore each part
        Of my hard heart
        Meets in this frame,
        To praise thy name.
    That if I chance to hold my peace,
    These stones to praise thee may not cease.
O let thy blessed S A C R I F I C E be mine,
And sanctifie this A L T A R to be thine.

The

"The Altar," from George Herbert's *Temple*,
Cambridge, 1633

(Pierpont Morgan Library)

The unity of this opening section is tightened by many different interlocking connections in detail. "The Altar" introduces a strand of imagery that runs through several other poems of this section: the imagery of the stony heart of man, cut by the power of God. This imagery is based partly upon the "tables of stone, written with the finger of God" (Exodus 31.18), but more particularly on the passage in 2 Corinthians (3.3), which refers to "the epistle of Christ ministered by us, written not with ink, but with the Spirit of the living God; not in tables of stone, but in fleshly tables of the heart." This imagery is touched upon in "The Sacrifice" (lines 90, 122–3), forms the basic metaphor of "Sepulchre," and rescues "The Sinner" from banality in its closing couplet:

> And though my hard heart scarce to thee can grone,
> Remember that thou once didst write in stone.

The imagery of writing in the heart then forms the basis of the second poem under the title "Good Friday," a poem which in its second stanza uses imagery of "lodging" also found in "Sepulchre," stanza 1; at the same time this "Good Friday" poem concludes with legal imagery of "possession" that prepares the way for the similar imagery of "Redemption," which immediately follows. Musical imagery runs throughout the section in the same interlocking way, especially notable in the parallel arrangement of the two poems that come under each of the titles, "Good Friday" and "Easter"; in both cases the first poem under the general title suggests a striving for some proper celebration of the occasion in song, as thus in "Easter":

> Awake, my lute, and struggle for thy part
>   With all thy art.
> The crosse taught all wood to resound his name,
>   Who bore the same.
> His stretched sinews taught all strings, what key
> Is best to celebrate this most high day.

And in each case the song follows, in nearly identical form: three quatrains in tetrameter, differing only in rime-scheme. This kind of connection by analogous verse-form is also operating in "Sepulchre," which has a form so similar to that of "The Sacrifice" that it appears as a continuation of the long meditation on the Passion. And finally, this section contains, at the beginning, and near the end, the two "shaped" poems of the *Temple*, "The Altar" and "Easter-wings": poems which, in their high formality of method, belong most appropriately to this ceremonial, liturgical section: their formality indeed serves as a frame enclosing the ritual movement from Gethsemane to Resurrection.

Now, with the sacramental center of "The Church" established, we are prepared to watch from this standpoint the "many spiritual Conflicts" of the soul attempting to make itself worthy of the Sacrifice: and to watch, throughout this struggle, the fulfillment of the promise made in "The Thanksgiving":

> My musick shall finde thee, and ev'ry string
>   Shall have his attribute to sing;
> That all together may accord in thee,
>   And prove one God, one harmonie.

2

It is a harmony, flexible, abruptly shifting, and subtle in its composition as those enigmatic last quartets of Beethoven. Nothing could have been easier for Herbert than to arrange the poems obviously according to themes or poetical methods, putting, say, the fifteen sonnets together, instead of dispersing them throughout the *Temple;* keeping the poems on "Nature" and "Grace" together, as they are in the Williams manuscript, instead of allowing fifteen pages between them; keeping "Mattens" and "Even-song" side by side in stanza-forms that match in reversed order, as they are in the Williams manuscript,[1] instead of rewriting "Even-song" and allowing the poem "Sinne" to come in between the two in the final version. Why not put the two "Jordan" poems together, along with other poems on theory of poetry, such as "The Posie," "The Forerunners," "The Quidditie"? Why not group together the five poems entitled "Affliction," or the three poems entitled "Love," as in the one such grouping that we have in the *Temple:* "Church-monuments," "Church-musick," "Church-lock and key," "The

1. See *Works of Herbert*, ed. Hutchinson, pp. liv, 203; the line-lengths match but the rime-schemes differ.

Church-floore," and "The Windows"? But even here the order
as Herbert evidently left it is not so regular as in the first edition
of the *Temple*. In the Bodleian manuscript, which Hutchinson takes
to be a fair copy of the "little book" that Herbert sent to Ferrar, the
anagram on the Virgin Mary comes in between "Church-musick"
and "Church-lock and key"; this is the only difference between
the order of the poems as given in this manuscript and in 1633.[2]
Here we seem to have the one place where Nicholas Ferrar made a
slight rearrangement, placing the poem instead just before the other
poem which deals so largely with the Virgin: "To All Angels and
Saints."

All such evidence suggests that Herbert has taken pains to avoid
any obvious, easy arrangement: chronological, thematic, or otherwise; and for reasons justified by the total implications of the *Temple* itself. The spiritual life (the *Temple* seems to say) will not fall
into such easy patterns: its unity is deeper and richer than this; and
therefore the beauty and harmony that Herbert sees in the book
which was, for him, incomparably the greatest of all books does not
lie in such arrangements, but rather in the subtle, "dispersed" "con-
figurations" which Herbert thus describes in his second sonnet
on the Scriptures:

> This verse marks that, and both do make a motion
>   Unto a third, that ten leaves off doth lie:
>   Then as dispersed herbs do watch a potion,
>   These three make up some Christians destinie:
>   Such are thy secrets, which my life makes good,
>   And comments on thee: for in ev'ry thing
>   Thy words do finde me out, & parallels bring,
>   And in another make me understood.

It is the method of the *Temple*, where one poem marks another, and
both make a motion toward a third, which may lie some ten or
twenty leaves away: but the reader strikes a chord, and understands the destiny thus offered. Sometimes, as several readers have
pointed out, the poems tend to run in short sequences thematically
linked, with one poem acting as an answer to the preceding. But
when this occurs the verse-forms are so various that any obvious

2. See *idem*, pp. li, lxx–lxxi, 77.

link is avoided, and indeed the linkage is often so light that it is easily overlooked.

One of the best of these sequences is found near the beginning of the "Church," in the group that follows from the poem "Nature." This poem is tied to the sacramental introduction, not only by contrast with Grace, but by a powerful continuation (in the last stanza) of the imagery of the stony heart, and of writing in the heart. We expect a poem on Grace to follow sooner or later, and when, some fifteen pages later, it occurs, the short sequence in which "Grace" appears is thus correlated with the short sequence begun by "Nature." The poem "Nature" is appropriately followed by the definition-sonnet, "Sinne" (1), which prepares the way for the next poem, "Affliction" (1), by its mention of

> Afflictions sorted, anguish of all sizes,
> Fine nets and stratagems to catch us in,

and especially by the final couplet,

> Yet all these fences and their whole aray
> One cunning bosome-sinne blows quite away.

This bosom-sin is then revealed in "Affliction" (1) as a blasphemous grumbling against God's justice, stemming from a desire for personal, worldly glory. All this is conveyed through the charge, first lightly implied, and then bluntly declared, that God has "enticed," tricked, and "betrayed" the speaker into a profitless life, stunted by bad health and personal disasters. Two lines here, through their imagery, tie this poem of affliction very closely to the sonnet "Sinne" (1):

> Thus thinne and lean without a fence or friend,
> I was blown through with ev'ry storm and winde.

The next poem, "Repentance," loses much of its force unless we keep it in its place: for it opens with the anguished cry, "Lord, I confesse my sinne is great," and pleads with God, "Cut me not off for my most foul transgression." The last three stanzas contain specific echoes of the preceding poem, especially in the lines,

> Sweeten at length this bitter bowl,
> Which thou hast pour'd into my soul;
> Thy wormwood turn to health, windes to fair weather . . . .

At the same time we notice that the irregular six-line stanza of "Repentance" is very similar to that of "Nature": in Herbert's usual way, the only difference lies in a variation of one foot in the third and fifth lines. The poem "Faith," which comes next, is an apt fulfillment of the promise of praise to God contained in the last stanza of "Repentance," which speaks of a song "Full of his praises,/Who dead men raises." "Faith," after many such praises, ends with explicit treatment of the resurrection of the body. This poem is really a meditation on the benefits conferred by Grace— "While grace fills up uneven nature"—and thus correlates with the first poem of the sequence, as well as with those ironical lines in the first stanza of "Affliction" (1), where the naive complainer speaks of his hopes of having

> my stock of *naturall* delights,
> Augmented with thy *gracious* benefits.

"Faith" provides the answer to this misunderstanding of the relation between Nature and Grace. And so we have a group of five poems which even in their bare titles suggest the progress of the soul: Nature, Sin, Affliction, Repentance, Faith.

After this comes at once the definition-sonnet, "Prayer" (1), which in its method of rapid analogy reminds one of the sonnet "Sinne"; and appropriately, since it deals with sin's antidote. At the same time it provides us with an account of prayer that serves to summarize all that lies before us in the *Temple*. This sonnet does not, like "Prayer" (2), deal primarily with prayer as petition: it includes this aspect, but goes beyond it to describe all the forms of prayer and meditation that have been discussed in the foregoing chapters, while the imagery suggests dozens of other poems in the *Temple*:

> Prayer the Churches banquet, Angels age,
>   Gods breath in man returning to his birth,
>   The soul in paraphrase, heart in pilgrimage,
> The Christian plummet sounding heav'n and earth;
> Engine against th' Almightie, sinners towre,
>   Reversed thunder, Christ-side-piercing spear,
>   The six-daies world transposing in an houre,

A kinde of tune, which all things heare and fear;
Softnesse, and peace, and joy, and love, and blisse,
    Exalted Manna, gladnesse of the best,
    Heaven in ordinarie, man well drest,
The milkie way, the bird of Paradise,
    Church-bels beyond the starres heard, the souls bloud,
    The land of spices; something understood.

The eucharistic imagery is first, and dominant; and especially appropriate here, since the next two poems of the "Church" are given under the title "The H. Communion." The second of these, a song of colloquy, bears a very close relation to this sonnet, a relation indicated by the fact that the song bore the title "Prayer" in its first version.[3] The second line of the sonnet recalls the obverse and perverse use of this "breath" related in "The Sacrifice" (69–71):

> Then they condemne me all with that same breath,
> Which I do give them daily, unto death.
> Thus *Adam* my first breathing rendereth . . . .

The "pilgrimage" suggests the poem by that title; "man well drest" suggests "Aaron"; line 7 looks forward to "Sunday"; the musical imagery of lines 7 and 8 carries on this central image of the *Temple*; while line 9 sums up the core of that Salesian spirituality which permeates the *Temple*:

> Softnesse, and peace, and joy, and love, and blisse.

At the same time line 3, "The soul in paraphrase, heart in pilgrimage," represents the two fundamental and complementary aspects of the meditative life: self-examination leading toward self-knowledge; and meditation leading on toward the love of God. As Hutchinson points out in a brilliant gloss, a paraphrase "clarifies by expansion; in prayer the soul opens out and more fully discovers itself." [4] In the same way the soul by meditation learns the art of "sounding heav'n and earth," and uses the weapon of mental communion which makes the sacraments flow from Christ's side. Such prayer "transposes" the workaday world, converts it, changes its profane note into a different musical key, into another "kinde of

3. See *Works of Herbert*, ed. Hutchinson, p. 52.
4. *Idem*, p. 493.

tune," after the manner described by Shakespeare: "Things base
and vilde, holding no quantity,/Love can transpose to form and
dignity." [5] And in these ways we come to the full fruit of prayer
and meditation: the "something understood," which Puente thus
sums up as the goal of meditation:

> the end of all the meditations, and discourses that shalbee put
> in the six partes of this booke, is to attaine to three notions,
> or knowledges. One of himselfe, and of his innumerable neces-
> sities and miseries of bodye and soule: The other of Christ
> Jesus our Lord, true God, and man, and of his excellent ver-
> tues, especially those which were resplendent in his Nativitye,
> Passion, and Death. And the third of almightie God Three, and
> One, and of his infinite perfection and benefits, as well naturall,
> as supernaturall that procede from him. (*1*, 30)

Such is the knowledge sought and discovered in two of the most
striking of the many paired poems of the "Church": "Longing"
and "The Bag." In the first of these the speaker in his affliction cries
out constantly for his Lord to "heare," "heare," ending with the
supplication:

> My love, my sweetnesse, heare!
> By these thy feet, at which my heart
> Lies all the yeare,
> Pluck out thy dart,
> And heal my troubled breast which cryes,
> Which dyes.

And the next poem answers, with allusion to the storm on the Sea
of Galilee (Matthew 8.23–7), and also to the poem, "The Storm,"
ten leaves before:

> Away despair! my gracious Lord doth heare.
> Though windes and waves assault my keel,
> He doth preserve it: he doth steer,
> Ev'n when the boat seems most to reel.

5. *Midsummer Night's Dream*, I. i. 246–7; cited by *OED*, "transpose," *v.* 1:
"To change (one thing) *to* or *into* another; to transform, transmute, convert."

> Storms are the triumph of his art:
> Well may he close his eyes, but not his heart.

The verse-forms add to both the variety and the correlation: both "Longing" and "The Bag" are written in six-line stanzas riming ababcc; but the irregular line-lengths of the "Longing" stanza, with its dying fall, form a sharp contrast with the firm and formal line-arrangement of "The Bag."

More important than the paired nature of these poems is the representative way in which each of them reaches out its tentacles of imagery and theme to "mark" dozens of other poems—ranging from the first to the last poem in the "Church." "Longing," for example, refers to the "furnace" of affliction in Isaiah (48. 10), and thus suggests not only the similar "fornace" of "Love unknown," but all the other poems of "Affliction." The lines,

> Lord JESU, heare my heart,
> Which hath been broken now so long,
> That ev'ry part
> Hath got a tongue!

are reminiscent of "The Altar"; while the allusion to Psalm 94. 9 ("Shall he that made the eare,/Not heare?) suggests the echoing answer based upon the same verse of this Psalm in the final poem of the "Church," "Love" (3): "Who made the eyes but I?" And this final poem is also involved with the reference here to the Communion table:

> Thy board is full, yet humble guests
> Finde nests.

At the same time, the reference to "God's board" [6] is followed in the next stanza by a bitter complaint that reminds one of "The Collar," lying only a leaf away:

> Thou tarriest, while I die,
> And fall to nothing: thou dost reigne,

6. This ancient phrase is preserved in a rubric for the Communion service in the Prayer-Book of Herbert's day: "Then shall the Priest kneeling downe at Gods board say, in the name of all them that shall receive the Communion, this prayer following." See *The Booke of Common Prayer*, London, 1604. For the use of the phrase see *OED*, "board," *sb.* 6.

> And rule on high,
> While I remain
> In bitter grief: yet am I stil'd
> Thy childe.

In its acceptance of the status of "childe," "The Collar" also provides its answer to this complaint.

Meanwhile, "The Bag" maintains this sacramental imagery by presenting a "storie" of the life of Christ: it briefly recounts Christ's incarnation, birth, suffering, and death, and closes with these stanzas on the Wound:

> But as he was returning, there came one
> That ran upon him with a spear.
> He, who came hither all alone,
> Bringing nor man, nor arms, nor fear,
> Receiv'd the blow upon his side,
> And straight he turn'd, and to his brethren cry'd,
>
> If ye have any thing to send or write,
> I have no bag, but here is room:
> Unto my Fathers hands and sight,
> Beleeve me, it shall safely come.
> That I shall minde, what you impart,
> Look, you may put it very neare my heart.
>
> Or if hereafter any of my friends
> Will use me in this kinde, the doore
> Shall still be open; what he sends
> I will present, and somewhat more,
> Not to his hurt. Sighs will convey
> Any thing to me. Harke, Despair away.

And so in this mode of a familiar tale, we hear once more the words of Christ from the Cross, but not the Reproaches. In this way, through a hundred different guises, the Communion imagery permeates the *Temple*, not only in poems explicitly devoted to praise of this sacrament, but also in dozens of brief references to the "feast," the "board," the "meat," the "banquet," the "blood," the Cross, the wounds, often woven into another context with a witty surprise, as in this stanza from "Affliction" (5):

> There is but joy and grief;
> If either will convert us, we are thine:
> Some Angels us'd the first; if our relief
> Take up the second, then thy double line
>> And sev'rall baits in either kinde
>> Furnish thy table to thy minde.

Here we move in a flash from Nativity to Crucifixion: from the angels of the Nativity with their tidings of great joy, to "our relief" which "takes up" the mode of grief; with simultaneous reference to the beneficial sufferings of the sinner and the way in which that relief was made possible by the Man of Sorrows. Joy and grief are then aligned with the two species or kinds of the Communion table: "baits" being used in the old sense of food, along with overtones of a fisherman's lure.

Read in the light of this all-embracing Image, many of Herbert's finest poems take on a deeper richness than they can ever hold when detached from their place in the *Temple*. The fabric of the *Temple* helps to define the meanings of the words that occur within it; provides the dramatic context in which the poems are best read. This is particularly true of "The Collar," where the blasphemy of the opening lines strikes with special force after we have read in preceding poems of that "board's" benefits; as in this address to "Conscience":

> And the receit shall be
> My Saviours bloud: when ever at his board
> I do but taste it, straight it cleanseth me,
>> And leaves thee not a word;
>> No, not a tooth or nail to scratch,
>> And at my actions carp, or catch.

In this context we are prepared for the tone of self-ridicule which dominates "The Collar," for we see the ironies latent in the worldly perversion of this imagery of thorn, blood, wine, and grain:

> I struck the board, and cry'd, No more.
>> I will abroad.
> What? shall I ever sigh and pine?
> My lines and life are free; free as the rode,

> Loose as the winde, as large as store.
> Shall I be still in suit?
> Have I no harvest but a thorn
> To let me bloud, and not restore
> What I have lost with cordiall fruit?
> Sure there was wine
> Before my sighs did drie it: there was corn
> Before my tears did drown it.

The ending of the poem "Peace" provides the perfect gloss upon this outburst: for here the speaker meets "a rev'rend good old man" who tells a story of Melchisedec, King of Salem, type of Christ; the story concludes, as Miss Freeman has noted, with echoes of the Communion ritual: [7]

> Take of this grain, which in my garden grows,
> And grows for you;
> Make bread of it: and that repose
> And peace, which ev'ry where
> With so much earnestnesse you do pursue,
> Is onely there.

In a different way, remembrance of the Passion illuminates the companion-poem to "Peace," "The Pilgrimage" (eight leaves away), which pursues the search for peace in a very similar stanza-form. The speaker here, struggling toward "the hill, where lay/ My expectation," comes to a place which has puzzled commentators:

> That led me to the wilde of Passion, which
> Some call the wold;
> A wasted place, but sometimes rich.
> Here I was robb'd of all my gold,
> Save one good Angell, which a friend had ti'd
> Close to my side.

A passage from the *Imitation of Christ* will, I believe, throw a good deal of light on this:

7. *Works of Herbert*, ed. Hutchinson, p. 521; Freeman, p. 159; Tuve, *Reading of Herbert*, pp. 161–3.

Thou errest greatlie, if thou seeke anye other thinge then to suffer: For all this mortall life is full of miseries, and is all beset about and marked with Crosses, and the more highlie that a man profiteth in spirite, the more painfull Crosses shall he finde, For by the soothfastnes of Christes love, wherein he daylie increaseth, daylie appeareth unto him more and more the paine of this exile. But neverthelesse, a man thus vexed with paine, is not left whollie without all comfort, for he seeth well, that great fruite and high rewarde shall growe unto him by the bearinge of his Crosse. And when a man freelie submitteth him selfe to such tribulation, then all the burden of tribulation is sodenlie turned into a great trust of heavenlye consolation . . . . And sometime the soule shall feele such comfort in adversities, that for the love and desire that it hath to be conformed to Christe crucified, it woulde not be without sorowe and trouble . . . . If thou desire to be a deare and well beloved frende of Christ, drinke effectuouslie with him a draught of the chalice of his tribulation . . . . and when tribulations come, take them as speciall consolations, sayinge with the Apostle thus: The passions of this world be not worthy of them selves, to bringe us to the glorye that is ordeined for us in the life to come . . . . (Bk. 2, chap. 12)

The "Passion" of Herbert's poem refers to "the passions" in this sense: that is, to "the sufferings of this present time" (Romans 8. 18); with simultaneous reference to the sufferings of Christ and to the similar "crosses" which the Christian must bear in the imitation of Christ. "Wilde," of course, suggests "wilderness," with overtones of the view of life found in the *Imitation*, which speaks of Christ as "the ioy and comfort of all christien people that are walking and labouring as pilgrimes in the wyldernes of this world." (Bk. 3, chap. 23: i.e., chap. 21) But the shift to "wold" localizes the wilderness, in Herbert's familiar way, calling to mind particular localities in England known as "the Wild" or "the Wold"—"a wasted place," [8]—"but sometimes rich" in its Passion, both through

8. See *OED*, "wild," B. *sb.* 3: "A wild or waste place . . . a wilderness." Cf. *OED*, "wold" and "weald": the three words were used interchangeably, as in the phrase, "the wild of Kent."

the value of the Sacrifice there made, and through those comforts and consolations which the Christian "sometime" feels amidst his own "passions." The "Angell" is coin of this realm, the guardian angel, and the consolations which this guardian angel, through Christ the friend, sometimes affords the soul, in order that it "may progress and advance from good to better." [9]

The advancement continues:

> At length I got unto the gladsome hill,
>> Where lay my hope,
>> Where lay my heart; and climbing still,
>> When I had gain'd the brow and top,
> A lake of brackish waters on the ground
>> Was all I found.

It is a Calvary: where else could this *via dolorosa* end but in a pool of tears? Yet the speaker misunderstands the meaning of this hill, and he cries out, stung with fears as with vicious insects arising from a stagnant pool:

> With that abash'd and struck with many a sting
>> Of swarming fears,
> I fell, and cry'd, Alas my King!
> Can both the way and end be tears?

It is so, yet something more lies beyond: the speaker has, we might say, mistaken Calvary for Mount Zion: and yet for all this, he has gone by the right road:

> Yet taking heart I rose, and then perceiv'd
>> I was deceiv'd:

> My hill was further: so I flung away,
>> Yet heard a crie
>> Just as I went, *None goes that way*
>> *And lives:* If that be all, said I,
> After so foul a journey death is fair,
>> And but a chair.

And finally, to take one more example of this kind, we find the presence of a "friend" in "Love unknown," combined with eu-

9. St. Ignatius, pp. 111–12.

charistic imagery and with other imagery that makes this one of the great nodal poems of the *Temple*, as well as one of Herbert's subtlest achievements in the art of colloquy. It works upon the basis found in so many of Herbert's poems: the guise of the naive complainer, who here pours out his tale of woe to a familiar companion; he doesn't expect much help, but sorrow will tell its story:

> Deare Friend, sit down, the tale is long and sad:
> And in my faintings I presume your love
> Will more complie then help.

His trouble is, as in the sonnet "Redemption," with a Landlord who exacts too hard a lease:

> A Lord I had,
> And have, of whom some grounds, which may improve,
> I hold for two lives, and both lives in me.
> To him I brought a dish of fruit one day,
> And in the middle plac'd my heart. But he
> (I sigh to say)
> Lookt on a servant, who did know his eye
> Better then you know me, or (which is one)
> Then I my self.

This would appear to be "a colloquy with one's own soul"—the "friend" is the speaker's other self, to whom he narrates the strange actions of this "servant":

> The servant instantly
> Quitting the fruit, seiz'd on my heart alone,
> And threw it in a font, wherein did fall
> A stream of bloud, which issu'd from the side
> Of a great rock . . . .

Again, as in "The Altar," the speaker's heart must be offered in combination with a memorial of the Sacrifice of Christ, the Rock, the suffering servant of Isaiah:

> I well remember all,
> And have good cause: there it was dipt and dy'd,
> And washt, and wrung: the very wringing yet
> Enforceth tears. *Your heart was foul, I fear.*

The friend, with his mild comment, shows that he understands
the situation—almost, we might say, seems to know the tale already;
but stranger things are to follow:

> After my heart was well,
> And clean and fair, as I one even-tide
> > (I sigh to tell)
> Walkt by my self abroad, I saw a large
> And spacious fornace flaming, and theron
> A boyling caldron, round about whose verge
> Was in great letters set *AFFLICTION*.

Here is an interesting combination of ingredients. The vision of
the flaming furnace seen during a lone walk "abroad" reminds one
very strongly of a love-poem by Robert Greene that appears in *Englands Helicon* (1600); [10] a vision here fused with the "furnace of
affliction" described in Isaiah, along with overtones of the many
other poems of "Affliction" in this *Temple*. But, the speaker continues, when he went "To fetch a sacrifice out of my fold," and
present it once more with his heart, the same thing happened as before: the sacrifice was neglected, the heart taken instead, and thrown
"into the scalding pan." "*Your heart was hard, I fear*," comments the
understanding friend. Yes, it was, the speaker goes on, but I found
a remedy for this spreading hardness:

> with a richer drug then scalding water
> I bath'd it often, ev'n with holy bloud,
> Which at a board, while many drunk bare wine,
> A friend did steal into my cup for good,
> Ev'n taken inwardly, and most divine
> To supple hardnesses.

But when at last he was able to reach home again, he found no peace,
for "some had stuff'd the bed with thoughts,/I would say *thorns*."
"*Your heart was dull, I fear*," says the knowing friend. And then, at
the close, all is revealed: the friend knows the meaning of all this,
and shrewdly explains the significance of every event:

10. See *England's Helicon*, ed. Hyder Rollins (2 vols., Cambridge, Harvard
University Press, 1935), *1*, 96–8.

> *Truly, Friend,*
> *For ought I heare, your Master shows to you*
> *More favour then you wot of. Mark the end.*
> *The Font did onely, what was old, renew:*
> *The Caldron suppled, what was grown too hard:*
> *The Thorns did quicken, what was grown too dull:*
> *All did but strive to mend, what you had marr'd.*
> *Wherefore be cheer'd, and praise him to the full*
> *Each day, each houre, each moment of the week,*
> *Who fain would have you be new, tender, quick.*

Thus the speaker, throughout the events of this sad-happy tale, has been working with the help of "love unknown"; and in fact, when the whole tale has been told, it appears that he has been conversing throughout with "Love unknown"; the friend is indeed his other self: the Christ who at the close reveals the full counsel of his "inward speaking."

3

So the whole *Temple* grows from this sacrament, the other images cluster round it, the strings and pairs of poems issue from and return into it, throughout this body of conflicts, until near the close of the "Church" we feel this central Image asserting itself with a stronger and stronger dominance. We have struggled toward what might be called a sacramental plateau, matching the section which I have called the sacramental introduction. The movement toward this "plateau" is marked, about thirty poems from the end of the "Church," by a tightly connected sequence of four quite different poems: "The Search," "Grief," "The Crosse," and "The Flower." The unity here is most remarkable in the answer which the last stanza of "The Flower" provides for the opening queries of "The Search":

> Whither, O, whither art thou fled,
> My Lord, my Love?
> My searches are my daily bread;
> Yet never prove.

.   .   .   .   .

> These are thy wonders, Lord of love,
> To make us see we are but flowers that glide:
>   Which when we once can finde and prove,
> Thou hast a garden for us, where to bide.

"The Search," as we would expect, is closely related to earlier poems
in the *Temple*, such as "The Starre," and the many poems of "sighs
and groans"; but more specifically it looks forward to the poem that
follows it:

> Since then my grief must be as large,
>   As is thy space,
> Thy distance from me; see my charge,
>   Lord, see my case.

The poem "Grief" continues this theme by echoing Jeremiah (9.1),
the Psalms, the Southwellian literature of tears, and of course the
tears of the Petrarchan lover. These last are recalled to us in the
closing lines lamenting that works of poetry are spoiled in this grief,
for reasons implied in the cry that bursts out and breaks the meter
of the poem at the close:

> Verses, ye are too fine a thing, too wise
> For my rough sorrows: cease, be dumbe and mute,
> Give up your feet and running to mine eyes,
> And keep your measures for some lovers lute,
> Whose grief allows him musick and a ryme:
> For mine excludes both measure, tune, and time.
>   Alas, my God!

After this, the opening words of "The Crosse" follow almost inevitably:

> What is this strange and uncouth thing?
> To make me sigh, and seek, and faint, and die,
> Untill I had some place, where I might sing,
>   And serve thee;

but with the words, "Thy will be done," the speaker makes his peace,
and, with symbolical suddenness, the spirit flowers:

> How fresh, O Lord, how sweet and clean
> Are thy returns! ev'n as the flowers in spring;

> To which, besides their own demean,
> The late-past frosts tributes of pleasure bring.
> Grief melts away
> Like snow in May,
> As if there were no such cold thing.

Thus in the profits and returnings of grace the plea of "The Search," "Turn, and restore me," is answered; the word "grief," which occurs in all three of the preceding poems, is erased; along with the storms and frosts which have provided the basic imagery for dozens of stanzas scattered throughout the whole preceding portion of the "Church." Instead, we have now the dominant image of the flourishing flower, to replace the image of the "blasted," "wasted" plant which has so often dominated earlier poems, as in "Employment" (1):

> If as a flowre doth spread and die,
> Thou wouldst extend me to some good,
> Before I were by frosts extremitie
> Nipt in the bud . . . .

But "The Flower" recalls the words of Job (14.7–9): "For there is hope of a tree, if it be cut down, that it will sprout again, and that the tender branch thereof will not cease. Though the root thereof wax old in the earth, and the stock thereof die in the ground; Yet through the scent of water it will bud, and bring forth boughs like a plant." The man is renewed, and poetry flows again, as part of the sensory joy of life:

> And now in age I bud again,
> After so many deaths I live and write;
> I once more smell the dew and rain,
> And relish versing: O my onely light,
> It cannot be
> That I am he
> On whom thy tempests fell all night.

"The Flower" is a poem of summation, of spiritual achievement. From here on, in the remaining twenty-eight poems of the "Church," griefs melt away: they are remembered, as traces and twinges of a serious illness, but with a tone of achieved calm and assurance, accepting the limitations of grief, exulting quietly in the assurance of love. Here, following "The Flower," we find the other poems which refer to the speaker's advancing age: "The Forerunners," where, like a poet in the *Paradise* before him,[1] he sees in his white hair the "harbingers" of his coming "winter"; "The Glance," with its reminiscence of the time

> When first thy sweet and gracious eye
> Vouchsaf'd ev'n in the midst of youth and night
> To look upon me . . . .

and memories of the period "since that time," when the soul has felt "many a bitter storm"; or "The Answer," the only poem here which approaches the earlier tone of lamentation:

> My comforts drop and melt away like snow:
> I shake my head, and all the thoughts and ends,
> Which my fierce youth did bandie, fall and flow
> Like leaves about me; or like summer friends,
> Flyes of estates and sunne-shine.

But he, and we, know the answer: it has already been given in "The Quip." All such references support the retrospective tone of renunciation which marks the perfect poise of "The Rose."

> Presse me not to take more pleasure
> In this world of sugred lies,
> And to use a larger measure
> Then my strict, yet welcome size.
>
> First, there is no pleasure here:
> Colour'd griefs indeed there are,
> Blushing woes, that look as cleare
> As if they could beautie spare.
>
> Or if such deceits there be,
> Such delights I meant to say;
> There are no such things to me,
> Who have pass'd my right away.

1. See *Paradise*, ed. Rollins, poem 48.

At the same time, in accordance with this retrospective atmosphere and with this rediscovered "relish" in versing, we find in this section a far heavier concentration of poems dealing with theory of poetry, than anywhere else in the *Temple*. Most notable is "The Forerunners," which throws more light on the attitudes toward poetry which have built this Temple than any other poem in its fabric. It accords much more exactly with the actual poetical achievement of the *Temple* than do either of the "Jordan" poems: for those poems had spoken in terms of a simplicity which might be interpreted as renunciation of all the subtleties of poetic effect, a renunciation which of course these poems qualify through their use of witty turns and images. The "Jordan" poems speak in the hyperboles of dedication; "The Forerunners" describes the actual achievement, in terms that show a fervent devotion to all the arts of poetry, properly used. The harbingers have come to dispossess him, as "Harbingers were sent in advance of a royal progress to purvey lodgings by chalking the doors": [2] they will put out ("dispark," in two senses) these "sparkling notions" of the brain from their estate. The poetical "Dulnesse" which he had berated in the poem by that title may now come to pass: "Yet have they left me, *Thou art still my God*": from Psalm 31.14. So all is well enough:

> Good men ye be, to leave me my best room,
> Ev'n all my heart, and what is lodged there:

as in the song for "Good Friday." Therefore he does not care

> what of the rest become,
> So *Thou art still my God*, be out of fear.
> He will be pleased with that dittie;
> And if I please him, I write fine and wittie.

True, and yet the poet deep within has his regrets for these arts which he has for so long cherished, and purified, and "simplified," in his own enriching way:

> Farewell sweet phrases, lovely metaphors.
> But will ye leave me thus? when ye before
> Of stews and brothels onely knew the doores,

2. *Works of Herbert*, ed. Hutchinson, p. 538.

> Then did I wash you with my tears, and more,
> > Brought you to Church well drest and clad:
> My God must have my best, ev'n all I had.

> Lovely enchanting language, sugar-cane,
> Hony of roses, whither wilt thou flie?
> Hath some fond lover tic'd thee to thy bane?
> And wilt thou leave the Church, and love a stie?
> > Fie, thou wilt soil thy broider'd coat,
> And hurt thy self, and him that sings the note.

Such beauties should not dress the songs of "foolish lovers":

> True beautie dwells on high: ours is a flame
> > But borrow'd thence to light us thither.
> Beautie and beauteous words should go together.

Yet if they go, the center of his love-song will remain:

> For, *Thou art still my God*, is all that ye
> Perhaps with more embellishment can say.
> Go birds of spring: let winter have his fee;
> > Let a bleak palenesse chalk the doore,
> So all within be livelier then before.

But what a world of reservation lies in that one word, so emphatically placed: "Perhaps"! The poet loves his art: the devout humanist cannot bring himself to renounce it utterly, though he continues to contemplate this possibility, in "The Posie":

> > Invention rest,
> Comparisons go play, wit use thy will:
> > *Lesse then the least*
> *Of all Gods mercies*, is my posie still,

he says, adopting a motto remarkably similar to a passage in the *Imitation of Christ*, though of course the Bible is the basic source.[3]

---

3. *Imitation of Christ*, Bk. 3, chap. 24 (i.e., chap. 22): "But I knowe and confesse it for truth, that I am not able to yeld to thee condigne thankinges for the least benefite that thou hast geven me, for I am lesse then the least benefite that thou hast geven." For the biblical sources see *Works of Herbert*, ed. *Hutchinson*, p. 540.

Or again, with the words "My joy, my life, my crown" (also paralleled in the *Imitation*),[4] he will make, as we have seen, "A true Hymne":

> Yet slight not these few words:
> If truly said, they may take part
> Among the best in art.
> The finenesse which a hymne or psalme affords,
> Is, when the soul unto the lines accords.

Lines which accord well with the immediately preceding poem, "The Sonne," in which he scorns the "fine varietie" of other languages and praises the neatness of his native tongue—as Sidney had done before him.[5] All these remarks are then summed up in a poem that occurs near the middle of the early manuscript, but now, appropriately, comes almost at the very end of the "Church": "A Wreath," which makes "A wreathed garland of deserved praise" in the repetitive fashion used by Southwell and by Sidney. In representing the "crooked winding wayes, wherein I live," the poem provides a convenient symbol of the "Church's" mode of wreathing unity: a mode which, like this poem, leads toward the ideal here expressed: "Give me simplicitie, that I may live."

At the same time this concluding section, appropriately, contains some of the most explicit examples of the art of sacred parody in the whole *Temple*: the echo-song, "Heaven"; the "Dooms-day" poem opening with the invitation of the lover's *aube*, "Come away";[6] a "Rose-song" in ballad measure; and the one poem in the *Temple* which is announced as "A Parodie," where Herbert, like Southwell, turns a well-known poem of profane love into a sinner's complaint. In the last Herbert reworks, with far greater freedom than Southwell used with Dyer, the song, "Soul's joy, now I am gone," some-

4. *Imitation of Christ*, Bk. 3, chap. 55 (i.e., chap. 50): "thou art my hope, my crowne, my ioye, and all my honor."

5. See "The Defence of Poesie," *Works*, ed. Feuillerat, 3, 43–4.

6. See the popular song in John Dowland's *First Booke of Songes or Ayres* (1597), printed in *Englands Helicon*: "Come away, come sweet Love,/The golden morning breakes." (*Helicon*, ed. Rollins, *1*, 158–9; *English Madrigal Verse*, pp. 413–14; for other love-songs using this opening, see *idem*, pp. 347, 480.)

times attributed to Donne, but probably a work by the Earl of Pembroke, resembling Donne's poems of valediction. Herbert's poem follows the original closely only for the first three lines, and then, using the same verse-form, moves off into almost complete freedom, utilizing only the general conception of grief and loss of light, together with a few small verbal echoes. The reader will find the Pembroke poem in the appendix to Grierson's standard edition of Donne: [7] the immense difference between the two, not only in subject, but in simplicity and directness of phrasing, can only be appreciated by a full and careful comparison. We ought to note, however, that Herbert's complaint here is not at all the same as his earlier lamentations for loss of the sense of "presence": here he is, in keeping with the mood of this section, speaking retrospectively, remembering the "stormie" times when he suffered from a sense of God's withdrawal. But his "souls joy" is supremely present here, and in this mood of confidence he realizes that the sense of absence which he has sometimes felt has been illusory: "Because thou dost abide with me,/ and I depend on thee."

Finally, the sense of full assurance in this closing section is reinforced by the ways in which the central Image of the *Temple* now appears with redoubled emphasis. Here, in this section, we have the two poems of the *Temple* in which the speaker clearly appears in the role of ordained priest. In the poem "The Priesthood," which comes just before "The Search," we have seen the speaker standing on the threshold of ordination, but hesitating, in view of the responsibility which forms the center of this office:

> But th'holy men of God such vessels are,
> As serve him up, who all the world commands:
> When God vouchsafeth to become our fare,
> Their hands convey him, who conveys their hands.

But now in "Aaron" we see the priest "well drest," calling the "people" to worship in the last line. And in "The Invitation" he issues the call to Communion, with touches of sacred parody:

> Come ye hither All, whose love
> Is your dove,

7. *Poems of Donne*, *1*, 429. For the term "parody" see above, p. 186 n.

And exalts you to the skie:
Here is love, which having breath
Ev'n in death,
After death can never die.

Parody of love-poetry plays an even greater part in the companion-poem, "The Banquet," which is filled with echoes of earlier poems in the "Church," such as "Praise" (1), with its lines:

I go to Church; help me to wings, and I
Will thither flie;
Or, if I mount unto the skie,
I will do more.

The plea is answered at the close of "The Banquet," where, with an echo of "The Collar" ("my lines and life are free"), the speaker rededicates his life and song to the service of religious love, in terms that remind us of the various addresses to his voice and lute that have occurred earlier, and also of the common Elizabethan love of "musical strife": [8]

Having rais'd me to look up,
In a cup
Sweetly he doth meet my taste.
But I still being low and short,
Farre from court,
Wine becomes a wing at last.

For with it alone I flie
To the skie:
Where I wipe mine eyes, and see
What I seek, for what I sue;
Him I view,
Who hath done so much for me.

Let the wonder of his pitie
Be my dittie,
And take up my lines and life:

8. See Ben Jonson's poem, "The Musicall strife; In a Pastorall Dialogue," *Ben Jonson, 8,* 143.

> Hearken under pain of death,
>   Hands and breath;
> Strive in this, and love the strife.

Amid this atmosphere of assurance, it is fitting that we should find here the one example of a translated psalm included in the *Temple*, and that it should be the twenty-third. Herbert has translated it in such a way as to combine the meter and phrasing of Sternhold and Hopkins with phrasing from both the Coverdale and the King James versions,[9] along with many touches of his own that make this version of the Psalm a perfect expression of the Salesian spirit of the *Temple*. Herbert's version adds the thematic word "love" in the first line, takes the second line verbatim from Sternhold and Hopkins, and echoes in the third line a verse from the Song of Solomon (2.16), "My beloved is mine, and I am his":

> The God of love my shepherd is,
>   And he that doth me feed:
> While he is mine, and I am his,
>   What can I want or need?

In the fifth stanza Herbert's phrasing serves to suggest the Communion table, especially through his addition of the word "wine":

> Nay, thou dost make me sit and dine,
>   Ev'n in my enemies sight:
> My head with oyl, my cup with wine
>   Runnes over day and night.

And the last stanza sums up the theme by throwing a special weight, once more, upon the key-word, "love":

> Surely thy sweet and wondrous love
>   Shall measure all my dayes;
> And as it never shall remove,
>   So neither shall my praise.

So we are prepared for the sequence of the last five poems, where we move, with a witty gaiety, through all the traditional "last things,"

9. See *Works of Herbert*, ed. Hutchinson, p. 537. I have used *The Whole Booke of Psalmes, Collected into English meeter by Thomas Sternhold, Iohn Hopkins and others*, London, 1604.

except, of course, Hell—thoughts of this terror have long since fallen away. We move from "Death," to "Dooms-day," to "Judgement," to "Heaven," and conclude there with that famous poetical achievement, "Love" (3), a poem in which all the central arts and symbols of the "Church" are summed up. I have noted earlier how this poem echoes the dialogue-technique found in a passage of Southwell's "Saint Peters Complaint": but fundamentally, the poem represents a perfect amalgamation of the Elizabethan love-dialogue with the meditations of mental communion, found at their best in the fourth book of the *Imitation of Christ*, where the speaker responds thus to his friend's invitation, "he shal dwell in me, and I in him":

> But Lorde, my sinnes feare me greatlie, and my conscience not pure to receave so great a misterie, draweth me sore abacke. The sweetnes of thy wordes provoketh me, but the multitude of mine offences charge me verie sore . . . . What meaneth this moste meeke worthynes, and this lovelie and frendly biddinge? howe shall I dare come unto thee, which knowe not that I have done any thinge wel?

> Thou arte the Saint of all Saints, and I am the filth of all sinners, and yet thou enclinest thy selfe to me, that am not worthye to looke towarde thee. Thou commest to me, thou wilt be with me, thou biddest me to thy feast, thou wilt geve me this heavenly meate . . . . (Bk. 4, chaps. 1, 2)

It is through the meditation of this presence that "Love" (3) achieves its subtle intimacy of tone, its restrained power of allusion, in a sacred parody which simultaneously represents the reception of the sacrament and the admission of the redeemed to the "marriage supper" of Revelation:

> Love bade me welcome: yet my soul drew back,
>   Guiltie of dust and sinne.
> But quick-ey'd Love, observing me grow slack
>   From my first entrance in,
> Drew nearer to me, sweetly questioning,
>   If I lack'd any thing.
>
> A guest, I answer'd, worthy to be here:
>   Love said, You shall be he.

> I the unkinde, ungratefull? Ah my deare,
> > I cannot look on thee.
> Love took my hand, and smiling did reply,
> > Who made the eyes but I?
>
> Truth Lord, but I have marr'd them: let my shame
> > Go where it doth deserve.
> And know you not, sayes Love, who bore the blame?
> > My deare, then I will serve.
> You must sit down, sayes Love, and taste my meat:
> > So I did sit and eat.

I can think of nothing that so well describes the effect of this poem, and of its placing in the *Temple*, as certain words that Yeats uses in his *Vision* to describe the "phase of complete beauty." (pp. 135–6) "Thought and will are indistinguishable, effort and attainment are indistinguishable; and this is the consummation of a slow process . . . ." Since the outset of the *Temple* "all images, and cadences of the mind, have been satisfying to that mind just in so far as they have expressed this converging of will and thought, effort and attainment." Since the outset of the *Temple*, "the *Creative mind* . . . has more and more confined its contemplation of actual things to those that resemble images of the mind desired by the *Will*." And now at the close, "contemplation and desire, united into one, inhabit a world where every beloved image has bodily form, and every bodily form is loved."

The Meditative Poem

it is the rehearsal
Of own, of abrúpt sélf there so thrusts on, so throngs the ear.

Hopkins, "Henry Purcell"

Toward the union of "the powers of the soul," Herbert's "simplicity," or Yeats's "Unity of Being"—toward such a principle, by disciplined effort, the meditative poet makes his way, while creation of the poetry plays its part in the struggle. There is, as Yeats has said, a close correspondence between this discipline and the creative imagination. Yeats describes the relation in terms of the theater, but his argument will apply also to poets as dramatic in their manner as those who have just been discussed. "There is," he says, "a relation between discipline and the theatrical sense. If we cannot imagine ourselves as different from what we are and assume that second self, we cannot impose a discipline upon ourselves, though we may accept one from others. Active virtue as distinguished from the passive acceptance of a current code is therefore theatrical, consciously dramatic, the wearing of a mask." [1]

Thus Herbert, revising his poems, changing his style from the "winding" of wit to a witty simplicity, might have agreed with the explanation Yeats gave to those who objected to his revision of his early, ornate poems:

> The friends that have it I do wrong
> Whenever I remake a song,
> Should know what issue is at stake:
> It is myself that I remake.[2]

1. W. B. Yeats, *Autobiography* (New York, Macmillan, 1938), pp. 400–1.
2. Yeats, *Collected Works in Verse and Prose* (8 vols., Stratford-on-Avon, 1908), epigraph to vol. 2.

It is the creation of this self that a meditative poem records: a self that is, ideally, one with itself, with other human beings, with created nature, and with the supernatural. Such a self Hopkins indicates by his famous terms, "instress" and "inscape": the first describing that active essence, that inner force, possessed by every individual thing; the second referring to the "design," the "pattern" —the unique "relation between the parts of the thing to each other and again of the parts to the whole"—by which a discerning observer grasps the unique nature of every thing.[3] That is, the instress of a thing is manifested by its inscape—by its style of being, we might say. Yet all this world of instress flows from one invisible principle: "All things therefore are charged with love, are charged with God and if we know how to touch them give off sparks and take fire, yield drops and flow, ring and tell of him." "All the world is full of inscape and chance left free to act falls into an order as well as purpose: looking out of my window I caught it in the random clods and broken heaps of snow made by the cast of a broom."[4] All things exist in this relation: and yet nothing ever loses its "selfbeing." "And this is much more true when we consider the mind; when I consider my selfbeing, my consciousness and feeling of myself, that taste of myself, of *I* and *me* above and in all things, which is more distinctive than the taste of ale or alum, more distinctive than the smell of walnutleaf or camphor. . . ."[5] It is all summed up perfectly in the great sonnet, "As kingfishers catch fire":

> Each mortal thing does one thing and the same:
> Deals out that being indoors each one dwells;
> Selves—goes itself; *myself* it speaks and spells;
> Crying *Whát I dó is me: for that I came.*

3. *The Letters of Gerard Manley Hopkins to Robert Bridges*, ed. Claude Colleer Abbott (London, Oxford University Press, 1935), p. 66; *The Notebooks and Papers of Gerard Manley Hopkins*, ed. Humphry House (London, Oxford University Press, 1937), p. 68. See the helpful discussion of these terms by W. A. M. Peters, *Gerard Manley Hopkins* (London, Oxford University Press, 1948), chap. 1.

4. Hopkins, *Notebooks*, pp. 342, 173-4.

5. *Idem*, p. 309.

I say móre: the just man justices;
Kéeps gráce: thát keeps all his goings graces;
Acts in God's eye what in God's eye he is—
Chríst—for Christ plays in ten thousand places,
Lovely in limbs, and lovely in eyes not his
To the Father through the features of men's faces.

Thus the self of meditative poetry speaks a language based on that of common men, but including whatever in its own experience is unique and individual. If the self is learned and theological in its bent, then common speech will be infused with learned, theological terms and ways of thought, as in the case of Donne. If this self is deeply devoted to the English Bible and the English liturgy, this language will glow through common speech, as in Herbert. Or if, in turn, the self finds itself inflamed with the hagiographic devotions of the Counter Reformation—these too will find their way through common speech and live within the baroque poems of a Crashaw. And if the self has been molded, in large part, by the writings of an earlier poet, that poet's idiom will make its way into the later poet's speech, as Herbert's language speaks through Vaughan. Meditative poems, being wrought out as part of a search for the common basis of humanity, must have common speech as a basis; yet being also part of a personal quest, the language must also express that one, essential personality that is every man's unique possession. Something of this, perhaps, is what Eliot suggests, when he says that a poem by Hopkins "may sound pretty remote from the way in which you and I express ourselves—or rather, from the way in which our fathers and grandfathers expressed themselves: but Hopkins does give the impression that his poetry has the necessary fidelity to his way of thinking and talking to himself." [6] It is poetry of a kind that Eliot, in his lecture on "The Three Voices of Poetry," would include within his category of the "first voice"—"the voice of the poet talking to himself—or to nobody." Here, in a context that mentions Vaughan, Marvell, Donne, Herbert, Rilke, and Valéry, Eliot discusses the inadequacy of the term "lyric poetry" and concludes: "I should prefer to say 'meditative verse.'" [7]

6. T. S. Eliot, "The Music of Poetry," *On Poetry and Poets* (London, Faber and Faber, 1957), p. 33.

7. *Idem*, pp. 89, 96–7.

Yet the meditative poetry of the seventeenth century, or of Hopkins, could seldom, if ever, be considered as addressed to nobody. For the self created in this poetry is one that tries to speak with full awareness of a supernatural presence, one that feels the hand of the supernatural upon himself and upon all created things. Thus the learning, the logic, the philosophy that help to form this individual self are easily joined with perceptions of a bird, or a broom, or a love-ballad: for all these things are viewed as issuing, though sometimes once-removed, from an omnipresent source of creative power. Such meditative poems, then, are composed in "current language heightened," [8] molded, to express the unique being of an individual who is seeking to learn, through intense mental discipline, how to live his life in the presence of divinity.

On the other hand, it is true that the term "meditation" designates a process of the mind, rather than a particular subject-matter: a full definition of the meditative poem, it seems, should be broad enough to include certain poems that are not concerned with the religious or the supernatural, in our usual sense of those words. The genre of meditative poetry should be broad enough to include some of the Odes of Keats or the later poetry of Wallace Stevens, as well as the unorthodox, though still religious, poetry of a Yeats or a Wordsworth or an Emily Dickinson.[9] It must include "The poem of the mind in the act of finding/What will suffice." [10]

It seems that in certain eras, under certain conditions of distress and disorder, some poets will inevitably be led to cultivate a unity of interior life through processes of thought that bear some degree of similarity to the meditative exercises of the seventeenth century. In the poetry of Hopkins, and in the later poetry of Yeats or Eliot, we may find that the individual ways of meditation are guided in part by traditional methods. We may find in their poems a total movement, a total structure, that shows a resemblance to the threefold method discussed at length in my opening chapter. As we might expect, the method is most evident in the Jesuit, whose

8. Hopkins, *Letters to Bridges*, p. 89.

9. For development of these ideas see my essay on Stevens in *Literature and Belief* (*English Institute Essays*, 1957), ed. M. H. Abrams, New York, Columbia University Press, 1958.

10. See *The Collected Poems of Wallace Stevens* (New York, Alfred A. Knopf, 1954), pp. 238-40.

sonnets, like Donne's, open with a firm, dramatic "composition," a "proposing" of the subject:[11]

> The world is charged with the grandeur of God.

> Sometimes a lantern moves along the night,
>   That interests our eyes.

> As a dare-gale skylark scanted in a dull cage
>   Man's mounting spirit in his bone-house, mean
>   house, dwells—

> Look at the stars! look, look up at the skies!

> Some candle clear burns somewhere I come by.
> I muse . . .

And then, in various ways, the analysis and the "affections" follow, as in the sonnet "Hurrahing in Harvest":

> Summer ends now; now, barbarous in beauty, the stooks arise
>   Around; up above, what wind-walks! what lovely behaviour
>   Of silk-sack clouds! has wilder, wilful-wavier
> Meal-drift moulded ever and melted across skies?

> I walk, I lift up, I lift up heart, eyes,
>   Down all that glory in the heavens to glean our Saviour;
>   And, éyes, heárt, what looks, what lips yet gave you a
> Rapturous love's greeting of realer, of rounder replies?

> And the azurous hung hills are his world-wielding shoulder
>   Majestic—as a stallion stalwart, very-violet-sweet! —
> These things, these things were here and but the beholder
>   Wanting; which two when they once meet,
> The heart rears wings bold and bolder
>   And hurls for him, O half hurls earth for him off under his feet.

One cannot find precisely the same development in Yeats or

11. For perceptive accounts of the importance of the *Exercises* in Hopkins' career see John Pick, *Gerard Manley Hopkins, Priest and Poet* (London, Oxford University Press, 1942), chap. 2; Alan Heuser, *The Shaping Vision of Gerard Manley Hopkins* (London, Oxford University Press, 1958), chap. 9; and David A. Downes, *Gerard Manley Hopkins: A Study of his Ignatian Spirit*, London, Vision Press, 1960.

Eliot, yet a generally similar development may sometimes be found: in the *Four Quartets*, which open with those symbolic landscapes (can we call them "compositions of place"?); or in "Byzantium," "Sailing to Byzantium," "Coole Park, 1929," "Coole and Ballylee, 1931," or "The Tower":

> I pace upon the battlements and stare
> On the foundations of a house, or where
> Tree, like a sooty finger, starts from the earth;
> And send imagination forth
> Under the day's declining beam, and call
> Images and memories
> From ruin or from ancient trees,
> For I would ask a question of them all.

Of Eliot's acquaintance with meditative, or contemplative, writers it is hardly necessary to speak: the commentaries on *Ash Wednesday* and the *Four Quartets* are full of clues. Eliot's own quotation from St. John of the Cross (in the epigraph to "Sweeney Agonistes") points the direction in which his poetry was developing. And even earlier than this, one might see in "Gerontion" a bitter parody of the traditional meditation on death, complete with "composition" ("Here I am, an old man in a dry month,/ Being read to by a boy, waiting for rain."), analysis ("Think now . . . Think now . . . Think. . . ."), and "affections"—of horror and despair!

> What will the spider do,
> Suspend its operations, will the weevil
> Delay? De Bailhache, Fresca, Mrs. Cammel, whirled
> Beyond the circuit of the shuddering Bear
> In fractured atoms.

"Gerontion" will not release its full irony unless we follow the lead of the epigraph, and see how the lost speaker is perverting the traditional materials of the meditation on death—as summed up by Shakespeare's Duke in the third act of *Measure for Measure*.

With Yeats the case may at first seem dubious: he renounced Christianity as he knew it; the best he could say for modern students of Christian spirituality was "get you gone, Von Hügel, though with blessings on your head" ("Vacillation"). Yet in Yeats's *Autobiography* and *Vision*, and in the studies of his career by Ellmann, Jeffares, or Henn,[12] we find a groping toward a method of meditation uncannily akin to the orthodox method that Hopkins had just been pursuing. This tendency is clear in Yeats's own account of his efforts, during the 1890's, to found an Irish Mystical Order, centered on an island-castle in Lough Kay:

> I planned a mystical Order which should buy or hire the castle, and keep it as a place where its members could retire for a while for contemplation, and where we might establish mysteries like those of Eleusis and Samothrace; and for ten years to come my most impassioned thought was a vain attempt to find philosophy and to create ritual for that Order. I had an unshakable conviction, arising how or whence I cannot tell, that invisible gates would open as they opened for Blake, as they opened for Swedenborg, as they opened for Boehme, and that this philosophy would find its manuals of devotion in all imaginative literature, and set before Irishmen for special manual an Irish literature which, though made by many minds, would seem the work of a single mind, and turn our places of beauty or legendary association into holy symbols. I did not think this philosophy would be altogether pagan, for it was plain that its symbols must be selected from all those things that had moved men most during many, mainly Christian, centuries.[13]

During this period, Yeats declares, he was obsessed with "the need of mystical rites—a ritual, system of evocation and meditation—to reunite the perception of the spirit, of the dream, with natural beauty." [14] He speaks also of the "methods of meditation" that he was at this time practicing with the "Hermetic Students of the Golden Dawn"—"the Cabbalistic Society, which had taught me

12. Richard Ellmann, *Yeats, The Man and the Masks*, New York, Macmillan, 1948; A Norman Jeffares, *W. B. Yeats, Man and Poet*, New Haven, Yale University Press, 1949; T. R. Henn, *The Lonely Tower*, New York, Pellegrini and Cudahy, 1952.

13. Yeats, *Autobiography*, pp. 217–18.

14. Ellmann, p. 123.

methods of meditation that had greatly affected my thought." [15]
Those methods, one gathers, consisted in concentrating upon visual
symbols until a state of imaginative trance occurred: "Occult
progress is achieved through study and practice, through self-
purification and isolation. Its steps are symbolized by a series of
initiations, each of them withdrawing the initiate further from
his ordinary self and bringing him, as his mind is winnowed of
impurities, more and more powerful and arcane knowledge. He
learns to fix his mind, with an intensity previously unknown to
him, upon the images he seeks to evoke." [16] Such a procedure represents an ancient underground current of Neoplatonic thought,
and is thus affiliated with more orthodox ways of achieving spiritual
progress; at the same time, this use of images seems to have an
affiliation—if only a psychological one—with the "composition of
place" upon which the writers of the seventeenth century concentrated their attention. Ellmann (pp. 188–9) prints from Yeats's
manuscripts a "symbolic meditation" written in 1909 that bears a
remarkable analogy—after allowance has been made for the gro-
tesqueries of the method—to the preludes of a seventeenth-century
meditation: the "composition of place" and the petition "according
to the subject matter."

Yet trance was not a state that could satisfy a Yeats or a Herbert:
it made one remote from common life, and any such tendency
worried Yeats, as he shows in his curious early poem, "To the Rose
upon the Rood of Time." Here he calls to the "Rose," "Come
near, come near, come near . . ."

> Lest I no more hear common things that crave;
> The weak worm hiding down in its small cave,
> The field-mouse running by me in the grass,
> And heavy mortal hopes that toil and pass;
> But seek alone to hear the strange things said
> By God to the bright hearts of those long dead,
> And learn to chaunt a tongue men do not know.

Yeats could not achieve poetry that satisfied him until he had
transformed his cabalistic, Rosicrucian methods into a more ra-

15. Yeats, *Autobiography*, p. 351.
16. Ellmann, p. 87.

tional and realistic form that would enable him to analyze the course of human history in general, and the qualities of individual men, both of the past and of the present. The transformation is presented in his *Vision*—Yeats's private handbook of meditation—which bears the same relation to his later poetry as the seventeenth-century handbook of meditation bears to religious poetry of that era. Both provide a method, a technique, a discipline, through which the powers of the soul may strive toward Unity of Being. Such a Unity, where "religious, aesthetic and practical life were one," Yeats found not only in ancient Byzantium, but also in what he calls "the eighth gyre," which "completes itself say between 1550 and 1650." [17]

So too, in her own original way, Emily Dickinson came to create a huge body of meditative poetry, out of the remnants of her Puritan heritage of self-scrutiny, out of an Emersonian concern with Nature, and out of her broad reading in the English poets of the seventeenth century.[18] But other meditative poems appear to have been created in a condition of almost complete independence from such traditional influences. Thus Wordsworth has told us in his famous Preface: "habits of meditation have, I trust, so prompted and regulated my feelings, that my descriptions of such objects as strongly excite those feelings, will be found to carry along with them a *purpose*." So, in the Tintern Abbey poem, the scene before him stirs the memory to recall certain vague and undirected feelings; then the understanding, with an associative, rather than a dialectical method, carefully explores the meaning and the purpose of these memories, until at the close of the poem, past and present are made one and the speaker's being lives in harmony with the universe.[19] It is, I believe, a method properly called meditation; it

17. Yeats, *Vision*, pp. 279, 293.

18. See the important article by Judith Banzer, " 'Compound Manner': Emily Dickinson and the Metaphysical Poets," *American Literature*, *32* (1961), 417–33.

19. These remarks on Wordsworth, along with an implied application to Coleridge and Keats, have been influenced by hearing an excellent lecture by M. H. Abrams on "The Greater Romantic Lyric." I am also indebted here to the new and brilliant critical study of the Romantic poets by Harold Bloom, *The Visionary Company* (New York, Doubleday, 1961), esp. pp. 127–36.

is not the same process as that followed by the men of the seventeenth century, but it represents the same essential effort to evoke and discipline the natural powers of the mind. Habits of meditation, as I suggested in my opening chapter (p. 39), appear to arise in answer to certain basic tendencies of the human mind; such habits do not create these tendencies, but they shape and cultivate, they "prompt and regulate" these tendencies, developing in gifted minds, in different ages and in different lands, kindred ways of mental action that manifest themselves in the genre of meditative poetry.

The meditative poem: can it be defined? We should not, I think, expect a much more precise definition than we can give for such established genres of literature as satire, comedy, tragedy, epic, mock-heroic, pastoral, or allegory. But this much, at least, may be said: a meditative poem is a work that creates an interior drama of the mind; this dramatic action is usually (though not always) created by some form of self-address, in which the mind grasps firmly a problem or situation deliberately evoked by the memory, brings it forward toward the full light of consciousness, and concludes with a moment of illumination, where the speaker's self has, for a time, found an answer to its conflicts. But perhaps a better definition might be made by adapting to this end a passage by Paul Claudel: in the true meditative poem, we might say, "everything takes place as if there were a motor-directive principle governing our organized matter, and as if there were in us someone who is master and who knows what he has to do with everything. It is not our body which makes us, it is we at each second who make our body and who compose it in that attitude adapted to every situation which we call sensation and perception. It is not movement which drags us along in an irresistible flow. Movement is at our disposal. We can exploit it. We who are able to oppose and stop it, and, by using a free and limitless choice, impose on our perceptions the firm pattern of a concept, of a figure, of a will." [20]

20. Claudel, *A Poet before the Cross*, trans. Wallace Fowlie (Chicago, Regnery, 1958), pp. 196-7.

Mauburnus, Hall, and Crashaw: the "Scale of Meditation"

THIS appendix provides a detailed examination of the relationship between three works of great importance among the meditative writings of this era: the *Rosetum* (Zwolle, 1494) of Joannes Mauburnus—Jean Mombaer; *The Arte of Divine Meditation* (London, 1606), by Joseph Hall, later Bishop of Exeter and Norwich; and Richard Crashaw's hymn, "To the Name above Every Name, the Name of Iesus," first published in 1648 (see above, Chap. 1, sec. 6).

The massive *Rosetum* of Mauburnus, though now a book whose labyrinths of meditation easily lose the reader, was in its time a book of considerable fame: it saw two editions early in the sixteenth century (Basle, 1504, and Paris, 1510), and two more early in the seventeenth (Milan, 1603, and Douay, 1620), the last of which is probably most significant for our interests here, since it was edited by the English Benedictine, Leander St. Martin. But the major importance of the book lies in the fact that it exerted a strong influence upon the meditative methods of García de Cisneros, Abbot of Montserrat, and thus, directly or indirectly, came to exert a strong influence upon the creation of the *Spiritual Exercises* of St. Ignatius.[1] While the *Rosetum* was thus playing a part in the meditative life of the Continent, its most important section, the explanation of the *Scala Meditatoria*,[2] was also making a strong impact upon England through the agency of Hall's treatise; for the

1. See the very judicious account of this problem by Watrigant, *Études*, 72, 195–216; 73, 199–228; also Debongnie, pp. 292–4.
2. See pp. 477–99 in ed. 1620; all references to the *Rosetum* throughout this appendix are made to this edition, which I have compared with that of 1494; there are no significant differences in the account of the *Scala*.

Arte of Divine Meditation quickly went through two more separate editions (1607, 1609) and was thereafter prominently included in Hall's collected works, of which there were at least thirteen editions by 1650. In that year the influence of Hall's *Arte*, along with other of his devotional writings, was manifested in the greatest of all the native English treatises on meditation: the fourth part of Richard Baxter's *The Saints Everlasting Rest*.[3] Thus, in their methods of meditation, Jesuit and Puritan came to be more closely related than either knew—or would admit. The relationship becomes even more striking when we realize that the *Scala* set forth by Mauburnus is not his own invention, but is, as he acknowledges (p. 477), the work of a certain nameless doctor: it is, as Debongnie (pp. 206–8) has shown, a very close transcription of the *Scala Meditationis* of Johan Wessel Gansfort, whom the Reformers claimed as their precursor, and whose works had been officially condemned in 1529. Gansfort's original version of the *Scala* was first published in the Protestant edition of his *Opera* that appeared at Groningen in 1614.

Joseph Hall does not conceal his indebtedness. In his dedication he acknowledges: "In this Art of mine, I confesse to have received more light from one obscure namelesse Monke, which wrote some 112. yeres agoe, then from the directions of all other Writers. I would his humilitie had not made him niggardly of his name, that we might have knowne whom to have thanked." Dating back from 1606 brings us to the year 1494, when the *Rosetum* appeared, anonymously; and that this is indeed the book referred to is manifested by Hall's whole treatise, which in places gives either a direct translation or a summary of the section in the *Rosetum* explaining the *Scala*. This is clearest in Hall's Chapter 16, where he writes:

> I have found a subtill scale of Meditation, admired by some Professors of this Art, above all other humane devices, and farre preferred by them to the best directions of *Origen, Austen, Bernard, Hugo*[,] *Bonaventure, Gerson,* and whosoever

3. For explicit reference to Hall's "excellent Treatise of *Meditation,*" see Baxter, Pt. 4, p. 162.

hath been reputed of greatest perfection in this skill. The severall staires whereof (lest I should seeme to defraude my Reader through envy) I would willingly describe, were it not that I feared to scarre him rather with the danger of obscurity, from venturing further upon this so worthy a businesse: yet, lest any man perhaps might complaine of an unknowne losse, my Margent shall finde roome for that which I hold too knotty for my Text.[4]

He then presents, with a few minor changes, the first eleven steps of the *Scala*, in the long marginal addition here reproduced. But since Hall regards this portion of the *Scala* as too "knotty" for the uninitiated readers to whom his treatise is addressed, he suggests instead what he regards as a simpler way of proceeding with steps of the understanding, through various logical categories that would, no doubt, have been familiar to many of his readers. When, however, he comes to deal with the "degrees of affection" and the "Conclusion," he tacitly returns to the *Scala* and follows it very closely for nine short chapters (28–36). In the following pages I have arranged Hall's explanation of these steps in tabular form, to match the outline of the *Scala*; the numbering, titles, and phrases of the table are taken from Hall's text and margin. The outline of the *Scala* facing Hall's version is here reprinted from the edition of 1620 (p. 479), since this expands the abbreviations of 1494, aligns the parts more accurately, and contains a few additional words that help to clarify the process.[5] Moreover, this edition of 1620 would be the one most likely to have come to Crashaw's attention during his residence on the Continent. These tables make it clear that in the latter part of his treatise Hall is following the *Scala* step by step, except that he has combined the steps of *Mensio* and *Consecratio* into his one step of "Enforcement," and has similarly combined the steps of *Commendatio* and *Permissio* into his one concluding step of "Recommendation."

4. I take my quotations from the *Arte* as published in Joseph Hall, *A Recollection of such Treatises as have bene heretofore severally published, and are nowe revised, corrected, augmented*, London, 1621.

5. For further clarity, I have made one change in alignment and a few changes in punctuation and spelling.

The Scale of Meditation of an Author,
ancient, but namelesse.

* *Degrees of Preparation.*

1 *Question.* { What I { thinke. / should thinke.

2 *Excussion.* { A repelling of what I should not thinke.

3 *Choice,* / *or* / *Election.* { Of what most { necessarie. / expedient. / comely.

* *Degrees of proceeding in the understanding.*

4 *Commemoration.* { An actuall thinking vpon the matter elected.

5 *Consideration.* { A redoubled Commemoration of the same, till it be fully knowne.

6 *Attention.* { A fixed and earnest consideration whereby it is fastned in the minde.

7 *Explanation.* { A clearing of the thing considered by similitudes.

8 *Tractation.* { An extending the thing considered to other points, where all questions of doubts are discussed.

9 *Diiudication.* { An estimation of the worth of the thing thus handled.

10 *Causation.* { A confirmation of the estimation thus made.

11 *Rumination.* { A sad and serious Meditation of all the former, till it may worke vpon the affections.

From hence to the degrees of affection.

"The Scale of Meditation," reproduced from Hall's *Arte of Divine Meditation* as printed in the *Recollection* of Hall's works (London, 1621), p. 105

(Yale University Library)

Per gradus ascendebatur in templum.

Modus recolligendi.

Quaestio,	Qua scilicet, quisque a se	*Exuscitativa.*
	requirat { Quid cogito. / Quid cogitandum.	

Gradus Praeparatorii.

Excussio,	Est repulsio eorum, quae minus cogitanda.	*Depulsiva obstantium.*
Electio,	Magis s[cilicet] cogitandorum,	*Assumptiva conferentium.*
	puta quae magis { Expediunt, / Conferunt, / Decent;	

Gradus Processorii, & mentis.

Commemoratio,	Est actualis electae & destinatae rei cogitatio.	*Haeret con- duplicatione.*
Consideratio,	Est sedula, & iterata commemoratio & inhaesio, donec proprie nosca-tur commemoratum.	*Penetrat.*
Attentio,	Est fixa & attenta consideratio, vel per[sp]ectio rei consideratae & commemoratae.	*Figit.*
Explanatio,	Est quaedam illustratio in atten-tione positorum.	*Illustrat.*
Tractatio,	Est rerum commemoratarum & c. ad alia quaedam extensio.	*Extendit.*

Gradus Processorii, & iudicii aut intellectus.

Dijudicatio,	Est qua pro dignitate sua suscepta res aestimatur.	*Aestimat.*
Causatio,	Est stabilitio factae dijudicationis, sicut confirmatio orationis.	*Stabilit.*
Ruminatio,	Est morosa superiorum cum com-memoratione tractatio, donec gustum attingat.	*Iterando inquirit.*

Will and Affections.

1 *Taste.*

Let the heart therefore first conceive and feele in it selfe the *sweetnesse* or *bitternesse* of the matter meditated: which is never done, without some passion; nor expressed, without some hearty exclamation.

2 *Complaint.*

Wherein the heart bewaileth to it selfe his owne poverty, dulnesse, and imperfection; chiding and abasing it selfe in respect of his wants and indisposition.

3 *Wish.*

An hearty and passionate *Wish* of the soule, which ariseth clearely from the two former degrees: For, that which a man hath found sweet, and comfortable, and complaines that hee still wanteth, hee cannot but wish to enjoy.

4 *Confession.*

Having bemoaned our want, and wished supply, not finding this hope in our selves, we must needs acknowledge it to him, of whom only we may both seeke and finde.

5 *Petition.*

Earnestly requesting that at his hands, which we acknowledge our selves unable, and none but God able to performe.

6 *Enforcement.*

From argument and importunate obsecration.

7 *Confidence.*

Wherein the soule, after many doubtfull and unquiet bickerings, gathereth up her forces, and cherefully rowzeth up it selfe.

Conclusion.

1 *Gratulation.*

The good heart cannot finde it selfe happie, and not be thankefull: and this thankefulnesse which it feeleth and expresseth, maketh it yet more good, and affecteth it more.

2 *Recommendation.*

Wherein the soule doth cheerefully give up it selfe, and repose it selfe wholly upon her Maker, and Redeemer; committing her selfe to him in all her wayes, submitting her selfe to him in all his waies.

Gradus Processorii amoris voluntatis & affectus.

Gustatio,	Est qua, sicut superioribus monemur ac docemur, ita hic nos affici sentimus.	*Videt exclamatione.*
Quaerela,	Est quaerentis impatientia, vel denunciatio displicentis.	*Deplangit lamentatione.*
Optio,	Qua quod dulce iudicat possidere desiderat; vel, est desiderium complacentis.	*Esurit desideratione.*
Confessio,	Est veritatis assensus, & publica agnitio.	*Congesta detegit.*
Oratio,	Est optionis ad Deum insinuatio.	*Exigit.*
Mensio,	Est oratorum collatio, & orantium.	*Animat.*
Consecratio,	Est cum sacrae rei attestatione oratio.	*Extorquet.*
Confidentia,	Est persensae & agnitae bonitatis argumentum, ad impetranda monens.	*Possidet.*

Gradus terminatorii.

Gratiarum actio,	Perceptorum verorum bonorum grandis aestimatio est.	*Refundit.*
Commendatio,	Desideriorum suorum in Dei bonitatem fiducialis remissio.	*Custodit.*
Permissio,	Est integra propriae voluntatis in Dei voluntatem resignatio.	*Holocaustat.*

The general resemblance of all this to the movement of Crashaw's hymn may be clarified by presenting, first of all, an outline of the poem, according to divisions that seem clearly marked within the sequence of the work itself:

I. (1–12) Introduction: proposal of the subject and introductory prayer (*modus recolligendi*).

II. (13–45) Preliminary self-address (*gradus praeparatorii*).

III. (46–87) Address to all creatures, asking for their assistance: "Help me to meditate mine Immortall Song" (*gradus processorii, & mentis*).

IV. (88–114) Self-address, justifying the speaker's own place in the celebration (*gradus processorii, & iudicii aut intellectus*).

V. (115–150) Invocation of the Name, calling for its appearance; first part of the "hymn," proper (*gradus processorii amoris, voluntatis & affectus:* steps 1–6).

VI. (151–196) Celebration of the appearance of the Name: second part of the "hymn," proper (*gradus processorii amoris, voluntatis & affectus:* final steps of *Consecratio* and *Confidentia*).

VII. (197–239) Conclusion: the faith of the ancient martyrs contrasted with the lack of faith at the present moment of history (*gradus terminatorii*).

The reader familiar with the rules of Renaissance oratory will perhaps see here some similarities to the "seven partes in every Oration" recommended by Thomas Wilson in his famous *Arte of Rhetorique:* Entrance (*exordium*), Narration (*narratio*), Proposition (*propositio*), Division (*partitio*), Confirmation (*confirmatio*), Confutation (*reprehensio*), and Conclusion (*peroratio*).[6] Certainly the common modes of rhetorical development are operating in this poem, especially in the Introduction and the Conclusion. Here, as elsewhere in this book, I do not wish to disregard the many other elements that enter into the poem; but I know of no rhetorical scheme that will bear so precise a resemblance to the sequence of Crashaw's poem as does the *Scala* of Mauburnus. Let us see how far this resemblance will hold in detail.

The poem opens, in the usual meditative fashion, with a clear, precise definition of the "Question," using the "proper" way of "entrance into this worke," as recommended by Hall (chap. 15): a way "wherein the minde, recollecting it selfe, maketh choise of that Theme or matter whereupon it will bestow it selfe for the present":

> I sing the NAME which None can say
> But touch't with An interiour RAY:

6. *Wilson's Arte of Rhetorique, 1560*, ed. G. H. Mair (Oxford, Clarendon Press, 1909), p. 7. This is a reprint of the edition of 1585.

> The Name of our New PEACE; our Good:
> Our Blisse: & Supernaturall Blood:
> The Name of All our Liues & Loues.

This is performed in conjunction with preparatory prayer, as Hall (chap. 14) and Mauburnus (p. 481) both advise; here the prayer is addressed to the souls of the blessed in heaven, in a way similar to that advised in the *Introduction* of St. François de Sales:

> My Philotheus, let us joine our harts unto these heavenlie spirits and happie soules: for as the little young Nightingales, learne to sing by chirping in companie of the old-ones: so by the holie association which wee frequent with the Saints and Angels of heaven, we shall learne farre better to pray and sing Gods divine prayses . . . . (p. 170)

> Hearken, And Help, ye holy Doues!
> The high-born Brood of Day; you bright
> Candidates of blissefull Light,
> The HEIRS Elect of Loue; whose Names belong
> Vnto The euerlasting life of Song;
> All ye wise SOVLES, who in the wealthy Brest
> Of This vnbounded NAME build your warm Nest.

After a pause, the preparatory steps follow, adopting the mode of self-address recommended by Mauburnus (pp. 480–1) for these steps, as well as for the preceding Quaestio: the soul asks itself questions and gives responses, for the purpose described by the word *exuscitativa*—awakening. Thus the poem proceeds to repel the less important matters that may impede the soul in its aim:

> Awake, MY glory. SOVL, (if such thou be,
> And That fair WORD at all referr to Thee)
> Awake & sing
> And be All Wing;
> Bring hither thy whole SELF; & let me see
> What of thy Parent HEAVN yet speakes in thee.
> O thou art Poore
> Of noble POWRES, I see,
> And full of nothing else but empty ME,

> Narrow, & low, & infinitely lesse
> Then this GREAT mornings mighty Busynes.
> One little WORLD or two
> (Alas) will neuer doe.
> We must haue store.
> Goe, SOVL, out of thy Self, & seek for More.

Already the Electio is under way, which proceeds thus with
the choice of those things that are "most necessarie, expedient,
comely": [7]

> Goe & request
> Great NATVRE for the KEY of her huge Chest
> Of Heauns, the self inuoluing Sett of Sphears
> (Which dull mortality more Feeles then heares)
> Then rouse the nest
> Of nimble ART, & trauerse round
> The Aiery Shop of soul-appeasing Sound:
> And beat a summons in the Same
> All-soueraign Name
> To warn each seuerall kind
> And shape of sweetnes, Be they such
> As sigh with supple wind
> Or answer Artfull Touch,
> That they conuene & come away
> To wait at the loue-crowned Doores of
> This Illustrious DAY.
> Shall we dare This, my Soul? we'l doe't and bring
> No Other note for't, but the Name we sing [.]

The act of choice could not be more clearly marked. But what is
this "great morning," this "illustrious day?" This is a hymn for a
special occasion, probably for a feast of the Holy Name. Though
this feast was not established for the Universal Church until 1721,
it was widely celebrated by various orders during the seventeenth
century: the Franciscans, for example, celebrated the feast on January 14, by right of a decree of 1530. The occasion of the poem

7. Unless it is otherwise noted, all subsequent quotations from Hall and
Mauburnus are taken (as this quotation is) from materials contained in the
tables under the appropriate heading.

may have been Crashaw's first participation in this relatively new devotion.

The matter of the meditation is now fully prepared, and the work of the three powers of the soul may now begin, as indicated by the threefold grouping of the *gradus processorii* in the table of Mauburnus: *gradus mentis, gradus iudicii, gradus affectus.* This distinction is obscured in Hall's version, since he groups the first two as steps of the "understanding." The process of the *mens,* of course, includes more than memory, but it proceeds from "Commemoration" and a "redoubled Commemoration": thus we have here once more that threefold movement that we have discussed in Chapter 1: the prototype of that movement. (Cf. Mauburnus, p. 481: "Post praeparatorios gradus sequuntur gradus procedendi, & hoc secundum tres partes imaginis; s[cilicet] mentis, intelligentiae & voluntatis; ita quod mens secundum se totam, intenta sit meditationi. Et ideo sunt gradus *monitionis,* quae mentem monent; *doctionis,* quae intelligentiam docent; *motionis,* quae voluntatem movent.")

We can follow the movement of the *mens* throughout the third section of the poem, the mood of which is clarified by the phrase "gradus monitionis" which Mauburnus uses to describe the purpose of these steps of the *mens:* admonition, with a mood of earnest exhortation. First, the Commemoratio, the "actuall thinking upon the matter elected"; a process that makes the matter "stick" by repetition (*haeret conduplicatione*):

> Wake Lvte & Harp
> And euery sweet-lipp't Thing
> That talkes with tunefull string;
> Start into life, And leap with me
> Into a hasty Fitt-tun'd Harmony.
> Nor must you think it much
> T'obey my bolder touch;
> I haue Authority in Love's name to take you
> And to the worke of Loue this morning wake you[;]
> Wake; In the Name
> Of Him who neuer sleeps, All Things that Are,
> Or, what's the same,

> Are Musicall;
> Answer my Call
> And come along;
> Help me to meditate mine Immortall Song.

The *Consideratio* follows, which recapitulates a dozen and more
of the words and images thus far introduced, repeating them with a
different inflection, entwining them in a continually richer context: exactly the manner suggested in the chart of Mauburnus,
which says that this step seeks to "penetrate" by "persistent and repeated remembrance of and clinging to" the matter, "until it is
thoroughly, intimately (*proprie*) known."

> Come, ye soft ministers of sweet sad mirth,
> Bring All your houshold stuffe of Heaun on earth;
> O you, my Soul's most certain Wings,
> Complaining Pipes, & prattling Strings,
>   Bring All the store
> Of Sweets you haue; And murmur that you haue no more.
>   Come, nere to part,
>   Natvre & Art!
>   Come; & come strong,
> To the conspiracy of our Spatious song.
>   Bring All the Powres of Praise
> Your Prouinces of well-vnited Worlds can raise;
> Bring All your Lvtes & Harps of Heavn & Earth;
> What e're cooperates to The common mirthe[:]
>   Vessells of vocall Ioyes,
> Or You, more noble Architects of Intellectuall Noise,
> Cymballs of Heau'n, or Humane sphears,
> Solliciters of Sovles or Eares . . . .

It is filled with subtle echoes of Herbert, woven into this more
rhapsodic texture: "mirth," "houshold stuffe," music as the soul's
wings, "prattling," "store." These, together with the witty play
on "conspiracy" and the pun on "Cymballs," create a sense of
Herbertian fun transposed to the mode of baroque celebration. But
now these persistent repetitions must be driven home (cf. *figit*),
through the following step of *Attentio*, which operates by a "fixed
and earnest consideration whereby it is fastned in the minde":

> And when you'are come, with All
> That you can bring or we can call;
> O may you fix
> For euer here, & mix
> Your selues into the long
> And euerlasting series of a deathlesse Song;
> Mix All your many Worlds, Aboue,
> And loose them into One of Loue.

So far, all seems in clear order; but now, in the fourth section, the poem modifies the strict sequence of the method—as indeed it must, I think, if it is to remain a poem, for these steps, as Hall suggests (chap. 16), may well involve too much repetition. It is perhaps significant that, just in this portion of the process, Mauburnus adds a comment designed to encourage the kind of freedom here displayed by Crashaw. At the close of the sequence of the *mens* (at the end of his commentary on the step of Tractatio), he warns: "Here, then, are the steps of the intellect, which are full of abundant possibilities; nevertheless, one must not put his trust in these things, but the sails of the mind must be unfurled to the winds of grace, and inspiration followed, rather than a set procedure." (p. 483)

The poem at this point appears to omit the steps of Explanatio and Tractatio, which, it seems, could only overextend the matter already so thoroughly considered. Instead, the poem moves ahead into the *gradus iudicii*, or the *gradus doctionis*, as Mauburnus calls them in the passage cited earlier: that is to say, these are the steps of instruction, of convincing, of proving, steps that will bring the matter home to the "heart" after the manner suggested by Mauburnus in his comments on the step of Ruminatio: "in order that the affection may arise more strongly, and the taste be felt more sweetly, it is necessary for rumination to go before, which is a careful discussion of the foregoing matters, thoughtfully lingering upon them, until the taste is reached; in order that we may, like Mary the mother of God, preserve these matters that have been considered and decided, let us draw them together in our hearts, and like the clean animals under the Law, let us chew the cud of these matters, until they grow sweet in our hearts." (p. 484) In Crashaw's poem the whole of the fourth section is such a rumination, including the steps of Dijudicatio and Causatio, with their "estimation of the worth of the thing thus handled," and a "confirmation of the estimation thus made"; and including as well a "sad and serious Meditation of all the former" steps on the Scale, "till it may worke upon the affections."

So, at line 88, the speaker turns to encourage himself:

> Chear thee my HEART!
> For Thou too hast thy Part
> And Place in the Great Throng
> Of This vnbounded All-imbracing SONG.
> Powres of my Soul, be Proud!
> And speake lowd
> To All the dear-bought Nations This Redeeming Name,
> And in the wealth of one Rich WORD proclaim
> New Similes to Nature.

The address to the soul here cancels out, under a new dispensation of Love, the rejection of the soul's powers performed in the Excussio: this was an act of humility, now rewarded with a deeper understanding of man's place in the scheme of things; a place firmly established also by the way in which the beginning of this fourth section matches metrically the opening of the third (dimeter, trimeter, trimeter, expanding into a longer line).

Now, with the proper tone of rumination (*morosa*, "sad and serious"), the speaker analyzes and defends with his judgment his right to play a part in this great song: addressing the heavenly spirits in words that echo all the preceding portion of the poem, and link especially with the introductory prayer:

> May it be no wrong
> Blest Heauns, to you, & your Superiour song,
> That we, dark Sons of Dust & Sorrow,
> A while Dare borrow
> The Name of Your Delights & our Desires,
> And fitt it to so farr inferior LYRES.
> Our Murmurs haue their Musick too,
> Ye mighty ORBES, as well as you,
> Nor yeilds the noblest Nest
> Of warbling SERAPHIM to the eares of Loue,

A choicer Lesson then the ioyfull BREST
     Of a poor panting Turtle-Doue.
And we, low Wormes haue leaue to doe
The Same bright Busynes (ye Third HEAVENS) with you.
Gentle SPIRITS, doe not complain.
     We will haue care
     To keep it fair,
And send it back to you again.

With this quiet, Herbertian note, the sequence of the "under-standing" ends. Now the celebration itself can begin; the hymn, properly speaking, may be sung; the affections may begin to move upward toward the top of the Scale, as Hall explains (chap. 28) in one of the most significant passages of his whole treatise:

> The most difficult and knotty part of Meditation thus fin-ished, there remaineth that which is both more lively, and more easie unto a good heart, to be wrought altogether by the affections: which if our discourses reach not unto, they prove vaine, and to no purpose. That which followeth therefore, is the very soule of Meditation, whereto all that is past serveth but as an instrument. A man is a man by his understanding part: but hee is a Christian by his will and affections. Seeing therefore, that all our former labour of the braine is onely to affect the heart, after that the mind hath thus traversed the point proposed through all the heads of reason, it shall en-deavour to finde in the first place some feeling touch, and sweet rellish in that which it hath thus chewed; which fruit, through the blessing of God, will voluntarily follow upon a serious Meditation. *David* saith, *Oh taste, and see how sweet the Lord is.* In Meditation we doe both see and taste; but we see before we taste: sight, is of the understanding; taste, of the affection: neither can we see, but we must taste; we cannot know aright, but we must needs be affected. Let the heart therefore first conceive and feele in it selfe the *sweetnesse* or *bitternesse* of the matter meditated: which is never done, with-out some passion; nor expressed, without some hearty exclama-tion.[8]

8. Hall is here freely elaborating upon the commentary of Mauburnus, pp. 484–5: the beginning of the sequence of the affections.

At line 115, then, the poem begins this sequence of the affections for which all the earlier portion has been so deliberately preparing. It opens with the Gustatio, the first taste of the sweetness of the matter, replete with passionate exclamations (cf. Mauburnus, p. 485: "fit exclamatione, interrogatione, dubitatione, & aliis coloribus & modis exuscitativis"):

> Come, louely NAME! Appeare from forth the Bright
>   Regions of peacefull Light[.]
> Look from thine own Illustrious Home,
> Fair KING of NAMES, & come.
> Leaue All thy natiue Glories in their Gorgeous Nest,
> And giue thy Self a while The gracious Guest
> Of humble Soules, that seek to find
>   The hidden Sweets
>   Which man's heart meets
> When Thou art Master of the Mind.
> Come, louely Name; life of our hope!
> Lo we hold our HEARTS wide ope!
> Vnlock thy Cabinet of DAY
> Dearest Sweet, & come away.

Now comes the second step: Quaerela, the "Complaint," in which the speaker laments "his owne poverty, dulnesse, and imperfection." Here again, the poem moves with great freedom through the established steps: the tone of the Complaint dominates the next twenty-two lines (129–50), while within this portion the poem flexibly includes the acts of Optio, Confessio, Oratio, and Mensio: the wish to possess the thing desired, hungering with the wish; a recognition of one's helpnessness; a prayer to God beseeching him to grant the wish; and a "measure," which, Mauburnus says (p. 486), is a "confirmation of the prayer by reasoning with comparisons." This step, as the table says, "animates" the spirit by setting together the things prayed for and the persons praying. And all this is done with the fluctuations of feeling thus described by Hall: "the minde is by turnes depressed, and lifted up: Being lifted up with our taste of ioy, it is cast downe with *Complaint:* lift up with *Wishes,* it is cast downe with *Confession* . . . ." (chap. 31)

> Lo how the thirsty Lands
> Gasp for thy Golden Showres! with long stretch't Hands
> Lo how the laboring EARTH
> That hopes to be
> All Heauen by THEE,
> Leapes at thy Birth.
> The'attending WORLD, to wait thy Rise,
> First turn'd to eyes;
> And then, not knowing what to doe;
> Turn'd Them to TEARES, & spent Them too.
> Come ROYALL Name, & pay the expence
> Of All this Pretious Patience.
> O come away
> And kill the DEATH of This Delay.
> O see, so many WORLDS of barren yeares
> Melted & measur'd out in Seas of TEARES.
> O see, The WEARY liddes of wakefull Hope
> (LOVE's Eastern windowes) All wide ope
> With Curtains drawn,
> To catch The Day-break of Thy DAWN.
> O dawn, at last, long look't for Day!
> Take thine own wings, & come away.

It is a daring exploit in the art of sacred parody: opening with allusion to the tale of Zeus and Danaë, moving on through the imagery
of *accouchement* into a lover's lament and a version of the lover's
dawn-song, "come away"—echoing here, as before, the Song of
Solomon. But more daring developments are to follow, as the Name
appears, and the affections come to rest in the steps of Consecratio
and Confidentia.

What is the "attestation of a sacred thing" with which this final
prayer is to be offered, and by which the prayer's answer is to be
"extorted" from God? Answer and attestation are given simultaneously by presenting the appearance of the Name itself (with perhaps
some overtones of the Elevation of the Host). This is presented
exactly as Mauburnus advises (p. 486): "per se, suos, sua"; that is,
first in itself, then in those beings who are united with it, and lastly
in those attributes which belong to it:

Lo, where Aloft it comes! It comes, Among
The Conduct of Adoring SPIRITS, that throng
Like diligent Bees, And swarm about it.
     O they are wise;
And know what SWEETES are suck't from out it.
     It is the Hiue,
     By which they thriue,
Where All their Hoard of Hony lyes.
Lo where it comes, vpon The snowy DOVE's
Soft Back; And brings a Bosom big with Loues.
WELCOME to our dark world, Thou
     Womb of Day!
Vnfold thy fair Conceptions; And display
The Birth of our Bright Ioyes.
     O thou compacted
Body of Blessings: spirit of Soules extracted!
O dissipate thy spicy Powres
(Clowd of condensed sweets) & break vpon vs
     In balmy showrs;
O fill our senses, And take from vs
All force of so Prophane a Fallacy
To think ought sweet but that which smells of Thee.

The last step of affection follows: Confidentia, in which the soul "possesses" its desire, through "evidence of a goodness deeply felt and fully recognized." And this is done with a tranquil fusion of the intellectual and the sensory, renewing first the witty legal image of "convening," and moving on into what may be called an "application of the senses":

Fair, flowry Name; In none but Thee
And Thy Nectareall Fragrancy,
     Hourly there meetes
An vniuersall SYNOD of All sweets;
By whom it is defined Thus
     That no Perfume
     For euer shall presume
To passe for Odoriferous,
  But such alone whose sacred Pedigree

Can proue it Self some kin (sweet name) to Thee.
SWEET NAME, in Thy each Syllable
A Thousand Blest ARABIAS dwell;
A Thousand Hills of Frankincense;
Mountains of myrrh, & Beds of spices,
And ten Thousand PARADISES
The soul that tasts thee takes from thence.
How many vnknown WORLDS there are
Of Comforts, which Thou hast in keeping!
How many Thousand Mercyes there
In Pitty's soft lap ly a sleeping!
Happy he who has the art
      To awake them,
      And to take them
Home, & lodge them in his HEART.

It is ornate to the verge of extravagance, but held from falling by the crisp control of wit, by the traditional allusions to the Song of Solomon, and by the quiet, Herbertian close, matching exactly, in its quatrain-form, the conclusion to the sequence of the "understanding."

There remain the *gradus terminatorii*, which, according to Mauburnus, consist in three degrees: first, the "action of graces," by which the soul restores all to God, through "a lofty estimation of the true good received" in this meditation; secondly, through Commendatio, which guards this good through a "confident remission of one's own desires to the goodness of God"; and lastly, through Permissio, which represents an act of self-immolation, "total resignation of one's own will to the will of God." (In the chart of 1494 reproduced in my first chapter, yet another step may appear to follow: the Complexio; but this, as Mauburnus explains (pp. 479, 487), is not really another step, but a *modus commorandi*—a way of prolonging the meditation, if time permits, by comparing one step with another and ruminating over the whole exercise. The Scale proper ends with the Permissio.)

In Crashaw's poem the terminal steps are clearly set off by a change of pace and theme which gives the last section—the seventh—the effect of epilogue. It falls into three parts, and I believe that, in a very general way, the threefold division accords with the procedure suggested by Mauburnus. This final section is a colloquy, in which the speaker, remembering the religious quarrels and persecutions of his age, ponders the perfect "action of graces," the perfect submission, the perfect resignation—by drawing a strong contrast between the faith of the ancient martyrs and the weakness of a world where everything he most values seems to be desecrated.

The key to the manner of the first part of this epilogue, and to some extent of the second as well, is found in the phrase of Mauburnus, "grandis aestimatio." "Grandis," in all the meanings of the word: "full," "abundant," "powerful," "weighty," or with regard to style: "great," "lofty," "dignified," "noble." The poetry changes from a mood of tranquil simplicity to one of militant elaboration; the feet march in long lines, with bold alliteration, in keeping with the theme, the action of grace in the Church Militant:

> O that it were as it was wont to be!
> When thy old Freinds of Fire, All full of Thee,
> Fought against Frowns with smiles; gaue Glorious chase
> To Persecutions; And against the Face
> Of DEATH & feircest Dangers, durst with Braue
> And sober pace march on to meet A GRAVE.
> On their Bold BRESTS about the world they bore thee
> And to the Teeth of Hell stood vp to teach thee,
> In Center of their inmost Soules they wore thee,
> Where Rackes & Torments striu'd, in vain, to reach thee.

At this point the poetry reverts to a quieter mode, in a quatrain that begins a new movement upward toward the grand style; this second part portrays in eucharistic imagery the justification for the trust which the martyrs displayed in reenacting the Sacrifice:

> Little, alas, thought They
> Who tore the Fair Brests of thy Freinds,
> Their Fury but made way
> For Thee; And seru'd therein Thy glorious ends.
> What did Their weapons but with wider pores
> Inlarge thy flaming-brested Louers
> More freely to transpire

That impatient Fire
The Heart that hides Thee hardly couers.
What did their Weapons but sett wide the Doores
For Thee: Fair, purple Doores, of loue's deuising;
The Ruby windowes which inrich't the EAST
Of Thy so oft repeated Rising.
Each wound of Theirs was Thy new Morning;
And reinthron'd thee in thy Rosy Nest,
With blush of thine own Blood thy day adorning,
It was the witt of loue o'reflowd the Bounds
Of WRATH, & made thee way through All Those WOVNDS.

Finally he emphasizes the need for this complete submission and resignation by setting the controversy over bodily posture in worship against the words of Philippians (2.9–11) from which the whole poem is fundamentally derived: "Wherefore God also hath highly exalted him, and given him a name which is above every name: That at the name of Jesus every knee should bow, of things in heaven, and things in earth, and things under the earth; and that every tongue should confess that Jesus Christ is Lord, to the glory of God the Father." Here, exhibiting the same control that has marked every movement toward excess throughout the poem, Crashaw concludes with a stern tone of warning that acts as a necessary antidote to the cloying richness of the blood-imagery in the preceding lines:

Wellcome dear, All-Adored Name!
          For sure there is no Knee
          That knowes not THEE.
Or if there be such sonns of shame,
          Alas what will they doe
          When stubborn Rocks shall bow
And Hills hang down their Heaun-saluting Heads
          To seek for humble Beds
Of Dust, where in the Bashfull shades of night
Next to their own low NOTHING they may ly,
And couch before the dazeling light of thy dread majesty.
They that by Loue's mild Dictate now
          Will not adore thee,

Shall Then with Iust Confusion, bow
And break before thee.

Thus it appears that in this poem the art of meditation has provided the fundamental unity of structure necessary to control the daring adventures of the baroque imagination. Crashaw's hymn stands with Donne's *Second Anniversary* as one of the great achievements in the poetry of meditation.

The Dating and Significance of Donne's Anniversaries

IT HAS long been known that Elizabeth Drury died in 1610: thus the natural assumption would be that the *Anatomie* was written for the first anniversary of her death, in 1611, and the *Progresse* for the second, in 1612. It seems clear that the combined edition of the two poems (the first edition of the *Progresse*) was published early in 1612, since Donne refers to current opinion of his *Anniversaries* in a letter dated April 14, 1612 (*Letters*, pp. 206–7). But we now know, more precisely, that Elizabeth Drury died in December, 1610: John Sparrow (*Times Literary Supplement* [March 26, 1949], p. 208) has pointed out that the registers of Hawsted Church record her burial on December 17, 1610: see Sir John Cullum, *The History and Antiquities of Hawstead, and Hardwick* (2d ed., London, 1813), p. 75. Thus the *Second Anniversary* appears to have been published only a little more than a year after her death. This dating accords with what the poems themselves indicate. In the opening of the *Anatomie* (line 39) Donne says, "Some moneths she hath beene dead"; and he begins the *Progresse* by saying that

> a yeare is runne,
> Since both this lower world's, and the Sunnes Sunne,
> The Lustre, and the vigor of this All,
> Did set; 'twere blasphemie to say, did fall.

That is, a year has passed since Elizabeth Drury died: the *Second Anniversary*, it seems, is being written sometime near December, 1611. The date is confirmed by other evidence: the poem's conclusion refers to the fact that the poet is writing in France; and R. E. Bennett has shown that Donne was living in France with the Druries from the end of November, 1611, until mid-April, 1612 ("Donne's

Letters from the Continent in 1611–12," *PQ*, *19* [1940], 66–78; see pp. 71–4 for the problems of dating the letters of mid-April in which Donne refers to the *Anniversaries*).

The title, *The First Anniversary*, was not used in the first appearance of the *Anatomie* in 1611: it was added when the poem was republished with the *Progresse* in 1612. The term "anniversary" is thus not a part of the original conception of the first poem; it is rather a device added to tie the two poems together. Nevertheless, Donne says at the close of the *Anatomie*:

> Accept this tribute, and his first yeares rent,
> Who till his darke short tapers end be spent,
> As oft as thy feast sees this widowed earth,
> Will yearely celebrate thy second birth,
> That is, thy death; (447–51)

and he offers the *Progresse* "for my second yeares true Rent." (520) What does the word "anniversary" mean in this context? In the first place it holds implications of the old ecclesiastical meanings of the term, thus summed up in Thomas Blount's *Glossographia* (London, 1656): "Those were of old called *Anniversary days*, whereon the martyrdoms or death-days of Saints were celebrated yeerly in the Church; or the days whereon at the yeers end, men were wont yeerly to pray for the souls of their deceased friends according to the continued custom of Roman Catholiques." At the same time, the word could also mean, "Enduring for or completed in a year" (*OED*, "Anniversary," *adj*. 3), and might also be used "for the *annale* or commemorative service performed daily for a year after the death of a person." (*idem, sb.* 3) I take it that the term "anniversary," as applied to these poems, indicates a whole year's commemorative tribute, paid in advance. "Rent" need not have the crass implications that some have seen in Donne's use of the word: it indicates, in context, an obligation due at a stated time—at the end of the year.

This dating, with its emphatic references within the poem to the recent death of the person celebrated, may help to comment upon the interpretations of the *Anniversaries* recently advanced by Marius Bewley in "Religious Cynicism in Donne's Poetry," *KR*, *14* (1952),

619–46; and by Marjorie Nicolson in *The Breaking of the Circle* (Evanston, Northwestern University Press, 1950), chap. 3. Miss Nicolson has made an important point in reminding us that the legend of Astraea plays a significant part in the poem; and Mr. Bewley seems on safe ground when he views the "girl-symbol" of these poems as "a symbol of what at one moment appears to be the soul's interior awareness of its own spiritual possibilities, and a moment later the objectification of those possibilities in terms of a theology." (p. 625) But both writers leap beyond these points to find in the poems a fundamental reference to Queen Elizabeth. Miss Nicolson regards her as the "central character" of the poems (p. 79), and Mr. Bewley finds allusions to the Virgin Queen in the course of developing his view that the poems deal basically with Donne's attitudes toward the Church: "Elizabeth Drury alive, Donne is saying, symbolized the Catholic Church; but she is dead, and he turns to contemplate the consequences of her death for the world. All is not hopeless, for her ghost still walks abroad, and in her ghost—or the image of Elizabeth Drury dead—we have the image of Anglicanism." (pp. 626–7) These interpretations seem to impose a meaning upon the central image instead of allowing a meaning to develop from this image in accordance with the poems' structure. One can arrive at these views, I think, only by treating the metaphors as literal statements. Thus, out of context, the following passage, cited by both Miss Nicolson and Mr. Bewley, may look like a reference to Queen Elizabeth:

> For shee made warres, and triumph'd; reason still
> Did not o'rthrow, but rectifie her will:
> And she made peace, for no peace is like this,
> That beauty, and chastity together kisse:
> She did high justice, for she crucified
> Every first motion of rebellious pride:
> And she gave pardons, and was liberall,
> For, onely her selfe except, she pardon'd all . . . .
>
> (*2 Ann.*, 361–8)

But in terms of the whole poem, this passage does not imply that the central figure was, literally, a monarch; the point is that the "she" of the passage has learned to rule herself, that inward rule—the self-control of true humility—is the greatest of all "dignities." The central point of both poems lies in the assertion that religious virtue is the greatest of all human values.

Donne's basic image, then, is that of a "maid" who has recently died an "untimely" (but a "religious") death, in her "youthfull age" (*2 Ann.* 68): still pure, still innocent. From this basis he proceeds to surround the central figure with imagery of value drawn from religious veneration of the Virgin and of the saints—until at the close of the *First Anniversary*, she can be called a "blessed maid" (443). Supporting the pre-eminence of such values, imagery of Petrarchan adulation and imagery of royalty are also used, with the result that the eulogies are bound to bear a strong resemblance to the kind of tributes paid to Queen Elizabeth. Certainly Donne would have been aware of such tributes—but his tribute here is not paid to monarch, monarchy, or institutional Church: he is celebrating the values of "interior peace":

> nothing
> Is worth our travaile, griefe, or perishing,
> But those rich joyes, which did possesse her heart,
> Of which she's now partaker, and a part. (*1 Ann.* 431–4)[1]

1. The whole biographical background of the *Anniversaries* has now been thoroughly explored by R. C. Bald, *Donne & the Drurys*, Cambridge University Press, 1959.

APPENDIX 3

Bibliography

THE FIRST section of this bibliography lists, for purposes of reference and acknowledgment, all editions of the works of the poets which have been used for quotations or referred to more than once in the course of this study; other editions and works of the poets are cited in individual footnotes (see index). The second and third sections list those other works which, after the first reference, I have identified simply by name of author or by short title. The bibliography does not include, then, all the works referred to in this book, nor all the works that have been helpful in its composition. I should like to have included here a number of works for which no specific reference has arisen, but which nevertheless have certainly aided my thinking upon these matters: articles such as L. C. Knights' fine essay on George Herbert in his *Explorations* (New York, George W. Stewart, 1947); broad surveys such as Douglas Bush's very helpful *English Literature in the Earlier Seventeenth Century* (Oxford, Clarendon Press, 1945); or such monumental works as the authoritative *Dictionnaire de Théologie Catholique*, ed. A. Vacant *et al.* (15 vols., 30 parts, Paris, 1909–50), a work of reference that ought to be more widely known among students of religious thought in this period. And of course I am deeply indebted to the *Short-Title Catalogue* of Pollard and Redgrave, and to its continuation by Wing. But these must suffice.

I have used the following abbreviations:

HLQ: Huntington Library Quarterly
KR: Kenyon Review
MLR: Modern Language Review
OED: Oxford English Dictionary
PMLA: Publications of the Modern Language Association of America

PQ: Philological Quarterly
RES: Review of English Studies

A. WORKS OF THE POETS

Crashaw, Richard. *The Poems, English, Latin and Greek, of Richard Crashaw*, ed. L. C. Martin. Oxford, Clarendon Press, 1927.

Donne, John. *The Poems of John Donne*, ed. Herbert J. C. Grierson. 2 vols., Oxford, Clarendon Press, 1912.

The Divine Poems, ed. Helen Gardner. Oxford, Clarendon Press, 1952.

Devotions upon Emergent Occasions, ed. John Sparrow. Cambridge, University Press, 1923.

Essayes in Divinity. London, 1651.

Letters to Severall Persons of Honour, ed. Charles Edmund Merrill, Jr. New York, Sturgis and Walton, 1910.

England's Helicon, ed. Hyder Rollins. 2 vols., Cambridge, Harvard University Press, 1935.

English Madrigal Verse, 1588–1632, ed. E. H. Fellowes. 2d ed., Oxford, Clarendon Press, 1929.

Herbert, George. *The Works of George Herbert*, ed. F. E. Hutchinson. 2d ed., Oxford, Clarendon Press, 1945.

All quotations from Herbert's works are taken from this edition.

The English Works of George Herbert, ed. George Herbert Palmer. 3 vols., Boston and New York, Houghton Mifflin, 1905.

Hopkins, Gerard Manley. *Poems of Gerard Manley Hopkins. The First Edition with Preface and Notes by Robert Bridges*, ed. W. H. Gardner. 3d ed., New York, Oxford University Press, 1948.

The Letters of Gerard Manley Hopkins to Robert Bridges, ed. Claude Colleer Abbott. London, Oxford University Press, 1935.

The Note-books and Papers of Gerard Manley Hopkins, ed. Humphry House. London, Oxford University Press, 1937.

Jonson, Ben. *Ben Jonson*, ed. C. H. Herford, Percy and Evelyn Simpson. 11 vols., Oxford, Clarendon Press, 1925–52.

Marvell, Andrew. *The Poems and Letters of Andrew Marvell*, ed. H. M. Margoliouth. 2 vols., Oxford, Clarendon Press, 1927.

Metaphysical Lyrics and Poems of the Seventeenth Century, ed. Herbert J. C. Grierson. Oxford, Clarendon Press, 1921.

Milton, John. *The Works of John Milton*, ed. Frank Allen Patterson. 18 vols., New York, Columbia University Press, 1931–38.

The Paradise of Dainty Devices (1576–1606), ed. Hyder Rollins. Cambridge, Harvard University Press, 1927.

Religious Lyrics of the XIVth Century, ed. Carleton Brown. Oxford, Clarendon Press, 1924.

Sidney, Sir Philip. *The Countesse of Pembrokes Arcadia*, London, 1598.

> Quotations from Sidney's sonnets are taken from this edition; quotations from Sidney's other works are taken from the next entry.

The Complete Works of Sir Philip Sidney, ed. Albert Feuillerat. 4 vols., Cambridge, University Press, 1912–26.

Southwell, Robert. *Saint Peters Complaint, Newly augmented With other Poems*. London, William Leake [1607–9?].

Moeoniae. Or, Certaine excellent Poems and spirituall Hymnes. London, John Busby, 1595.

The Complete Poems of Robert Southwell, ed. Alexander B. Grosart. London, 1872.

> Quotations from Southwell's poetry present a difficult problem, since no adequate modern edition exists, and the priority among the early editions is uncertain. Grosart's edition, based on the Stonyhurst manuscript, is helpful, but his text is marred by excessive capitalization and punctuation, and he has made his own arrangement of the poems which violates the significant arrangements found in the early editions and in the manuscripts. *Saint Peters Complaint* saw three editions in 1595, two by John Wolfe, and one by Gabriel Cawood. McDonald (pp. 73–5) tends toward the opinion that the shorter Wolfe edition is the first; but this is a badly printed volume, lacking eight poems contained in the other two editions of 1595. Moreover, none of these contains the most famous of Southwell's poems, "The burning Babe," which was first printed in a

group of seven poems added to the "augmented" edition of the *Complaint* issued by Cawood in 1602. Or so it appears. There is also the "augmented" edition of the *Complaint*, undated, and published by William Leake; McDonald (p. 89) makes out a good case for dating this in 1607–9. This last is a carefully printed volume which corrects some misprints in the edition of 1602; I have used this volume as the basis for my quotations from the poems which it contains, but to guard against corruptions I have compared my quotations with the Cawood texts of 1595 and 1602 as well as with the variants from the manuscripts as listed by McDonald. *Moeoniae* is in some ways easier to deal with: there were two issues in 1595, both published by John Busby, and without significant variations. I have based my quotations from the poems in this volume on what appears to be the first issue (see McDonald, pp. 101–5); but this is a badly printed volume which ignores all stanza-divisions: in my quotations I have arranged what appear to be the proper divisions into stanzas. I have kept to the readings of the early editions except in places where a change in punctuation seems essential for clarity, and in a few other places where the printed text seems clearly to be corrupt. Most of the verbal emendations are based on the manuscript variants recorded by McDonald. Needless to say, my quotations make no claim to textual authority; but they at least represent substantially the form in which the poems were read during the early part of the seventeenth century. James McDonald is at work on a definitive edition of the poems, which is badly needed.

Marie Magdalens Funeral Teares. London, Gabriel Cawood, 1591.

A Short Rule of Good Life. [London? 1598?]

Spiritual Exercises and Devotions of Blessed Robert Southwell, S.J. Edited for the first time from the Manuscripts, with intro. by J.-M de Buck and translation by P. E. Hallett. London, Sheed and Ward, 1931.

Tottel's Miscellany, 1557–1587, ed. Hyder Rollins. 2 vols., Cambridge, Harvard University Press, 1928.

Vaughan, Henry. *The Works of Henry Vaughan*, ed. Leonard

Cyril Martin. 2 vols., Oxford, Clarendon Press, 1914.

Watson, Thomas. *Poems*, ed. Edward Arber. London, 1870.

Yeats, William Butler. *The Collected Poems of W. B. Yeats*. New York, Macmillan, 1933.

    The Autobiography of William Butler Yeats. New York, Macmillan, 1938.

    A Vision. New York, Macmillan, 1938.

B. DEVOTIONAL WORKS

Antonio de Molina. *A Treatise of Mental Prayer* [trans. J. Sweetman. St. Omer], 1617.

Baxter, Richard. *The Saints Everlasting Rest*. 4th ed., London, 1653.

Bellarmine, Robert. *The Ascent of the Mind to God by a Ladder of Things Created . . . . In the first English Translation, by T. B. Gent. Published at Doway, 1616*, with intro. by James Brodrick. London, Burns, Oates, and Washbourne, 1928.

Bernard of Clairvaux, St. *Saint Bernard His Meditations: or Sighes, Sobbes, and Teares, upon our Saviours Passion . . . . Also His Motives to Mortification, with other Meditations*, trans. "W. P." 4th ed., London, 1631–2.

    The Twelve Degrees of Humility and Pride, trans. Barton R. V. Mills. London, S. P. C. K., 1929.

Bonaventure, St. *The Franciscan Vision: Translation of St Bonaventure's Itinerarium Mentis in Deum, with an introduction by Father James*. London, Burns, Oates, and Washbourne, 1937.

    Opera Omnia. 11 vols., Quaracchi, 1882–1902.

The Booke of Common Prayer. London, 1604.

Bunyan, John. *Grace Abounding to the Chief of Sinners*, ed. John Brown. Cambridge, University Press, 1907.

Camus, Jean Pierre. *A Spirituall Combat: A Tryall of a Faithfull Soule or Consolation in Temptation* [trans. Thomas Carre, i.e., Miles Pinkney]. Douay, 1632.

Castello, Alberto. *Rosario della gloriosa vergine Maria*. Venice, 1564.

Chambers, Sabin. *The Garden of our B. Lady. Or A devout manner, how to serve her in her Rosary*. [St. Omer], 1619.

Dent, Arthur. *The Plaine Mans Path-way to Heaven. Wherein every man may clearely see, whether he shall be saved or damned.* London, 1601.

Diego de Estella, *The Contempte of the World, and the Vanitie thereof*, trans. "G. C." [Douay?], 1584.

Directory. See under St. Ignatius.

Francisco de Osuna. *The Third Spiritual Alphabet*, trans. "By a Benedictine of Stanbrook." Westminster, Md., Newman Bookshop, 1948.

François de Sales, St. *An Introduction to a Devoute Life* [trans. John Yakesley]. 3d ed., Rouen, 1614.

> Unless it is otherwise noted, all references to St. François de Sales indicate this work and this edition. A few references, specially noted, are made to the following two items.

Introduction à la Vie dévote, ed. Charles Florisoone. 2 vols., Paris, Éditions Fernand Roches, 1930.

A Treatise of the Love of God [trans. Thomas Carre, i.e., Miles Pinkney]. Douay, 1630.

Gansfort, Johan Wessel. *Opera.* Groningen, 1614.

Gibbons, Richard. "The Practical Methode of Meditation," prefixed to Gibbons' translation: *An Abridgment of Meditations of the Life, Passion, Death, and Resurrection of our Lord and Saviour Iesus Christ. Written in Italian by the R. Father Vincentius Bruno of the Society of Iesus.* [St. Omer], 1614.

> I assume that Gibbons is the author of the prefixed treatise on meditation, which seems clearly addressed to an English audience; but it may be by some other hand. The dedication is signed "I. W. P.," perhaps indicating a John Wilson, Priest, who was at this time issuing works under this signature from St. Omer.

Hall, Joseph. *The Arte of Divine Meditation*, London, 1606.

> I have used this first edition, but have taken my quotations from this treatise as it appears in the next item.

A Recollection of such Treatises as have bene heretofore severally published, and are nowe revised, corrected, augmented. London, 1621.

Ignatius Loyola, St. *The Text of the Spiritual Exercises of Saint Ignatius, Translated from the Original Spanish*, with preface by John Morris. 4th ed., Westminster, Md., Newman Book-shop, 1943.

I refer to this edition because it is both authoritative and easily available; but I have also made extensive use of the next item, with its superb commentary and its translation of the Jesuit *Directory* of 1599.

The Spiritual Exercises of Saint Ignatius of Loyola, Translated from the Spanish with a Commentary and a Translation of the Directorium in Exercitia, by W. H. Longridge. 4th ed., London, A. R. Mowbray, 1950.

The Imitation of Christ. From the First Edition of an English Translation Made c. 1530 by Richard Whitford, ed. Edward J. Klein. New York, Harper, 1941.

This is a convenient and useful edition, but since it is modernized I have taken my quotations from the edition of 1585. In some places Klein's division into chapters differs from that of 1585; where this occurs I have given an alternative chapter-reference to Klein's edition.

The Folowing of Christ [trans. Richard Whitford. Rouen?], 1585.

Juan de Bonilla. *Pax Animae:* for translation used see under *Spiritual Combat.*

Juan de Ávila. *The Audi Filia, or a Rich Cabinet Full of Spirituall Iewells* [trans. Sir Tobie Matthew. St. Omer], 1620.

Loarte, Gaspar. *The Exercise of a Christian Life* [trans. Stephen Brinkley. Rheims?], 1584.

Instructions and Advertisements, How to meditate the Misteries of the Rosarie, [trans. John Fen. London? 1579?]

Louis de Blois. *A Book of Spiritual Instruction: Institutio Spiritualis,* trans. Bertrand A. Wilberforce. 2d ed., London, Art and Book Co., 1901.

Luis de Granada. *Of Prayer, and Meditation* [trans. Richard Hopkins.] Douay, 1612.

Mauburnus, Joannes (Jean Mombaer). *Rosetum exercitiorum spiritualium et sacrarum meditationum,* ed. Leander St. Martin. Douay, 1620.

Meditations on the Life of Christ, attributed to St. Bonaventure, trans. Sister M. Emmanuel. St. Louis, B. Herder, 1934.

Patrologiae cursus completus . . . Series [latina], ed. Jacques Paul Migne. 221 vols., Paris, 1844–65.

Pedro de Alcántara, San. *Treatise on Prayer and Meditation*, trans. Dominic Devas. Westminster, Md., Newman Press, 1949.

    I have also used the old translation by Giles Willoughby, published with the title, *A Golden Treatise of Mentall Praier*, Brussels, 1632.

Persons, Robert. *A Christian Directorie.* [Rouen], 1585.

The Psalter or Psalmes of David, after the translation of the great Byble. London, 1575.

Puente, Luis de la. *Meditations upon the Mysteries of our Holie Faith, with the Practise of Mental Prayer touching the same* [trans. John Heigham]. 2 vols., St. Omer, 1619.

Regulae Societatis Iesu. Rome, 1590.

Richeome, Louis. *The Pilgrime of Loreto*, trans. "E. W." Paris, 1629.

Rodriguez, Alphonsus. *Practice of Perfection and Christian Virtues*, trans. Joseph Rickaby. 3 vols., Chicago, Loyola University Press, 1929.

Savonarola, Girolamo. *De Simplicitate Christianae Vitae.* Strassburg, 1615.

The Societie of the Rosary. Newly Augmented. [St. Omer? c. 1600].

The Spiritual Combat [attributed to Lorenzo Scupoli] *and a Treatise on Peace of the Soul* [by Juan de Bonilla], translation revised by William Lester and Robert Mohan. Westminster, Md., Newman Bookshop, 1947.

    I have also used the old translation, entitled *The Spiritual Conflict*, Rouen, 1613 (apparently a second edition).

Stafford, Anthony. *The Femall Glory: or, The Life, and Death of our Blessed Lady.* London, 1635.

Stimulus Divini amoris: That is The Goade of Divine Love [trans. B. Lewis Augustine]. Douay, 1642.

    This treatise was for long attributed to St. Bonaventure, but is now believed to be the work of Jacobus Mediolanensis.

Tomás de Villacastín, *A Manuall of Devout Meditations and Exercises, Instructing how to pray mentally. Drawne for the most part, out of the spirituall Exercises of B. F. Ignatius* [trans. H. More. St. Omer], 1618.

Vita Christi. London, 1525.
Nicholas Love's adaptation of the pseudo-Bonaventure's *Meditations on the Life of Christ* (see above).
Worthington, Thomas. *The Rosarie of our Ladie.* Antwerp, 1600.

C. SECONDARY WRITINGS

Bennett, Joan. *Four Metaphysical Poets.* Cambridge, University Press, 1934.

Bremond, Henri. *A Literary History of Religious Thought in France,* trans. K. L. Montgomery. 3 vols., London, S. P. C. K., 1928–36.

Coffin, Charles Monroe. *John Donne and the New Philosophy.* New York, Columbia University Press, 1937.

Debongnie, Pierre. *Jean Mombaer de Bruxelles.* Louvain, Librarie Universitaire, 1927.

Eliot, T. S. *Selected Essays, 1917–1932.* New York, Harcourt, Brace, 1932.

Ellmann, Richard. *Yeats, The Man and the Masks.* New York, Macmillan, 1948.

Empson, William. *Seven Types of Ambiguity.* 2d ed., London, Chatto and Windus, 1947.

Freeman, Rosemary. *English Emblem Books.* London, Chatto and Windus, 1948.

Gilson, Étienne. *The Mystical Theology of Saint Bernard,* trans. A. H. C. Downes. New York, Sheed and Ward, 1940.
The Philosophy of St. Bonaventure, trans. Illtyd Trethowan and F. J. Sheed. New York, Sheed and Ward, 1938.

Gosse, Edmund. *The Life and Letters of John Donne.* 2 vols., London, Heinemann, 1899.

Haller, William. *The Rise of Puritanism . . . 1570–1643.* New York, Columbia University Press, 1938.

Janelle, Pierre. *Robert Southwell the Writer.* London, Sheed and Ward, 1935.

Knappen, M. M. *Tudor Puritanism.* Chicago, University of Chicago Press, 1939.

McDonald, James H. *The Poems and Prose Writings of Robert Southwell, S. J. A Bibliographical Study.* Oxford, Roxburghe Club, 1937.

Maycock, Alan L. *Nicholas Ferrar of Little Gidding*. London, S.P.C.K., 1938.

Pourrat, Pierre. *Christian Spirituality*, trans. W. H. Mitchell and S. P. Jacques. 3 vols., London, Burns, Oates, and Washbourne, 1922–7.

Simpson, Evelyn. *A Study of the Prose Works of John Donne*. 2d ed., Oxford, Clarendon Press, 1948.

Smith, Hallett. "English Metrical Psalms in the Sixteenth Century and their Literary Significance," *HLQ*, 9 (1946), 249–71.

Southern, A. C. *Elizabethan Recusant Prose, 1559–1582*. London, Sands, 1950.

[*Stationers' Register.*] *A Transcript of the Registers of the Company of Stationers of London; 1554–1640*, ed. Edward Arber. 5 vols., London, 1875–94.

Thurston, Herbert. "Catholic Writers and Elizabethan Readers. III.—Father Southwell, the Popular Poet," *The Month, 83* (1895), 383–99.

"Our Popular Devotions. II.—The Rosary. V. The Fifteen Mysteries," *The Month, 96* (1900), 620–37.

Tuve, Rosemond. "On Herbert's 'Sacrifice,' " *KR, 12* (1950), 51–75.

A Reading of George Herbert. London, Faber and Faber, 1952.

Walton, Izaak. *Lives*. World's Classics, London, Oxford University Press, 1936.

Warren, Austin. *Richard Crashaw, A Study in Baroque Sensibility*. Louisiana State University Press, 1939.

Watrigant, H. "La genèse des Exercices de Saint Ignace de Loyola," *Études, 71* (1897), 506–29; 72, 195–216; 73, 199–228.

White, Helen C. *English Devotional Literature [Prose],1600–1640*. University of Wisconsin Studies in Language and Literature, No. 29. Madison, 1931.

The Tudor Books of Private Devotion. University of Wisconsin Press, 1951.

Wright, Louis B. *Middle-class Culture in Elizabethan England*. Chapel Hill, University of North Carolina Press, 1935.

Index

(Since the Conclusion to this book has been revised and reset for the second edition, the Index is no longer accurate for pages 321–30.)